RAF Strike Command
1968–2007

RAF Strike Command 1968–2007

Aircraft, Men and Action

Kev Darling

Pen & Sword
AVIATION

First published in Great Britain in 2012 by
Pen & Sword Aviation
an imprint of
Pen & Sword Books Ltd
47 Church Street
Barnsley
South Yorkshire
S70 2AS

Hardback ISBN: 978 1 84884 898 6

A CIP catalogue record for this book is available from the British Library.

Typeset in 11pt Ehrhardt by
Mac Style, Beverley, E. Yorkshire

Printed and bound in the UK by CPI Group (UK) Ltd, Croydon, CRO 4YY

Pen & Sword Books Ltd incorporates the Imprints of Pen & Sword Aviation,
Pen & Sword Family History, Pen & Sword Maritime, Pen & Sword Military, Pen
& Sword Discovery, Wharncliffe Local History, Wharncliffe True Crime,
Wharncliffe Transport, Pen & Sword Select, Pen & Sword Military Classics, Leo
Cooper, The Praetorian Press, Remember When, Seaforth Publishing
and Frontline Publishing.

For a complete list of Pen & Sword titles please contact
PEN & SWORD BOOKS LIMITED
47 Church Street, Barnsley, South Yorkshire, S70 2AS, England
E-mail: enquiries@pen-and-sword.co.uk
Website: www.pen-and-sword.co.uk

Contents

Introduction

W hen Bomber and Fighter Commands were shoehorned together many thought
that this particular marriage would not work. Fortunately for Britain's defence
Strike Command would play its part well. This book is dedicated to those men
and women that made Strike Command function: to the aircrew, some of whom lost their
lives on active service, the ground crew who stopped the foregoing being no more than
an expensive walking club and to all those support personnel who could supply anything
from a bolt to a boiled egg, frequently at very short notice. I count myself lucky to have
served alongside many of them.

Like most military organizations the command was subject to financial stringencies,
some were imposed by politicians looking to further their own agendas while others
occurred due to the cost of new equipment. The latter increased in price due to the
complexity of emerging technologies, although once proven they would remain in
service; sometimes well past their sell by date. Possibly the low point in the history of
Strike Command would come in the mid-1970s when, due to financial stringencies,
morale was at an all time low. Fortunately NATO came to the rescue with its insistence
that all countries adopt a low profile for their aircraft and their support infrastructure.
Extra money had to be found to carry out this task, and fortunately it was.

With nearly everything painted green the old routine of training for a war that no one
hoped would happen was resumed, although it was rudely interrupted by the Falklands
War in 1982. This revealed a few deficiencies in equipment that were quickly dealt with
while the type of training carried out by all personnel was mostly vindicated. New
equipment was also coming on stream; the Sepecat Jaguar was settled in service, and new
versions of the Harrier were being developed, while the Panavia Tornado was starting to
enter service. The service also said farewell to some old favourites such as the Avro
Vulcan that had performed so well during the Falklands War.

The fall of the Berlin Wall and the collapse of communism in November 1989 led the
leaders of the West to declare a misguided 'peace dividend'. There followed a short
period of base closures, cancelled programmes and personnel being made redundant.
Much of this would be put on hold in August 1990 when Iraq invaded Kuwait; the
author first heard this news courtesy of the BBC World Service at 30,000 feet on the
flight deck of Tristar ZE705 en route to Mount Pleasant from Ascension Island. The
world's response was impressive; not only would all the nations of the West band
together, they were quickly joined by the Arab nations in the region. The premise behind
the war was not only to establish complete air superiority, but to use massive air power

to destroy and thoroughly demoralize the Iraqi forces. Not only was this successful, it also allowed the ground forces to carry out their counter invasion with little let or hindrance.

During the remaining seventeen years of Strike Command's existence the squadrons have hardly had time to draw breath between conflicts before packing up and moving onto the next conflict. Not bad for an organization formed to protect Britain against one particular enemy. Unfortunately, the chosen name for the replacement organization was the rather anonymous Air Command. Would Air Expeditionary Command have been better and more accurate?

Obviously, such a work as this requires the help of others even though it is but a primer on the subject. Therefore, I would like to thank my old friends Bob Archer and Robbie Shaw for their help with illustrations. I would especially like to thank my old friend and boss Wing Commander Mel James for his assistance with Operation *Corporate* information and photographs.

Kev Darling
Wales 2012

Chapter 1

Fighter Command – the Final Decade

As the day dawned bright and sunny over the airfields of Britain little did those who scurried to work on that Friday realize that ten years from 30 April 1958 the command that had won the Battle of Britain would cease to exist. Thus as shift bosses chivvied their troops into hangars and onto the flight line, as young pilots dreaming of derring-do entered the briefing rooms daydreaming of future glories, little did they realize that some of them would be in senior positions to take the nascent Strike Command into the future.

Fighter Command had embraced the jet fighter with alacrity very early on in its career. Success with the Gloster Whittle powered by a Whittle/ Power Jets centrifugal engine on 5 March 1943 had led to the development and deployment of the Meteor F1 to Specification F9/40. Production deliveries of the first production machines, later to be named Meteor, took place in July 1944, No. 616 Squadron being the recipient. Powered by Welland engines, the new fighter was deployed on V-1 'Doodle Bug' interception patrols. Codenamed 'Diver' these flights took place from Manston with the unit scoring its first success in August. While much of the squadron remained in Britain one flight was detached to Nijmegen in the Netherlands, although the Meteor was banned from flying over enemy territory thus two of the significant aircraft in jet aircraft development failed to meet in combat. The deployment lasted throughout January 1945, this first version of the Meteor being withdrawn from use soon afterwards.

This first venture in to the realm of the jet fighter was followed by the Meteor Mk 3 whose various improvements included higher thrust and more reliable engines, a ventral fuel tank, plus a sliding canopy. No. 616 Squadron would be the first recipient with No. 504 gaining their complement soon afterwards. The follow-on would be the Meteor F Mk 4, this being the first version to enter mass squadron service, a total of twenty-four units being thus equipped. No. 92 Squadron would be the first to equip in May 1948 while based at Duxford whereas No. 245 Squadron would achieve a measure of fame when some of their machines were fitted with in-flight refuelling probes for aerial refuelling trials.

Having delivered three versions of the Meteor to the Royal Air Force, Glosters would then go on to manufacture the most prevalent model, the Meteor F Mk 8, a total of 1,079 aircraft being delivered. In contrast with the earlier machines this version featured an extended nose, clipped wings, modified tail unit and a Martin-Baker ejection seat. At its height the F8 equipped thirty squadrons, including ten assigned to the Royal Auxiliary

Air Force. The final front-line Meteor F8 was retired by No. 245 Squadron in April 1957 having flown various marques of the Meteor continuously from August 1945.

Also in the race to deliver the first jet fighter to the RAF was de Havilland with its Spidercrab, later given the slightly more sensible service name of Vampire. Already well known as the builder of the 'Wooden Wonder', the Mosquito, de Havilland would enter the DH 100 in answer to Specification E.6/41. The powerplant for this diminutive fighter would be the Halford H1 designed by Major Frank Halford. This was a simpler and slightly smaller version of the Welland engines specified for the Gloster Meteor; in fact, the first Halford H1s would be fitted into some aircraft from the early Meteor production in order to test them for future usage. The first DH 100, LZ548/G, the 'G' indicating that the aircraft required guarding when away from home base, undertook its maiden flight on 20 September 1943 some six months after its Gloster rival had flown. In appearance the Vampire series was a small single-seat twin boom fighter that still featured wood in much of its construction. The pilot plus engine was housed in a short pod as were the four 20mm cannon. The first production of the Vampire F Mk 1, TG274, made its maiden flight on 20 April 1945 with first deliveries being undertaken to No. 247 Squadron during March 1946. Changes took place throughout delivery, thus from the fortieth aircraft a more powerful Goblin, as the Halford H1 had become, was fitted, while from the fifty-first aircraft the F1 featured a bubble canopy and cabin pressurization. Eventually, a total of eleven front-line units were equipped with this model.

Given its diminutive size it was no surprise that the short endurance of the Vampire needed to be addressed and quickly, therefore the next model would be the F Mk 3 to Specification F3/47. Although underwing tanks had been introduced with the F1 this later version also had increased tankage in the wing panels. In its initial iteration the extra wing fuel caused some instability, which was cured by lowering the tailplane and extending its chord while the fin and rudder were reworked to increase the available surface area. The first prototype first flew on 4 November 1945 and was subject to a prolonged development and testing period before first deliveries were undertaken to No. 54 Squadron in April 1948. Eventually, a total of thirteen units were equipped with the type.

While the Vampire proved to be a stable platform it was obvious that any further development as a fighter would be limited by its size and space limitations thus any further models should be dedicated to ground attack only. To that end de Havilland reworked a redundant F1 as the FB5 prototype. To cope with the differing demands of the ground attack role the new model featured a strengthened structure that allowed the carriage of two 1,000lb bombs or eight rockets. The wings were also clipped to improve the roll rate. The undercarriage was also altered, having an increased stroke to compensate for the increased weights involved. The prototype undertook its maiden flight on 29 June 1948 with deliveries to the first operational squadron, No. 54 Squadron, at Odiham during October 1959. Eventually, a total of forty-one squadrons were equipped with this model, most employing the type for ground attack purposes. The final Vampire fighter bomber was the FB Mk 9 that was intended for tropical usage thus it added a conditioning unit to the basic FB5 airframe, which resulted in an increase of eight inches to the starboard wing root fillet. The first deliveries were undertaken during January 1952, the redundant FB5s being returned to Britain for training duties. Overall, twenty-four fighter bomber units were equipped with this version.

It had become obvious by 1953 that the Meteor and Vampire had been totally outclassed by the emerging crop of Soviet Union fighters. Unfortunately, the next British fighter was still in the development stage and therefore a stop gap was needed in a hurry. The only available candidate was the North American F-86E Sabre that had already proven its worth in Korea. It would be Canadair who would build the RAF fighters under licence from North American Aviation (NAA). Altogether, some 430 aircraft were built for Britain, which were flown across the Atlantic by pilots from No. 1 Long Range Ferry unit as part of Operation *Beechers Broo*k. While the majority of the new fighters were delivered to the units based in Germany, two units in Fighter Command were equipped with the type these being Nos 66 and 92 Squadrons. The F-86 Sabre F Mk 4 was withdrawn from service in 1956, the majority being refurbished for further use by other nations.

The first British swept wing fighter to enter service was the Supermarine Swift, which could trace its ancestry in a tortuous way back to the Spitfire. Unlike its more illustrious ancestor, the Swift was an unmitigated disaster in its earliest form. Developed to meet Specification F105, the first Type 541, Swift F Mk 1, undertook its maiden flight on 25 August 1952. This version was equipped with a pair of 30mm Aden cannon, a fixed tailplane plus a Rolls-Royce Avon engine without reheat. Development problems delayed service entry until 13 February 1954 when No. 56 Squadron traded in its trusty Gloster Meteor F8s. The pilots were then faced with an aircraft that was beset by flight restrictions that included gun firing, maximum speed and altitude. This was compounded by a spate of accidents that caused the type to be grounded in August of that year. By the end of that month the squadron had received the next model, the Swift F2, which was supposed to be a better aircraft. Unfortunately, the opposite was true as two aircraft were lost due to uncommanded pitch-ups. By this time the RAF had lost patience and ordered the withdrawal of the extant fleet from flying in March 1955. Only one version would enter unit service in appreciable numbers, the Swift FR5 that would operate with Nos 2 and 4 Squadrons in Germany.

It would be the Hawker Aircraft Company that would produce the next RAF fighter, the Hunter. Having already delivered the Hurricane, credited with the highest number of kills during the Battle of Britain, the Typhoon that became an outstanding ground attack aircraft plus the Tempest that was an outstanding fighter bomber, it came as no surprise that the Hunter was greeted with delight by the waiting squadrons. The first Hunter F1, WT555, undertook its maiden flight on 16 May 1953. This was followed by a total of 113 aircraft at Kingston while a further 26 were built at the Blackpool factory. Flight testing would show that a ventral airbrake was needed to improve handling, which delayed service entry until July 1954. No. 43 Squadron would be the first to equip, quickly followed by Nos 54 and 222 Squadrons. While its looks were graceful this first model suffered some problems, the greatest of which was engine surging at high altitude when the guns were fired, also the links ejected during firing causing damage to the aircraft's skin. The next Rolls-Royce Avon-powered Hunter to enter service would be the F Mk 4, which had increased fuel capacity in the wing while the airframe was capable of carrying a far greater weapons load. The first F4 undertook its maiden flight on 20 October 1954 with 188 being built at Kingston while a further 177 were constructed at Blackpool. The F4 entered service with Nos 54 and 111 Squadrons in March 1955. Eventually, a total of twenty-three squadrons would equip with the type, the majority of the aircraft being fitted with the Rolls-Royce Avon 115 engine that finally cured the surging problem caused by gun firing.

The Hunter also brought with it an improvement in flying standards. No longer were pilots told to go off on an aimless flight; they were given proper flight briefings that included the use of cine gun cameras while the standards in air-to-air firing also improved. Pilots were also expected to complete a set number of flying hours per month during which a set number of exercises were completed. Proper post-flight debriefings were also established as normal practice with pilots being expected to tell the ground crew of any faults that needed rectification. Although the Hunter was a good visual day fighter only being hampered by a lack of flying tailplane, the Distance Measuring Equipment (DME) mounted in the nose was regarded as virtually useless. Curing this required improved servicing plus the addition of improved voltage regulators that turned the DME system into a viable proposition.

The definitive fighter, the Hunter F6, would make its first flight on 22 January 1954 with 264 being built. The first production model flew on 25 March 1955, followed by a further 119 machines by Armstrong Whitworth. As production progressed the aircraft were fitted with an extended wing outer section that improved handling while the gun links would be collected in blisters under the gun pack. The final F6 was delivered on 9 July 1957. Eventually, twenty front-line fighter units were equipped with this model and after leaving service it saw extensive use by second line units. Support for trainee fighter pilots was provided by the Hunter T7, examples of which were used by twenty-nine squadrons.

The final Avon-powered version of the Hunter delivered to the RAF was the FGA9, which as its designation shows was dedicated to the ground attack role. Based on the earlier F6, the first aircraft, XE617, undertook its maiden flight on 3 July 1959. Modifications applied to this model included a tail brake parachute compartment above the jet pipe fairing, the fitment of 230-gallon underwing tanks on the inboard pylons plus strengthened wings capable of carrying an increased weapons load, improved cockpit ventilation and an air conditioning system. Eventually, nine squadrons of Fighter Command were equipped with this version, although the greater majority were delivered to the various overseas commands. Two other models of the Hunter were

Assigned to Flt Lt JT Hall this Hawker Hunter FGA9 XG296 'A' was on the inventory of No. 43 Squadron at Leuchars. By June 1961 the squadron had transferred to the Near East Air Force. *(John Ryan Collection)*

No. 1 Squadron was assigned to No. 38 Group when Hawker Hunter FGA9 XG130 'E' was photographed at West Raynham. *(John Ryan Collection)*

manufactured, these being the F2 and F5. The primary difference between this and the other models was the fitment of a Sapphire engine, the intention being to give the Hunter another powerplant should there be a shortfall in Avon manufacture given that this engine in its various forms was proving a very popular unit. The Hunter F2 was manufactured by Armstrong Whitworth with forty-five being built. Only two units would be equipped, Nos 257 and 263 Squadrons. The next model would be the F Mk 5 that was equivalent to the Avon-powered F Mk 4 and would be delivered to six front-line Fighter Command units. Both of the Sapphire-powered versions would be withdrawn from use by 1958, although the F5 would see action during the Suez Crisis in 1956.

While the RAF was reasonably well equipped with day fighter aircraft there was a greater need for an aircraft that could operate in all weathers and at night. To that end Glosters would put forward the GA5 in response to Specification F4/48. The Air Ministry would select this design for further development in July 1952 in competition with the de Havilland DH 110. The Javelin would be the first delta wing twin-engined fighter in the world. The aircraft was designed to have high performance, good endurance and be capable of intercepting incoming bombers flying at high altitudes and high subsonic speeds. The onboard avionics had to be capable of detecting intruders in all weathers in either night or day.

The first Javelin prototype, WD804, undertook its maiden flight from the company airfield at Moreton Valance on 26 November 1951, followed by a further two machines. The third aircraft, WT827, was the first to be fitted with the intended gun armament, four 30mm cannon. The test flights of the prototypes revealed some instability during parts of the flight regime, although these were quickly cured by modifying the wing to have a compound taper on the leading edge. The first production aircraft, XA544, flew on 31 October 1955, although service entry was delayed due to accidents suffered by the prototypes. Eventually, No. 46 Squadron based at Odiham received their allocation from the forty built in February 1956. These machines were powered by Sapphire Sa6 engines while the radar system was the A117 system. Only one other squadron would receive the FAW1, the Germany-based No. 87 Squadron.

The initial FAW1 was quickly followed by the FAW2 of which thirty were built. These were similar to the preceding version although the radar system was the American-built

AI22, APQ-43, unit. Three units would be equipped with the type, Nos 46 and 89 Squadrons, the latter being renumbered No. 85 Squadron. On 19 September 1955 the next version of the Javelin, the FAW4, undertook its maiden flight. This marque differed from the previous aircraft in that it featured an all-flying tailplane for pitch control. Only fifty FAW4s were built, which were operated by Nos 3,11, 23,41, 72, 87, 96 and 141 Squadrons at various times. The FAW4 was quickly followed by the FAW5, the major change applied to this version being the incorporation of extra wing tankage that increased available fuel by a further 250 gallons. Units issued with the FAW5 included Nos 5, 11, 41, 72, 87 and 151 Squadrons. The following version was the FAW6, which incorporated all of the previous modifications applied to the preceding marques. The FAW6, of which thirty-three were constructed, was fitted with the AI22 American-built unit and would be issued to the same units that were flying the FAW2, both types being operated concurrently.

The arrival of the FAW7 was a quantum leap over the earlier marques as it featured Sapphire Sa7 engines of increased thrust rated at 11,000 lb st each. Provision for drop tanks was built into each wing pylon while the rear fuselage was extended to cope with the revised engine exhausts. Changes were also made to the wings as vortex generators were fitted to the outer wing panels while the ailerons had their trailing edges thickened. The armament was also updated to include the Firestreak air-to-air missiles and it was intended to reduce the number of cannon to two, although due to delays in the missiles development early aircraft were delivered with the original quartet of cannons installed.

The final production Javelin to be produced was the FAW8 that featured Sapphire Sa7R engines with a limited reheat while the radar system employed was the American AI22 that was coupled to a Sperry autopilot. The FAW8 also featured a revised wing complete with a drooped leading edge and a double row of vortex generators, while the flight control surfaces were fitted with yaw and pitch dampers. Other modifications included a simplified engine starting system plus improved windscreen rain dispersal. While the limited reheat was of value at high altitude its operation at lower altitudes in fact caused a loss of thrust due to the fuel system pumps being unable to pump enough fuel through when requested. The first airframe undertook its maiden flight on 9 May 1958, a total of forty-seven being built. When the final FAW8 rolled out of the door it was in fact the last machine to be built at the Gloster factory, although modification and repair would keep the work force in business for a few more years. Only two units were equipped with the type, Nos 41 and 85 Squadrons. The final Javelin models were rebuilt FAW7s of which 124 were converted to FAW9 standard while 40 were rebuilt as FAW9R models. The FAW9 incorporated slightly drooped wing leading edges, an autopilot coupled to the radar system, jet pipes with variable area nozzles and full reheat, belly-mounted full tanks, sometimes known as Sabrinas, plus an improved radar system. The FAW9R was fitted with modified pylons so that four 230-gallon fuel tanks could be carried for ferry flights. The FAW9/9R was operated by Nos 5, 11, 23, 25, 29, 33, 60 and 64 Squadrons.

The arrival of the Javelin would see the gradual retirement of the de Havilland NF10 night fighters fitted with the AI Mk 10 radar. The first production aircraft entered service in July 1951 and remained in service use until being withdrawn in 1954. The Vampire NF10 was operated by Nos 23, 25 and 151 Squadrons. De Havilland would also be the manufacturers of the Venom NF2 and NF3 night fighters. Based on the earlier FB1 Venom the NF versions featured an extended and enlarged pod that housed the pilot and navigator– radar on side-by-side seating while the radar unit was mounted in the extreme nose. As with the earlier Vampire NF10 the four 20mm cannon armament was carried in the nose. A total of sixty Venom NF2s were eventually delivered to Fighter Command, although service entry was delayed for nearly three years while various handling and technical faults were rectified. Following on from the Venom NF2 was the NF3, which featured an improved radar system, power-operated ailerons to improve manoeuvrability at high Mach altitude, redesigned rudder surfaces, a frameless canopy to improve all-round visibility plus ejection seats. A total of 129 aircraft were built, the first having made its maiden flight on 22 February 1953. The NF2 was flown by Nos 23, 33, 219 and 253 Squadrons while the NF3 was flown by Nos 23, 89, 125, 141 and 151 Squadrons. While the Venoms were very much interim night fighters they operated alongside the newly arrived Javelins during Exercise Beware in 1955, both types operating from RAF Coltishall.

Operating alongside the de Havilland Venom were the night fighter versions of the Gloster Meteor. As Gloster's were overloaded with producing the day fighter versions the construction of these aircraft was transferred to another company within the Hawker group, Armstrong Whitworth. The first version, the Meteor NF11, was designed to Specification F24/28. This model featured an elongated nose that housed the pilot and navigator plus the radar system, this being the American AI10, an updated version of the Westinghouse SCR-720. The wings were of the long span variety as applied to the early fighter models; this gave the aircraft greater stability at altitude. As the nose was occupied by the radar system the cannon armament was relocated into the wings while fuel was increased by the addition of underwing tanks and a ventral tank. The prototype Meteor NF11 undertook its maiden flight on 31 May 1950 while the first production machine flew the following November. Eventually, 358 aircraft were manufactured, most of which served with the RAF. This marque would serve with Nos 5, 11, 29, 46, 68, 85, 87, 96, 125, 141, 151, 219, 256 and 264 Squadrons. The Meteor NF11 remained in operational usage until replaced by the Javelin in June 1960.

Although the single-seat day fighter Meteors had long left service the night fighter squadrons still retained their aircraft. Armstrong Whitworth-built Meteor NF14 WS779 'T' was being operated by No. 72 Squadron at Church Fenton. *(John Ryan Collection)*

The following version was the NF12, which was a development of the NF11, although it featured an American-supplied APS 21 radar system that required a fuselage extension of 17 inches. This nose extension required an increase in fin size to maintain longitudinal stability. Eventually, a total of 100 aircraft were built and served with Nos 25, 29, 46, 64, 72, 85, 152 and 153 Squadrons. The final model of the Meteor night fighter was the NF14, of which 100 were manufactured. The first NF14 undertook its maiden flight on 23 October 1953 while the last was delivered on 31 May 1954. The NF14 differed from the earlier models as it featured an even longer nose that housed the American-built AN/APQ-43 radar system while to maintain stability yaw dampers were fitted to the rudder. The most visible change, however , was the completely clear canopy that replaced the previously framed assemblies. Although the NF14 left front-line service in 1961 when replaced by the Javelin it did serve with Nos 25, 33, 46, 60, 64, 72, 85, 96, 152, 153, 213 and 264 Squadrons.

The final pure fighter to enter the service of Fighter Command was the iconic English Electric Lightning, the only fighter that was capable of sustained supersonic flight, although in common with many British fighters it had seriously short 'legs' and it was therefore limited on range. As the development of the Lightning continued however, this shortfall was taken care of by the fitment of an in-flight refuelling probe, an increased size belly tank and for the F Mk 6 the installation of overwing fuel tanks sometimes called overburgers.

Designed by WE Petter and subject to an extensive development programme, the Lightning was nearly cancelled by the Sandys Defence White Paper of 1957, its execution only stayed by the first flight of one of the pre-production aircraft. The first production Lightning F Mk 1 first flew on 30 October 1959 with the early production aircraft being delivered to the Central Fighter Establishment at Coltishall. Unlike previous RAF aircraft the Lightning was the first that was able to sustain supersonic speed in level flight; it was also unusual in that it was designed from the outset as an integrated weapons system and not purely as a gun platform. To that end the airframe, flight controls, engines, armament and autopilot were all carefully tailored to match each

No. 33 Squadron based at Leeming had originally been No. 264 Squadron before renumbering. Meteor NF14 WS790 'H' complete with red rudder sits on the flight line awaiting its next crew. *(John Ryan Collection)*

other. The core of the Lightning was the Ferranti AI23, ARI 5897, AIRPASS radar that allowed the pilot to search in front of the aircraft for possible targets. Automatic lock on was later added to allow the radar to track the target and to guide the pilot to the target. Once in range the system would signal the pilot when it was apposite to launch a missile. In contrast to later marques the early tall fin Lightnings were also equipped with nose-mounted cannon just in case the further targets appeared once the paltry amount of missiles had been fired.

When the Lightning F Mk 1 had completed its time with the AFDS, Air Fighting Development Squadron, at Coltishall the aircraft were transferred to No. 74 Squadron, also based at Coltishall, in June 1960. Following the F1 came the F1A, featuring an in-flight refuelling capability courtesy of a detachable probe that could be mounted under the port wing. The radio system was also changed from VHF to UHF while changes to the missile wiring resulted in the fitment of external conduits to carry the extra wiring. The engines were also enhanced these being the Rolls-Royce Avon 210R with a four position reheat selector. Only two units were equipped with the type these, Nos 56 Squadron in December 1960 and 111 Squadron in April 1961, both being based at Wattisham. The last of the tall tail Lightnings to be manufactured was the F Mk 2, the first of which flew on 11 July 1961. Differences from the two earlier marques included improved navigation systems, a liquid oxygen breathing system instead of the earlier gaseous system, an offset TACAN, a steerable nose wheel and a variable nozzle reheat. The only visible difference between the F1 and the F2 was the fitment of a small ventral intake on the spine to provide cooling for the DC standby generator. Only two units would ever fly the F2, Nos 19 and 92 Squadrons. No. 19 Squadron would receive their

When the English Electric Lightning first entered service the first few were delivered to the Air Fighting Development Squadron at West Raynham. This is F1 XM137 complete with badge and inscription on the fin. *(BBA Collection)*

No. 74 Squadron would receive the EE Lightning F1 in June 1960 while based at Leuchars. This is XM144 'J', one of the early production machines. Later on their aircraft would become more colourful. *(BBA Collection)*

complement at RAF Leconfield in December 1962 while the No. 92 Squadron deliveries would begin in April 1963. Both would retain the type as their mounts after their transfer to Germany and after many of the F2s had been rebuilt to F2A standard.

Following on from the F2 English Electric came the F3, although by this time the company had been absorbed into the British Aircraft Corporation. This newest marque would be the fastest built as it had a superb power-to-weight ratio, the grunt being provided by a pair of Rolls-Royce Avon 301Rs. While extra speed might seem to be the ultimate the operational pilots had a different conclusion as the removal of the cannon armament reduced the fighter's firepower and its effectiveness. The primary armament was therefore the Red Top collision course missiles, which were matched to the AI23B radar. Externally the most obvious change was the introduction of the square-topped fin that increased the area by 15 per cent although the aircraft still retained the original small ventral tank, which reduced the available range. Further changes were wrought in the cockpit where the OR946 Integrated Flight Instrumentation System was installed in place of the earlier arrangement. The first unit to receive the F Mk 3 was No. 23 Squadron based at Leuchars in August 1964 followed by Nos 29, 56, 74 and 111 Squadrons.

Following the F3 came the F3A, which drew on the earlier model but added a larger ventral tank and cranked leading edges to the wings. Later redesignated F6 Interim, the design was finalized as the F Mk 6, the prototype, XP697, first flying on 17 April 1964. The interim models would later be updated to full F6 standard. While the enlarged ventral tank would increase the aircraft's range the cambered wings also helped by reducing drag and improving range at subsonic speeds. The use of the ventral tank required two ventral fins to restore stability. The production F6 aircraft also had plumbing for overwing wing pylons and fuel tanks to be carried; initially these were seen as range extenders although in the fighter's latter years they were carried as standard. The lack of cannons was seen as a major deficiency especially as the RAFG equivalent, the F2A, still retained them. The answer was to build a two-cannon gun pack into the leading section of the ventral fuel tank with aircraft being modified from 1970 onwards. The F3A, F6 Interim and F6 were operated by Nos 5, 11, 23, 56, 74 and 111 Squadrons.

No. 74 Squadron would also operate the Lightning F3, gaining their new mounts in 1964. One would be XP753 'J'. *(BBA Collection)*

Fighter Command was formed from the Fighting Area, Air Defence of Great Britain in July 1936 with Air Chief Marshal Sir Hugh Dowding in command. As such Fighter Command ceased to exist from November 1943 to October 1944 as it became Air Defence of Great Britain for that period. Fighter Command would resume its identity from that date and by 1958 the Air Officer Commanding was Air Marshal Sir Thomas Pike who would be replaced by Air Marshal Sir Hector McGregor in July 1959.

Below Fighter Command Headquarters at RAF Bentley Priory came the operational groups, the most important of which was No. 11 Group whose headquarters was Uxbridge. Having been the major fighter group during the Second World War, it came as no surprise to find this organization as the primary for the defence of Britain. Following the war No. 11 Group continued to be a key formation within Fighter Command although by December 1951 it had been split into two sectors, the Southern and Metropolitan. Within this set-up the Hawker Hunter was the primary day fighter. Odiham was the Home of No. 54 Squadron flying the Hunter F Mk 6 while No. 1

Having disbanded in Germany in 1966 No. 111 Squadron reformed as a Lightning operator at Leuchars in 1967. The F3s were received in 1967, XP895 'O' being one such. *(BBA Collection)*

Squadron had traded in its Sapphire-powered F5s for the Hunter F6. Flying alongside this squadron was No. 34 Squadron, which continued to fly the F5 until disbanded in 1958. No. 56 Squadron based at Waterbeach had also operated the Hunter F5 until it was replaced by the Hunter F6. This marque was already well established with No. 63 Squadron at Waterbeach, the unit having received its first examples in November 1956. Also an established F6 operator was No. 65 Squadron, although this unit had received its inventory at Duxford in November 1956 as had No. 111 Squadron operating from North Weald. No. 263 Squadron had operated various models of Gloster Meteor and the early marques of Hunter before receiving the F6 at Wattisham in July 1956. The final unit to receive the Hawker Hunter F6 was No. 247 Squadron based at Odiham, the squadron having run through the Vampire, Meteor and the earlier Hunters to reach this point.

The night fighter/all weather fighter units were operating the Armstrong Whitworth-built Meteor and the Gloster Javelin, the last de Havilland Venom NF2 unit, No. 253 Squadron, having disbanded in September 1957. The final Meteor in service was the NF14, the operating units being Nos 25, 85, 153 and 152 Squadrons. The first three flew from West Malling while No. 152 Squadron was based at Wattisham. All four units would relinquish their Armstrong Whitworth mounts in mid-1958 with Nos 153 and 152 Squadrons being disbanded although the former would be renumbered as No. 25 Squadron at Waterbeach. The replacement for the Meteor was the Gloster Javelin, the first operator of which was No. 46 Squadron based at Odiham the aircraft arriving in February 1956. This unit would also fly the Javelin FAW 2, received in August 1957, and the FAW6 that arrived in May 1958. The squadron would operate the FAW2 and FAW6 side by side until the latter was relinquished in October of that year. No. 46 Squadron would move to Waterbeach in July 1959 before disbanding in June 1961, although a cadre would remain available to ferry Javelins to the Far East to equip No. 60 Squadron. Another unit that operated the FAW2 and FAW6 was No. 89 Squadron based at Stradishall. The FAW6 arrived in September 1957 with the FAW2 arriving during the following month. No. 89 Squadron would disband in November 1958 being renumbered No. 85 Squadron. This unit had previously been a Meteor NF14 operator at Stradishall

Gloster Javelin FAW4 XA808 'V' was on the strength of No. 46 Squadron when photographed at Waterbeach. *(John Ryan Collection)*

and would operate both versions of Meteor side by side until March and June 1960 respectively. In 1959 No. 85 Squadron would move bases to West Malling in 1959, this being its home base when the two earlier models were replaced by the Javelin FAW8 in March 1960. The squadron would retain its heavyweight deltas until March 1963 although it had been flying from West Raynham where it would disband.

The Javelin FAW4 would join No. 23 Squadron based at Horsham St Faith in March 1957, although a transfer to Coltishall took place in June 1959. Joining No. 23 at Coltishall would be No. 41 Squadron this unit having been renumbered from No. 141 Squadron, the unit had received the Javelin FAW4 in February 1958. No. 23 Squadron would relinquish its FAW4s in July 1959 while No. 41 Squadron would say farewell in February 1960. No. 141 Squadron had also been based at Horsham St Faith when it received the Javelin FAW4 in February 1957 before transferring to Coltishall where it was renumbered No. 41 Squadron as recounted earlier. The final Fighter Command unit to operate the FAW4 was No. 72 Squadron, which previously operated the Meteor NF14. In April 1959, while based at Church Fenton, the squadron received the FAW4 and would continue to operate them until June 1961. No. 72 Squadron was also a Javelin FAW5 operator using this marque alongside the FAW4. Both types had transferred to Leconfield in June 1959 and were still there when the unit disbanded in June 1961. While still equipped with the FAW4 Nos 23 and 141 Squadrons undertook Operation *Fabulous* during which a battle flight of aircraft were placed on the platform at the end of the runway. Crews were changed hour by hour with ground crews in attendance. Two other Javelins were also placed on a lower state of readiness should the primary pair be despatched.

No. 23 Squadron would also take part in Exercise Dragon for which they were deployed to Cyprus during October 1958. The Cyprus-based fire crews were not used to the Javelin thus the volcanic eruption of the fighter's starter system frequently resulted in the appearance of fire engines on the dispersal.

Following the FAW4/5 came the FAW6, which arrived at Acklington for No. 29 Squadron in November 1957 when it replaced the Meteor NF11. A transfer to Leuchars

No. 85 Squadron would operate a veritable mix of Javelins at Stradishall, West Malling and West Raynham. This is FAW8 XA815 'E', the squadron also flying the FAW2 and FAW4 models. *(John Ryan Collection)*

took place in July 1958 as the concrete hardstanding at Acklington was no longer capable of supporting the weight of the Javelin due to subsidence caused by mining operations, the squadron transitioning to the Javelin FAW9 in April 1961. Having moved to Leuchars the squadron was involved in Exercise Yeoman during May 1960. Unfortunately, the exercise was marred when two aircraft collided. Fortunately, both crews managed to survive after ejection. The two other units that would use the FAW6 have already been mentioned as they also operated the FAW2 indiscriminately. Only four units would fly the FAW7, the first numerically being No. 23 Squadron based at Coltishall where the new marque would replace the FAW4. When No. 153 Squadron was renumbered as No. 25 Squadron in July 1958 the unit was flying Meteor night fighters from Waterbeach. When the Gloster delta fighter arrived on the scene No. 25 Squadron would receive the FAW7 in December 1958 retaining this model until January 1961. From December 1959 the squadron also operated the Javelin FAW9, taking the latter model to Leuchars in October 1961. Two other units would also be operating the Javelin FAW7, No. 33 Squadron and No. 64 Squadron. The former had originally flown the Meteor NF14 at Leeming having been renumbered from No. 264 Squadron. The Javelin FAW7 would replace the Gloster night fighter in July 1958 moving to Middleton St George in September. The FAW7 would remain in service with No. 33 Squadron until January 1962. Another Meteor NF14 unit that would transition to the Gloster Javelin FAW7 would be No. 64 Squadron based at Duxford in April 1958, the unit retaining this model until October 1960, although the Javelin FAW9 had started to equip the squadron in July 1960.

Only Nos 41 and 85 Squadrons would operate the Javelin FAW8. No. 41 Squadron based at Coltishall had previously operated the FAW4/5 before receiving the FAW8s that arrived in November 1959 and would retain them until December 1963 when the unit was disbanded. No. 85 Squadron, previously No. 89 Squadron, had traded in its earlier FAW2/6 inventory in March 1960 while based at West Malling. No. 85 Squadron and its FAW8s would move to West Raynham in September 1960, the unit disbanding there in March 1963.

Javelin FAW9 XH725 'L' would serve with No. 29 Squadron at Leuchars before the unit transferred to Nicosia in 1963. XH725 would later transfer to No. 60 Squadron in the Far East. (*John Ryan Collection*)

No. 41 Squadron would take part in Malta Adex 60 (Malta Air Defence Exercise) where they provided air defence for the island while undertaking courtesy visits to both Greece and Turkey. The next big exercise for No. 41 Squadron was Exercise Fawn Echo, undertaken during August 1962 in Norway.

The final version of the Javelin was the FAW9 and this would be flown by four units in No. 11 Group. No. 23 Squadron had already operated the Javelin FAW4/7 before the FAW9R model was received in April 1960, the squadron moving to Coltishall in July 1960. The squadron had retained a handful of FAW7s during 1962 for crew conversion purposes until these were withdrawn for conversion to FAW9 standard. No. 23 Squadron would decamp to Leuchars and No. 12 Group in March 1963, the squadron dispensing with its mighty deltas in October 1964. During 1960 the squadron undertook Exercise Dyke, which involved a refuelled flight to Singapore via Gan and required meticulous planning by Nos 23 and 214 Squadron who would provide the Valiant tankers. As the Javelin had no long-range navigation equipment they were dependent upon the tankers there of which there were two in attendance in case there was a fault with the drogue. Having completed this exercise successfully the squadron was involved in Exercise Pounce, which was intended to be a more realistic warlike deployment. This required a rapid deployment of fighters and tankers to Bahrain routeing via Karachi and Cyprus. No sooner had the squadron returned to Britain than they turned around and were deployed for real to Cyprus due to the threatened invasion of Kuwait by Iraq. As this was for real the aircraft were equipped with live Firestreaks and this presented its own set of problems. As there were no proper facilities for missile storage the weapons were left on the aircraft, their noses being covered by red rubber noddy caps. Unfortunately, the heat welded the caps to the glass panels in the nose, which came off when the caps were removed and rendered the missile useless. While No. 23 Squadron utilized a few FAW7s for conversion purposes No. 33 Squadron would operate both the FAW7 and FAW9 versions at Middleton St George. The FAW7 would remain in service between July 1958 to January 1962 while the FAW9 was flown between October 1960 and November 1962.

Gloster Javelin FAW9 XH880 'JHW' was one of the few to carry personalized initials on the fin even though it was assigned to No. 25 Squadron at Waterbeach. In this case the code stands for Wing Commander Jim Walton. *(John Ryan Collection)*

To convert crews to the Javelin the T3 was manufactured by Glosters. This example is XH395 'D' of No. 46 Squadron. *(John Ryan Collection)*

By 1960 the number of operation squadrons on the No. 11 Group roster had shrunk considerably as had the number of aircraft operated. Only three units continued to operate the Hawker Hunter F6 – Nos. 56 and 111 Squadrons based at Wattisham plus No. 65 Squadron based at Duxford. The only other type in service was the Gloster Javelin flown by four squadrons. Still flying the FAW2 was No. 46 Squadron while this marque plus the FAW6 was flown by No. 85 Squadron. The two other units flying the FAW7 were Nos 25 and 64 Squadrons based at Waterbeach and Duxford respectively.

Although the 1957 Defence White Paper was touting the white hot bleeding edge of technology the reality was that missiles were not the be all and end all of Britain's defence requirements. While there was a massive culling of units within the RAF, fortunately some of the fighter projects already in full-scale development managed to survive, the most important of these being the English Electric Lightning supersonic fighter. It would be No. 74 'Tiger' Squadron that would introduce the Lightning to squadron service while based at Coltishall in June 1960. Flying the F1 version the unit would find itself participating in numerous exercises acting out the scenarios developed for the type by the Air Fighting Development Squadron. However, this first iteration of the Lightning would suffer from a few problems, the major one being a tendency to develop a dangerous fuel leak between the ventral fuel tank and the aircraft. This required urgent attention by the manufacturers while the defence alert aircraft remained available minus the ventral tank whose fuel air and electrical connections were blanked off.

As the F1 was used to iron out any operational problems there were high hopes that the next version, the F1A, would be more reliable. Having delivered nineteen F Mk 1 Lightnings to the RAF English Electric would then manufacture a slightly improved model, the F1A. Although only twenty-eight of this model were delivered they did equip two squadrons. The first unit to receive its complement was No. 56 Squadron based at Wattisham with the aircraft arriving in December 1960 at Wattisham, while No. 111 Squadron also based at Wattisham would see its first Lightnings in April 1961. Both units would trade in their early machines in 1965, the survivors finding further employment with the target facilities flights at Binbrook, Leuchars and Wattisham. The next production model was the Lightning F2, of which forty-four were built, which were

As the RAF was more colourful in the 1960s it is hardly surprising that No. 74 Squadron soon applied extra colour to their new mounts as exemplified by the black fin spine, fin badge and nose bars on each side of the nose roundel of the XM137 'D'. *(BBA Collection)*

flown by Nos 19 and 92 Squadrons. Both units were based at Leconfield and were equipped with Hawker Hunters, however No. 19 Squadron traded in Hawker's finest for the Lightning F2 in December 1962 while No. 92 Squadron became supersonic in April 1963. In 1965 both squadrons were transferred to RAF Germany while their mounts were modified into the excellent F2A.

When English Electric delivered the Lightning F3 it was a quantum leap in performance, however it was not the aircraft it could have been. Introduced with this version was a larger square-tipped fin, more powerful Avon engines, an improved AIRPASS radar system, provision for the carriage of overwing tanks plus the introduction of the Red Top all-aspect missile that replaced the earlier Firestreak that was only capable of locking onto an aircraft's hot spots such as jet pipes. Unfortunately for the front-line pilots the F3 was missing some vital systems such as built-in cannon

When No. 111 Squadron received the Lightning F1A it also painted its aircraft in bright colours of black and yellow as seen on XM190 'G' at Leuchars. *(BBA Collection)*

armament, the already available integrated interception system plus the already available overwing tanks. These omissions did not stop the RAF purchasing sixty-three aircraft for use by seven fighter squadrons. The first unit to equip within No. 11 Group was No. 56 'Firebirds' Squadron based at Wattisham whose inventory was delivered throughout March 1965, and also at Wattisham was No. 111 Squadron, which traded in its Lightning F1As for the F3 from December 1964. No. 29 Squadron, also based at Wattisham, was a late comer to the F3 community, not receiving its aircraft until May 1967. No. 56 Squadron would achieve a certain measure of fame when it was allowed to form the Firebirds aerobatic team for which purpose its aircraft were repainted in a red and white scheme with a chequered tail fin. No. 56 Squadron would be the first unit to lose its F3s as it transitioned to the far more superior Lightning F6 with which it transferred to Akrotiri in 1967 as part of the Near East Air Force. The other two units would lose their F3s in 1974; No. 29 Squadron would move to Coningsby to work up on the MDD F-4 Phantom FGR2 while No. 111 Squadron would transition via the Lightning F6 onto the FGR2 at Coningsby before departing for Leuchars. Unlike other fighters that had previously served with the RAF the Lightning trainers, the T4 and T5, would not only serve with the Operational Conversion Unit (OCU) and the operational squadrons. The Lightning T4 was the two-seat equivalent of the F1A and F2/F2A fighters while the T5 was originally intended to support the F3, although it was later upgraded for the Lightning F6.

During the period that No. 11 Group existed between 1958 and 1968 it was commanded by the following senior officers: Air Vice-Marshal VS Bowling assumed command on 16 January 1956 and was replaced by Air Vice-Marshal A Foord-Kelcey on 12 January 1959. He in turn was replaced by Air Vice-Marshal HJ Maguire on 1 January 1961 while the final group commander was Air Vice-Marshal GTB Clayton who took over on 13 January 1962 and remained in command until 30 April 1968. It would be Air Vice-Marshal Foord-Kelcey who would oversee the rationalization of Fighter Command in 1960 thus 11 Group was disbanded on 31 December 1960. The reasons for these

The next model of Lightning to enter service with Fighter Command was the F3 that quickly replaced the earlier F1A. No. 56 Squadron had originally flown the F1A from Wattisham, although this was replaced by the F3 in 1965. Sporting aerobatic 'Firebird' markings is XP746 'K'; a similar scheme had been worn by the F1As. *(BBA Collection)*

No. 111 Squadron would also receive the Lightning F3, although these were initially plainer than previous F1As. *(BBA Collection)*

changes were two fold, one was as ever financial while the other was strategic. While the RAF could do little about the former the latter would see the fighter squadrons moving further north to counter the Warsaw Pact threat, the premise being that the first line of defence for the south was RAF Germany. Should any intruders break through this barrier fighter defence could have been deployed further south courtesy of the tanker squadrons. No. 11 Group was not dormant for long as it reformed one day later when No. 12 Group was renumbered as No. 11 Group. On 1 April 1963 the Group was renamed No. 11 (Northern) Sector. This incarnation lasted until Fighter Command was

Fighter Command would receive the Lightning F6 to augment and in some cases to replace the Lightning F1As and F3s. Heading this line-up is XR760 'H' of No. 23 Squadron. *(BBA Collection)*

No. 11 Squadron would be one of the last operators of the EE Lightning F6. Pictured here is F6 XR723 'L' on the line at Binbrook. *(BBA Collection)*

absorbed into the new Strike Command on 30 April 1968. On the day that Fighter Command was merged into RAF Strike Command, 30 April 1968, Group Headquarters was moved to RAF Bentley Priory in north-west London taking full responsibility for the UK Air Defence Region (UK ADR).

The other fighter organization that was dedicated to the defence of Britain was No. 12 Group whose responsibility was the protection of the Midlands, North England, Scotland and Northern Ireland. Originally, the group had its headquarters at Newton until August 1959 before moving to Horsham St Faith and remaining there until the group was renumbered as No. 11 Group at the start of April 1963.

One of the day fighter units in No. 12 Group was still flying the Hawker Hunter F Mk 4 thus No. 43 Squadron at Leuchars clung onto this model until July 1958 before they were replaced by the more capable Hunter F Mk 6 while No. 19 Squadron at Church

When the F-4 Phantom joined Fighter Command the majority of type conversion and training was undertaken at Coningsby. Pictured here is No. 41 Squadron undergoing that process. *(BBA Collection)*

One of the earliest bases to receive the Phantom was Leuchars. Being a dedicated air defence station the resident units aircraft were configured for this role as shown by this No. 43 Squadron aircraft. *(BBA Collection)*

Fenton had already equipped with this version in October 1956. Another unit that received the Hunter F6 during the same time period was No. 66 Squadron at Linton-on-Ouse. Joining the F6 club slightly later was No. 92 Squadron, which received its complement of aircraft during March 1957 at Middleton-St-George.

The all weather and night fighter element of No. 12 Group was covered by the Javelin FAW4, operated by Nos 23 and 141 Squadrons. Both Javelin units were based at Horsham St Faith before moving to Coltishall in May 1957. No. 23 Squadron would later equip with the Javelin FAW7 in April 1959 with which it would transfer back to Horsham St Faith. By 1960 the squadron was operating the Javelin FAW9R, the unit

No. 56 Squadron at the other end of the country was also optimized for the air defence role. XV452 'L' was amongst the batch of airframes received by No. 56 Squadron in June 1976. *(BBA Collection)*

then returning to Coltishall. Some Javelin FAW7s were added to the inventory in April 1962, although these were only operated until September 1962. In the meantime No. 23 Squadron had decamped to Leuchars in March 1963 with its deltas.

The Armstrong Whitworth-built Meteor night fighters were still on strength in 1958. No. 29 Squadron based at Acklington would remain a Meteor NF12 operator until July 1958 before transferring to Leuchars in that same month. By April 1961 the unit was flying the Javelin FAW9, although its area of operations would change in March 1963 when a transfer to Akrotiri and NEAF took place. Another NF12 operator, although with a fair sprinkling of NF14s in the line-up, was No. 72 Squadron based at Church Fenton, both types remaining in service until June 1959. The Meteors were replaced by a mix of Javelin FAW4/5s, the squadron changing base to Leconfield at the same time. No. 72 Squadron would relinquish its all-weather mounts in June 1961 when the unit was disbanded.

When 1958 arrived the de Havilland Venom night fighters had disappeared to be replaced by Gloster Javelins. No. 33 Squadron had flown the Venom night fighters and their Armstrong Whitworth-built Meteor night fighters from Leeming before equipping with the Gloster Javelin FAW7 in July 1958. A move to Middleton St George followed in September, the squadron receiving the Javelin FAW9 in October 1960. The unit operated the FAW9 until it disbanded in November 1962. The Venom NF3 was also operated by No. 89 Squadron at Stradishall until they were replaced by a mix of Gloster Javelin FAW2/6 all weather fighters in late 1957, although the squadron would disband in November 1958 when it was renumbered as No. 85 Squadron.

By 1960 the two fighter groups, although extant, had changed radically. The most obvious change was the obvious contraction in the number of squadrons available to each group, of which No. 11 Group was now the smallest. Three units were still flying the Hunter F6 even though it was already out-classed by its Warsaw Pact opposition. Wattisham was home to Nos 56 and 111 Squadrons while Duxford was graced by No. 65 Squadron. Duxford was also the base for the Gloster Javelin FAW7-equipped No. 64 Squadron. Also operating the FAW7 at this time was No. 25 Squadron at Waterbeach while Nos 46 and 85 Squadrons were still flying the Javelin FAW2/6 models.

Hawker Hunter FGA9 XG161 'H' was assigned to No. 54 Squadron when photographed at West Raynham. This unit too was assigned to No. 38 Group for troop support duties. *(John Ryan Collection)*

Hawker Hunter F6A XE584 'W' was on the strength of No. 1 Squadron when photographed at West Raynham. The aircraft was later upgraded to FGA9 standard. *(John Ryan Collection)*

As its area of responsibility was greater No. 12 Group had a larger aviation component. Three of the units still flew the Hawker Hunter F6. They were No. 19 Squadron, based at Leconfield, and No. 66 Squadron at Acklington while No. 92 Squadron was flying its mounts from Middleton St George. One other unit was also flying the Hunter and this was No. 43 Squadron based at Leuchars that flew a mix of F6 and FGA9s. The Gloster Javelin was the main aircraft type equipping the units of No. 12 Group, two of which were based alongside No. 43 Squadron at Leuchars these being Nos 29 and 151 Squadrons flying the Javelin FAW6 and FAW5 respectively. Four units within the group were also equipped with Javelin. Coltishall was home to Nos 23 and 41 Squadrons, which flew the FAW7 and FAW8 respectively while No. 33 Squadron was based at Middleton St George also with the FAW7. The final Javelin unit was No. 72 Squadron based at Leconfield with the FAW4. Change was on the horizon though as the first English Electric Lightning F1 unit was already operational with No. 74 Squadron at Coltishall.

Fighter Command had one other air defence role comprising the units operating the Bristol Bloodhound Mk 1. The Bristol Bloodhound was a long-range surface-to-air missile that had come to fruition during the 1950s courtesy of the Bristol Aircraft Company. Bristol was responsible for the management of the programme and manufacturing the hardware while Ferranti developed the onboard guidance system. The development of the Bloodhound had started with Project 1220 in 1949. This was a Bristol project to develop a surface-to-air guided weapon that was intended to protect the V bomber fleet bases from Soviet attack. As Project 1220 came to fruition it was assigned the codename Red Duster by the Ministry of Supply.

So that a decent range was available for the missile, Bristol decided to employ a ramjet engine design instead of the easier to develop rocket power commonly in use at the time. Development of the ramjet engine progressed rapidly with Bristol working in close harmony with Boeing Aircraft and the Royal Aircraft Establishment. As with most new weapons systems initial service trials of the new missile did not go overly well as the range was restricted by the ramjet combustor design that used a flare to maintain combustion. This in turn meant that the ramjet could only operate for the duration of the flare burning time. As a result of this failure the RAF cancelled its order for the Red Duster opting instead for the English Electric-developed Red Shoes programme, later to be called Thunderbird Mk 1.

The Red Duster ramjet problem was fixed by altering the combustor design to one developed by the National Gas Turbine Establishment (NGTE). This design used a separate pilot combustor to keep the main combustor alight instead of the previous system. With this design incorporated the missile entered RAF service as the Bloodhound Mk 1 in 1958. It was deployed with eleven Air Defence Missile Squadrons of RAF Fighter Command to protect the V bomber and Thor bases. However, the Ferranti-designed Type 83 pulsed radar was susceptible to jamming, and could be confused by ground clutter, limiting its low–level capability, thus this system was seen as an interim measure until a more advanced model could be provided.

The Bloodhound squadrons were managed by four wings whose headquarters were at Lindholme, No. 21 Wing, based Watton, No. 24 Wing, based at North Coates, and Nos 148 and 151 Wings at North Luffenham. No. 21 Wing controlled Nos 94, 112 and 247 Squadrons based at Misson, Breighton and Carnaby. No. 24 Wing covered Nos 242, 263 and 266 Squadrons based at Marham, Watton and Rattlesden respectively while No. 148 Wing controlled Nos 141, 222 and 264 Squadrons, which were based at Dunholme Lodge, Woodhall Spa and North Coates. The final controller was No. 151 Wing, which managed Nos 62 and 257 Squadrons based at Woolfax Lodge and Warboys. Each Tactical Control Unit at Wing HQ was equipped with the Type 82 Orange Yeoman radar, which would track incoming hostile aircraft and transmit data to a missile fire unit once it was within range of its Type 83 target illuminating radar. Target data could then be fed to the launch control post from where the missiles would be launched.

Strangely enough given the desire by Duncan Sandys to do away with manned aircraft the Bloodhound Mk 1 was nearly slated for cancellation, although the modifications to the combustor system changed the outcome. Even so, the lack of radar performance meant that an improved model was desperately needed thus engineers from Bristol and Ferranti hatched a plan to improve the breed. From a political point of view such a proposal was good for Ferranti as the government auditors had decided that the Ferranti had made excess profits from the original Bloodhound Mk 1 deal.

The Bloodhound Mk 2 featured a more powerful Thor engine along with a stretched fuselage that increased fuel storage. These changes dramatically extended range from about 35km to 80km, pushing the practical engagement distance out to 50km. The Mk 2 was guided by either the Ferranti Type 86 Firelight radar for mobile use, or the larger fixed Marconi Type 87 Scorpion. In addition to its own illumination and tracking antennas, the Scorpion also added one of the receiver antennas out of a missile body on the same frame. This antenna was used to show what the missile's own receiver was seeing, which was useful for jamming detection and assessment. The new radar system eliminated problems with ground clutter reflections, allowing the missile to be fired at any visible target, no matter how close to the ground. Combined with the new engines, the Mk 2 had an extended altitude performance between 150ft and 65,000ft.

The use of a CW radar would present a problem for the missile semi–automatic guidance system. Continuous wave radar relies on the Doppler effect to detect moving targets, comparing returned signals to the reference signal being broadcast. However, in the Bloodhound Mk 2's case the missile was moving away from the reference signal as fast, or faster than, the target would be approaching it. The missile would then need to know the velocity of the target as well as its own airspeed in order to know what frequency to look for, however this information was known only to the radar station on the ground as the missile did not broadcast any signals of its own. To solve this problem the radar site also broadcast an omnidirectional reference signal that was shifted to the frequency that the missile's receiver should be looking for, taking into account both the target and missile speed. Thus the missile only had to compare the signal from its nose mounted receiver with the signal from the launch site. Testing began on the Mk 2 in 1963 and it was cleared for RAF service in 1964. Unlike the Mk 1 that had limited performance advantage over an incoming aircraft the Mk 2 was a much more formidable weapon with capabilities against Mach 2 aircraft at high altitudes. To cater for an increased strength several new Bloodhound bases were set up for the Mk 2 while some of the Mk 1 bases were updated to host the new Mk 2.

As the Bloodhound Mk 2 entered service some of the earlier missile units would be disbanded, No. 264 Squadron would disband in November 1962 while No. 94 Squadron would cease operations in June 1963 with No. 247 Squadron closing down in December. The following year would see the majority of Bloodhound Mk 1 units stand down: Nos 112 and 141 Squadrons disbanded in March 1964, and No. 266 Squadron closed down in June while Nos 64, 242 and 222 Squadrons finished in the September. The final unit to stand down would be No. 263 Squadron, which ceased operations in June 1966. Replacing this plethora of units were four UK-based units – Nos. 25, 41, 85 and 112 Squadrons.

Formed in October 1963 No. 25 Squadron received its complement at North Coates although in 1970 the complete unit was transferred to the RAFG base at Bruggen. No. 25 Squadron returned to Britain upon the closure of Bruggen, setting up shop at Wyton with flights detached to Barkston Heath and Wattisham. With the wind down of the Bloodhound force in progress No. 25 Squadron reformed as Tornado F3 unit in 1989. Having flown the Javelin FAW8 in defence of Britain the next task for No. 41 Squadron was as a Bloodhound Mk 2 missile operator. The unit activated in September 1965 at West Raynham, although it would cease operation some five years later. No. 112 Squadron had originally operated the Bloodhound Mk 1 from Church Fenton and Breighton between August 1960 and March 1960 before moving to Woodhall Spa later that year to work up on the Bloodhound Mk 2. By October 1967 the unit had moved to the sunnier climes of Cyprus and remained active until disbanding in July 1975.

The major operator of the Bloodhound Mk 2 was No. 85 Squadron. Previously a target facilities unit the new equipment was received in December 1975, the main headquarters being at West Raynham. Also based here was A Flight while B Flight was located at North Coates and C Flight was stationed at Bawdsey. By October 1989 No. 85 Squadron had absorbed No. 25 Squadron thus the missiles at Barkston Heath became D Flight while those at Wattisham became E Flight and F Flight was at Wyton. In December 1990 B, C, D and F Flights would be disbanded while the remaining flights and the headquarters ceased operations in July 1991.

In contrast with the missiles designed to shoot down incoming enemy aircraft the advent of the jet aircraft into Fighter Command had been marred by a continuously growing number of accidents, many of them fatal. Part of the problem was a carryover from the Second World War; aircraft from that period were designed primarily to undertake a given task thus safety considerations were not to the fore, with just enough done to get crews to and from their targets. Allied to this were the problems some pilots had in converting to the new fangled aircraft types while the ground crew also faced similar problems in assimilating to the new technology en masse. Once aircraft manufacturers and aircraft operators had grasped that changes had to be made the accident safety record improved dramatically. These improvements were reflected in the number of crashes recorded in the last ten years of the command's existence even though the aircraft coming into service had perforce increased in complexity. The final month of operations would see only a pair of Lightning F6s being lost, both from No. 5 Squadron; this was in complete contrast with 1958 when ten aircraft were lost, all being Javelins.

When the final day of Fighter Command dawned there were many within and without the organization who were set against it, however the reality of the situation was that the armed forces were, as ever, under financial strictures while Fighter Command had shrunk to no more than a handful of squadrons, a far cry from the glory days of yore. Thus it was inevitable that a merger with Bomber Command initially and later Coastal and Transport Commands was inevitable.

Chapter 2

Bomber Command – the Last Ten Years

Unlike Fighter Command their counterparts in Bomber Command were slow to adopt jet-powered aircraft. This was not down to a lack of desire, but to a lack of technology. In contrast with a fighter a bomber required range, altitude and the ability to carry a decent bomb load to a target. Not only were conventional bombs in the inventory, but the first nuclear weapons were becoming available, however, unlike the slick slim beasties available today these early weapons were big bulky shapes that required carriage by the only aircraft available. Until the arrival of V Force the only platforms available were the Avro Lincoln, a development of the Lancaster, and the Boeing B-29 Washington, also known as the Superfortress in USAF service.

It was the arrival of the English Electric Canberra B2 that brought Bomber Command into the jet age with a bang. Over 40 squadrons would be equipped with the type, at least 430 having been constructed. Having been designed to satisfy Specification B.3/45 the first prototype, VN799, undertook its maiden flight with Wing Commander Roland Beamont at the controls on 13 May 1949. Likened from the outset to a jet-powered Mosquito replacement the Canberra was designed without defensive armament, relying instead on high speed to evade any enemy. Allied to the aircraft high speed was the low aspect ratio wing that gave good fuel economy at the highest possible altitude, which in turn gave the Canberra great manoeuvrability.

The Canberra was originally intended for radar-guided bombing with a crew of two, however the specification was changed to visual bombing with a crew of three. To that end the fifth prototype, VX165, was reworked to Specification B.5/47. The first production machine, WD929, undertook its first flight on 23 April 1950. Production continued at a rate that was high enough to allow the formation of the first operational unit, No. 101 Squadron based at Binbrook in May 1951. After that deliveries were rapid, allowing all those units still flying the piston-powered Avro Lincoln to convert to the new type. Following on from the B2 came the Canberra B6 that featured more powerful engines and increased fuel content, which in turn increased the type's range. In contrast with the B2 this later version only equipped fifteen units and its tenure in Bomber Command was short as the first V bombers were becoming available. This was not the end of the Canberra's career however, as it was reworked for tactical strike duties with the Near East Air Force based on Cyprus.

Of the surviving units to operate the Canberra B2 No. 35 Squadron had previously operated the Avro Lincoln and the Boeing B-29 Washington before converting to the Canberra in April 1954. Initially based at Marham the squadron transferred to Upwood in 1956, remaining there until disbanding in September 1961. The oldest Canberra unit was No. 50 Squadron, which had converted from the Lincoln in August 1952 at their new base at Binbrook, although later joining No. 35 Squadron at Upwood and disbanding by October 1950. Both units would eventually reform as Avro Vulcan squadrons.

Other units that operated the Canberra B2 included those that had previously operated the Douglas Aircraft PGM-17 Thor. The first of these was No. 97 Squadron, which took up its allocation of Canberras in May 1963. These were operated from Watton alongside the Varsity T1 and the Hastings C2 until the unit disbanded in January 1967. Also an ex-Thor missile operator was No. 98 Squadron, which would replace No. 97 Squadron at Watton in October 1976, although its operating base by this time was Cottesmore as relocation had taken place in April 1969. No. 100 Squadron would have two bites at the Canberra cherry. The first was in April 1954 when both the B2 and B6 plus a handful each of the PR7 reconnaissance model and the interdictor strike B(I)8 were flown. Throughout this period until disbandment in September 1959 the squadron was based at Wittering, although detachments were supplied to Wyton and Christmas Island, the latter in support of Operation *Grapple* between 1956 and 1958. The second bite began in February 1972 when No. 100 Squadron reformed at West Raynham being equipped with the Canberra B2, E15, TT18, T19 and the reconnaissance PR7. The Canberras were dispensed with in 1991, the unit having moved twice in that period, to Marham in January 1976 and to Wyton in January 1982.

Unlike the Thor missile operators No. 139 Squadron had previously flown a variety of de Havilland Mosquitos before transferring to the Canberra B2 in November 1952, these aircraft lasting until July 1955. The B2s would be replaced by the superior B6 from February 1955. A year later No. 139 Squadron moved to Binbrook, the unit finally disbanding in December 1959. Only two other units would still be flying the Canberra B2 in April 1958. The first was No. 245 Squadron based at Watton, having been renumbered from No. 527 Squadron, receiving its complement of aircraft in August

Bomber Command would operate the Canberra in the nuclear strike role before the V bombers became available. Such an aircraft was B6 WT213 of No. 9 Squadron based at Binbrook. (*John Ryan Collection*)

1958 and moving to Tangmere soon afterwards. Disbandment came in April 1963 when the unit was renumbered No. 98 Squadron. Also at Wyton was No. 1323 Flight, which was renumbered as No. 542 Squadron in November 1955. During this period both the Canberra B2 and B6 were operated from November 1955 and remained in service until October 1958. During this period the unit moved to Hemswell in March 1957 and to Upwood in July 1958 before being renumbered as No. 21 Squadron.

Some squadrons after operating the Avro Lincoln and the Canberra B2 would move onto the far superior Canberra B6. The first of these would be No. 9 Squadron at Binbrook, which received its Canberra B6s in September 1955, finally relinquishing its B2s in January 1956. The B6s would be gone in July 1961 when the squadron disbanded in July 1961 in preparation for the Avro Vulcan. Also based at Binbrook and destined to become a Vulcan unit was No. 12 Squadron; the unit relinquished its B2s in June 1955 having received the B6 in May 1955. The squadron disbanded in July 1961 at Coningsby to begin training for the Vulcan.

When No. 542 Squadron was disbanded its crews and aircraft were taken over by No. 21 Squadron based at Upwood in October 1958. The squadron had a short existence and disbanded in October 1959, although it did find time to send detachments to Laverton, Western Australia, in support of nuclear weapons trials. Another unit that was heavily involved in supporting nuclear weapons development was No. 76 Squadron, which had received the Canberra B6 while based at Weston Zoyland, although moves to Hemswell took place in April 1957 and to Upwood in July 1958. From each of these bases the squadron would send detachments to Pearce and Edinburgh Field in Australia plus to Christmas Island in support of Operation *Grapple*. The final unit flying the Canberra B6 was No. 192 Squadron based at Watton. The unit's principal role was electronic reconnaissance and warfare to which end the Canberra B2, Vickers Varsity T1 and Canberra B6(RC) and later the DH Comet C2(RC) were flown between July 1957 and August 1958 when the squadron was disbanded.

Although the Canberra was regarded as an interim measure until the arrival of the V bombers the crews trained to undertake the roles forecast for the heavies on the horizon. Originally the training revolved around the use of Gee-H, the primary blind bombing aid. Over half the missions flown by the Canberra crews would end with a Gee-H attack. However, this system proved less than reliable as it could be jammed by a basic radio counter measures (RCM) system. This was not the main defect as the system had serious reliability issues, not only did the aircraft receivers fail at inconsiderate moments but the ground stations also failed on occasion. Given the possibility of system failure it would come as no surprise to find the Canberra crews relying more on visual bombing courtesy of the onboard optical bomb sight.

Exercises played a primary part in the lives of the Canberra crews, the main one being Exercise Skyhigh where each squadron would allocate a number of aircraft to the exercise. Unlike some of the smaller exercises Skyhigh stopped just short of actual gunfire but even so full RCM jamming was employed by the attackers while the defenders used their own RCM systems to jam the incoming Gee-H signals to the bombers while also trying to generate spoof signals to cause chaos in the incoming bomber fleet. With all these complications the crews were expected to complete their night navex (navigational exercise) and undertake a Gee-H bombing attack.

These simulated attacks would be followed by a fully loaded take-off complete with live bombs; some of these attacks were Gee-H while others were purely visual. The ranges involved with these sorties included Jurby, Donna Nook, the Wash and Nordhorn. Exercise Skyhigh would also involve Fighter Command in the defensive role, although the Canberras were limited by the exercise instructions, plus the top speed was limited to 365 knots when wingtip tanks were fitted. Even so, when working within these confines the Canberras could easily outfly the available British, which gave rise to great concern to those charged with Britain's air defence. While the aircraft manufacturers strove to create fighters capable of intercepting incoming bombers there were also developments happening in the world of bomber defence. The first such system applied to the Canberra and also Valiant was the Orange Putter, ARI 5800, active tail warning radar. Fitted in the tail cone this unit was designed to detect incoming fighters preparing to undertake a tail on attack. A similar system had been tried on bombers during the Second World War and had proved unpopular then as it did later with the Canberra crews. Not only was Orange Putter an active radar, it was also very unreliable with no more than a 20 per cent detection rating. Other exercises undertaken by the Canberra squadrons included the regular Kingpin monthly training, Coronet, Phoenix (designed to give the Royal Navy training against aerial attacks) plus those in the Mediterranean, these being designated Green Pivot and Medflex Fort where the US Navy 6th Fleet was the recipient of the Canberra's attentions, the units taking part being deployed to Luqa, Malta, for that purpose.

Although the British-based Canberras did undertake some low-level training this was mainly in support of possible operations over Germany should the RAFG units need reinforcement. Overall, the British crews continued their normal training, but there were attempts to improve the defensive systems fitted to the aircraft. While Orange Putter had fallen out of favour, the increasing capability of Warsaw Pact defensive systems meant that other methods had to be found to protect the bombers and to

When No. 109 Squadron received the Canberra B6 it was a quantum jump from the DH Mosquitos flown earlier. In this photograph are B6s WJ771, WJ778, WJ780 and WT371 heading home to Hemswell. *(John Ryan Collection)*

improve their blind bombing capability. One defensive system that never reached the Canberra force was an automatic window dispenser designed to spread chaff in a hostile radar environment. A self-contained blind bombing system was the real need as the Gee-H system was increasingly vulnerable to jamming. The answer would be the 'Blue Shadow', ARI 5868 sideways-looking airborne radar. Initial trials originally gave a good report of the system, however continued use in service revealed that it required extensive preparation by the crews before an operation was undertaken. The conclusion by Bomber Command was that Blue Shadow should be used only by aircraft dedicated to the target marker while the remaining Canberras would revert to their normal visual bombing practice.

Obviously the normal high-speed visual attack run was not a viable option when nuclear weapons became part of the Canberra force inventory. The answer would be to adopt the American Low Altitude Bombing System (LABS), which had been adopted by the USAF in 1954. Instead of buying the already available Honeywell developed system it was decided that the British would develop their own system in-house. In typical British fashion there were the inevitable delays thus a number of Honeywell systems were purchased as a stop gap.

The first unit to send its aircraft for modification was No. 9 Squadron based at Binbrook whose aircraft were sent away in batches to No. 39 MU (Maintenance Unit) at Colerne for modification. The conversion process was quite slow thus No. 9 Squadron received a handful of Canberra B2s for continuation training. It was therefore February 1959 before the squadron began serious training with their new equipment. As deliveries of the converted aircraft continued LABS became the main method of weapons delivery for all the remaining strike/attack Canberra squadrons. Part of the conversion process included airframe modifications to cope with the stresses of this form of low-level attack; not only was the structure generally strengthened, the bomb doors were increased in strength to cope with the buffeting caused by the increased attack speed while baffle plates were installed to cope with the turbulence when the doors were open. The technique for a LABS attack involved the pilot utilizing an already established landmark from which point the aircraft undertook a timed run towards the target at the lowest height possible. With the onboard timer running the pilot would pull the control column back to climb the aircraft. At a preset angle, and with the bomb doors open, the weapon would be released to travel a parabolic arc to the target. In the meantime the Canberra had completed its half loop followed by a roll off the top, after which the aircraft dropped down as low as possible and flew back to base as quickly as possible.

It would be No. 9 Squadron that was chosen to give the LABS system a full work out before full adoption across the remaining Canberra units. Throughout March 1959 the unit dropped over 1,400 25lb practice bombs while operating from Idris in Libya. The following month No. 12 Squadron arrived at Idris to undertake its LABS workup period; this unit's aircraft had also been modified at Colerne. After the squadrons had returned from Idris both would eventually end up at Coningsby where they would provide the only British force utilizing this form of attack. Obviously, this type of manoeuvre required constant practice thus both squadrons ranged all over Britain carrying out dummy attacks on selected target, and both units also tested the Royal Navy using the LABS manoeuvre. LABS did have its down side, as one of its lesser faults was an occasional bomb release failure, although the bomb did drop out after the pull out – an embarrassment to all concerned. It would be the number of crashes and lost crews

One of the earliest units to equip with the Canberra B2 was No. 10 Squadron at Honington. B2 WD965 is seen in the original Bomber Command scheme of grey and black with the Honington rising pheasant badge on the fin and squadrons red speedbird on the tip tanks. *(BBA Collection)*

and aircraft that caused greater concern, many being lost at low level in marginal conditions.

Having perfected the LABS technique, Nos 9 and 12 Squadrons were obliged to provide a standing Quick Reaction Alert (QRA), which came into effect during October 1960. Other problems were also coming to the fore, the primary one of which was an increase in airframe fatigue consumption plus the appearance of cracks in areas of the structure that were not designed for such manoeuvres. To manage the fatigue lives of each airframe they were fitted with 'g' fatigue meters that were read after each sortie. While each aircraft was monitored via the meter the crews were charged following a series of requirements. These covered flying at a reduced speed wherever possible, fuel management to ensure that the wing fuel contents were as low as possible before undertaking violent manoeuvres, both low-level manoeuvring and low-level flying were to be undertaken near the end of the flight and 'g' manoeuvres were to be restricted to no more than 4 'g'. While this directive was a touch restrictive, within the context of airframe fatigue management, it was found to be a necessity although in times of war such hampering of flying would be removed.

Photo reconnaissance was a vital part of Bomber Commands needs, as not only were sorties required to track down and confirm possible targets, their efforts were also required to photograph targets post strike. All of Bomber Command's reconnaissance assets were contained within No. 3 Group, the headquarters for which was located at Mildenhall. The group was commanded by Air Vice-Marshal KBB Cross until May 1959 when he was replaced by Air Vice-Marshal MH Dwyer. Air Vice-Marshal Dwyer remained in post until replaced by Air Vice-Marshal BK Burnett in October 1961. He in turn was replaced by Air Vice-Marshal DF Spotswood in August 1964. The final incumbent was Air Vice-Marshal DG Smallwood who took up his duties in November 1965 and remained in post until No. 3 Group was absorbed by No. 1 Group in 1967. Both of the latter officers would eventually serve as Commanders in Chief of Strike Command.

The aircraft types flown by No. 3 Group were variants of the Vickers Valiant and the English Electric Canberra PR7. The Canberra PR7 was flown by a single unit within the

As well as the bomber version of the Canberra, Bomber Command also received the photo-recce model. This is Canberra PR7 WJ820 of No. 58 Squadron based at Wyton. *(BBA Collection)*

group, No. 58 Squadron. Based at Wyton No. 58 Squadron had cut its reconnaissance teeth on the DH Mosquito PR34 before moving to Wyton to equip with the Canberra PR3, which was replaced in January 1955 by the more capable PR7 version. For a short period the squadron also operated the Canberra PR9 between January 1960 and November 1962. The Canberra PR7 remained in service with No. 58 Squadron until the unit disbanded in September 1970.

No.58 Squadron was the only survivor of the original four strong reconnaissance Canberra wings that remained at Wyton. To them fell all those tasks that were undertaken during periods of peace. As well as the full range of photo-based navigation exercises both at home and overseas the squadron also undertook less well known tasks. One of these was photographing areas for town and country planning agencies plus Ordnance Survey for the purpose of making more accurate maps. The squadron also sent detachments to Singapore during the Malaysian emergency, which lasted until 1960. The overall campaign was known as Operation *Firedog* while the reconnaissance detachment rejoiced in the name of Operation *Planter's Punch* initially and continued until the end of the emergency. No. 58 Squadron also sent detachments to Kenya in support of the Mau Mau operations.

The Canberra also found favour in other roles as there were only so many overseas sales possible for redundant Canberra B2s and PR3s. One area where the Canberra served well was that of electronic warfare and electronic intelligence gathering better known as ELINT. In a post-war Europe it would be the latter role that would become the most important as a previous erstwhile ally, Russia, created the iron curtain to differentiate between the so-called degenerate and the purity of a communist empire. With the world now polarized into two distinct factions those nations within the Western Union, later to evolve into NATO, were rightly concerned about advances in Russian arms technology especially as it appertained to a possible invasion of Europe. Although much photo-mapping of Europe, and where possible those countries that later became part of the Warsaw Pact, had been undertaken as part of Project Casey Jones after 1945, great tracts of Russia remained undiscovered. Project Casey Jones had been undertaken by the 381st Bomb Group whose Boeing B-17s had been disarmed with an array of cameras being installed instead. As the Russian air defence system had improved year on year the act of photo reconnaissance still remained very important, although great interest had arisen in the frequencies used in radio communications and those of radar arrays. To that end No. 192 Squadron at Watton eventually used small quantities of Avro Lincolns, Boeing B-29 Washingtons and Vickers Varsities for this task, although all suffered from a major fault, that of being too slow to evade any enemy fighters. The Lincolns would disappear in March 1953 with the Varsity going in April 1956. The heavily modified Washingtons would continue in service until February 1958 before a seriously falling serviceability rate saw them being withdrawn from use. Fortunately a replacement was on the horizon – the de Havilland Comet C2(RC). In April 1957 the first of No. 192 Squadron's de Havilland Comet C2(RC)s, XK663, arrived at Special Radio Installations Flight, in 3 Hangar at Watton, for fitting out with the full ELINT package.

No.192 Squadron had been non-operational since December 1957 awaiting the delivery of the Comet aircraft. Therefore no operational flights were undertaken during the month of January. In early February Comets XK663 and XK659 were delivered to No. 192 Squadron from Special Radio Installations Flight (SRIF), beginning operational flying immediately. By the end of the month both Comets had completed operational 'Border' ELINT flights, one of the duties of retired Washingtons. The Comets were frequently deployed on 'electronic ferret' missions over the Barents Sea north of Norway along the Baltic. Detachments were also undertaken to Cyprus where the aircraft were charged with monitoring activity, the Black Sea then being an area of particular interest as it was home to the Soviet Black Sea Fleet. The crew consisted of two pilots, two navigators and a flight engineer with up to ten electronic specialists in the main cabin of the aircraft where they operated the monitoring and recording equipment, the majority of which was manufactured in the USA. Eventually the squadron operated four ELINT Comets while other standard aircraft were used for crew training.

No.192 Squadron was also the recipient of four EECo Canberra B6(RC)s that were taken on strength in July 1954. These were heavily modified Canberra B6s with tail

The Canberra did not cover just the bomber and photo-recce roles. WH670 was originally built as a B2 although it was delivered to Signals Command, later No. 90 Signals Group. Of note is the large aerial just aft of the nosewheel doors. *(BBA Collection)*

warning equipment, sensors in the nose and a pair of ARI.5856 Blue Shadow Side Looking Airborne Radar (SLAR) that operated in the X-band. Also installed in these aircraft was the Green Satin Decca Doppler radar. Very little is known about the missions of these aircraft, a feature of much secret squirrel work.

In August 1958 the RAF decided, in the face of a contracting service, to move the number plates of younger squadrons to those of a greater age, thus No. 192 Squadron was renumbered as No. 51 Squadron. Initially No. 51 Squadron continued to operate from Watton although by March 1963 the squadron had completed its move to its new base at Wyton. During its final years as part of No. 90 Signal Group the squadron continued to operate the Canberras and Comets and for a short period some Handley Page Hastings.

Another function for which redundant Canberras were well suited was in the electronic warfare role. During 1963 the threat of Soviet air strikes accompanied by extensive ECM protection was becoming a reality. To counter this potential threat it was decided to create an aircraft that could simulate an incoming ECM attack. To that end design work for the systems required began in 1963 while the chosen platform would be retired Canberra B2s, these being redesignated the T17 after conversion. The conversion work was undertaken at Salmesbury and saw ECM power units mounted in the bomb bay space while the ECM aerials were mounted in a much modified nose cone that sported extra bumps to cover the aerial horns. Further equipment was mounted around the tail cone while chaff dispensers were also installed. Eventually, a total of twenty-three airframes were converted to this new version. To operate the new version No. 360 Squadron was formed in April 1966, formed by merging No. 97 Squadron, RAF, and No. 813 Naval Air Squadron, which had previously operated Fairey Gannets in a similar role. Throughout its existence the squadron had a mixed RAF and RN make up while the commanding officer alternated between the services.

Initially based at Watton No. 360 Squadron took over some of the duties of No. 97 Squadron using Canberra B2s and B6s. The first T17 prototype arrived at Watton for trials in January 1967, although it departed soon afterwards. Consolidation of the T17's systems took longer than expected thus the first operational aircraft did not appear until December of that year. As No. 360 Squadron was working up to full operational status another unit was in the process of being created to provide similar services in the Far East. However, this was yet another period of contraction for the Armed Forces thus No. 361 Squadron was formed at Watton in January 1967 being disbanded in July of that year, a victim of the 1967 defence review.

The purpose of No. 360 Squadron was to create an electronic warfare environment for land, sea and air units as needed. In reality their role was to create as much mayhem as possible for those charged with guiding fighters to their targets, this was followed by creating a similar picture for the fighter pilot desperately searching for the incoming opposition only to see his radar screen descend into a fuzzy mess. In order to improve the aircraft's capabilities some of the Canberras were upgraded to T17A standard, which featured improved navigation aids, a spectrum analyser and a powerful communications jammer. No. 360 Squadron was later moved to Cottesmore in April 1969 before decamping to its final base at Wyton in September 1975 to make way for the incoming Panavia Tornado. Eventually, the Canberra T17s were coming close to replacement, however the government decided that it would be cheaper and easier to farm the role out to a private concern. The result of this decision was that No. 360 Squadron was disbanded in October 1994.

The use of atom bombs to bring the Second World War to a swift and explosive conclusion would change the shape of aerial bombardment for ever. While conventional bombing would remain a vital part of the arsenal the power of the atom bomb delivered by air would become the ultimate deterrent. Allied to this change in warfare would be the dissolution of alliances built on the need for mutual victory over Germany. Once a cautious and suspicious ally the Russian influence would spread over eastern Europe and create the Warsaw Pact, while in the USA the Manhattan Project, creators of the first atom bombs, would be wound down and the British scientists sent home, allegedly without taking any secrets with them, while closer to home Bomber Command had realized quite quickly that their stalwart Avro Lancaster and its follow-on Lincoln replacement were already obsolescent especially as this was the emergence of the jet engine age. In response to these two separate acts both the government and RAF recommended that Britain should have the best weaponry available to defend the country throughout this period, better known as the Cold War.

After the war pressure within Britain was being put upon the government by both scientific and military groups who were pushing for a quick decision concerning the development of a British atom bomb. Such a push by political, military and scientific communities plus the expectations of the general population meant that the acquisition of such a bomb was almost inevitable and that it must be the best possible. The Prime Minister at the time was Clement Attlee who had been Deputy Prime Minister during the war period and was more than aware of the capabilities of the atomic bomb, thus he would preside at all meetings concerning major defence matters. It was believed that the creation of the bomb and its ability to be dropped from great height on any target in the world might have fostered greater hopes of peace through the newly created United Nations, but this was not to be as the USSR was determined to develop its own weapon and the aircraft to carry them. As this was the period before the creation of NATO the McMahon Act in the United States banning the export of such technologies to other nations meant that Britain needed its own bomb to stay on a par with the Americans. To that end the Chiefs of Staff would put forward their first requests for an atom bomb in August 1946. Supporting this request would be a report personally crafted by William Penney, the chief scientific advisor, that proposed how such a bomb could be manufactured in Britain. As the procurement of such a weapon was extremely secret in nature it came as no surprise to find that discussions of such things were restricted to as few people as possible.

Three people would have primary responsibility for creating the British atom bomb, Professor J Cockroft at Harwell, Sir William Penney who would oversee the manufacture and testing of the bomb and Christopher Hinton at Risley whose responsibility included the design and construction of the reactors required to produce the fissile material. All of this research and development was later concentrated at Fort Halstead in Kent, home of the Ministry of Supply (MoS) Armament Research Department whose location was quickly removed from any British maps. This conglomerate of scientists, engineers and technicians had only one purpose, which was to develop the core of a plutonium-based bomb known as the 'gadget'. A move from Fort Halstead to the ex-RAF airfield at Aldermaston would take place in 1950 during which period the gas-cooled reactor at Windscale in Cumberland went critical. Both of these events would lead the development team to predict that the testing of the first British atomic bomb could take place as early as October 1952 under the codename Operation *Hurricane*.

These successes would see the weapon ready in May 1952 after which it was loaded aboard HMS *Plym*, a naval frigate, for transportation to the test site close by the Monte Bello Islands. The successful conclusion of Operation *Hurricane* would be achieved on 3 October 1952 when the bomb, still aboard HMS *Plym*, was detonated.

Although Britain was facing a period of post-war austerity the development of the bomb had cost some £150 million over the seven-year development period, a fraction of the total defence budget. To ensure total security throughout this period the costs had been covered by the Civil Contingencies Fund under the title of The Public Buildings of Great Britain. For those who knew where to look some of the clues to the nuclear programme were available thus the shortage of stainless steel was courtesy of the development programme while shortages of highly skilled labour meant that there were shortages in some British industries.

All of this would lead to the successful explosion of an atomic device, but the bomb itself would have its specification formulated in 1946, subsequently becoming known as Blue Danube. As such bombs were complicated in nature the RAF took the unusual step of creating a specialist team that would work alongside their civilian counterparts to simplify the operation of Blue Danube. The co-operation would lead to the creation of good training and maintenance facilities for the Blue Danube and the writing of the manuals in support of same. However, ensuring that a nuclear device could be made to explode and creating a workable deliverable weapon would be an entirely different prospect, thus four years would pass before Blue Danube became a reality, although this period was put to good use for developing the aeroplanes needed to carry such a weapon.

With the bomb undergoing development attention would now turn to creating the bomber to carry the weapon. At the time Bomber Command was reliant on the Lancaster, a stalwart of the war effort, and the Lincoln, a later development. Joining the strength of Bomber Command would be a large quantity of Boeing B-29s known in RAF circles as the Washington. All three aircraft had serious shortcomings, the Avro-built machines being slow, not overly manoeuvrable and still toting defensive machine guns in turrets while the American built aircraft suffered from short-length bomb bays that would not be able to accommodate any British-built weapon. To ensure that Bomber Command was equipped with an aircraft that was capable of flying into the Warsaw Pact to drop its weapon the Air Ministry issued Specification B.35/46, which called for a medium bomber to Operational Requirement OR.229. The specification required that the competing manufacturers develop an aircraft that was capable of carrying a 10,000lb bomb over a range of 1,500 miles from a friendly base anywhere in the world. The manufacturers were also made aware of the possibility that for much of the aircraft's flight it would be tracked by ground based radar thus any aircraft developed to this specification had to be capable of avoiding destruction by both air- and ground-based attackers. To satisfy these needs the bomber had to have a high cruising speed, be manoeuvrable at high speeds and altitudes, have a high cruising altitude, be capable of carrying sufficient warning devices and have adequate self defence systems.

The required performance called for a continuous power output between altitudes of 35,000 and 50,000 feet at a consistent speed of 500 knots. This in turn required that the maximum speed in level flight should be as high as possible. Further details within the same specification required the bomber to be able to fly in all weathers and that it should have a still air range of 3,350 nautical miles at a height of 50,000 feet carrying a 10,000lb bomb. The total bomb load needed to be 20,000lb maximum that could comprise a

10,000lb or 6,000lb high-explosive bomb, 1,000lb bombs or a single special bomb. The crew would consist of two pilots, two navigators who would share bomb aiming and radar operating duties, and a single wireless operator who would also manage the onboard warning and protective devices. The engine installation was also quite flexible, although there was a restriction set on the number, which could be between four and six depending on the power output available at that time. Navigation equipment had to consist of a long-range direct reckoning and fixing system using the H2S radar system to help pinpoint specific ground features while a completely automatic astro navigation system was to be developed. The radio and radar systems would include the H2S radar with a navigation and bombing computer, Rebecca/ BABS or the SCS51, which was to be used in conjunction with the autopilot. Multi-channel UHF and VHF was also required as were radar-warning devices that had to be capable of detecting the launch and approach of air- and ground-launched missiles.

Six firms responded to the B.35/46 specification: Armstrong Whitworth, Avro with the Type 698, Bristol with the Type 172 design, English Electric, Handley Page and Vickers. By August 1947 the Minister of Defence had decreed that there would be a slowdown in the overall development speed of new weapons as it was highly unlikely that there would be any major conflict in the following five years while a further five-year period of grace, with some rising tension, would exist before any full-scale war erupted. This hiatus would give all of the country's aircraft manufacturers time to ponder in depth the technology surrounding the integration of jet engines, swept wings and high speed flight. The Chiefs of the Defence Staff were also grateful for this break as it had proven impossible to determine the number of atomic weapons that Britain required but their one assurance was that possession of such and the means to deliver a weapon would act as a deterrent to any future enemies.

Eventually, six tenders were delivered to the Ministry of Supply in May 1947. That tender from English Electric would resemble a slightly enlarged Canberra with slightly swept back wings while the Vickers' proposal featured an airframe with a long fuselage carried on a high aspect wing with a 26 degree sweep back. These two proposals were

The Vickers Valiant B1 was the first of the V bombers to enter service. Still wearing the unpainted finish of the early aircraft is WZ370 that spent some time engaged in Blue Steel trials in Australia. *(John Ryan Collection)*

quickly discarded as not being advanced enough for 1957 thus the other four were given greater consideration. All would feature sweep back, delta wings, crescent and flying wings but all were too slightly advanced for an Air Ministry that was just accepting the Avro Lincoln into service. The answer was to pass all of the information to the Royal Aircraft Establishment at Farnborough for further evaluation and guidance.

The ongoing process of selection would soon see the more advanced flying wing designs from Shorts and Armstrong Whitworth rejected even though they would be lighter than more conventional designs and would offer a greater maximum altitude. This process of elimination would leave only two concept designs in front of the group these being the crescent winged Handley Page HP80 and the delta winged Avro Type 698. As both of these aircraft were destined to be at the cutting edge of design technology in the 1950s the Bomber Project Group felt able to recommend that a third less advanced design be pursued. This would allow the introduction of a large jet bomber into RAF service at an earlier date than was possible with the other aircraft types. In fact, this option would be based upon two entirely different aircraft that had been built to the original specification. The first for consideration would be the Short SA4 Sperrin while the second aircraft to be presented at a lower technology level would be the Vickers Valiant. This had been put forward to the RAF, the MoS and the Advanced Bomber Project Group as the Type 660. This was recommended by the bomber group as having fewer development problems especially as the wings would be of reduced sweep back. The guaranteed production time scale put forward by George Edwards, the chief designer at Vickers, was enough to convince the RAF and the Air Ministry to issue a new specification, B.9/48, in April 1948. Construction of the two Valiant prototypes would be undertaken at the Fox Warren experimental shops for two reasons. The first was for security reasons, the second was due to Weybridge, the main production works, being jammed with Viscounts, Valettas and Vikings. The first prototype, WB210, would undertake its maiden flight on 18 May 1951.

The Vickers Valiant was a four-engined high-winged monoplane with a mid-mounted tailplane. The power was courtesy of the Rolls-Royce Avon 204/205 series engines that also provided pneumatic and electrical power to the aircraft systems. While described as a simple aircraft the Valiant featured some interesting innovations, as not only were the flaps and undercarriage electrically driven, the main gear units were tandem in design, although each wheel was mounted on a separate undercarriage leg. The crew were housed in a pressurized cabin and consisted of two pilots, two navigators and a signaller, later upgraded to an air electronics operator. Various versions of the Valiant were delivered, including the B Mk 1 pure bomber variant and the B(PR), a bomber/photo-reconnaissance aircraft that had been considered from the start and therefore this particular batch of aircraft could accommodate a removable crate in the bomb-bay, carrying up to eight narrow view/high resolution cameras and four survey cameras. Also delivered was the B(PR)K1, a bomber/photo-reconnaissance/tanker aircraft, plus the B(K)1, a bomber/tanker aircraft. Both tanker variants carried a removable tanker system in the bomb-bay, which featured fuel tanks and a hose-and-drogue aerial refuelling system.

In 1960 the Lockheed U-2 flown by Gary Powers was shot down over Russia, which revealed that the SAM threat was greater than first realized and led the V-Force to train for low-level attacks. Unfortunately, low-level operations proved too much for the Valiant and on 6 August 1964 there was a failure of a rear spar in WP217, an OCU aircraft from

Vickers Valiant BK1 XD828 was on the inventory of No. 7 Squadron based at Honington and sports an all white scheme. *(BBA Collection)*

Gaydon. The aircraft landed safely back at Gaydon but without a flap due to damage in the rear of one wing. Later inspection of the aircraft showed the fuselage skin below the starboard inner wing section had buckled, popping the rivets; the engine door had cracked and the rivets had been pulled and the skin buckled on the top surface of the mainplane between the two engines.

Inspection of the entire fleet showed that the wing spars were suffering from fatigue at between 35 per cent and 75 per cent of the assessed safe fatigue life, probably due to low-level turbulence. After this inspection, the aircraft were divided into three categories: Cat A aircraft continuing to fly, Cat B to fly to a repair base, and Cat C requiring repair before flying again. The tanker squadrons had the highest proportion of Cat A aircraft because their role had been mainly at high level. However, in early 1965 the Wilson government decided that the expense of the repairs could not be justified and the fleet was permanently grounded on 26 January 1965.

Although the Valiant prototype, WP210, had been lost in a crash in January 1952 Vickers were given a production contract for their new aircraft. Eventually, a total of 114 aircraft were delivered to equip ten squadrons with the first delivery taking place in January 1955 to No. 138 Squadron based at Gaydon. By July the squadron had transferred to Wittering and eventually had a strength of eleven Valiants. Either side of the Suez War in October 1956 the squadron undertook overseas proving trials designated Operation *Too Right*, while Exercise Rejuvenate took place afterwards and tested the defences of the north-west of Britain. After seven years of operations No. 138 Squadron was disbanded in April 1962. During its existence No. 138 Squadron had operated the standard version, the B Mk 1, a reconnaissance version of the B(PR) Mk 1, a combined reconnaissance and tanker version, the B(PR)K Mk,1, and the bomber tanker version, the BK Mk,1. Following No. 138 Squadron came No. 49 Squadron, which reformed at Wittering in May 1956. Soon after formation the squadron became involved with Operation *Buffalo*, the dropping of Britain's first atomic bombs codenamed Blue Danube. A move to Marham took place in June 1961 with the squadron being declared to Superme Allied Commander Europe (SACEUR) in 1961 while the unit was declared ready in the operational role in August 1962. Disbandment took place in May 1965. In common with No. 138 Squadron, No. 49 Squadron would operate the full range of Valiant versions during its existence.

Honington was the home of No. 7 Squadron when it reformed as a Valiant unit in October 1956. Although the squadron was involved with the numerous Bombex (bombing exercise) flights it also undertook various astro navigation and NBS (Navigation/Bombing System) trials. During June 1958 the squadron took part in Exercise Full Play. Having flown the full gamut of Valiant models the squadron would disband in October 1962, although one flight was retained to represent Bomber Command at the Ugandan independence celebrations. Just before No. 7 Squadron formed No. 148 Squadron had been reformed at Marham in July 1956. The squadron would join No. 138 Squadron in Malta during the Suez Crisis, undertaking bombing attacks on Almaza and Fayid airfields, each being the recipient of twelve 1,000lb bombs from each of the participating aircraft. Having returned from active service No. 148 Squadron became involved in Exercise Green Epoch in February 1957. This exercise was designed to give the US Navy 6th Fleet and its defences a good workout. Both day and night attacks were undertaken successfully; the only interception made during this period was made by a pair of Grumman F9F Cougars. Flag waving was always part of the Bomber Command scenario thus two Valiants were dispatched to the Gold Coast in 1957 to take part in independence celebrations, the country being renamed Ghana at the same time. When NATO required that the V bombers be declared to SACEUR No. 148 Squadron was declared operational in April 1963. Its sojourn with NATO was short as the unit was disbanded in April 1965.

Honington was home to two other units, Nos 90 and 199 Squadrons. No. 90 Squadron was reformed in January 1957 with the majority of its aircraft coming straight off the production line. After a period of working up the squadron undertook a tour of the Far East in March 1958, calling at Singapore, the Philippines and South Vietnam. After the majority of aircraft had wended their way home a single machine, XD862, carried on to Australia and New Zealand returning to Britain soon afterwards. Two aircraft were dispatched to Marshalls of Cambridge in April 1958 for RATOG and water methanol equipment fitment and trials. By 1962 the squadron had become a flight refuelling unit in April 1962, although it was disbanded three years later. Also based at Honington was No. 199 Squadron, which had been engaged in ECM work since 1952, although after the

Vickers Valiant BK1 XD867 was on the strength of No. 90 Squadron from Honington when photographed. *(BBA Collection)*

move to Honington the Canberras were joined by Valiants that were fitted with American-provided ECM equipment that included the APT-7 and APT-16A jammers plus APR-9 and APR-4 search receivers. The aircraft were also fitted with chaff dispensers. All of the Valiants flown by C Flight of No. 199 Squadron were disbanded in December 1958 although within two days, on 17 December, the flight was used to form the core of No. 18 Squadron. This new unit would decamp to Finningley and would remain operational until disbandment in April 1963.

In 1956 two further units would form at Marham to operate the Valiant, all major versions being flown. The first would be No. 214 Squadron, which reformed in January. By October the unit was based in Malta to undertake bombing raids in support of the Suez crisis. Attacks were undertaken against El Adem, Almazara and Abu Sueir, all of which received their fair share of 1,000lb bombs. Further raids were carried out against Kasfrit, Huckstep Barracks and El Agami. During 1958 No. 214 Squadron became involved in the trials for the proposed in-flight refuelling system for which purpose a dispensing system was fitted in the bomb-bay. The unit took over this role permanently in 1962 and continued in this role until the Valiants were grounded in 1965. No. 207 Squadron would reform at Marham in April 1956. After working up the unit would take part in bombing raids against Egyptian targets during the Suez Crisis. Targets attacked by the Valiants of No. 207 Squadron included Kabrit, Kasfareet and El Agami. Upon its return to Britain No. 207 Squadron took part in Exercise Red Pivot, during which the Valiants undertook mock attacks against the US Navy 6th Fleet. No. 207 Squadron took part in the 1960 Annual Bomber Command Competition, in the process winning the Laurence Minot and Armament Officers' Trophies. The following year the squadron won the Medium Bomber Squadron Efficiency Trophy. During 1958 the squadron would transfer, along with the other Valiant units, to the low-level role operating as low as 100 feet on some occasions. The unit would receive the American Mk 43 nuclear weapons in 1962 after which it was declared to NATO remaining available to them until disbandment in 1965.

Vickers Valiant BK1 XD829 heads this line-up of camouflaged aircraft at Gaydon. Not long after this portrait was taken the entire fleet was grounded after a wing spar failure. *(BBA Collection)*

Illustrating the Valiant's final role is XD812 of No. 214 Squadron from Marham seen refuelling AWA Argosy C1 XN814, which was undertaking trials. *(BBA Collection)*

The final operational unit to fly the Valiant was No. 543 Squadron, which reformed in September 1956 at Gaydon, although by November the squadron had transferred to Wyton. During 1958 the unit took part in Operation *Record Book* and Exercise Freshwind. In common with the other squadrons No. 543 Squadron would lose its Valiants in 1965, although the unit would remain active as it received Handley Page Victor SR2s as replacements. Other units would also fly Valiants at various times, including No. 2 Air Trials Unit, which operated a lone aircraft, WP206, to undertake trials of the Blue Steel standoff weapon inertial guidance platform. This unit was finally disbanded in 1960 with the Valiant being dispatched to Australia to join the Blue Steel trials unit. The Bomber Command Development Unit based at Gaydon also operated some Valiants between February 1955 and March 1956. During this period the allocated aircraft undertook intensive flying trials aimed at revealing any persistent defects that needed rectifying before the aircraft entered service. Supporting the flying units was No. 232 Operational Conversion Unit, also based at Gaydon. The unit was formed in February 1955 and charged with providing trained crews to the Valiant fleet as well as standards checking. The OCU lost its aircraft in 1965, although the number plate would later be used by the Victor OCU. The final unit to operate the Valiant was No. 1321 Flight whose job was to undertake trials involved in Blue Danube. The aircraft assigned to these trials was WP201, the third prototype, and the dropping trials of the inert Blue Danube were undertaken on behalf of the Atomic Weapons Research Establishment acting in concert with the Royal Aircraft Establishment. The flight was disbanded in March 1956, the trials being taken over by No. 138 Squadron, also based at Wittering.

The aircraft that would survive the longest in the bombing role was the Avro Vulcan. Designed to fulfil Operational Requirement 229 the aircraft that would become the Type 698 would be designed to cover both the conventional and nuclear bombing roles. The first prototype, VX770, undertook its maiden flight on 30 August 1952 piloted by Wing Commander Roly Falk. The second prototype, VX777, would join the flight test programme on 3 September 1953, followed quite quickly by some of the early production Vulcan B1s. The crew in all of the production versions consisted of a captain, co-pilot, navigator radar, navigator plotter and air electronics operator. Crews would meet up at 230 OCU, first at Finningley and later at Scampton, and would eventually be posted to flying units as a group.

Early on in the Vulcan's career a major problem reared its head; in level flight at high speed the aircraft showed a tendency to pitch up and therefore much effort was expended on curing this fault. The answer was a cranked and kinked wing plus auto stabilizers that would considerably reduce the pitch problem; most of the fleet would either have this modification embodied or would be delivered with it as standard. The Vulcan B1 was intended to carry either the Yellow Sun or Red Beard free fall nuclear weapon that would be dropped from high altitude, and to that end it was finished in gloss white anti-flash white paint. Unfortunately, those that designed the colour scheme forgot that dark colours on such things as national markings and the tail numbers would absorb heat and flash from the bomb and burn through the airframe. Also lacking in the early B1 was a dedicated ECM installation, which was catered for by installing the ECM equipment in the bomb bay, although to support this a turbo generator was installed to cover the electrical requirements. Obviously, when conventional bombs were loaded the ECM equipment had to be off loaded to make room.

Only thirty-five Vulcan B1s would be built as this version was seen as an interim model; the B2 that would emerge in August 1958 was a far more advanced machine. Powerplants were more powerful and the initial model was the Olympus 200 series engine in place of the earlier Olympus 100 series engines. The airframe also underwent significant changes; the wings had their span extended while the leading edge was also cranked as per the earlier model. The fuselage also underwent some changes; the ECM equipment was installed in a purposely designed tail cone while a refuelling probe was installed in the nose. Both of these modifications were embodied in the earlier B1s, these being redesignated B1A after conversion. Other changes included the installation of powered flying control units (PFCUs) for the flight control surfaces, these being self-contained units unlike the previous B1, which gained its power supply from the aircraft's hydraulics. The electrical installation also underwent a radical overhaul being changed to 28V dc and 200v AC. This change was backed up by the installation of a ram air turbine

When the Blue Steel stand-off weapon was deployed one of the recipient units was No. 617 Squadron at Scampton whose XL321 is seen here. *(John Ryan Collection)*

Even with snow and ice on the ground the Blue Steel Vulcans still required maintenance. Suffering the icy blast is XL444 of No. 27 Squadron at Scampton. *(BBA Collection)*

(RAT) and an airborne auxiliary power plant (AAPP), both of which could supply electrical power in case of emergency; the latter system could also supply power on the ground should no external source be available. Initially the Vulcan B2s were delivered in anti-flash white finish with the correct pale-coloured national markings.

Initially the B2s were slated to carry the same nuclear weapons as the B1s, however the improvements in Soviet air defences meant that the Vulcan fleet was more vulnerable therefore another means of delivery was needed. The answer would be the Blue Steel standoff weapon. The project was led by Avro whose sub contractors would provide a very capable inertial navigation system while the powerplant was the Bristol-designed Stentor engine whose fuel was the highly volatile hydrogen peroxide. After numerous trials at home and Australia the first weapons were issued to No. 617 Squadron in

The first version of the Vulcan to enter service was the B1. This is XH478 undertaking refuelling trials with Vickers Valiant WZ376. *(John Ryan Collection)*

September 1962, although these weapons were designated for national emergency use only until the fully developed version was available. When the decision was taken to swap the Vulcan to the low-level role in 1964 the aircraft were repainted in upper surface camouflage while the Blue Steel delivery tactics were altered to suit.

The Blue Steel weapon, while adequate for its purpose, was due for replacement thus the RAF cast around for a more viable replacement. It was during this period that the Douglas Aircraft Corporation was developing an intermediate range ballistic missile for the USAF. Known as WS, or weapons system, 138A the weapon was later designated AGM-87A Skybolt and was seen as a better proposition than the Blue Steel Mk 2 as its range was far greater. Discussion at governmental level began in 1960 with a Memorandum of Understanding being signed on 6 June. Skybolt was beset by problems from the beginning but each problem was cleared and each launch article behaved closer to the desired profile. Ironically the weapon would be cancelled in November 1962 on the very day that a Skybolt performed faultlessly. To replace Skybolt the Americans would offer the Polaris missile system as a replacement.

While Blue Steel remained in service the problem of delivering the weapon safely at low level was becoming one of great concern as flying into the ground with your country's deterrent aboard was undesirable. The answer would be the Terrain Following Radar system that was test flown aboard XM606 during 1966. The system was housed in a small pod and was mounted in an extreme nose just under the in flight refuelling probe.

Given the complexity of the Vulcan it was the conversion unit that formed first, therefore in May 1956 No. 230 OCU was reformed at Waddington to prepare for the entry into service of the Vulcan B1. The first aircraft was officially handed over on 20 July 1956, although it was quickly returned to Avro for further trials thus the first aircraft delivered to the OCU didn't turn up until September. Proper crew training finally started in January 1957 with the first crews from A Flight being hived off to form the basis of No. 83 Squadron. When the Vulcan B2 entered service B Flight was formed in July 1960 to train aircrew for this version. A Flight was still in existence flying a mix of

With the increase in the strength and accuracy of the Warsaw Pact air defences Bomber Command instituted a programme of adding ECM to the fleet. Showing the modifications that created the Vulcan B1A is XH482. *(BBA Collection)*

Vulcan B1 and B1A aircraft, and this earlier model remained with the OCU until it was retired in November 1965. The entire organization decamped to Finningley a year later, remaining there until a final move was made to Scampton in December 1969. By this time the OCU was flying Vulcan B2s and the handful of Handley Page Hastings T5s used for NBS training, better known as No. 1066 Squadron. No. 230 OCU was finally disbanded in August 1981 as there was no further need for Vulcan crews as the force was winding down.

The first operational unit to form with the Vulcan B1 was No. 83 Squadron based at Waddington whose first aircraft arrived in July. As the first operational unit No. 83 Squadron found itself heavily involved in developing tactics for the new aircraft and proving that it was more than capable of doing the job it was designed for. Once fully operational the squadron was declared as part of Britain's nuclear deterrent. Initially the Vulcans were configured to deliver Blue Danubes, although these were later replaced by Violet Clubs.

In 1960 No. 83 Squadron moved to Scampton minus its Vulcan B1s in order to prepare for the Vulcan B2. By October the squadron was declared operational on its new mount, although its primary role initially was that of free fall weapons delivery both in the strike and attack modes. By 1963 the squadron's role changed to that of Blue Steel delivery and the unit remained in this role until being disbanded in August 1969.

Hard on the heels of No. 83 Squadron would be No. 101 Squadron, which would trade in its Canberra bombers for the Vulcan B1. Based at Finningley the unit reformed as a Vulcan operator in October 1957. After being declared operational the unit undertook numerous detachments, the most notable of which was to South America during May 1960. By March 1961 the Vulcan B1s were being replaced by the more capable B1A. With the new model in service the squadron moved to Waddington and undertook training to deliver the Yellow Sun nuclear weapon in the free fall role. The squadron would receive its first Vulcan B2 during 1967 and would retain the model until disbanding in August 1982 having provided crews for the recapture of the Falklands.

Bomber Command realized that at some point the effectiveness of Blue Steel would lessen. The answer appeared to be the Douglas Skybolt, however as America preferred to utilize submarine-launched weapons the programme was cancelled. XH537 is captured rolling along the taxiway with a pair of dummy missiles under the wings. *(John Ryan Collection)*

Possibly the best known bomber squadron was No. 617 'Dambusters' Squadron, which traded in its Canberras and reformed with the Vulcan B1 at Scampton in May 1958. By September 1960 the squadron was equipped with the Vulcan B1A, although these were dispensed with in August 1961 being transferred to Waddington to equip No. 50 Squadron while No. 617 Squadron received the Vulcan B2 as replacements. This squadron would also be equipped to carry the Blue Steel standoff missile and retained this role until the weapon was retired in favour of Polaris. With their aircraft restored to the free fall role No. 617 Squadron trained for the strike mission with the WE177B nuclear free fall weapon while in the attack role the aircraft was used to drop a variety of high-explosive bombs.

One other unit (No. 83 Squadron) also flew from Scampton with the Vulcan B2, reforming in April 1961. Initially deployed in the free fall role the unit flew with Blue Steel rounds aboard until the weapon was retired, after which the squadron returned to the free fall role until disbanded in March 1972.

Over at Waddington two units would form to fly the Vulcan B1, the first was No. 44 Squadron, which was basically the original No. 83 Squadron renumbered. By July 1961 the unit was equipped with Vulcan B1As, retaining these plus the Yellow Sun free fall weapon until 1967 when the B2 was received. By this time the Vulcan squadrons were learning about flying at low level, although the bomber still needed to make a rapid climb to 12,000 feet to release the weapon. No. 44 Squadron finally disbanded at Waddington in December 1982. Also at Waddington was No. 50 Squadron, which gained its Vulcan mix from No. 617 Squadron in August 1961 and had already adapted to low-level operations in 1964 before the Vulcan B2 arrived in December 1965. The squadron used its aircraft in both the free fall strike and attack roles before changing its role completely in 1982 when six aircraft were converted to single point tankers. No. 50 Squadron disbanded in March 1984.

In common with the remainder of the V Force aircraft the Vulcan fleet soon received upper surface camouflage as shown here on B2 XM650 of the Waddington Wing. *(BBA Collection)*

Coningsby would be the home for the final three Vulcan operational units. No. 9 Squadron would receive its Vulcan B2s in March 1962, although the entire wing decamped to Cottesmore in November 1964. Initially the squadron was trained to deliver the Yellow Sun free fall nuclear weapon, although this was replaced later by the WE.177B weapon. When the strike task ended for the Cottesmore Wing No. 9 Squadron was dispatched to Akrotiri as part of the NEAF Strike Wing. Also at Coningsby and later Cottesmore was No. 12 Squadron whose operational history with the Vulcan B2 was similar to that of No. 9 Squadron. When Polaris became part of Britain's nuclear deterrent No. 12 Squadron was disbanded in December 1967 and later reformed as a Buccaneer unit in October 1969. The final Coningsby / Cottesmore wing unit was No. 35 Squadron, which received its aircraft in December 1962. In common with the two other units No. 35 Squadron trained on both the Yellow Sun and WE.177B free fall nuclear weapons before transferring to Akrotiri as part of the NEAF Strike Wing. The Vulcan would also be operated by other units in various roles. The Bomber Command Development Unit was the main one. Based initially at Wittering the unit originally covered the Canberra before taking on the Valiant. After a move to Finningley the BCDU concentrated its efforts on the Vulcan and remained active until December 1968.

The final member of the V bomber triumvirate to join the RAF would be the Handley Page Victor. Beaten into the air by the Vulcan prototype that flew on 30 August 1952 those building the Victor had to wait until Christmas Eve to get their contender into the skies. Although the Victor prototypes performed within design specifications there were a few design miscalculations that eventually led to the loss of WB771 on 14 July 1954, when the tailplane detached whilst making a low-level pass over the runway at Cranfield. This caused the aircraft to crash with the loss of the crew. The tailplane was attached to the fin using three bolts thus more stress than had been anticipated was generated and the three bolts failed due to metal fatigue. Also adding to the loading problems the aircraft were tail heavy due to the lack of equipment in the nose, although this was remedied by placing large ballast weights in that area. The fin on production aircraft was

Handley Page Victor B1 XA936 'A' performs a flyby in its white anti-flash finish. This aircraft was operated by Nos 10 and 15 Squadrons at Cottesmore. *(John Ryan Collection)*

This excellent portrait shows Victor B1 XA927 of No. 57 Squadron from Honington at altitude. Like many of its ilk it was later converted to a tanker. *(BBA Collection)*

shortened to eliminate the potential for flutter while the tailplane attachment was changed to a stronger four-bolt fixing arrangement.

Production B1 Victors were powered by the Armstrong Siddeley Sapphire ASSa.7 engines and was originally configured to deliver the Blue Danube nuclear weapon, later re-equipping with the more powerful Yellow Sun weapon when it became available, although Victors were also capable of carrying the American-owned Mk 5 nuclear bombs that were made available under the Project E programme while the British Red Beard tactical nuclear weapon was added to the inventory when it became available. A total of twenty-four were later upgraded to B1A standard by the addition of Red Steer tail warning radar in an enlarged tail cone and a suite of ECM jammers between 1958 and 1960.

The RAF later recognized a requirement for a higher ceiling for its bombers, and a number of proposals were considered for improved Victors to meet this demand. Handley Page proposed using Sapphire 9 engines to produce a Phase 2 bomber, which was followed by the Phase 3 Victor with much greater wingspan and powered by Bristol Siddeley Olympus or Rolls-Royce Conways. The Sapphire 9 was later cancelled while the heavily modified Phase 3 aircraft would have delayed production. The interim Phase 2A Victor was therefore proposed and accepted, powered by the Conway engine with the airframe having minimal modifications. The Phase 2A proposal was accepted by the Air Staff as the Victor B2 powered by the Conway; these required enlarged and redesigned intakes to provide greater airflow. The wingspan was increased to 120 feet. In contrast with the B1, the B2 featured distinctive retractable elephant ear intakes on the rear fuselage forward of the fin that fed ram air to turbine-driven alternators. In the event of a high altitude flameout or other engine problems that caused the loss of electrical or hydraulic power the RAT scoops would open and provide sufficient electrical power to work the flight controls until the main engines could be relit. The right wing root also incorporated a Blackburn Artouste airborne auxiliary powerplant (AAPP). This small engine could provide high pressure air for engine starting, electrical power on the ground, or in the air as an emergency backup in the event of main engine failure. The aircraft also featured a fin extension at the base that contained the ECM cooling equipment.

With its airbrakes extended Victor B2 XL163 of No. 139 Squadron performs a flyby at Wittering. *(John Ryan Collection)*

The first prototype Victor B2, serial number XH668, undertook its maiden flight on 20 February 1959. The aircraft had flown 100 hours quite safely when on 20 August 1959 while undertaking high-altitude engine tests for the Aeroplane and Armament Experimental Establishment it disappeared from radar screens and crashed into the sea off the coast of Pembrokeshire. An extensive search operation was initiated to locate the aircraft and the wreckage was finally discovered in November 1960 with the accident investigation report concluding that the starboard pitot head had failed during the flight, causing the aircraft's flight control system to force the aircraft into an unrecoverable

When it was decided that the Victor fleet would be camouflaged the first recipient was XL513. Originally the dividing line finished as shown, although it would soon drop further down the fuselage. *(John Ryan Collection)*

dive. Only minor changes were needed to resolve this problem thus allowing the Victor B2 to enter service in February 1962.

A total of twenty-one B2 aircraft were upgraded to the B2 Blue Steel standard with Conway engines of increased thrust while fitments were incorporated to allow the carriage of a Blue Steel standoff nuclear missile. The aircraft's wings were modified to incorporate two pods or Küchemann carrots that were anti-shock bodies that reduced wave drag at transonic speeds. They were also used as a convenient place to house chaff dispensers. Handley Page proposed building a further refined Phase 6 Victor with more fuel and the capability of carrying up to four Skybolt ballistic missiles on standing airborne patrols, although this proposal was later rejected. Later it was agreed that some of the Victor B2s on order would be fitted to carry two Skybolts, although this idea was later abandoned when the United States cancelled the whole Skybolt programme in 1963. With the move to low-level penetration attack profiles the Victors were fitted with air-to-air refuelling probes above the cockpit, large underwing fuel tanks receiving a two tone camouflage finish in place of the original anti-flash white. Trials were also conducted with terrain-following radar and a side scan mode for the bombing and navigation radar but neither became operational.

Nine B2 aircraft were converted for strategic reconnaissance purposes as the SR2 to replace the Valiants that had been withdrawn due to wing fatigue, with delivery beginning in July 1965. They received the capability for a bomb bay camera crate or a bomb bay-mounted radar mapping system plus air sniffers mounted at the front of the under wing tanks to detect particles released after nuclear testing. The long-range photographic reconnaissance role for the Handley Page Victor began in 1964 when Victor B2 XL165 became the prototype for the Victor B(SR)2, this later being changed to SR2. XL165 undertook its maiden flight in February 1965 with deliveries of the aircraft beginning in May to No. 543 Squadron at RAF Wyton. The squadron undertook reconnaissance missions sorties far and wide, also carrying out high-level survey photographs for various governments. It was said that one Victor SR2 could photograph the whole of the UK in a single two-hour sortie.

Not only were bomber versions of the Victor delivered to the RAF, they also acquired a handful of SR2s for reconnaissance and air samples collection. Based at Wyton these aircraft were operated by No. 543 Squadron. *(John Ryan Collection)*

The photographic systems fitted to the SR2 were housed in a crate that was located within the bomb bay. This crate could have various camera combinations fitted to match the task thus for daylight reconnaissance this would normally be four F49 survey cameras and up to eight F96 cameras were fitted to take either vertical or oblique images. For undertaking night photography, F89 cameras would be fitted. As time passed it was a clear fact that the Shorts-built Canberra PR9 was cheaper to operate than the Victor thus the SR2 relinquished its photographic reconnaissance role and the nine Victor SR2s concentrated on maritime radar reconnaissance operations. On 24 May 1974, No. 543 Squadron was disbanded, three aircraft went to be converted to K2 tankers, and three other aircraft remained at Wyton at the Victor flight, used to monitor the French nuclear testing in the Pacific until that was discontinued in May 1976.

The withdrawal of the Valiant fleet due to metal fatigue in December 1964 saw the RAF with no front-line tanker aircraft and with the B1/1A aircraft now judged to be surplus in the strategic bomber role they were refitted for this duty. To get some tankers into service as quickly as possible Handley Page converted six B1A aircraft to B(K)1A standard, although these were later redesignated B1A (K2P). The version received a two-point system with a hose and drogue carried under each wing while the bomb bay remained available for weapons. Handley Page worked day and night to convert these six aircraft with the first being delivered on 28 April 1965, and No. 55 Squadron becoming operational in the tanker role in August 1965. While these six aircraft provided a limited tanker capability suitable for refuelling fighters, the Mk 20A wing hose reels could only deliver fuel at a limited rate therefore they were not suitable for refuelling larger aircraft. Work therefore continued to produce a definitive three-point tanker conversion of the Victor Mk 1. Fourteen further B1As and eleven B1s were fitted with two permanently fitted fuel tanks in the bomb bay plus a high-capacity Mk 17 centreline hose unit with three times the fuel flow rate as the wing pods, these being designated K1A and K1 respectively. The remaining B2 aircraft were not as suited to the low-level strike mission as the Vulcan with its strong delta wing. This, combined with the change of the nuclear deterrent from the RAF to the Royal Navy using submarine launched Polaris missiles meant that the Victor B2s were now surplus to requirements. Therefore twenty-four B2s were modified to K2 standard. Similar to the earlier K1/1A conversions the wingspan was reduced to reduce stress while the nose glazing was plated over.

The Victor was the last of the V bombers to enter service with the first deliveries of B1s to No. 232 Operational Conversion Unit RAF based at RAF Gaydon before the end of 1957. The first operational bomber squadron, No. 10 Squadron, formed at RAF Cottesmore in April 1958 while a second squadron, No. 15 Squadron, formed before the end of the year. Four Victors, fitted with Yellow Astor reconnaissance radar, together with a number of passive sensors, were used to equip a secretive unit, the Radar Reconnaissance Flight at RAF Wyton. The Victor bomber force continued to increase with No. 57 Squadron forming in March 1959 while No. 55 Squadron formed in October 1960.

Deliveries of the improved Victor B2 started in 1961, with the first B2 Squadron, No. 139 Squadron forming in February 1962 with a second, No. 100 Squadron, forming in May 1962. These were the only two bomber squadrons to form on the B2, as the last twenty-eight Victors on order were cancelled. The prospect of Skybolt ballistic missiles, with which each V-bomber could strike at two separate targets, meant that fewer bombers would be needed, while the government were unhappy with Sir Frederick Handley

Page's resistance to their pressure to merge his company with competitors. In 1964–1965 a series of detachments of Victor B1As was deployed to RAF Tengah, Singapore, as a deterrent against Indonesia during the Borneo conflict. The detachments fulfilled a strategic deterrent role as part of Far East Air Force, while also giving valuable training in low-level flight and visual bombing. In September 1964, with the confrontation with Indonesia reaching a peak, the detachment of four Victors was prepared for a rapid scramble with two aircraft loaded with live conventional bombs and held at one-hour readiness, however they were not required to fly combat missions therefore the readiness alert finished at the end of the month.

With the Victor B2 fleet now redundant Handley Page prepared a modification scheme that would see the Victors fitted with tip tanks, the structure modified to limit further fatigue cracking in the wings and ejection seats provided for all crew members. The Ministry of Defence delayed signing the order for conversion of the B2s until after Handley Page went into liquidation. The contract for conversion was instead awarded to Hawker Siddeley who produced a much simpler conversion than that planned by Handley Page, with the wingspan shortened to reduce wing-bending stress and thus extending airframe life.

An accident review for 1959 covering all three V bombers revealed some disturbing trends. As the first to enter service the Valiant fleet had seen its losses and major incident rates drop as experience was gained. During 1955 WP211 had experienced a rough running No. 3 engine; this had then been shut down at which point the fire warning light had illuminated. The Graviner fire bottles for the engine were then fired, which in turn caused the warning light to go out. After landing safely No. 3 engine was inspected and the failure of a compressor seal was discovered as the source of the fire. A similar set of circumstances befell WP212, which landed back at base after the No. 1 engine compressor seal had failed. Less lucky were the crew of WP222. Having departed for a cross country flight the aircraft was seen to turn to port instead of starboard as expected. Although the crew were obviously attempting to correct the bank the nose continued to turn towards the ground. The entrance door was jettisoned and the signaller baled out, although he did not survive. The Valiant continued towards the ground at a speed of 300 knots before crashing and killing the remaining crew members. The cause was determined to be either a stuck switch or a runaway actuator. Modification covering both of these faults was quickly carried out while the remaining Valiants were inspected and repaired as needed. One of the most telling incidents occurred on 29 April 1957 to Valiant WB215, which was being used by the Ministry of Supply. The aircraft was tasked to undertake Super Sprite rocket trials. During a run of the drop range the pilot banked away during which a lurch and muffled bangs were felt and heard. Although the crew suspected a problem they carefully nursed the aircraft back to base at which a normal landing was made. Post flight inspection revealed that the starboard mainplane rear spar near the wing break joint had failed close to the undercarriage bay.

The Vulcan also had its fair share of incidents, some of which were almighty cock-ups. The greatest of these involved B1 XA902, which was cleared to land on a runway that was bordered by snow banks. After touchdown the brake parachute was deployed, followed by a wild swing into one snow bank and a collision with the other bank. The result of this collision was the collapse of the port undercarriage and sideways slide off the runway. The subsequent investigation criticized the uncleared runway, the lack of proper self briefing by the crew and a failure by the Air Ministry to adequately provision major airfields with enough snow-clearing equipment.

Possibly one of the most serious incidents to overtake the Victor in its early years happened on 16 April 1958 when XA921 was undertaking trials for the Ministry of Supply. The crew were briefed to undertake bomb door and store release trials at various heights and speeds. During one of these bomb door cycles the installed close circuit television switched off, and the crew opted to return to base. During the post-flight inspection it was discovered that the rear bomb bay bulkhead had completely collapsed, which in turn had caused the false bulkhead at frame 804 to break up and the debris entered the bomb bay causing damage to the hydraulic and electrical systems in the bomb bay. All in-service Victors were then issued with an in-flight restriction concerning bomb door opening, although this was subsequently cancelled by Modification 943 being applied to all the extant aircraft.

In a similar manner to Fighter Command its heavier counterpart also had missiles in its inventory, although those of Bomber Command were of the strategic variety instead of the air defence type operated by Fighter Command. The ballistic missile supplied to the RAF was the Douglas Thor Intermediate Range Ballistic Missile. This had been designed and developed in nine months under a crash programme in 1955–6. By April 1962 144 had been launched, of which 114 were successful. In 1957 the new British Prime Minister Harold Macmillan visited President Eisenhower both in Bermuda and Washington as part of his efforts to patch up Anglo–American relations after the Suez Crisis in 1956. The Americans were worried that Warsaw Pact forces were setting up bases with missiles aimed at the USA. In response the Americans were keen to base Thor missiles within range of the Soviet Union. Britain was offered sixty missiles for free as Project Emily, although the defence budget would have to provide the bases, but the warheads would remain under American control with a US officer attached to each launch team. His responsibility was to hold the second key to arm the nuclear warhead thus ensuring that Britain could not launch a missile without US approval. Launching of the missile required the keys of both the RAF and USAF Launch Control Officers

When the TSR2 programme was cancelled a rather tortuous route led to the Blackburn Buccaneer. One of the first units to receive the type was No. 15 Squadron based at Honington whose XV350 is seen here. *(BBA collection)*

Showing what else the Buccaneer could do is XT270 releasing a full load of rockets from the SNEB pods under the wings. *(John Ryan Collection)*

(LCOs), however during some training exercises the USAF officer failed to turn up. As experience was gained with the systems it was discovered that the USAF LCO was not required as judicious use of a screwdriver, a copy of the RAF key or even hitting the lock could change the status of the missile from peace to war status.

The first Thor was delivered to No. 77 Squadron at RAF Feltwell on 19 September 1958 and deployment was completed by March 1960. Each of the twenty squadrons had three missiles and they were divided into four complexes around Driffield, Feltwell, Hemswell, and North Luffenham. Originally it was intended that there would be four squadrons with each squadron controlling five out-based flights of three missiles. These flights were subsequently renumbered as separate squadrons. The four missile groups were headquartered at Driffield, Feltwell, Hemswell and North Luffenham, with their satellite bases in close proximity. The Thors were air transportable and were delivered using Douglas C-124 Globemaster IIs and Douglas C-133 Cargomasters. The missiles were initially flown into Driffield, Hemswell later replaced by Scampton, Lakenheath for the Feltwell complex, and North Luffenham. All were then transported by road under armed guard to the outer sites. All the bases used to house the missile complexes had been retained on care and maintenance, and some had not been used since wartime. The RAF crews were trained in the US and the first live firing by an RAF crew was on 16 April 1959 at Vandenberg AFB, California.

The Thor missile force was designed to attack targets in the Soviet Union with the missiles arriving before the V-Bomber strike force reached their targets. In one exercise it was reported that fifty-nine of the sixty Thors were operational and ready to launch. The fifteen-minute delay in launching made them vulnerable on the ground and this was the reason given when it was announced on 1 August 1962 that the Thors would be withdrawn in the following year. The last Thor was withdrawn from service on 15 August 1963 and the missiles returned to the USA in Globemasters and Cargomasters, many later being used in further research programmes. The operating squadrons were then disbanded, none of them to reform. Most of the bases reverted to care and maintenance and subsequent disposal, although Feltwell and North Luffenham saw some use for non-flying activities.

The Feltwell Missile Group had its squadrons based at Feltwell (No.77 Squadron), Shepherds Grove (No.82 Squadron), Tuddenham (No.107 Squadron), Mepal (No.113 Squadron) and North Pickenham (No.220 Squadron). The unit at Feltwell became operational in January 1959 with the remainder coming on line during that July. The Helmswell Missile Group was home to No. 97 Squadron while Ludford Magna, Bardney, Coleby Grange and Caistor were the bases for Nos 104, 106, 142 and 269 Squadrons respectively. The Helmswell group operational dates were similar to those of the Feltwell group. The Driffield Missile Group housed No. 98 Squadron while Full Sutton, Carnaby, Catfoss and Breighton housed the Thor missiles allocated to Nos 102, 150, 226 and 240 Squadrons. Driffield and its outstations all came on line during January 1959 as did the North Luffenham group. The final Missile Group was based at North Luffenham, this being home to No. 144 Squadron, while Nos 130, 223, 218 and 254 Squadrons were based at Polebrook, Folkingham, Harrington and Melton Mowbray respectively. All four groups were stood down between April and August 1963, and the missiles were returned to the United States.

Chapter 3

Coastal and Transport Commands

Coastal Command had really earned its spurs during the Second World War; not only were its allocated squadrons involved hunting U-boats, they also carried out attacks on surface shipping and introduced a fully fledged search and rescue service to the great benefit of those it rescued. Having risen greatly throughout the war Coastal Command would be afflicted by a great contraction immediately afterwards. As many of the command's aircraft were American Lend Lease, such as the Catalina, their operating units quickly disappeared. Also disappearing almost overnight were those units whose personnel were mainly drawn from the Commonwealth; they decamped home in many cases taking their aircraft with them. Changes were also wrought upon the strike squadrons as they disbanded very quickly.

These changes also set the course for the command's future thus anti-submarine, search and rescue plus meteorological fights became the post-war duties of Coastal Command. The majority of service aircraft would also be scrapped as the majority were war weary. Beaufighters, Mosquitoes and Halifax patrol aircraft would be rounded up

Coastal Command would also operate a small fleet of Hastings Met1 aircraft for weather reporting and other meteorological duties. These were acquired in October 1950 and remained in use until 1964. TG566 would be operated by No. 202 Squadron from Aldergrove and would be written off there in September 1962. *(John Ryan Collection)*

and reduced to produce. These aircraft were replaced by new build Avro Lancasters for use in the General Reconnaissance and air-sea rescue roles while the Short Sunderland was used in a similar role over longer ranges. Joining the Lancaster and Sunderland would be the Handley Page Hastings MR1, which equipped No. 202 Squadron based at Aldergrove while detachments were undertaken to North Front, Gibraltar. Originally the maritime reconnaissance tasks were assigned codenames, which were Epicure from St Eval, Nocturnal from Gibraltar and Bismuth from Aldergrove. When the eight Hastings came into service only the Bismuth task force remained and these were divided into tracks labelled A to O. Sorties were selected by the Chief Meteorological Officer and, on a normal day, only one track was selected and flown. Things changed during exercises and alerts when more missions were undertaken, some of them at night. The Bismuth sorties were being flown when weather satellites were no more than just a dream thus the Met flights were providing very important data not only to the military, but to the nascent and burgeoning airlines starting to cross the Atlantic en masse. The squadron continued to provide this service until August 1964 when it was disbanded.

While the Avro Lancaster GR3 was undertaking sterling work it had become obvious that it was becoming long in the tooth thus a more capable replacement was sought. Initially a version of the Avro Lincoln was mooted, however the potential lack of growth in what was basically a bomber design saw this idea sent back to the drawing board. To fill the gap between the Lancaster and its replacement an approach was made to the United States to provide Lockheed Neptunes under the Mutual Defence Aid Programme (MDAP). The version of Neptune supplied to the RAF was equivalent to the US Navy P2V-5 and came complete with nose and tail gun turrets although these were soon improved by the fitment of a clear Plexiglas nose while the tail turret was replaced by a Magnetic Anomaly Detector (MAD), sting tail. The first of fifty-two Neptunes were delivered to No. 217 Squadron based at St Eval in January 1952, although by April the squadron had moved to Kinloss. This first Neptune squadron was quickly joined by No. 210 Squadron based at Topcliffe in February 1953 while No. 203

Lockheed Neptune MR1 WX505 'J' would be flown by No. 217 Squadron based at St Eval. The squadron would disband in 1957 having decamped to Kinloss while WX505 was passed onto the Brazilian Air Force. *(John Ryan Collection)*

Squadron, also at Topcliffe, received its complement by March 1953. No. 36 Squadron was the final unit to form, also at Topcliffe, was reforming in July 1953.

Although the Neptune squadrons were declared operational there were numerous technical problems experienced with the aircraft. Not only did the weapons systems fail to work correctly but some of the electronic systems were not fitted before delivery and the Americans were slow to deliver the missing boxes preferring to give priority to their own forces. By 1955 the Neptunes were fully modified and operational thus they were able to take part in a major exercise over the Bay of Biscay called Centre Board. While the majority of Neptunes concentrated on the maritime reconnaissance role four were utilized for a completely different role that would have far reaching consequences for the future. On 1 November 1952, four Lockheed Neptune MR Mk 1s formed the inventory of Vanguard Flight of Fighter Command based at RAF Kinloss. Their purpose was to research and develop tactics for use by Airborne Early Warning aircraft.

Although disbanded in June 1953 the four Neptune aircraft of Vanguard Flight were reformed as No. 1453 (Early Warning) Flight at RAF Topcliffe in Yorkshire. Despite their anonymous role the Neptunes of No. 1453 Flight appeared like normal aircraft to the public as they retained the full armament of the P2V-5 variant with nose, dorsal and tail turrets. Details of No. 1453 Flight's operations are scant, leading to speculation that they may have been involved in highly classified reconnaissance missions over or near the Eastern Bloc countries in a similar manner to the US Navy's Martin P4M Mercator ELectronic INTelligence (ELINT) aircraft, and the 'Ghost' North American RB-45 Tornados that flew with RAF crews and markings from RAF Sculthorpe, over eastern Europe to provide radar images of potential targets for RAF and Strategic Air Command (SAC) bombers.

By 1957 there were sufficient replacements available to allow the Neptunes to be returned to America. No. 36 Squadron would disband in February 1957, although No. 203 had gone by August 1956. Other 1957 disbandments included No. 210 Squadron in January while No. 217 Squadron relinquished its aircraft two months later. No. 1453 Flight would end its mission in June 1956 with its machines returning home first.

Not only were the aircraft of Coastal Command changing so were its areas of responsibility. When NATO became operational in April 1951 the AOC-in-C Coast Command also became Allied Air Commander-in-Chief, Eastern Atlantic. This change resulted in HQ Command issuing its projected mid-1953 deployment and equipment. The planned eight Shackleton squadrons covering long-range patrol and maritime reconnaissance were deployed thus: four were allocated to South Western Approaches, three to North West Approaches and a single unit to Gibraltar. All eight units had an aircraft inventory of eight aircraft each. The Short Sunderland was still in service at this time and its deployment included two squadrons each deployed to the southern and northern approaches. As all four units were due to be disbanded or re-equipped their inventory stood at five aircraft each. The Neptune squadrons were concentrated to the east; one was allocated to the north-eastern approaches while the remainder covered the Eastern approaches. In common with the Shackleton units each Neptune squadron was equipped with eight aircraft. Meteorological duties were covered by five Hastings aircraft based at Aldergrove and their duties were set by the Chief Meteorological Officer. By this time the command was operating helicopters for short-range rescue and communications duties, as the operating squadron was divided into flights the sixteen helicopters were dispersed around the country.

Another unit to operate the Lockheed Neptune MR1 was No. 210 Squadron that flew its aircraft from Topcliffe. WX516 'T' would be retired when No. 210 Squadron disbanded. *(John Ryan Collection)*

Coastal Command also had an extensive support network; most of it was active during peacetime although some organizations were wartime only. Providing training for the front-line squadrons was the School of Maritime Reconnaissance (SoMR) and the Anti-Submarine Warfare Development Unit, both of which moved into St Mawgan when it reopened in January 1951. Should war break out No. 16 Group would be reformed at Chatham to manage the three Neptune units charged with patrolling the eastern approaches while No. 17 Group would reform at Benson for training purposes with No. 19 Group moving to Liverpool to cover the port facilities. The duties of the SoMR included giving sprog maritime aircrew their initial training during a three-month period when 100 hours of training were flown, leaving the Operational Conversion Units to concentrate upon the individual aircraft.

It would be the arrival of the Shackleton that would bring a great leap in capability to Coastal Command. The progenitor of the Shackleton was designed by Roy Chadwick as the Avro Type 696. It was based on the Lincoln bomber and Tudor airliner, both derivatives of the successful wartime Lancaster heavy bomber, one of Chadwick's earlier designs, which was the current MR aircraft. The design utilized the Lincoln centre wing section and tail unit assemblies bolted to which were the Tudor outer wings and landing gear. These in turn were married to a new wider and deeper fuselage while power was provided by four Rolls-Royce Merlin engines. It was initially referred to during development as the Lincoln ASR3. The design was accepted by the Air Ministry as Specification R.5/46. The tail unit for the Shackleton differed from that of the Lincoln while the Merlin engines were replaced by the more powerful Rolls-Royce Griffons driving contra-rotating propellers. The Griffons were necessary due to the increased weight and drag and having a lower engine speed; they provided greater fuel efficiency for the long periods in the denser air at low altitudes that the Shackleton was intended for when hunting submarines better known as loitering.

The first test flight of the prototype Shackleton GR1, VW135, was undertaken on 9 March 1949 at the hands of Avro's Chief Test Pilot J.H. Jimmy Orrell. In the anti-submarine warfare role, the Shackleton carried sonobuoys, electronic warfare support measures, an Autolycus diesel fume detection system and for a short time an unreliable

Following the Neptune into service was the Avro Shackleton MR1. VP256 would be assigned to No. 269 Squadron at Ballykelly coded B-A. *(BBA Collection)*

magnetic anomaly detector (MAD) system. Available weaponry included nine bombs, three torpedoes or depth charges, while defensive armament included two 20mm cannon in a Bristol dorsal turret. The aircraft was originally designated GR1, although it was later redesignated the MR1. The Shackleton MR2 was an improved design incorporating feedback from the crews' operational experience. The radome was moved from the earlier position in the nose to a ventral position, which improved radar coverage and minimized the risk of bird-strikes. Both the nose and tail sections were lengthened while the tailplanes were redesigned and the undercarriage was strengthened.

Although the Shackletons were originally delivered in the old wartime finish of white and grey they soon started to appear in a dark grey scheme with a white upper fuselage. One such was MR1 VP288 'K' of No. 210 Squadron based at the Shackleton haven of Ballykelly. This unit had originally been No. 269 Squadron flying Neptunes before renumbering. *(John Ryan Collection)*

The Avro Type 716 Shackleton MR3 was a radical redesign of the aircraft in response to crew complaints. A new tricycle undercarriage was introduced while the fuselage was lengthened. Redesigned wings with better ailerons and tip tanks were introduced, although the span was slightly reduced. To improve the crews' working conditions on fifteen-hour flights, the sound proofing was improved and a proper galley and sleeping space were included. Due to these upgrades the take-off weight of the RAF's MR3s had risen by over 30,000lb and assistance from Armstrong Siddeley Viper Mk 203 turbojets was needed on take-off, although these extra engines were not added until the aircraft went through the Phase 3 upgrade. This extra weight and increased fatigue consumption took a toll on the airframe thus the service life of the RAF MR3s was sufficiently reduced that they were outlived by the MR2s. In an attempt to take the design further the Avro Type 719 Shackleton IV was proposed. Later redesignated as the MR4 this was a projected variant using the extremely fuel efficient Napier Nomad compound engine. Unfortunately for Avro the Shackleton IV was cancelled in 1955 as the RAF was shrinking as financial cuts and a contraction of responsibilities was taking place.

The Shackleton MR1 entered service with the Coastal Command Operational Conversion Unit at Kinloss in February 1951. Even as the first Shackletons were entering service with the newly created No. 236 OCU the Royal Navy was trying to scupper the whole of Coastal Command. Their plan was to scrap Avro's finest and replace them with a fleet of Fairey Gannets operating off small aircraft carriers in mid-ocean while further aircraft would cover the inshore areas. Once the idea had been fully costed it was obvious that the whole plan was fundamentally flawed. Within the command itself the flying boat lobby was also reacting vociferously putting forward the type as a more flexible design, however this too was shot down in flames when it was pointed out that rough sea conditions would either stop them flying or actually wreck the aircraft. Also, flying boats were inherently slow and heavy and the proliferation of runways of sufficient length were springing up all over the world and many of these countries were still susceptible to British entreaties.

No. 224 Squadron based at Aldergrove would be the first unit to receive the Shackleton MR1 in July 1951 replacing the unit's weary Handley Page Halifax GR6s. Other units that received the Shackleton MR1 included No. 220 Squadron, which initially formed at Kinloss in September 1951 although the unit moved to St Eval in November. In May 1952 No. 269 Squadron based in Gibraltar received its allocation of MR1s while its crews were formed from the nucleus of No. 224 Squadron. By March, however, the entire squadron had returned to Britain taking up residence at Ballykelly. No. 120 Squadron had already been equipped with the Shackleton MR1 in March 1951 while based at Kinloss, although this tenure was short as the entire unit decamped to Aldergrove in April 1952. While at Aldergrove No. 120 Squadron provided the nucleus for No. 240 Squadron, which was also based there. The squadron quickly moved to its new base at St Eval for a few weeks before settling at Ballykelly. No. 240 Squadron would later be renumbered as No. 203 Squadron in November 1958, although this unit would be equipped with the MR1A version that featured slightly more powerful engines amongst other improvements. The Shackleton MR1A was also used by No. 42 Squadron based at St Eval retaining this model until July 1954. No. 206 Squadron was also based at St Eval when it re-equipped with the MR1A in September 1952; the squadron retained this model until May 1958. The last unit to equip with the MR1A was No. 204 Squadron, which traded in its more advanced Shackleton MR2s for the less capable

Following on from the MR1 Avro would provide Coastal Command with the MR2. This was a far more capable aircraft and in many cases would outlive the later MR3. WL754 'F' was flown by No. 42 Squadron from St Evan, then St Mawgan. WL754 would later have a second career as an AEW2. *(John Ryan Collection)*

MR1As in May 1958 while stationed at Ballykelly. The MR1As remained in use until February 1960, although by this time the squadron had received some MR2Cs that it retained until March 1971.

The arrival of the Shackleton MR2 would improve the capabilities of the MR squadrons and, in most cases, this new marque would replace the MR1/1A in use. Deliveries to operational units began in 1953 with first deliveries being made to No. 42 Squadron. Initially the squadron retained some of its complement of MR1As until July 1954 as the entry of the MR2 into service was slow, although once the technical problems had been ironed out the type served until 1966. No. 206 Squadron would receive some MR2s in February 1953, although they were dispensed with in June 1954, the unit retaining its complement of MR1As throughout this period. In January 1958 No. 206 Squadron departed St Eval for St Mawgan, remaining there until July 1965 when a further transfer was made to Kinloss. In March 1953 two units would start to accept deliveries of Shackleton MR2s. The first would be No. 240 Squadron based at Ballykelly, although their tenure was short as they were dispensed with in August 1954, the unit resuming operations with MR1s. By November 1958 No. 204 Squadron had been renumbered as No. 203 Squadron still at Ballykelly. No. 203 Squadron would later receive MR2s in April 1962, retaining them until December 1966. The other unit that gained MR2s would be No. 269 Squadron, also based at Ballykelly. The initial allocation lasted until August 1954, the squadron resuming operations flying its original MR1s, which remained the case until October 1958 when a new batch of Shackleton MR2s was received. By December No. 269 Squadron had been renumbered as No. 210 Squadron as part of the contraction of the RAF and the desire of Coastal Command to retain significant unit number plates. No. 210 Squadron would remain as part of Coastal Command and into the early days of Strike Command before disbanding on 31 October 1970 only to reappear the following day as a Near East Air Force squadron.

No.120 Squadron was based at Aldergrove and had a bit of a hit and miss affair with the Shackleton MR2. The first deliveries were made in April 1953, although all had been returned by August 1954, the unit resuming operations with its MR1s. The squadron received another allocation of MR2s in October 1956 and retained these until November 1958. No. 224 Squadron had slightly better luck with its MR2 allocation that was taken on charge in May 1953, retaining them until disbandment in October 1966.

Ballykelly would also be home to No. 204 Squadron, which had last been in existence as a Vickers Valetta unit before renumbering as No. 84 Squadron in February 1953. The squadron would receive its complement of MR2s in January 1954, which remained in use until May 1958 when they were replaced by Shackleton MR1As. These remained in service until February 1960 by which time the first of the replacement MR2s had arrived. No. 204 Squadron retained its MR2Cs until disbandment in March 1971. The MR2C model differed from the basic MR2 in that it was fitted with the avionics suite from the later MR3. Instead of a base transfer No. 204 Squadron would be disbanded on 1 April 1971 reforming on the same date at Honington. The squadron would supply detachments to Majunga, Tengah and Masirah – the unit had originally been known as the Majunga Detachment Support Unit. The purpose of the Majunga, Madagascar, detachment was to provide aircraft for the blockade of Rhodesia. When the Rhodesian blockade was withdrawn in 1972 No. 204 Squadron was disbanded, its Tengah and Masirah patrols being covered by other units on rotation.

The Shackleton MR2 underwent extensive trials of its avionics and remedial work on its engines, which had a tendency to throw spark plugs from their cylinder heads and required an overhaul every 400 hours. Trials were carried out with the MR2 at the Anti Submarine Warfare Development Unit (ASWDU) covering the performance of the ASV Mk 13 and extensive trials of the RCM/ECM suite before they were cleared for use. The Autolycos diesel fume detection system was also put through its paces before being cleared for service use. Other trials undertaken by the MR2 included the Glow Worm illuminating rocket system, the Shackleton replacing the last Lancaster in operational use. At least one MR2 was utilized for MAD sting trials, although both it and the rocket were dropped. However, the former would equip the later MR3 once all the bugs had been ironed out. Fortunately, the Orange Harvest ECM system, homing torpedoes and the various sonic buoys at least were successful.

The final model of Shackleton developed by Avro was the MR3. Pictured here is MR3 WR984 'L', which was on the inventory of No. 201 Squadron based at St Mawgan before moving to Kinloss in 1965. *(John Ryan Collection)*

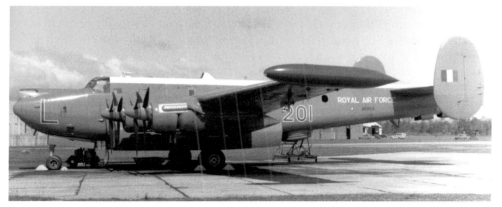

The genesis of the Shackleton MR3 would rest upon the need for Coastal Command to cover its projected strength of 180 front-line aircraft by 1956. Although other projects had been put forward the Air Staff finally plumped for the Avro product, issuing OR.320 in January 1953. The first Shackleton MR3 made its maiden flight on 2 September 1955, although production aircraft did not reach service until 1957 by which time some of the contracts had been cancelled. The MR3 was a complete contrast to the earlier models in that it was carried on a tricycle undercarriage, had wing-tip mounted fuel tanks, modified ailerons, a clear view canopy and a sound proofed wardroom to help alleviate the effects of long patrols. Defensive armament consisted of a pair of nose-mounted 20mm cannon, the upper turret being deleted. During 1966 a programme was instituted to upgrade the MR3, the most obvious change being the fitment of a Bristol-Siddeley Viper engine in each outboard engine nacelle resulting in the type being designated the MR3/3.

First deliveries were made to No. 220 Squadron based at St Mawgan in August 1957, although the unit retained some of its MR2s. The squadron had a short existence as it was renumbered as No. 201 Squadron in October 1958. This unit would last a lot longer than its predecessor as it remained as a Shackleton operator until 1970 having moved to Kinloss in December 1965. Close on the heels of No. 220 Squadron to equip with the Shackleton MR3 was No. 206 Squadron, also based at St Mawgan. This unit traded in its 5/3 mix of MR1As and MR2s for a similar number of the new model in January 1958. No. 206 Squadron would also move to Kinloss, departing St Mawgan in July 1965 and remaining there until re-equipping in August 1970.

St Mawgan was also the home for No. 42 Squadron, although this unit would continue to fly some of its MR2s alongside the MR3s after their delivery in November 1965, retaining them until replacement in September 1971. Ballykelly and No. 203 Squadron would be the final recipient of the Shackleton MR3 in June 1966 having first used this model between December 1958 and July 1962. No. 202 Squadron would leave Coastal Command in February 1969 when it was transferred to Luqa, Malta, as part of Near East Air Force (NEAF).

Development of weaponry for the Shackletons continued apace with the Mk 30 Homing Torpedo finally being cleared for service in March 1955 after a period spent trying to get the delicate mechanisms to work properly under operational conditions. With this weapon in service it would see the final demise of the depth charge as the primary anti-submarine weapon. To complement the Mk 30 development work was also taking place on an active homing torpedo codenamed Petane. Unfortunately, delays in clearing the torpedo for service use would result in cancellation and its replacement by the American Mk 43 weapon although the latter's strike rate was less than that of the British weapon. Also missing from the Shackleton fleet was an airborne lifeboat that had been prominent under the Lancaster GR3s. Although a boat was planned for the Shackleton it was never developed and the fleet was supplied with Lindholme gear that became a standard throughout the command. Avionics for the Shackleton were also under continual improvement, Orange Harvest was constantly being improved while a Doppler system known as Blue Silk was also developed, which was an improvement on the Green Satin system. The primary radar system installed in the Shackleton was the AN/ASV-21 developed for submarine detection; this too was in a state of constant development in order to improve its capability and its ease of operation.

This period was also one of confusion, while the Neptunes and Shackletons remained a constant Coastal Command was also looking at extending the lives of ten of the command's Short Sunderlands however as the type would need extensive and expensive upgrades to its avionics and weapons systems. Another Short product, the Seamew, was also intended for Coastal Command use, the intention being to base flights at St Mawgan and Ballykelly. However, this was a period of defence cuts thus all programmes were put under close scrutiny. The result of this was the cancellation of the Sunderland life extension while the Seamew programme was cancelled as its handling, performance and overall usefulness was questioned.

The Shackleton was also accumulating secondary roles such as trooping, which was tested to the full during Operation *Encompass* undertaken during January when 1,200 troops were flown to Cyprus to counter terrorist activity. Colonial policing also became a Shackleton role, being allocated to No. 42 Squadron, which took over the task from Bomber Command. These extra duties helped the AOC-in-C to counter the desire of the Air Ministry to reduce the overall strength. Initially it was proposed that the entire force would be four active units although Coastal Command would counter with a need for a minimum of nine squadrons operating in the MR role, one covering MR and Met while sixteen older MR1/T4s would be operated by the Maritime Operational Training Unit, formed from No. 236 OCU and the SMR at Kinloss on 1 October 1956, while a further three aircraft would be used for trials work.

1957 was a tumultous year for Coastal Command. The Sunderlands had finally retired resulting in the final closure of Pembroke Dock while St Eval would suffer a similar fate as Nos 220 and 228 Squadrons would move to St Mawgan to prepare for the Shackleton Mk 3 as St Eval was not capable of supporting this model. When No. 42 Squadron departed for colonial policing duties in Aden this sounded the death knell thus St Eval was finally closed in 1959.

Coastal Command underwent further contractions as some of the Shackleton MR1s were converted to T4 trainers, although some aircraft were gained when the Joint Anti-Submarine School was disbanded releasing a handful of aircraft for front-line duties. Although the MR3 had been cleared for squadron use it was restricted until some of the problems such as hydraulic malfunctions and engine fading were ironed out. It had been intended that No. 228 Squadron would be the first to re-equip, although the deteriorating state of the aircraft flown by No. 220 Squadron hastened their replacement. Even so, given the problems experienced with the MR3 the squadron continued to operate the MR1 alongside the newer machine. Maintaining the operational front-line strength for Coastal Command was becoming more difficult as the extra duties piled up. Not only were colonial duties carrying on longer than expected, other aircraft were being diverted to protect the zone in the Hebrides missile range.

In March 1957 the Jordanian government severed the long-standing treaty ties with Britain therefore over the next few months the British started to remove stores from the two RAF bases and from Aqaba. By 6 July 1957 a ceremonial guard from the 10th Hussars and the Middlesex Regiment handed over the base to the Jordan Arab Army. During July 1958 a call for assistance came from King Hussein of Jordan and the 16th Para Brigade responded sending the 2nd Battalion Para to Amman airfield on 17 July courtesy of some Coastal Command Shackletons. A flight of Hawker Hunter fighters followed in the afternoon, followed by Blackburn Beverly transports with the 33rd Para Field Regiment aboard. Their task was to defend the hills overlooking the runway of Amman's aerodrome. By mid-October the situation had eased thus the paratroops were withdrawn on 2 November.

In June 1958 intensive flying trials began with the Shackleton MR3, the plan being to fly 1,000 hours in nine weeks. Taken into consideration was the projected fatigue life of 3,000 airframe hours, although it was thought that none of the airframes would ever reach that figure. Even so, it was planned that modifications to the MR3 would include airframe strengthening when the Phase 1 modification programme was undertaken. While the MR3 was undertaking its flight trials revised fatigue life figures for the earlier models had been calculated. Unlike more modern aircraft the fatigue life for such aircraft was calculated on the life of the main spar structure. Without any modifications the spar life for both the MR1 and MR2 would be limited to between 2,500 and 2,700 hours. This put Coastal Command in a difficult position as the MR3 was still not fully up to speed while the earlier models required major upgrading to continue in service. Adding to the woes of the AOC-in-C Coastal Command had been informed that it was intended to reduce the command to only six squadrons flying thirty-six aircraft with a handful of spares to cover overhauls.

At the beginning of 1959 No. 42 Squadron was replaced by No. 224 Squadron for colonial policing duties the former returning home to St Mawgan. By March 1959 the Coastal Command strength had dropped to twenty-four aircraft but nevertheless No. 120 Squadron despatched aircraft to take part in Exercise Dawn Breeze IV, which was followed by preparations for Calypso Strait, a tour of the Caribbean, although this was extended due to unrest in British Honduras, better known as Belize. By mid June the Shackleton fleet was in trouble again as all those aircraft that had more than 2,150 hours on the clock were grounded due to cracks in the main spars. This affected all of the earlier versions thus a substitute had to be found to keep the pilots current. To that end the squadrons were supplied with a handful of Vickers Varsities while MOTU crew training was carried out using Shackleton MR3s that were still cleared for flying. With no replacement in sight an accelerated programme of modifications was put in place, the intention being to relife the spar for a total life of 5,000 hours. This programme saw the first reworked aircraft return to their squadrons in August 1959 with the entire fleet being back in service by October.

The early months of 1960 saw the Phase I update programme completed, which was immediately followed by the start of Phase II, although this concentrated on updating the aircraft's avionics and the weapons capability, with the American Mk 44 torpedo being added to the incumbent Mk 30 torpedo. Even as the Shackleton fleet was being upgraded the Air Ministry was undertaking the machinations of selecting a replacement. However, this was not the easy task as it first seemed, as not only was the RAF looking for a replacement, NATO and the US Navy were also on the hunt for a replacement for the venerable Lockheed P-2 Neptune. Like many of the proposed joint programmes none of the participants could agree on exactly what was required. The outcome was that the United States selected another Lockheed product, the P-3 Orion, while those interested parties in NATO selected the Breguet 1150 Atlantique. Both these designs were rejected by the RAF and Air Ministry; the P-3 was considered too slow while the Atlantique was rejected as it only had two engines and was considered to have too low a safety margin for long-range operations. Eventually OR.350 was issued, requesting a new aircraft to be ready for service in 1960, although as with most projects it would be subject to time slip.

Exercises would occupy the Shackleton squadrons during the 1960s. In July 1960 three Shackletons from No. 204 Squadron departed Ballykelly to undertake Operation

Calypso Stream III that involved visiting Bermuda, Jamaica, British Honduras and Trinidad, the distance covered being 10,000 miles. Having returned home to Ballykelly No. 204 Squadron would join the rest of Coastal Command and Bomber Command in preparing for Exercise Fallex 60. This was a large NATO exercise that combined numerous exercises into one. This involved Blue Shield First/Second Watch, anti-submarine and shipping exercises, Sword Thrust, Bomber Command attacks plus Coffer Dam and Ballast One. Also involved in this exercise were units from the RCAF plus the carriers USS *Saratoga* and *Shangri La* from the US Navy. The Fallex exercises that followed were all of a similar nature, however Fallex 62 was a completely different matter. This was a full simulation of an all-out attack against NATO complete with an armoured attack backed up by a full range of nuclear weapons. Within the first few days the entire exercise had come to a shuddering halt as the projected loss of life inflicted by the enemy orange forces, between 19–15 million dead in Britain alone, revealed that NATO was completely unprepared for such an assault.

On a lighter note the Aird Whyte Competition between the squadrons of Coastal Command was revamped as the Fincastle Trophy. This would, and still does, involve crews and aircraft from Britain, Australia, Canada and New Zealand. 1961 was also notable for a threatened invasion of Kuwait by an unstable Iraq regime. As Britain was still providing security for the country Operation *Vantage* was launched to provide troops, aircraft and naval forces. For the Shackleton squadrons this meant that No. 42 Squadron would be placed on standby while Nos 203 and 204 Squadrons would be used to transport some equipment for Bomber Command. Fortunately for the Iraqis they had the sense to withdraw from the border while the Arab League would take over the security of Kuwait.

1963 was also an exciting year for the Shackleton squadrons. In August No. 201 Squadron sent a detachment to Nassau their brief being to deter Cuban forces attempting to capture refugees seeking political asylum. During their eight-week detachment the squadron undertook general surveillance and anti-smuggling patrols plus flew relief supplies into Mayaguana Island after it was devastated by a hurricane. A further detachment, this time provided by No. 210 Squadron, was deployed to Cyprus in December due to yet another round of trouble between the Greeks and the Turks. The trouble between the two ethnic groups continued until August 1964, resulting in the squadron having to send a rotating detachment to keep the aircraft flying. During this same period the Shackletons of Nos 120, 201, 204 and 206 Squadrons undertook Operation *Adjutant*, which was intended to assess the movements of Russian submarines passing through the choke area to the north of Britain. During this period over 2,000 hours were flown until August when the operation was completed.

September 1964 would see the whole of Coastal Command involved in Exercise Teamwork, which included the crews and senior students from MOTU that became the shadow unit No. 220 Squadron for the period. Most of the squadrons operated around Britain although No. 204 Squadron would fly to Norway from Gibraltar and operate out of Bodø while part of No. 203 Squadron would also travel north but only as far as Kinloss. A reshuffle of the Shackleton squadrons would take place in early 1965 as it had been determined that the greatest threat to shipping approaching the British Isles was from the Soviet Northern Fleet. To that end No. 201 Squadron was transferred from St Mawgan to Kinloss in July 1965 while MOTU came the other way. Kinloss thus became the home for No. 18 Group's assets while St Mawgan was home to No. 42 Squadron, the sole operational unit of No. 19 Group. From October the Kinloss-based squadrons took over the Affluent detachments, incorporating the Hornet Moth patrols. To Coastal Command these patrols in this undeclared war with Indonesia were a drain of resources. Fortunately the confrontation would eventually end in August 1966.

Exercise Calpurnia held during December 1965 involved all of the Coastal Command squadrons and required the crews to detect and carry out mock attacks against submarines provided by the Royal Navy. As ever the command was operating under financial constraints thus the planning staff had to contend with the day-to-day running and increasing overseas commitments, very much a case of doing more with even less. To that end more overseas detachments were undertaken in order to give the crews as much experience as possible. 1966 would also see No. 42 Squadron undertaking the final Exercise Capex to South Africa; these detachments were discontinued due to increasing pressure from the rest of the world concerning apartheid. No. 42 Squadron would also take over the Mizar patrols operating from Majunga in support of the Rhodesian blockade during which they acted in conjunction with Royal Navy patrols.

The operational squadrons had already received their initial allocation of Phase III Shackletons, which allowed some of the earlier MR2s to be modified to Phase III standard. Some of these aircraft would be transferred to MOTU to replace the outmoded Shackleton T4s. It was also at this time that centralized servicing and wing pooling of aircraft became a fact of life. Conceived as yet another means to save money both these ideas would result in loss of morale in both aircrew and ground crew. Adding to the work load of the Coastal Command stations was the news that Britain would withdraw from Aden in 1967. This news would see internecine fighting between the various tribal factions and increased attacks on British forces in theatre. As with all such conflicts in the Middle East the trouble soon spread to the remainder of the Persian Gulf. In order to monitor the possibility of illegal weaponry entering the area a MARDET (Maritime Detachment) was established at Sharjah, the crews and aircraft coming from the Kinloss wing. Not aiding the situation was further trouble in Cyprus that required more reinforcements from Britain.

From January 1968 the Shackleton T2 Phase IIIs entered service with MOTU, although the last T4 would hang onto July. The re-equipment of MOTU would bring benefits to Coastal Command as the new aircraft were equipped to the same standard as the operational units as No. 38 Squadron had just disbanded. This coupled with an increase in Soviet naval activity in the Mediterranean required that a detachment be sent to Luqa, Malta, from No. 42 Squadron for three months before No. 203 Squadron was permanently transferred to NEAF in February 1969.

On the re-equipment front both the British Aircraft Corporation and Hawker Siddeley Aircraft presented responses to OR.350. By June 1963 it had been revamped by the Ministry of Defence as Air Staff Target 357 and this was to be based upon existing designs thus the Trident and VC 10 and the Comet were in the running. Eventually, Hawker Siddeley won the competition and utilized two redundant Comet 4 airframes to create the HS801 prototypes. Both airframes flew in 1967, although the Nimrod did not enter service until 1968.

Coastal Command would be a pioneer in the use of the helicopter in the role of air-sea rescue. The first machine utilized was the Bristol Sycamore, a small batch of four being delivered to St Mawgan for trials with the ASWDU for anti-submarine and rescue

Coastal Command would also be responsible for the air–sea rescue helicopter fleet. The first type to enter service was the Westland (Bristol) Sycamore HAR12. This aircraft is WV781 'F-Z' assigned to the ASWDU at St Mawgan. *(John Ryan Collection)*

trials. No. 22 Squadron would reform at Thorney Island in March 1955 and take over the four Sycamore HC12s as their first equipment, retaining them until January 1956. While No. 22 Squadron was developing search and rescue techniques the Air Ministry was authorizing the use of the Westland Whirlwind as the primary aircraft in this role. The squadron received its first Whirlwind HAR2s in June 1955 while still based at Thorney Island. The HQ and A Flight were based at Thorney Island while B Flight was based at Martlesham Heath and Felixstowe with C Flight located at Valley. Twelve months later the HQ and A Flight had moved to St Mawgan with an outstation at Chivenor that had originally been part of No. 257 Squadron. The other flights were located at Felixstowe, Tangmere and Coltishall, all part of B Flight. C Flight had aircraft based at Valley while

After the Sycamore, Coastal Command would receive the Westland Whirlwind HAR10 for ASR duties. XP351 was operated by No. 202 Squadron whose headquarters were at Leconfield. *(John Ryan Collection)*

D Flight had aircraft operating at Thorney Island, Manston and Brawdy. The HAR2s were retained until August 1962 when the turbine-powered Whirlwind HAR10s were received, remaining in service until November 1981. On 27 November 1969 Air Marshal Sir John Lapsley would take the flypast salute at St Mawgan on the disbandment of Coastal Command, comprising two Westland Whirlwinds, nine Shackletons and a single Nimrod. The following day No. 18 (Maritime) Group took over the assets at Northwood while the existing headquarters at Pitreavie Castle, 18 Group, and Mount Devon, No. 19 Group, became the headquarters of the Northern and Southern Maritime Air Regions respectively.

Transport Command would really come into its own during the Second World War. Prior to its formation the RAF had very little use for fully dedicated transport squadrons preferring instead to utilize aircraft that could carry personnel and cargo or alternatively could drop bombs. By 1943 it had become obvious that aerial warfare had changed completely, all over the globe where the British military were in evidence the need for aircraft to support both aerial and ground operations was becoming obvious. This would lead to Ferry Command being renamed Transport Command that year.

At war's end Transport Command in common with other RAF organizations was subject to the obligatory rundown and contraction. Even so the command was still well equipped, mainly with the ubiquitous Douglas C-47 Dakota. Supplementing the C-47s would be two squadrons of Vickers Valettas, although their tenure would be short lived. It would be the arrival of the Handley Page Hastings that would vastly improve the command's capability. Designed to Air Ministry Specification C3/44 the Hastings was intended to replace the Avro York. Both prototypes made their maiden flights in 1946 with production aircraft entering service in October 1948. By 1958 the Hastings still equipped No. 511 Squadron based at Lyneham. The squadron had received its complement of Hastings C1s in 1949 while the C2s were acquired in 1952. No. 511 Squadron would disband in September 1958 being renumbered as No. 36 Squadron. The squadron would move to Colerne flying both models of Hastings until a move to Lyneham in July 1967 presaged re-equipment with Lockheed C-130 Hercules C1s.

Another early starter with Hastings was No. 99 Squadron at Lyneham, which received its complement of C1s in August 1949 while the C2s arrived in May 1952. Both types were retired in June 1959 being replaced by Bristol Britannias. No. 114 Squadron at Colerne would receive its allocation of Hastings in April 1959, as before a mix of C1s and C2s were on strength. In September 1961 the squadron disbanded only to reform the following month at Benson in preparation for the Armstrong Whitworth Argosy. No. 24 Squadron would trade in its Vickers Valetta in February 1950 moving to Lyneham in November in anticipation of receiving the Hastings C1. Some C2s were received in June 1951, both versions remaining in service until January 1968. The squadron decamped to Topcliffe in February 1951, receiving a handful of Hastings C4s for VIP use. These remained in service until June 1960 by which time the squadron was based at Colerne. Other users of the Hastings included No. 151 Squadron. Originally part of Fighter Command flying Gloster Javelins, the squadron was reformed from the Signals Development Squadron at Watton and would operate both the Hastings C1 and C2 between January 1962 and May 1963. No. 151 Squadron would be renumbered as No. 97 Squadron in May 1963, the Hastings C2s remaining in use until January 1967 when the unit disbanded. The final user of the Hastings was No. 114 Squadron, which reformed at Colerne in April 1959 and received both the C1 and C2 and retained them until

C1 was the first proper transport aircraft built for Transport Command. WJ333 was a C1 on the strength of No. 99 Squadron based at Lyneham. Of note is the radio call sign code on the fuselage. *(John Ryan Collection)*

September 1961. One month later the squadron would reform at Benson preparing for the Argosy C1.

In the mid-1950s it had become obvious that the current fleet of transport aircraft needed either replacing or supplementing. The first of these was the Blackburn Beverley developed from the earlier General Aircraft GAL60 Universal Freighter, Blackburn having purchased General Aircraft in 1949. The first GAL60 Universal Freighter was dismantled at the GAL Feltham, Middlesex, factory being transported to Brough in Yorkshire and undertaking its maiden flight on 20 June 1950. This, the second, GAL65 featured changes from the original. These included clamshell doors that replaced the combination of a door and ramp while the tailplane boom, increased in size, gained seating for thirty-six passengers and a para drop door. The original Bristol Hercules engines were replaced by Bristol Centaurus engines coupled to reverse pitch propellers. This feature gave the aircraft a short landing distance plus the ability to reverse under

The Westland Whirlwind would also join Transport Command in the tactical transport role. HAR10 XR454 'Q' was operated by No. 230 Squadron based at Odiham. *(John Ryan Collection)*

The arrival of the Comet C2 brought Transport Command into the jet age. XK696 was flown by No. 216 Squadron based at Lyneham and was withdrawn for scrapping in 1969. *(John Ryan Collection)*

its own power. The RAF would place an order in 1952 for forty-nine Beverley C1s, all aircraft being built at Brough.

The first production aircraft from an original order for twenty from the RAF flew on 29 January 1955 with the first operational aircraft being delivered to No. 47 Squadron based at Abingdon in March 1956. No. 53 Squadron, also based at Abingdon, received its complement of Beverleys in early 1957, although it was later absorbed into No. 47 Squadron in June 1963. These were flown until October 1967 when the squadron disbanded. No. 30 Squadron received its Beverleys in April 1957 while at RAF Dishforth, although it would subsequently deploy to Eastleigh, Kenya and Muharraq, Bahrain, remaining there as part of NEAF until disbanded in September 1967.

1956 would see the RAF become the first military jet transport in the world. Although the early DH Comet had suffered a number of fatal crashes the next model, the Comet Mk 2, was a better prospect as its engines were Rolls-Royce Avons instead of the earlier Ghost centrifugal engines. The RAF would take up the option of an initial ten aircraft, the first two being designated as Comet T2s for crew training. The first arrived at Lyneham in July 1956 with the transport models arriving a little later to form the equipment of No. 216 Squadron. Three other Comets were delivered to No. 90 Signals Group for ELINT duties. The squadron undertook some memorable assignments with their new machines, one of the earliest being a trip to Moscow on 23 June 1956 taking the British Air Minister for Soviet Air Force day. The Comets also undertook flights to Cyprus and Malta during the Suez crisis while other trips were made to Australia and Christmas Island in support of Operation *Grapple*.

De Havilland would deliver the Comet C4 to No. 216 Squadron at Lyneham during February 1962. The arrival of this version allowed the squadron to carry double the number of passengers and allowed the Comet C2s to be retired in April 1967. Altogether a total of five aircraft were delivered and they undertook a full range of duties including transporting members of the Royal Family to various destinations around the globe until the unit was finally disbanded in June 1975.

Transport Command would also receive its first turboprop aircraft in the shape of the Bristol Britannia. In civil guise the Britannia had first flown in August 1952 and would

No. 216 Squadron would later receive the Comet C4. This example is XR398 from Lyneham. *(John Ryan Collection)*

be ordered by the RAF in November 1955 when the projected Vickers V1000 pure jet transport was cancelled. Initially six aircraft were ordered in January 1956, later being increased to ten and later to twenty aircraft. The first C1 made its maiden flight from Belfast in December 1958 while the final aircraft was delivered in December 1960. A further three aircraft, designated C2, were delivered during 1959. No. 99 Squadron, based at Lyneham, was the first unit to receive the Britannia C1 and C2 in 1959, retaining them until they were retired in January 1976. Lyneham would also be the home of the next Britannia unit, No. 511 Squadron, which received its aircraft in December. No. 511 Squadron would retain its aircraft until December 1975, although by June 1970 both units had moved to Brize Norton with the aircraft being pooled between both squadrons. The author remembers well travelling by Britannia to various destinations in

While the Hastings was an excellent platform for moving troops and smaller stores a larger aircraft was needed to shift bulkier items. The answer was the Blackburn Beverley, the example shown being XM122 'D' of No. 30 Squadron based at Dishforth. *(BBA Collection)*

The Bristol Britannia C1 would mainly be used in the troop transport role, although it did have a cargo door fitted in the port front fuselage. XM489 was operated by Nos 99 and 511 Squadrons based at Lyneham. *(John Ryan Collection)*

support of Vulcan operations. While the Britannia in its later days was slow in comparison with its more modern civilian counterparts it was basically a reliable aircraft, although on at least one occasion a Britannia C1 lurched into Akrotiri, Cyprus, with failing electrics.

While the Beverley was utilized as a heavy transport Transport Command decided that it needed another aircraft in the tactical role. The aircraft chosen to fulfil this role was the Armstrong Whitworth Argosy C1. The Argosy was capable of carrying sixty-nine troops, medical litters plus loads the size of a Ferret or Saracen armoured car. A total of fifty-six aircraft were delivered these equipping five squadrons. All the designated units were formed at Benson before departing for their overseas bases, the exceptions being Nos 114 and 267 Squadrons, which remained at Benson as part of Transport Command. No. 114 Squadron had previously been a Hastings unit based at Colerne before reforming as a Argosy operator at Benson in October 1971. Joining No. 114 Squadron at Benson would be No. 267 Squadron this unit receiving its aircraft in November 1962. The latter unit would disband in June 1970 while No. 114 Squadron would disband in October 1971, both being victims of defence cuts. Also stricken in these defence cuts was the T2 trainer programme, which was an attempt to utilize redundant Argosies in another role. Only two would be converted as navigation trainers before the contract was cancelled. Although most of the Argosies ended up at No. 5 MU Kemble awaiting disposal, mainly to the civilian market, a handful were retained for airfield and flight-checking duties. A total of nine were converted for this role, entering service with No. 115 Squadron in 1971, initially at Watton and then Cottesmore.

Transport Command would have to wait until the mid-1960s before receiving more modern equipment. And like buses four came along at the same time. In 1960 the Ministry of Defence issued Specification C239 for a strategic transport, which resulted in an order being placed with Vickers in September 1961 for an initial five VC 10s. The order was increased by a further six in August 1962 while a further three aircraft from a cancelled BOAC order were added in July 1964. The military version, Type 1106, was a combination of the standard combi airframe with the more powerful engines and the fin fuel tank of the Super VC 10. This version also had a detachable in-flight refuelling probe on the nose plus an auxiliary power unit in the tailcone.

The first RAF aircraft, VC 10 C1, was delivered for testing by A&AEE in November 1965, with deliveries to No. 10 Squadron beginning in December 1966 being completed by August 1968. The VC 10s were named after Victoria Cross medal holders, this being displayed above the forward passenger door. All VC 10 C1 aircraft were supplied to the RAF with a forward freight door and a rolla deck floor. One aircraft, XR809, was later leased to Rolls-Royce for flight testing of the RB211 turbofan between 1969 and 1975. When returned to the RAF it was found that the airframe had become distorted, due to the increase in power from the RB211 fitted to one side of the fuselage over the Conways fitted to the other side. Considered uneconomical to repair, part of the fuselage was retained at Brize Norton for load training while the remainder was scrapped.

The first overseas training flight was undertaken to Hong Kong in August 1966 with routine flights starting in July 1967. Since that date the VC 10s of No. 10 Squadron have travelled worldwide transporting families to join their serving husbands, moving service personnel to detachment bases for such exercises as Sunflower, a Vulcan deployment to the Far East. As the pride of the Transport Command it is no surprise that the VC 10 took over the starring role from the Comet C4 as VIP and VVIP carriers. Not only did the aircraft convey various members of the Royal Family about the globe they also transported Prime Ministers, popular or otherwise, to various destinations. Preparing an aircraft for such a trip required the complete revamping of the interior while the outside underwent a complete wash and polish, the latter being tins of Wadpol applied by the unwilling, namely those assigned to the SWO's working party. For all the glamour the VC 10 fleet was capable of transporting injured and wounded personnel while, after removal of the forward seating, the aircraft could also be used as a freighter.

Although the Argosy was capable of delivering most payloads to their required destinations, Transport Command still lacked a tactical transport with a go anywhere capability. The aircraft selected for the role was an extensive rework of the Hawker Siddeley HS748. Designated the HS780, this new version was capable of STOL take-off and landings this allowing the type to undertake trooping, paratrooping, aerial freight dropping and aero med. In contrast with the civilian version the Andover C1 featured more powerful Dart turboprops, a fuselage of increased length, beaver tail doors and a unique kneeling undercarriage. Coupled to these features was a strengthened fuselage that gave the Andover the capability to operate from roughly prepared airstrips, ploughed fields and desert conditions. This allows the type to operate in strips down to 300 yards.

The first Andover C1 made its maiden flight in July 1965 with first deliveries being made to No. 46 Squadron at Abingdon. Eventually, a total of thirty-one aircraft delivered to the RAF, the majority of which were used by overseas commands. Another round of defence cuts saw No. 46 Squadron being disbanded in August 1975, the unit having moved to Thorney Island in September 1970. A handful of the C1s were transferred to No. 32 Squadron at Northolt for communications duties. A further four aircraft were converted to E3 standard for use by No. 115 Squadron replacing the earlier Argosies.

With the impending disappearance of the Beverley and Argosy the RAF was in the market for a heavy lift aircraft. The chosen design came from Shorts of Belfast who based their project on the Britannic, a design from 1957. This utilized the wings and powerplants from the earlier Bristol Britannia allied to a larger fuselage. The resultant

Transport Command would eventually require a faster long-range heavy lift transport. This would be the Shorts Belfast C1. The example shown here, XR394, would be operated by No. 53 Squadron at Fairford and later Brize Norton. *(John Ryan Collection)*

aircraft was named the Belfast and was developed to meet operational requirement ASR.371, which called for a freighter capable of carrying a wide range of military loads over long ranges. The prototype Belfast, developed from the Britannic 3A design, first flew on 5 January 1964. The aircraft was also notable for being only the second aircraft type to be built equipped with autoland blind landing equipment. The original RAF requirement had foreseen a contract for thirty aircraft, but this number was significantly reduced as a result of the Sterling Crisis of 1965. The British government required support for its loan application to the IMF, which the United States provided. As a result of this crisis the initial order was reduced to ten aircraft. The Belfast entered service with No. 53 Squadron in January 1966 initially based at RAF Fairford. By May the following year they had been moved to RAF Brize Norton.

Following entry into service it became apparent that a major drag problem was preventing the initial five aircraft attaining the postulated performance. Suction drag on the tail and rear fuselage was so severe that the operators gave the aircraft the nicknames The Dragmaster and the Slug. Modification and wind tunnel testing were carried out resulting in a new rear fairing being fitted that improved the aircraft's cruising speed by 40mph. Yet again the RAF was subject to shrinkage as further defence cuts were implemented, allied by the reorganization of the new RAF Strike Command. This was to have a repercussion on the Belfast fleet when No. 51 Squadron was disbanded in September 1976. By the end of that year the Belfast fleet had been retired and flown to No. 5 MU at Kemble for storage and disposal.

It would be the arrival of the Lockheed C-130 Hercules that would give Transport Command a quantum leap in technology and capability. The first C-130 for the RAF undertook its maiden flight from Lockheed Marietta in Georgia in October 1966. The first of the sixty-six aircraft order would arrive at Colerne in December. At Colerne each aircraft underwent a full range of pre-release checks that included the wing fuel tanks as trouble had been reported with aircraft on delivery flights. Once the wing tanks had been drained inspection revealed a myriad of foreign objects lurking within that included overalls, someone's lunch and the three-legged stools used for work in the tanks. The first unit to receive the Hercules in their sand and stone and black undersurfaces was No. 36 Squadron based at Lyneham in July 1967, being joined by No. 24 Squadron in February 1968. The other two squadrons, Nos 30 and 47 Squadrons, were based at Fairford, both equipping during May 1968. Both units would move to Lyneham in 1971 when the Comets retired and the Britannias had transferred to Brize Norton. Also based in Britain was No. 242 OCU at Thorney Island, becoming the Hercules conversion unit in April 1967.

Alongside the regular squadrons Transport Command still maintained an aircraft ferry organization, two flights were home based while the other two covered the remaining commands. While the ferry system was still regarded as a useful adjunct to normal operations it was felt by Air Chief Marshal Sir Walter Dawson, the Air Member for Supply and Organization, that a centralization and rationalization of the ferry flights would be in order. To that end all four original ferry units would be concentrated at Benson as Nos 147 and 167 Squadrons. Both units formed in April 1953 and remained active until they re-emerged as the Ferry Squadron in September 1958. The ferry unit remained operational until disbandment in 1960. Although the ferry unit gave good value for money it was felt that the possibility of putting the task out to civilian contract might be in order. Investigation revealed that the excellent record of the ferry units could possibly be compromised by variable standards. Also, ferry pilots, in contrast with normal service pilots, were used to flying aircraft that might not be fully equipped to operational standards. By July 1959 the situation had changed in favour of the squadrons, although this was limited to squadron pilots ferrying aircraft to and from Maintenance Units and the manufacturers as needed.

Transport Command would also enter the helicopter field as it had been determined that the type would be useful in the tactical transport role. To that end a decision by the Air Council in September 1959 would result in the Joint Experimental Helicopter Unit based at Andover becoming No. 225 Squadron in January 1960. The aircraft on strength at that time included nine Westland Whirlwinds and four Bristol Sycamores, all of which had been purchased from the Army budget. When the squadron was formed the Air Ministry was then faced with the prospect of purchasing the helicopters from the Army. Eventually, the paperwork was sorted out, the squadron was formed and almost immediately moved bases to Odiham in May 1960. No. 225 Squadron remained part of Transport Command until the unit transferred to Seletar in 1963 complete with Whirlwind HAR10s.

Changes also took place within the transport fleet with the arrival of the Bristol Britannia. Instead of retiring the Hastings and Beverley it was proposed that they be dedicated to the tactical transport role in support of Army operations. Supporting the argument for such a command was the increase in training exercises that were expected to reach fifty by 1960. The proposed organization would require a commander of air vice marshal rank plus a separate headquarters plus staff to manage the operational requirements of both the RAF and Army. After the usual wrangling between politicians and the military the decision was reached that the new organization would be created as No. 38 Group headquartered initially at Upavon, although it would later move to Odiham as this placed the group in closer proximity with their primary customer, the Army. No. 38 Group came into existence on 1 January 1960, the first AOC being Air Vice Marshal PG Wykeham. Initially the group's aircraft strength was very limited, consisting

The first tactical helicopter to join No. 38 Group Transport Command was the Westland Belvedere HC1. No. 72 Squadron based at Odiham was the British-based unit and XG482 'H' would be operated by this unit until replaced by the Wessex. *(John Ryan Collection)*

of two units with Scottish Aviation Pioneers/Twin Pioneers and Sycamores/ Whirlwinds, Nos 230 and 225 Squadrons, based at Odiham, while No. 118 Squadron was detached to Aldergrove with Sycamores.

The aircraft strength was increased in 1962 when a combat component was added consisting of Nos 1 and 54 Squadrons both operating the Hawker Hunter FGA9s. Also joining the group was No. 72 Squadron with the Westland (Bristol) Belvedere. Although not directly under the control of No. 38 Group the tactical transport units, No. 114 Squadron at Benson, Nos 24 and 36 Squadrons with Hastings at Colerne, Nos 47 and 53 Squadrons with Beverley's at Abingdon, were frequently tasked by No. 38 Group HQ as needed. Illustrating this point were the three major exercises undertaken in 1960 these being Starlight, Holdfast and Nation, all of which required the tactical transports of No. 38 Group to be successful. Starlight involved the movement of over 4,000 troops, 300 vehicles, 175 tons of equipment and fourteen helicopters to an area south of Tobruk. The primary airhead was at El Adem while the in country base was Tmimi. The entire force was transported during January, the heavy equipment was deployed using Beverleys and Hastings while most of the troops were flown out using Bristol Britannias. Also deployed were the Hunters of No. 54 Squadron while the Royal Navy contingent consisted of Sea Venoms from HMS *Albion*. The return was undertaken throughout April and included returning the helicopters and light transports of No. 38 Group back to base.

The Westland Belvedere, originally a Bristol Aircraft Company product, was the first helicopter designed from the outset to be a troop carrier. Unlike previous helicopters delivered to the British military the Type 192 was a twin engined, twin rotor machine that could operate on a single rotor should one of the powerplants fail. Capable of carrying a maximum of eighteen fully equipped troops, the first aircraft flew on 5 July 1958. Although the majority of Belvederes were deployed overseas No. 72 Squadron based at Odiham would receive their complement in November 1961, operating them until withdrawal in August 1964.

While the Belvederes were not deployed during Starlight another innovative item was. Although it was not much to look at a new type of container pallet was deployed that

No. 1 Squadron, in concert with No. 54 Squadron, based at West Raynham, was the firepower for No. 38 Group. XG130 'E' is sporting the unit's badge on its nose. *(John Ryan Collection)*

used nylon webbing in its construction and was capable of carrying a 1,000lb load. As soon as Starlight was completed No. 38 Group would begin the planning for Exercise Holdfast that would start in September 1960. The premise was that No. 16 Parachute Brigade would land at a Drop Zone near the Kiel Canal that was being defended by German and Danish forces against the incoming Orange forces. The planning for Holdfast was complicated by the need to pressure Transport Command into providing enough Beverley and Hastings aircraft to move the troops and their supplies as there was conflicting tasking at the time. Post Holdfast a report on the exercise determined that the Hastings and Beverleys would be better under the control of No. 38 Group as they were tactical in nature while Transport Command should manage the Britannia and Comet fleets.

The transfer would take place in time for Exercise Fabulist, which took place in April–May 1961. No. 38 Group would provide the Beverleys and Hastings while Transport Command would provide Bristol Britannias. The location for the exercise was Cyprus and it was designed to test the capability of the RAF and Army in the mounting of an airborne assault from an overseas base. To that end 1,864 troops from No. 16 Para Brigade, 77,712lb of stores and 52 pallets of equipment were delivered. To move this impressive amount required four Britannias, ten Beverleys plus nine Hastings. Also deployed were eight Hunter FGA9s from Stradishall to provide air support for the ground forces.

Exercises, while a major part of No. 38 Group's work, were also matched by other tasks such as moving over 1,500 officers and men of the Ghanian army plus 60 tons of supplies and 45 vehicles from Ghana to the Congo where they would act as part of the United Nations peace keeping force. Assisting in this task were the aircraft of Transport Command who moved further stores, supplies and equipment at the request of the UN. The reason for this effort was the civil war that was ravaging the Congo after the mineral-rich province of Katanga broke away.

The Defence White Paper for March 1961 revealed the number of aircraft available to Transport Command and No. 38 Group to cover both Strategic and Tactical tasks. Available for strategic tasking were twenty-three Britannias, and ten Comet C2s (about to be replaced by the improved C4), while for the tactical role forty-eight Hastings,

This fine aerial shot is of AWA Argosy C1 XN849 sporting Transport Command titles. This aircraft would be delivered to Benson in 1962 and would serve with all the units based there. *(BBA collection)*

thirty-two Beverleys, thirty-two Pioneers/Twin Pioneers, and four Percival Pembrokes were available. The helicopter fleet consisting of Westland Whirlwinds, Bristol Sycamores and Westland Belvederes was also available.

When the Armstrong Whitworth Argosy entered service at a much rebuilt Benson the recipient of the first few aircraft were delivered No. 242 OCU. When No. 114 Squadron was formed in February 1962 a pool of fully trained pilots, navigators and engineers was already available to man the aircraft. Once declared operational No. 114 Squadron was allocated to No. 38 Group. The first exercise that the Argosy took part in was Owl Song when three aircraft were deployed in support of No. 54 Squadron whose aircraft and personnel were transported from Waterbeach to Kemble, returning home four days later. September 1962 would see No. 114 Squadron taking part in a joint exercise/competition in September 1962. Two aircraft were despatched to Luqa, Malta, and Larissa, Greece to take part in the Lord Trophy Competition and Exercise Falltrap respectively. No. 114 Squadron would win the Trophy at the first attempt, beating all of the other tactical transport squadrons. Exercise Falltrap was part of Exercise Fallex 62 and was aimed at the destruction of Orange forces that had supposedly entered northern Greece. The aircraft of No. 38 Group would be utilized in the para dropping role successfully delivering their charges on time and place.

One role not mentioned in public for the Whistling Wheelbarrow was that of supporting the aircraft of Bomber Command during the annual Exercise Mickey Finn. This would see groups of V bombers plus logistic support sent to dispersal airfields. At the conclusion of the 1964 exercise the Chief of the Air Staff was pleased to report that all of the seventeen Transport Command aircraft required to move each units personnel and equipment to their dispersal bases arrived exactly on time, a great tribute to the air and ground crews of Transport Command.

In October 1964 a Labour Administration took charge and as is the wont of an incoming government they undertook an in-depth defence review. The first project to be cancelled was the Hawker Siddeley HS681, a jet-powered STOL transport. Requested under Specification C.241 to Operational Requirement 351 Armstrong Whitworth and the British Aircraft Corporation would respond. The Armstrong Whitworth design would be declared a winner, although by this time the company had been absorbed by Hawker Siddeley. The irony is that the design would be resurrected in a refined form as the BAE 146 transport.

To replace the HS681, the Beverley, the Hastings and later the Argosy the Lockheed C-130 Hercules was selected. Still regarded as one of the best tactical transports ever manufactured, the C-130 had already proven itself a winner with USAF and other nations. The initial order was for forty-eight aircraft, although this was increased to sixty-six in January 1966. The advent of a new transport type meant that bases had to be refurbished for their usage. Lyneham would be the chosen main base for Hercules operations while Brize Norton would be refurbished for the Britannia, Belfast and VC 10 fleets. Another survivor of the Labour Defence Review was the Hawker Siddeley Andover, both the tactical and the newly ordered VVIP versions being survivors. Two of the aircraft ordered for the VIP role would be allocated to the Queen's Flight.

The Shorts Belfast was also causing problems, as not only was the drag reducing the aircraft's performance, but limitations to the engine anti-icing systems had reduced the altitude that the aircraft could reach thus the payload had to be reduced to compensate. Eventually both the defects would be rectified with the Belfast giving good years of service until retirement. The Belvedere was also giving rise to concern. Not only were the engines liable to fail during start up, which frequently caused fires, but once started they could fail without warning and laminated rotor blades had a tendency to disintegrate without warning. Although this might mark an aircraft for withdrawal the usefulness of the type would see a full-blown modification programme put into action even though the RAF was looking for a replacement.

1966 would be the big year for Transport Command. In January 1966 the first Shorts Belfast was handed over to No. 53 Squadron at Brize Norton. Crew training and conversion would enable the squadron to undertake its first overseas flight to Malta, El Adem and Cyprus in May. Their conversion was slowed slightly when the squadron was temporarily transferred to Fairford as the runway at Brize Norton required a complete rebuild to cope with heavier aircraft and more importantly the projected intensive flying for training and

Captured on approach to Fairford is Lockheed C-130 Hercules C1 XV301. The type entered service in 1968 and is still in service. *(BBA Collection)*

trips overseas. No. 53 Squadron was finally declared fully operational in December 1966 and to celebrate the squadron sent an aircraft to the United States for route training.

While No. 53 Squadron was bringing its new aircraft to fruition the two Britannia squadrons, Nos 99 and 511, were undertaking a most unusual duty. When Ian Smith's government in Rhodesia declared UDI (Unilateral Declaration of Independence) in 1965 their first act was to cut the oil pipeline that connected Zambia to the rest of Africa. Beginning in December 1965 the Britannias flew a constant airbridge with drums of oil aboard, initially from Tanzania. After local opposition in Tanzania the operation transferred to the Zambian bases at N'dola and Lusake. The airbridge operation would continue until the final sortie was flown on 31 October 1966.

The third unit to form for transport operations at Brize Norton was No. 10 Squadron who received their first Vickers VC 10 in July 1966. Fitted out to airline standards plus a strengthened freight floor the VC 10 added a new dimension to the capability to Transport Command. Not only could personnel and families be transported at speed, badly injured patients could be moved to better medical facilities while the freight floor allowed the transport of freight and spares to arrive at their destinations quicker. Support for squadron deployments was also one of the squadron's tasks. Frequently carried out in concert with a Britannia or two the plan was the Britannia would carry the advance and transit servicing parties, TSP, the latter being dropped off en route to receive and despatch the deploying aircraft. The VC 10 would leave a couple of days later carrying the main party, the intention being to collect the TSPs as the VC 10 passed through. Occasionally the plan would need revising if one of the aircraft developed a technical fault; one of the favourite places for such an occurrence was Hawaii.

Transport Command would also gain another new type in 1966 when the HSA Andover tactical transport entered service. The only-home based unit to receive the type was No. 46 Squadron based at Abingdon in September, although it would transfer to Thorney Island in September 1970 finally disbanding in August 1975. The first crews arrived from the Andover Conversion Course in November 1966 bringing the three aircraft used for conversion with them. By the time the squadron was revealed to the press it had nine aircraft on strength.

When Transport Command required a tactical transport they would be equipped with the HSA Andover C1. The only British unit to fly the type was No. 46 Squadron whose XS601 is shown here. *(John Ryan Collection)*

The initial task assigned to No. 46 Squadron was flying aeromedical flights to Germany, followed by an exercise on Salisbury Plain. During this exercise the Andovers dropped a mix of fuel and ammunition totalling of 80,000lb. By the early months of 1967 the squadron was fully involved with No. 38 Group taskers. Their first task scheduled by No. 38 Group was to undertake a trip to El Adem carrying a mix of Army and RAF personnel plus forward air controllers for a training exercise, followed by a deployment of a Bloodhound missile unit to the same base. After this the Andovers undertook trials involving the one-ton container in the air drop role, which quickly became an established technique.

Even as the three new aircraft types were coming into service there were moves afoot to re-order Transport Command. This had started soon after the Labour Party had come into office in October 1964 and, typical of all such power changes, the new incumbents set about making their mark. Unfortunately, like most defence reviews it was the usual case of cuts while increasing the workload of the remaining personnel. Transport Command would also undergo a title change, becoming Air Support Command, although the Defence Reviews confused the issue by referring to Air Mobility Forces. The new command also became responsible for the tanker force although it was more of a paper transfer as tasking was still given by the planners at Bomber Command.

From the point of view of those undertaking the daily transport tasks very little had changed, the biggest difference being the RAF Air Support Command titles on the fuselage. Commanding the new organization would be the ex-Dambuster pilot Air Vice Marshal HB Martin who assumed command from Air Vice Marshal PC Fletcher on 1 July 1967. The aircraft inventory of the new command included ten Andovers, ten Belfasts, five Comet C4s, fourteen Hastings, nine C-130s with more to follow, fourteen VC 10s, twenty-three Britannias, twenty-four Hunters, plus twenty Wessex and ten Whirlwinds. This varied and versatile force would remain autonomous until 1 September 1972 when it became part of Strike Command. Having been a separate command the changes reduced the force to two groups, No. 38 Group for tactical support and No. 46 Group for strategic support.

The Nimrod MR1 would be a large leap in technology when the first examples were delivered to Coastal Command. XV226 was the first production machine and would finally be withdrawn to Bruntingthorpe for preservation in 2010. (*John Ryan Collection*)

Chapter 4

Strike Command is Born

It was becoming obvious during the 1960s that the cost of running the offensive side of the RAF in its current form was becoming financially unviable. Included in the costings were the aircraft, aircrews, ground crews, support personnel and equipment and the real estate that was needed to park the whole lot. Not helping the situation were the various governments who regarded the armed forces as an easy target for restrictions and cuts even though the workloads were never reduced to match; in many cases they were increased. Also under serious scrutiny were Britain overseas commitments that placed an extra strain upon resources. By 1967 plans were put in place to rationalize the number of operational commands within the home-based RAF. Thus on 31 April 1968 Fighter and Bomber Commands were merged as part of phase one to become Strike Command.

The Fighter Command component would become No. 11 Fighter Group within Strike Command being commanded by Air Vice Marshal I V Jones, a former fighter pilot. His counterpart, Air Vice Marshal MH LeBas, brought with him the bomber component that would form No. 1 Bomber Group. Also coming with the purview of Strike Command was No. 38 Group under the command of Air Vice Marshal HB Martin. This group was a mixture of ground attack aircraft plus tactical and strategic transports all being dedicated to the deployment and support of ground forces that needed to be deployed to one of the worlds trouble spots in a hurry.

Once the obligatory flypasts had been undertaken the various groups settled down to operating under the new regime whose headquarters were at High Wycombe. Fortunately the NATO tone down (in which everything was painted green) was still some way off thus the fighters dedicated to the defence of the British Isles were still allowed to sport the colourful markings of yore. All of the Lightning units were based in the east of the country; No. 5 Squadron had been resurrected in October 1965 having disbanded at Geilenkirchen in 1962 while still operating the Gloster Javelin FAW9. Equipped with the English Electric, BAC, and Lightning F6 the squadron sported the unit's red bars on either side of the nose roundel, a stylized five on the fin plus a Canadian maple leaf badge. For four years No. 5 Squadron was the only occupant of the former bomber airfield at Binbrook, although it was joined in March 1972 by No. 11 Squadron. This unit had reformed at Leuchars with the Lightning F6 in April 1967 having previously been a Javelin FAW9 unit at Geilenkirchen alongside its compatriot. These two squadrons and Binbrook were destined to be the last home of the Lightning force. No. 11 Squadron Lightnings sported their customary yellow and black nose bars with their twin eagles on the fin.

When No. 11 Squadron departed from Leuchars the only interceptor unit remaining on base was No. 23 Squadron. Originally based in England No. 23 Squadron had previously operated the Gloster Javelin at Coltishall before reforming on Lightning F3s in April 1964. These had remained in service until replaced by the Lightning F6. The role of the Binbrook-based units was to patrol and intercept incoming Russian Bears and Badgers testing Britain's air defences while that of the Leuchars squadron was to cover the Faroes Gap against similar Russian intruders. This unit's nose bars were blue and red bars with a red bird of prey on the fin. Covering the south of the country would be Nos 29 and 111 Squadrons both based at Wattisham. No. 29 Squadron had also been a Gloster Javelin operator until May 1967 when the big delta fighters were replaced by the EE Co Lightning F3 retaining this model until December 1974. In contrast No. 111 Squadron had flown numerous marques of the Gloster Meteor before receiving the EE Co Lightning F1A in April 1961, although these were replaced by the more capable F3 in December 1964. The final model, the Lightning F6, would enter service in May 1974, the squadron disbanding in September 1974. Throughout its Lightning period No. 29 Squadron sported its famous three-X nose bars with yet again birds of prey on the fin badge.

The Hawker Hunter still had a small role to play in the front-line RAF as two units still flew the type in its FGA9 form. Based at Wittering No. 1 Squadron had received its complement of FGA9s in January 1960 while based at Stradishall before ending up at Wittering having moved through Waterbeach and West Raynham to get there. The time that the squadron spent operating its Hunters from its new home was limited as disbandment took place in July 1969 in preparation for re-equipment. No. 54 Squadron had also been based at Stradishall when the Hunter FGA9 had been received in May 1960. This squadron also moved two more stations before ending up at Coningsby having been based at the same bases as No. 1 Squadron. Disbandment took place in September 1969, this being another squadron preparing for re-equipment.

English Electric Lightning F6 XS922 'H' was based at Binbrook with No. 5 Squadron. The aircraft would spend much of its time with the squadron until it transferred to No. 11 Squadron when No. 5 Squadron disbanded. *(John Ryan Collection)*

No. 54 Squadron based at West Raynham was still part of No. 38 Group when Hunter FGA9 XF517 'V' was photographed. *(John Ryan Collection)*

The bomber component of the newly created Strike Command centred around the Avro Vulcan B2, the remaining front-line Vulcan B1As having been retired in late 1967. This left the remaining bomber squadrons operating the B2 model only. Based at Scampton were Nos 27 and 617 Squadrons while across the other side of the City of Lincoln, Waddington housed Nos 44, 50 and 101 Squadrons. Support for the operational squadrons was provided by No. 230 OCU based at Finningley when Strike Command came into existence. A move to Scampton took place in December 1969 where the Vulcans were joined by the Hastings T5s from the Bomber Command Bombing School at Lindholme. Later renamed the Strike Command Bomber School the Hastings arrived at Scampton in September 1972 where they were promptly renamed 1066 Squadron. Originally eight converted Hastings were operated by the unit although four were retired from use in 1974 while the remainder struggled on until June 1977. Although normally dedicated to the training of navigators in the mysteries of the H2S radar on occasion the aircraft were utilized for other tasks one being to fly some Waddington Line personnel, including the author, to Valley to recover an errant Vulcan.

Away from the merger of Fighter and Bomber Commands the spectre of financial restraint and the fallout from the 1957 Defence White Paper were being felt. The major programme that would eventually feel the full force of politicians trying to control the budget was the iconic British Aircraft Corporation TSR2. This Mach 2 tactical strike and reconnaissance aircraft was intended to replace the various versions of English Electric Canberra that were serving with squadrons in RAF Germany and Britain.

In addition to the 1957 White Paper argument over the need for manned aircraft, additional political interference was complicating the project. During September 1957 the Ministry of Supply informed the Chief Officers of the competing aviation companies that the only acceptable proposals would be those issued by design teams from more than one company. As there were a large number of competing aircraft manufacturing companies in the UK competing for ever decreasing orders the government fostered co-operation between the various companies and encouraged mergers between them. Also not helping matters was the mutual distrust between the RAF and the Royal Navy. Even as GOR339, the TSR2 specification, was being defined, the Royal Navy was in the midst of developing the NA39 project that would later emerge as the Blackburn Buccaneer.

This aircraft was to be a low-altitude subsonic attack aircraft, designed for over-water as opposed to overland use. The savings involved in both services using a common aircraft were seen as considerable. To that end Blackburn offered the RAF a version of the NA39 that would cover some of the GOR339 requirements. The Chief of Defence Staff, and former First Sea Lord, Lord Mountbatten was a strong proponent of the Buccaneer claiming that five of the Blackburn aircraft could be purchased for the same price as one TSR2. As expected the RAF rebuffed the proposal stating that it was unsuitable due to a poor take-off performance while the avionics were not capable of delivering the desired accuracy. Or to put it another way as an RAF senior officer declared 'If we show the slightest interest in the Blackburn NA39 we might not get the GOR339 aircraft.'

Design work on the GOR339 proposals continued, with a submission deadline of 31 January 1958. Many proposals were entered; English Electric had teamed up with Short Brothers and submitted its P17A along with the Shorts P17D, a vertical lift airframe that would give the P17 a VTOL capability while designs were also received from Avro, Blackburn, de Havilland, Fairey, Hawker and Vickers-Armstrongs. The Air Ministry eventually selected the EE P17A and the Vickers-Armstrongs Type 571 for further consideration. The Ministry was particularly impressed with the Vickers submission that included not only the aircraft design, but a total systems concept outlining all the avionics, support facilities and logistics needed to maintain the aircraft in the field. This idea was already in use in the United States and was supposed to allow the primary contractor to have more control over the programme. Opinions within the Ministry of English Electric's management capability found it decidedly lacking in comparison with Vickers, although the two in combination was felt by officialdom to be a useful coalition therefore the development contract was awarded to Vickers, with English Electric as sub-contractor. The existence of the GOR339 programme was revealed to the public in December 1958 during a statement to the House of Commons. Under pressure by the recommendations of the Committee on Estimates, the Air Ministry examined ways that the various project proposals could be combined, and in January 1959 the Minister of Supply announced that the TSR2 would be built by Vickers working in concert with English Electric the initials coming from Tactical Strike and Reconnaissance, Mach 2.

On 1 January 1959, the project was given an official go-ahead; in February, it came under the new designation Operational Requirement 343, which firmed up the requirements of GOR339. Throughout 1959 English Electric and Vickers worked on combining the best of both of their designs in order to put forward a joint design with a view to having an aircraft flying by 1963. At the same time both organizations were working on merging the companies under the umbrella of the British Aircraft Corporation. During the design process there were some problems with realizing the design as some of contributing manufacturers were employed directly by the Ministry rather than through BAC, which in turn led to communication difficulties and cost overruns. However, at two Cabinet meetings held on 1 April 1965, it was decided to cancel the TSR2 on the grounds of projected cost, and instead to obtain an option agreement to acquire up to 110 General Dynamics F-111 aircraft with no firm commitment to buy. This decision was later announced in the budget speech on 6 April 1965. A week later, the Chancellor defended the decision in a debate in the House of Commons, saying that the F-111 would prove cheaper.

To replace the TSR2 the Air Ministry initially placed an optional order for the F-111K, a modified F-111A with F-111C enhancements including the extended wings but also considered two other choices: a Rolls-Royce Spey conversion of the Dassault Mirage IV plus an enhanced Blackburn Buccaneer S2 with a new nav-attack system and reconnaissance capability, referred to as the Buccaneer 2 Double Star. In the event neither proposal was actively pursued as a TSR2 replacement although a final decision was reserved until the 1966 Defence Review. Defence Minister Denis Healey's memo about the F-111 and the Cabinet minutes regarding the final cancellation of the TSR2 indicated that the F-111 was the preferred option.

Following on from the 1966 Defence White Paper, the Air Ministry decided on two aircraft types, the F-111K with a longer term replacement being a joint Anglo–French project for a variable geometry strike aircraft – the Anglo French Variable Geometry Aircraft that was later to morph via various steps into the Panavia Tornado. A censure debate followed on 1 May 1967 during which Denis Healey claimed the cost of the TSR2 would have been £1,700 million over fifteen years including operational costs, compared with £1,000 million for the F-111K/AFVG combination. Eventually, ten F-111Ks were ordered in April 1966 with an additional order for forty being placed in April 1967. However, the F-111 programme suffered an enormous cost escalation and this coupled with the devaluation of the pound eventually exceeded that of the TSR2 projected

The introduction of the Tornado GR1 would herald the rundown of the Buccaneer and the Vulcan fleets. This view shows the first production Tornado on its rollout at Warton. *(John Ryan Collection)*

figures. Many technical problems were still unresolved with the F-111, including engine and swing structural safety, prior to operational deployment. Therefore, faced with lower than projected performance estimates the order for fifty F-111Ks was eventually cancelled in January 1968. Having appeared to be a lemon the F-111 would go on to be one of the most capable attack aircraft in the USAF inventory; the RAAF were also enamoured with the type and were very reluctant to retire them.

After the demise of the TSR2 and the F-111K order the RAF was left with a quandary: what to purchase to fulfil the roles that the cancelled aircraft were supposed to cover. The replacement was two pronged: to cover the fighter, bomber and reconnaissance roles the Ministry of Defence contracted the McDonnell Douglas F-4 Phantom II, which was already on order for the Royal Navy. Based on the US Navy F-4J airframe the two versions destined for Britain were reworked to accommodate the Rolls-Royce Spey engine plus a suite of British designed and built avionics. Had the RAF gone shopping for the Phantom on its own it is highly likely that the preferred purchase would have been the long nosed F-4E model with a cannon mounted under the nose. The version that both service operators received was rumoured to be the slowest and most thirsty model of the Phantom ever built. The foregoing notwithstanding the first Phantom FGR2 was delivered to No. 23 Maintenance Unit (MU) at Aldergrove, part of which was established to receive and prepare the Phantom for British usage. No. 23 MU received the first aircraft on 20 July 1968, despatching it to No. 228 OCU at Coningsby on 23 August 1968. Eventually, all 168 British Phantoms would pass through Aldergrove on their way to either the Fleet Air Arm or the RAF.

The first unit to receive the FGR2 for operational purposes was No. 6 Squadron, which had disbanded as a Canberra operator in January 1969 while a cadre was established at Coningsby to prepare for the new aircraft type. No. 6 Squadron was officially reformed in May being declared ready not long afterwards. Their assigned role was to provide the offensive support for No. 38 Group Air Support Command where they replaced the Hunters of Nos 1 and 54 Squadrons. One of those Hunter units, No. 54 Squadron, would also form at Coningsby as a Phantom operator in September 1969; both units would remain as F-4 units until 1974 when they swapped their two-seat

No. 1 Squadron was the other Hunter unit that was charged with providing air support in company with No. 54 Squadron and was also based at West Raynham. *(BBA Collection)*

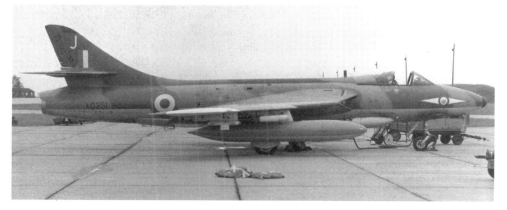

Although the Canberra had mainly left service at least one unit still operated the type this being No. 360 Squadron with the T17 version. *(Bob Archer Collection)*

mounts for the Sepecat Jaguar. The RAF also acquired twenty of the FG1 aircraft intended for the Royal Navy. These would be used to equip No. 43 Squadron at Leuchars in September 1969 having disbanded as Hunter FGA9 unit in October 1967. The F-4 was also directed to the majority of Lightning squadrons within Britain as it was becoming obvious that the Lightning F3 was becoming incapable of handling the new generation of Warsaw Pact attack aircraft; not only were they lightly armed in comparison with the newer machines, they suffered from having too short a range and thus endurance even with in-flight refuelling. The units that would trade in their Lightning included Nos 23, 29, 56 and 111 Squadrons. No. 23 Squadron had disbanded at Leuchars in October 1975 with a designate cadre forming at Coningsby in the same month in preparation for operating the Phantom FGR2. Declared operational in November at Coningsby the squadron soon decamped to it permanent base at Wattisham

When the political regime changed in Malta in 1978, with the country swinging towards Gaddafi's Libya, the British forces pulled out. This resulted in No. 13 Squadron returning to Wyton whose WJ825 is pictured here. *(John Ryan Collection)*

No. 39 Squadron remained a constant for Strike Command aerial reconnaissance as exemplified by Canberra PR9 XH175 complete with the squadron commander's pennant on the nose. *(BBA Collection)*

in February of the following year. A similar story concerned No. 29 Squadron based at Wattisham, which disbanded in October 1974, although a cadre would form at Coningsby as a designate unit, the squadron becoming fully operational in January 1975. Another Wattisham unit that would convert to the Phantom was No. 56 Squadron, which disbanded in March 1976. As before a cadre was established at Coningsby with the squadron becoming operational in June 1976; it would then move back to Wattisham in July 1976. The final unit that converted from the Lightning F3 to the F-4 Phantom was No. 111 Squadron, another Wattisham based unit. The Lightnings left service in September 1974 with a cadre forming at Coningsby in October 1974. No. 111 Squadron was declared operational in October 1974 before taking up residence at Leuchars in November 1975. Unlike the Phantoms assigned to Air Support Command those assigned to replace the Lightning were dedicated purely to the air defence role.

When No. 56 Squadron relinquished its Lightnings they were replaced by Phantom FGR2s. XV469 'A' would join the unit once it was at its operating base of Wattisham, the squadron having formed at Coningsby for working up. *(Bob Archer Collection)*

Coningsby would see No. 41 Squadron forming with the Phantom in 1972, the type remaining in service until 1977 when the Jaguar was received. *(John Ryan Collection)*

Although the majority of squadrons were equipped with the FGR2 version of the Phantom the excess FG1s ordered originally for the Royal Navy were delivered instead to No. 43 Squadron. Having flown models of the Hawker Hunter from 1954 to October 1967 while based at Leuchars and finally at Khormaksar, the squadron was reformed at Leuchars in September 1969 to operate the FG1 Phantom in the air defence role. This model Phantom remained in service until July 1989, although the unit's strength was bolstered during May to November 1988 by some FGR2 Phantoms. When No. 892 NAS was disbanded in December 1978 after the paying off of HMS *Ark Royal* its aircraft were flown to St Athan for rework. The refurbished fighters were allocated to No. 111 Squadron, also based at Leuchars, slowly replacing the incumbent FGR2 model, the last one departing in October 1979.

They say it pays to advertise as shown by Buccaneer S2 XX981 of No. 12 Squadron. The advert is carried on the inner face of the rotating bomb door, a concept that was borrowed from the Martin XB-51/ B-57 aircraft. *(BBA Collection)*

The other aircraft that replaced the defunct TSR2/F-111K and AFVG programmes was the Blackburn Buccaneer. Having proven itself with Fleet Air Arm strike squadrons in its S Mk 2 version this model was chosen for RAF service. An initial order for twenty-six aircraft was quickly followed by a further order for another seventeen airframes. No further new aircraft were ordered for the RAF, the service having to depend on the disbandment of the Fleet Air Arm units to increase their available aircraft and operational squadrons. As no new-build aircraft were available No. 736 NAS of the Fleet Air Arm was tasked with training the first RAF crews. An RAF flight was formed at Lossiemouth comprising three pilots, two attack instructors and three navigators. All of these were RAF officers who had flown the Buccaneer on secondment with Navy squadrons. Due to the increase in training requirements several redundant S1s were taken out of storage to supplement the few available S2s. The graduating crews were destined to form the cadres of the first two RAF Squadrons originally based at Honington, these being No. 12 Squadron that was formed in October 1969 while No. 15 Squadron was formed one year later in October 1970. These first-build aircraft were capable of launching the Martel missile, which was a bonus for Shiny Twelve as their primary role was that of anti-shipping.

The Martel was originally developed for the Royal Navy, the need for such a weapon being realized as ship board defences were improving year on year. The programme was developed by Hawker Siddeley, later BAES, in collaboration with Matra of France, and started in 1964. The Martel missile upon delivery was a tried and tested system that was available in both the Anti-Radar, AS37, and Anti-Ship, AJ168, TV-guided versions. Though the projected service life of the Buccaneer S2 was relatively short it was decided to press ahead with the weapon's development. However, to accommodate the missiles changes were made to allow for the clearance of the missiles fins; the outer pylons were moved outboard by approximately two feet allowing a full four missile load to be carried. The original build weapon pylons employed single point suspension with a single vertical ejector ram, however in order to reduce pylon depth a general-purpose standard weapon pylon was developed utilizing a two-point suspension system with a horizontal ejector ram operated by a linkage from the vertical rams.

The extra weight of the Martels meant that the aircraft's wings could not be folded with the missiles still mounted, although this was later rectified by modifying the wing fold hydraulic jacks. Also undergoing modifications were the undercarriage units and their mountings as if the missiles had not been fired the overall landing weight would be too high for the original units and the missiles were deemed too expensive to jettison. Other modifications required to launch and guide the Martel were incorporated in the navigator's cockpit. These comprised a television display, necessary to guide a TV Martel to its target. Due to the limited available space, the display was mounted on the floor between the navigator's legs. This in turn necessitated the splaying out of the thigh guards on the rear ejection seat. Additionally, a small control column and elbow rest were mounted on the right-hand console of the navigator's cockpit for the manual control of the missile.

In operation the TV-guided Martel flew a pre-determined mid-course trajectory at a reasonable altitude, which allowed for target acquisition. Flying at this kind of height allowed the data link to be maintained with the launch aircraft. The missile was fitted with a Marconi Vidicon camera in the nose that transmitted TV imagery back to the data link pod carried by the aircraft. This in turn transmitted control inputs given by the

Buccaneer's navigator using the small control stick. The AJ168 anti-ship missile, unlike its successor the Sea Eagle, was not designed to attack targets at sea level. Instead, the missile climbed then dived from height, which would later render it vulnerable to advancing shipborne defence systems.

The trials programme for evaluation of the AJ168 Martel began with the launch of the first article in February 1970. From that date until the end of firing trials in July 1973, a total of twenty-five missiles had been fired. No. 22 Joint Services Trials Unit based at A&AEE, Boscombe Down, would undertake the evaluation programme with live firings taking place from Aberporth, Cardigan Bay, Wales.

Although the Martel was initiated by the Royal Navy, it was the RAF that became the first Maritime Strike force to be fully Martel equipped due to the delivery of new-build Buccaneer S2Bs in 1972, which incorporated Martel carriage and capability from the outset. During September and October 1974 two Buccaneers from No. 12 Squadron were deployed to the French Air Force base at Cazaux, near Bordeaux, for a four-week service trial of the AS37 Martel. No. 12 Squadron later flew further service trials of the AJ168 'TV' Martel in October 1974 at Aberporth. From its resurrection to disbandment on 30 September 1993, No. 12 Squadron was the RAF's dedicated Maritime Strike unit that was declared to SACLANT, Supreme Allied Commander, Atlantic, as part of the maritime attack force within NATO.

During this period, the Martel missile system was the weapon of choice for radar suppression using the AS37 missile and this remained the case until the Buccaneer's retirement from service on 31 March 1994. The anti-ship missile remained in service with No. 12 Squadron until early 1988, when it was replaced by the Sea Eagle missile. The Sea Eagle is a true fire-and-forget weapon, powered by a jet engine rather than a rocket. This new powerplant increased the range fourfold over of the TV-guided Martel, this allowing the attacking Buccaneers to fly their attack profile, launch their Sea Eagles, and then return to base without ever appearing on the enemies' radar screen.

A small number of Hawker Hunters remained in service during this period. This T7 was one of a handful of the type assigned to the Buccaneer squadrons for pilot conversion purposes complete with the Integrated Flight Instrumentation System. This example was flown by No. 208 Squadron. (*John Ryan Collection*)

For Red Flag undertaken at Nellis AFB, Nevada, the Buccaneers were given this camouflage finish. Note the lack over the rear fuselage as it was inclined to get dirty due to jet efflux. *(BBA Collection)*

Only one other British-based unit would fly the Buccaneer – No. 208 Squadron. No. 15 Squadron had decamped to RAF Germany where it was later joined by No. 16 Squadron, both squadrons replacing the original Canberra B(I)8s. This unit had last existed as a Hawker Hunter operator in the Middle East, disbanding in September 1971. No. 208 Squadron reformed at RAF Honington in 1974 with Blackburn Buccaneer S2s. These were assigned to SACEUR and operated in the low-level strike role. The squadron's Buccaneers were declared operational to SACEUR from 1975 armed with WE177 nuclear weapons. The squadron was tasked with supporting land forces resisting an advance by Warsaw Pact forces into Western Europe by attacking enemy forces plus logistics and infrastructure targets beyond the forward edge of the battlefield. Initially these attacks were made with conventional munitions, although nuclear weapons would be used in the event of an escalation. The allocation of the British-owned WE177 to this role freed the squadron from the time-consuming burden of obtaining clearance to use American-owned nuclear weapons normally held in US custody. The squadron

Even the Buccaneer fleet could 'jazz it up' as shown on S2 XN976 of No. 208 Squadron bedecked with the unit's markings writ large. *(Robbie Shaw Collection)*

When the HSA Harrier GR1 entered service with No. 1 Squadron it replaced the venerable Hawker Hunter. When the new type entered service the squadron relocated to Wittering. *(John Ryan Collection)*

continued in this role based at RAF Honington until July 1983, when it moved to Lossiemouth and was reassigned to SACLANT for maritime strike duties. The squadron's allocation of WE177 nuclear weapons was then reduced to twelve, one per aircraft, although the Buccaneer was able to carry two in its internal bomb bay. The squadron continued in this role until late 1993 when it relinquished its nuclear weapons as the WE177 was being phased out. No. 12 Squadron was one of the last squadrons to operate the Buccaneer before it left service in 1994, the squadron disbanding on 31 March 1994.

Strike Command was the recipient of two further new aircraft during the late 1960s and early 1970s. The first of these was the radical Hawker Siddeley Harrier that had begun life as the Hawker P1127. The first recognizable design would be sketched at Hawker Kingston in October 1957. This initial sketch underwent full detail design over the following year with the Bristol BE53 vectored thrust engine at the core of the design. Leading the Hawker team was Sir Sydney Camm while the Bristol engine team was under the guidance of Dr SG Hooker. The Hawker input was a privately funded project while much of the funding for the Bristol engine came from the United States via the Mutual Weapons Development Programme who provided 75 per cent of funding. Once the design had been fully detailed NATO military staffs prepared a design requirement for a lightweight Vertical/ Short Take Off and Landing (V/STOL) fighter based on the P1127 design. The new aircraft was intended to replace the Fiat G91.

Construction of the first P1127 using private funding began in 1959, although the Ministry of Aviation later gave backing for the construction of two prototype aircraft. Construction continued apace with first hover trials taking place during October 1960 while the first conventional flight was undertaken in March 1961. First flight nozzle transitions took place in September by which time the Air Ministry had written Operation Requirement, OR.345, for a service version of the P1127. During this period Kingston was also developing a supersonic version, the P1154 in response to a NATO requirement. Although NATO were very keen to purchase this model the organization had no funds of its own to purchase the aircraft. Kingston also continued developing the P1127 design, the interested parties being Britain, the United States and West Germany.

The result was an order for nine improved models known as the Kestrel these being destined for the Tripartite Evaluation Squadron based at West Raynham. Flight trials were conducted over East Anglia throughout 1965, during which six hundred hours were completed. When the squadron was disbanded the unit's aircraft were split between the participating nations with America having the largest total of six machines, these being designated XV-6A.

In February 1965 the government decided to cancel the P1154 project, however they did announce that the Kestrel would be subject to further development intended for service with the RAF as a close support aircraft. The aircraft designed for the RAF would be named Harrier in 1969 entering service that same year. The aircraft that entered service was a vastly improved aircraft over the P1127 and the aircraft it replaced, the Hawker Hunter. At the core of the Harrier was the Pegasus engine that vented through four nozzles, two each side of the fuselage. All four nozzles were driven by air drawn from the compressor; this removed the need for hydraulic and electrical power supplies all of which reduced the weight of the aircraft. Great efforts were made from the start to make the engine reliable and safe, to achieve the latter the air motors that drove the nozzles were duplicated and ensured that the nozzles remained symmetrical at all times. To keep the weight of the airframe down a ruthless programme was initiated as every extra pound would reduce the Harrier's chances of taking off vertically. Obviously, this could not be taken too far as the aircraft still had to be capable of doing its job. Fortunately, the Kingston design team proved that they were more than capable of achieving this target. Great care was also taken in ensuring that the Harrier could operate

Part of the Harrier's uniqueness was its ability to operate with minimal support thus No. 1 Squadron spent a lot of time operating from the hides around Wittering. *(BBA Collection)*

safely from unprepared surfaces and minimal prepared surfaces without causing damage to the airframe.

From the pilot's point of view his primary system was the Ferranti FE541 inertial nav/attack system, a lightweight, self-contained unit. The data was supplied to the pilot via a Specto Head Up Display (HUD) system that was capable of displaying navigation data, weapon aiming plus night and VTOL flying. Also in the cockpit were the navigation display and computer that also fed its data into the HUD. The core of this system is the moving map display that is driven by the inertial system at the aircraft's ground speed.

One of the first non-flying units to become involved with the Harrier was the Central Servicing Development Establishment at Swanton Morley whose role was to ensure that the Harrier would not be excessively difficult to maintain under all conditions. The result of this input was that Kingston made strenuous efforts to create an aircraft that was a parallel to a modern car; it can be parked outside in an unprotected environment for long periods and it will start at the first push of a button. Originally the RAF were concerned about removing the entire mainplane for an engine change; here again Kingston made great strides in making this task as easy as possible by developing easily transportable equipment for that very purpose.

The result of these development trends was that the Harrier would only see the inside of a hangar at the 200-hour point for a minor servicing and 800 hours for a major servicing. To speed up the diagnostic process in the field as much built-in test equipment as possible was included and as far as possible line replaceable units were the norm. Recognizing that the RAF might want to operate their new aircraft in basically filthy environments the airframe and systems needed protection against such conditions while the aircraft itself should be able to operate for short periods with little or no ground support equipment. Overall, this engineering effort during the design phase would result in at least one American Naval aviator remarking that the low man-hours needed to maintain the Harrier were better than anything the USN had and that it matched the same man-hours needed to look after a captured MiG 21.

Of course, the primary role of the Harrier was to pop out of concealment and let loose its weaponry at its designated targets. This was only possible due to the aircraft's design and its ability to operate from semi or unprepared strips. During a war scenario the Harrier force could be widely dispersed in hides that with careful concealment were virtually undetectable, unlike conventional aircraft that require the full gamut of support facilities in order to be operable. To that end the Harrier was equipped with a pair of pods under the fuselage that were home to a pair of 30mm cannons. Between the pods was the centreline pylon that could carry either weaponry or a reconnaissance pod. Other weaponry could be carried on the four underwing pylons with the inner pylons being plumbed for the carriage of fuel tanks. Even as production was building up Rolls-Royce would purchase the engine manufacturer, Bristol Siddeley engines, from the Hawker Siddeley group, complying with the government's wish for a contraction and merging of the British aircraft industry.

The RAF would originally order sixty airframes comprising fifty single-seat aircraft plus ten two-seat conversion airframes, although the final total would reach 131 airframes. The second contract would include further GR1 airframes plus twenty-four GR3s and seventeen extra two-seaters. The GR1A featured an uprated Pegasus powerplant and after converting the remaining original GR1s a total of fifty-eight aircraft were available. Prior to service delivery the first six airframes were being flown hard by pilots from the manufacturers and the A&AEE at Dunsfold and Boscombe Down respectively. During this period the weapons delivery systems were put through their paces under all expected conditions. A great fillip was given to the Harrier's future at this time when Israel launched a pre-emptive strike against the airfields of the surrounding Arab nations during which they were virtually wiped out. This action by the Israelis vindicated the development and deployment of the Harrier given its ability to operate away from conventional support facilities.

In order to improve the aircraft's capabilities the Harrier was updated to the GR3, which had the Ferranti developed and manufactured Laser Rangefinder and Marked Target Seeker (LRMTS). As the name implies the aircraft's system calculates the closure rate and distance of a specified spot via the laser detector and detects the illuminated target. Although this improved the aircraft's combat options it still relied upon the target being illuminated by another external source. This version also featured an uprated engine plus a slight rearrangement of the cockpit to allow for the new equipment, which also included the ARI.18228 passive warning system mounted on the fin and rear fuselage. The two-seaters followed a similar path, the first version was the T2, followed by the T2A. This also had an uprated Pegasus engine, although the fin required an increase in size to counter the thrust. When the LRMTS equipment was installed in the two-seaters they were redesignated T4s and also featured the ARI.18221 equipment on the upper fin and rear fuselage extension.

Four units were equipped with the early Harriers, Nos 1, 3, 4 and 20 Squadrons, although the latter three were based in Germany. Initially training was carried out by the Harrier Conversion Unit based at Wittering that had formed in January 1969, although this was later redesignated as No. 233 Operational Conversion Unit in October 1970 also at the same base. Initially, the Harrier CU flew single-seat Harriers and Hawker Hunters, with the fledgling pilots also undertaking some helicopter training to get a feel for vertical take-offs and landings. The conversion unit would become a fully fledged OCU when the two-seaters became available.

The only Harrier unit that would be based in Britain would be No. 1 Squadron based at Wittering where it would become part of No. 38 Group of Air Support Command. Prior to equipping with the Harrier the squadron had been flying another Hawker product, the Hunter. The first commander of No. 1 Squadron was Wing Commander Ken Hayr and the operational unit would operate alongside the OCU for many years. On 16 May 1969 four Harriers arrived at Wittering where the Hunter Squadrons were converted one flight at a time. VTOL and transition training was undertaken at West Raynham using the old Kestrel pads as the Wittering concrete was not yet up to standard. As yet there were still no two-seater trainers and extra training sorties were necessary. The Harrier was not overly difficult to fly, however it did offer fierce acceleration. The use of the nozzles was instinctive but the need to add power during vertical landings, rather than pulling the nose up, was not.

The first Harrier-converted pilots became the staff of 233 OCU, which really got into its stride when the first two-seat T Mk 2As arrived in October 1970. The OCU course lasted six months with one week of helicopter flying, ground school, flight simulator and seventy-five hours of Harrier flying. The Basic Squadron covered V/STOL, instrument, formation, night and air combat flying, while the Advanced Squadron added low-level navigation, attack profiles, reconnaissance, port oblique and pod, weapons, cannon, SNEB rockets and cluster bombs. Short take-offs were practised from taxiways, roads and strips, while vertical landings were carried out using MEXE landing pads and rolling vertical landings were undertaken using semi-prepared strips.

The Harrier GR Mk 1 was released for service use in April 1969 and shortly afterwards would participate in the *Daily Mail* Trans-Atlantic Air Race organized to commemorate the fiftieth anniversary of Flight Lieutenants Alcock and Brown's first non-stop flight across the Atlantic. On 5 May Squadron Leader Tom Lecky-Thompson took off vertically in XV741 from St Pancras railway station and utilizing in-flight refuelling landed vertically in New York's Bristol Basin. The race was from the top of the London Post Office Tower to the top of the Empire State Building. The winning flight time was 6 hours 11 minutes. From west to east Squadron Leader Graham Williams flying XV744 completed the crossing in a flight time of 5 hours 49 minutes, although it was beaten by a Fleet Air Arm Phantom. Ferry wing tips, the 18-inch development versions, were used to improve cruise performance, the only time they were used in service. The British military participation in the air race was co-ordinated by an RAF team under the codename Blue Nylon and included aircraft and crews of the Harrier Conversion Unit Hawker Siddeley Harrier (No. 55 and No. 57 Squadrons), Handley Page Victor tankers (No. 72 Squadron), Westland Wessex (No. 543 Squadron), Victor SR2 reconnaissance aircraft, and No. 892 Squadron Fleet Air Arm, equipped with McDonnell Douglas Phantom FG1s.

With the excitement of the transatlantic race behind them No. 1 Squadron settled down to the usual round of exercises, training flights and armament practice camps for which they were based at Akrotiri, Cyprus. While the RAFG Harriers were dedicated to close air support and battlefield reconnaissance No. 1 Squadron was working up as part of No. 38 Group's rapid reaction force. During 1970 the unit undertook a detachment to Cyprus while Norway was the venue during September. The squadron would be equipped with the GR1A in quick order and would receive the GR3 during November 1973, retaining this model until 1989.

In 1975 No. 1 Squadron despatched six Harrier GR1As to the British colony of Belize in Central America as neighbouring Guatemala had yet again been threatening another incursion across the border, although this time the threat was real as troop and equipment were seen gathering on the border. After five months of flying armed along the border the Harriers returned home as the Guatemalan forces had withdrawn back to their barracks. The respite was short however as by June 1977 the Guatemalans were threatening to invade thus a more permanent force was established, designated No. 1417 Flight based at Ladyville airport using hides as standard practice. The Harrier force took with them a full range of live cannon shells, SNEB rocket pods, standard 1,000lb high-explosive and cluster bombs. All of these were given an airing using isolated swamps as targets although those chosen were close enough so that Guatemalan watchers could see clearly. The initial hides ranged from Alpha to Juliet although this was soon reduced to four hides that later acquired hardened hides plus a full range of facilities for both air and ground crews. Including the Rapier defence units the number of deployed personnel was around 300.

The Harriers and personnel were drawn alternately from Nos 1 and IV(AC) Squadrons, the rotation taking place every six months. While the support personnel travelled to their destination aboard an RAF transport the replacement Harriers transited via RAFSU Goose Bay, Canada and Bermuda. During these deployments three aircraft were lost; one to a bird strike, and one after failing to gain enough height during

One of the deployments supported by the Harrier force was the air defence needs of Belize. No. 1417 Flight continued in existence until July 1993. *(BBA Collection)*

a vertical take-off while the final crash involved a collision with the local trees. Fortunately all three pilots escaped safely. Two other Harriers suffered damage; the first collided with a large native vulture that went down the engine intake and promptly trashed the engine while the other got caught in a brown out while attempting a landing on St George's Cayes, a small island off the coast of Belize.

Given the British determination to protect Belize the Guatemalans decided that diplomacy might be a better course. The first step was taken in 1991 when Guatemala recognized that the people of Belize should determine their own future. This was followed in 1992 with the President of Guatemala recognizing the independence of Belize and establishing diplomatic relations between both countries. During 1993 with the peace in the area seemingly settled it was decided to withdraw No. 1417 Flight. This marked the end of the Harrier GR3 in RAF service as the more advanced GR5 was in the process of being delivered, of which more later.

Strike Command would also be the recipient of another strike attack aircraft, although this one arrived by a more circuitous route to enter service. Unusually both Britain and France were looking for a similar kind of aircraft that was intended to be a supersonic trainer for the *Armée de l'Air* and the RAF. The former was looking for an aircraft to replace both the Folland Gnat and the Hawker Hunter while the latter was intended to fill the gap between the Fouga Magister and the Dassault Mirage III. In France the Breguet Br121 would be declared the winner of the French competition. The aircraft intended for RAF use had been laid out in Air Staff Target 362 issued by the Ministry of Defence in 1964. The contenders were Hunting, Folland, Hawker Siddeley and English Electric, later the British Aircraft Corporation whose design was designated the P45.

1964 was also the year when international co-operation began in earnest. As both Britain and France were looking for a similar kind of aircraft it made sense for both countries to combine their efforts. After all submissions had been considered by both countries' defence departments the eventual winner was declared to be the Breguet Br121 that would be modified slightly to cater for the differing needs of both air forces. To that end a Memorandum of Understanding was signed on 17 May 1965 with Breguet nominated as the French partner while the British partner was BAC. In order to integrate the efforts of both countries a new organization was formed, therefore in May 1966 SEPECAT was born, Société Européene de Production de l'Avion d'École Combat et d'Appui Tactique. The entire organization would be co-managed by MBC Vallières of Breguet and Sir Fredrick Page of BAC Preston who were supported by seconded personnel from the Ministry of Defence, Ministry of Technology, Delegation Ministerelle pour l'Armament plus the Etat-Major de l'Armée de l'Air et Aeronavale. The initial contracts, covering 150 aircraft for each country, were issued by the Direction Technique de Construction Aeronautique. The French order covered seventy-five single-seat machines, appui or support, and seventy-five two-seat trainers, ecole, while the British order was purely for 150 two-seat training models. The powerplants were also a joint effort between Rolls-Royce and Turbomeca, resulting in the Adour engine.

From the outset both nations wanted aircraft with differences; the French required a fairly simple aircraft while the RAF was looking for a more sophisticated machine that had to be supersonic with a superior avionics fit. To cater for these alterations the Br121 was altered to feature a single-piece thinner wing, an area ruled fuselage, and an increase in the available weapons load while the rear cockpit was raised to improve the instructor's line of sight. These changes resulted in a much heavier machine that required increased engine power to cater for these changes. The British order for the Jaguar would change subsequently when the next joint project, the Anglo French Variable Geometry Aircraft, would fall by the wayside. Not only was there a severe disagreement between the partners, but the UK government was hacking and slashing its way through numerous aviation projects already in development.

All of these changes would result in the RAF being left without any kind of dedicated strike aircraft to satisfy its immediate needs. To cater for this the British order was changed by a Memorandum of Understanding issued in January 1967 that altered the British requirement to 90 single-seat strike aircraft and 110 two-seaters. Fortunately, altering the already extant design to this configuration was a relatively simple task. By 1970 the RAF was under government pressure to rationalize its requirements thus the order was changed again to 165 single-seaters plus 35 two-seat trainers. Added to this was a caveat for a further three two-seaters if they were required and the reduced number of this version indicated that the RAF was no longer interested in the type as an advanced trainer. Instead, one of the designs put forward by the other competing conglomerates, Hawker Siddeley, would later fill the role – the Hawk. And as for the new joint strike aircraft it would be named the Jaguar, which was announced in time for the 1965 Paris Air Salon.

The aircraft destined for the RAF was the Jaguar S. This was the single-seat version that was fitted with a Martin-Baker Mk 9 ejection seat, a pair of 30mm Aden cannon, five external store pylons, a nav attack system based around an inertial navigation platform, a central navigation digital computer, projecting moving map display, a laser rangefinder LRMTS, head up display, TACAN, internally carried in-flight refuelling probe and an arrestor hook. The two-seater was designated Jaguar B, and had a pair of Martin-Baker Mk 9 ejection seats, a single Aden cannon, five stores pylons, the same nav attack system as in the S and an arrestor hook. No LRMTS was installed in this model.

The first British prototype, S-06 XW560, was rolled out at Warton on 18 August 1969 making its first flight in the hands of Jimmy Dell on 12 October. The second aircraft, S-07 XW563, made its first flight in June 1970 and featured a mock-up of the LRMTS nose. The final British prototype was the eighth to fly overall and was B-08 XW566, a

The arrival of Sepecat Jaguar would improve Strike Command's attack capability. This is prototype XW560, pictured undertaking flight trials. *(John Ryan Collection)*

two seater. By the time this airframe flew it was constructed of 80 per cent of production components. During the development phase test flying various changes were proposed and later adopted; the short nosewheel door of the original was extended to cover more of the nose leg although it was still home to the twin landing lights, the intake splitter plates were deleted, and the rear lower fuselage airbrakes were given perforations while the original short fin was increased in height thus improving stability.

At the completion of the test and evaluation phase the first British production machine, XX108, undertook its maiden flight on 12 October 1972, while the second aircraft, XX109, flew in November. This aircraft was heavily involved in the development of the LRMTS and the full avionics package. Following on from the initial two machines the next production machines were involved in clearing the various systems for service use. Once these had been completed production aircraft deliveries began to the RAF. The majority of these airframes would be delivered to RAF Germany where they displaced the majority of F-4 Phantoms and one of the Harrier squadrons. The Phantoms were used to equip air defence squadrons within Strike Command and two in RAFG while the Harriers were dispersed amongst the remaining Harrier operators. Three operational units within Strike Command would receive the Jaguar plus No. 226 OCU. The latter unit was assigned to SACEUR during wartime utilizing twelve aircraft; their available weaponry included the WE177 nuclear weapon plus the full range of conventional weapons. The three front-line units had previously been equipped with the F-4 Phantom II at Coningsby. When the Jaguar became available Nos 6, 41 and 54 Squadrons would all congregate at Coltishall, their base until the type left service. Two of the three units, Nos 6 and 54 Squadrons, would work up at Lossiemouth on their new mounts while No. 41 Squadron would undertake its transition at Coltishall.

Prior to the creation of a full-blown OCU the first Jaguar to reach the Jaguar OCU was XX111, which was delivered to Lossiemouth in May 1973 their first task being to undertake training of the ground crew. Two further Jaguars were delivered to

Of the three Jaguar units based at Coltishall No. 41 Squadron had tactical reconnaissance as its primary role. Complete with reconnaissance pod on the centreline is XZ119 'G' posing for the camera.*(John Ryan Collection)*

Lossiemouth in September, allowing the unit to start the pilot conversion process. No. 226 OCU would come into existence in 1974 taking over the number plate from the Lightning OCU. No. 54 Squadron would reform on 29 March 1974, although they were forced to utilize the aircraft from JOCU until their own aircraft were delivered. Strangely enough the first unit to reveal a new build aircraft in Squadron colours was No. 6 Squadron that had reformed at Lossiemouth in September by which time No. 54 Squadron had decamped to Coltishall in August. No. 54 Squadron was declared fully operational in January 1975 being quickly followed by No. 6 Squadron that had moved to Coltishall in November becoming operational not long afterwards. No. 41 Squadron would join the Coltishall wing in April 1977, although their primary role was reconnaissance unlike the others whose primary was attack.

Not long after being declared ready for service No. 54 Squadron took part in their first NATO exercise, Bold Guard, held in September 1974. All three squadrons were

No. 41 Squadron also undertook missions over Norway and to that end this spotty dog finish was applied in an effort to break up the aircraft's outline. *(John Ryan Collection)*

declared to NATO when No. 1 Group cleared them for operations. Within NATO the wing was intended for Regional Reinforcement plus the Allied Commander Europe's Mobile Force, being capable of rapid deployment overseas during a time of crisis. Planned maintenance had originally taken place at No. 60 MU at Leconfield and was the case between 1974 to 1976. A move to Abingdon followed the Jaguars receiving attention in the old Belfast hangar, although Abingdon would later be rationalized in 1992 the planned maintenance moving to St Athan. When St Athan underwent rationalization the majors were moved to Coltishall where they remained until the Jaguars were withdrawn.

Given the complexity of the Jaguar the work of No. 226 OCU was vitally important for delivering fully trained pilots to the operational squadrons within Strike Command and RAFG. Lossiemouth on the Moray Forth in Scotland proved to be the ideal location for such training as the ranges of Tain and Rosehearty were close by. These ranges were cleared for the use of LRMTS thus both Jaguars and Harriers would undertake training there. Like much of Britain, Scotland is a rather lumpy place that has plenty of hills and valleys that allowed the Jaguars to operate down to 250 feet Above Ground Level (AGL) normally. One area of Scotland known as No. 14 Tango Tactical Training Area would see the Jaguars operating down to 100 feet AGL, although each sortie required special clearance to fly at this height. Once the operational squadrons had been fully equipped the OCU aircraft inventory shrank, although the unit still trained pilots and undertook post graduate courses that included Weapons Instructor and Instrument Rating Examiner.

Crashes and smashes are a fact of low flying in combat aircraft thus there should be no surprise that both the Harrier and Jaguars suffered some losses in their early years of service. The first Harrier loss for No. 1 Squadron occurred on 6 October 1970 when the pilot was forced to eject after the engine had flamed out and could not be relit. No. 1 Squadron was also unlucky during August 1971 when two aircraft were lost. Both were being flown by USAF exchange pilots who unfortunately lost their lives having ejected outside the parameters of the ejection seat. It would be April and May 1972 when No. 1 Squadron lost another pair of aircraft; the first was lost courtesy of a bird strike while the second was lost due to a loss of control although both pilots escaped successfully. The perils of low-level combat flying training came to the fore in September when an aircraft from No. 233 OCU crashed into the ground.

The Jaguar fleet also had its fair share of accidents in the early days; the first involved a T2 from the OCU that was damaged beyond repair after the undercarriage failed on landing. Another T2 from the OCU was lost in April 1975 when the pilot experienced a loss of control when Foreign Object Damage (FOD) fouled the control column. The operational units experienced their first losses in 1976: No. 6 Squadron lost a GR1 when the pilot experienced a loss of control while low flying over Germany while No. 54 Squadron saw one of their aircraft fly into the sea off Denmark. Unfortunately, both pilots were killed. Fortunately, the Strike Command squadrons would improve their accident rate as familiarity with both types of aircraft improved thus the loss and fatality rate would drop.

With the disbanding of the bomber wings at Coningsby and Cottesmore Strike Command inherited five squadrons and an OCU of Vulcan B2s. The majority of the aircraft were based at Waddington with Nos 44, 50 and 101 Squadrons while Scampton was home to Nos 27 and 617 Squadrons plus 230 OCU, which included No. '1066' Squadron and its Handley Page Hastings T5s used for the training of navigators. At both

By 1966 the Vulcan B2 fleet , with a few exceptions, had been fitted with a terrain-following radar carried in a small pod at the extreme nose. B2 XL425 sports the fin badge of No. 617 Squadron based at Scampton. *(BBA Collection)*

bases the regime of centralized servicing was the order of the day while the aircraft were devoid of unit markings, although those assigned to No. 617 Squadron frequently had the unit's dayglo lightning flashes on the fin while many of the Waddington aircraft sported the 'Liney' pig badge on the fin much to the chagrin of many senior officers. Only the aircrew were actually assigned to individual squadrons.

Even with these considerations the Vulcans plus their air and ground crews were subject to a full regime of exercises and deployments, although those crews and aircraft assigned to Quick Reaction Alert with the Blue Steel long-range missile were obviously exempt from such excitements. As the Blue Steel missile was based at Scampton the

By 1975 the Vulcan fleet had undergone further changes when the squadrons were reformed, which immediately improved the morale of the ground crew. Other changes were technical, the most obvious being the installation of the ARI.18228 receivers in the fin cap. XM655 was one of the initial aircraft assigned to No. 101 Squadron and is seen parked on Delta 15 at Waddington. *(BBA Collection)*

Barksdale was one of the favourite places for the Vulcan units to visit as this was the base for Giant Voice. This close up is of XM602 that is wearing the badge of No.1 Group on its nose although it was on loan from No.101 Sqdn. *(John Ryan Collection)*

entire missile support facility was based near Scampton as was the facility that dealt with the maintenance of the Vulcan ECM equipment. By this time all of the Vulcans were wearing a coat of camouflage; the uppers were finished in grey and green with white underneath, all being gloss finished. The majority of Vulcans were also flying with a terrain-following radar, this being carried in a small pod mounted in the extreme nose just under the refuel probe. Only a few aircraft from the early batch were never fitted with this system. The ECM equipment was also undergoing changes, with the Red Steer tail warning radar being updated. Not only was the performance improved, but the charging gas was changed from air to nitrogen. The ECM system was also undergoing improvement; adding to the Vulcan's capability was the fitment of an X-Band jamming system that operated in the 8–12Ghz frequency range. Also under development was the ARI 18228 passive warning system that would be mounted in the fin tip fairing. Although the system was very capable there was always interference when the Red Steer radar was switched on.

The Vulcan squadrons undertook numerous local and NATO-orientated exercises, all being designed to hone the air and ground crews skills. The local exercises included Tactical Evaluation (Taceval) where each station was put through its paces. For the ground crews on both the line and in Mechanical Aircraft Engineering Squadron (MEAS) were tasked with generating as many aircraft as possible as well as deploying the four needed for the Operational Readiness Platform at the end of the runway. MEAS would attempt to generate as many aircraft as possible from the hangars for operational flying. Originally these exercises were purely about generating aircraft and getting them armed. As NATO reacted to the increased Warsaw Pact threat these exercises changed and defending the station while operating the aircraft fleet with minimal personnel became the norm. Taceval normally lasted the greater part of a week and would end with a scramble of the four aircraft from the ORP. Other exercises included deployments to dispersal bases around the country, the intention being to move the bombers away from their main bases for safety's sake. Each deployment would see at least four aircraft plus air and ground crews deploying to a rough and ready base, on some occasions a full range of cooks, fire crews and as always RAF policemen were also deployed. Some of these deployments were called as part of an exercise while others were pre-planned.

The RAF would hand over its nuclear deterrent role to the submarines of the Royal Navy in 1970. With this change the Blue Steel fitted Vulcans were flown to the manufacturers to be restored to the conventional bombing role. The Blue Steel set-up had originally been designed as a quick change package, however the amount of electrical, hydraulic and cooling systems in the bomb bay plus the fin gap and modified bomb doors rendered this impossible. After being returned to normal configuration the ex-Blue Steel Vulcans were returned to service. Although Blue Steel had been relinquished the Vulcan still had a nuclear, strike role using the WE177 freefall weapon while in the conventional role the full range of free fall explosive bombs could be utilized in the attack role. No. 27 Squadron would remain operational for two years in this new role until disbanding in 1972.

NATO and UK Air Defence Region exercises included Exercises High Jupiter and Rum Keg in 1968 while the following year saw the aircraft involved in Town House. 1970 saw Castor Oil and Opal Digger being undertaken while in 1972 Exercises Whiskey Sour, Top Limit and Dry Martini were undertaken. As a sop to both air and ground crews various overseas deployments were undertaken. Those to Malta were codenamed Sunspot while the Far East deployments were codenamed Moon Flower and Sun Flower. Moon Flowers saw the Vulcans, normally four in number, heading westwards on deployment and returning home eastwards on the return journey. Sun Flowers followed an opposite course and both deployments would enjoy a short stopover in Hawaii. In 1975 the Vulcan fleet would undergo some changes as will be detailed later.

The other V Bomber still in service was the Victor B2, although both the Blue Steel Units were disbanded in late 1968 while No. 543 Squadron based at Wyton continued to fly their SR2 reconnaissance aircraft until 1974. All the withdrawn aircraft were placed in store at Radlett while their fate was discussed. With the withdrawal of the earlier

Prior to the Victor B2 bombers being converted to tankers the Tanker Wing at Marham flew the Victor K1A whose XA937 was nominally assigned to No. 214 Squadron. *(BBA Collection)*

The Victor SR2s remained in service with No. 543 Squadron until the unit was disbanded in May 1974, although some sorties were flown afterwards. XL161 would later be converted to K2 standard for the Marham tanker squadrons. *(BBA Collection)*

Victor K1A tankers due for withdrawal in 1975–76 and the desperate need the RAF had for tanker aircraft it was decided to convert twenty-four of the remaining Mk 2 Victors to three-point tanker configuration. The conversion work would be undertaken at Woodford as the original contractor and designer, Handley Page, had gone into liquidation in 1970. The modifications involved fitting semi–permanent fuel tanks into the bomb bay and the rear equipment bay, reducing the wing span to reduce wing loading plus the fitment of a Flight Refuelling unit on the centreline and a pod under each outer wing panel.

The Victor K1A tankers had originally been flown by Nos 55, 57 and 214 Squadrons plus 232 OCU. However, as only twenty-four Victor K2s were being made available it was decided that No. 214 Squadron would not reform on the new type thus leaving Nos 55 and 57 Squadrons as the only operators. Even 232 OCU would not reform with aircraft utilizing some from the squadrons as required. As a footnote XL232 bore the fin marks

K2 XL190 of No. 57 Squadron is representative of the Victor tankers. It is seen approaching Marham with everything out and down before landing. *(BBA Collection)*

The Victor K2 was still the primary tanker and is seen here in its element as XH671 refuels a pair of Lightning F6s of No. 11 Squadron. *(John Ryan Collection)*

of the OCU although the aircraft was operated by one of the squadrons. The replacement tankers were utilized mainly in the fighter support role, one being launched every time the Lightning QRA was scrambled. Even though many of Strike Command's aircraft sported refuel probes they were not utilized much.

Chapter 5

Integrations and Further Changes

With the bomber and fighter units integrated it was the turn of Coastal Command to become part of Strike Command. Coastal Command was then renamed 18 Group, the change occurring on 28 November 1969. Within Strike Command the new formation's title was No. 18 (Maritime) Group, the first commander being Air Marshal Sir Robert Craven. From that date AOC 18 Group held the NATO post of Commander, Maritime Air, Eastern Atlantic, reporting to C-in-C, Eastern Atlantic at the Northwood Headquarters in London. AOC 18 Group also held the corresponding post within the NATO Channel Command.

Submarine hunting was a vital part of the Nimrod's mission. To that end many training sorties were flown against Royal Navy vessels at the conclusion of which the submarine would surface to exchange banter with its ASW hunter. *(John Ryan Collection)*

While the MR version of the Nimrod was an outstanding success the AEW model would be plagued by difficulties. Like many programmes before it success was on the horizon when the entire project was cancelled. *(John Ryan Collection)*

Upon absorption there were seven squadrons all flying various models of the Avro Shackleton. Nos 42, 120, 201, 203 and 206 Squadrons flew the MR3 model, although No. 42 Squadron also flew some MR2s. Only two units were equipped with the Shackleton MR2 these being Nos 204 and 210 Squadrons. The Shackletons were located at four bases, the largest being at Ballykelly in Northern Ireland. Located at this most important Atlantic guard point were No. 203 Squadron with the MR3 while Nos 204 and 210 Squadrons were equipped with the MR2 model. Another unit was also based in Northern Ireland – No. 120 Squadron, which operated out of Aldergrove near Belfast. On mainland Britain the Shackletons operated from two bases. In the southern part of the country St Mawgan was the home of Nos 42 Squadron with its mixed inventory and No. 201 Squadron equipped purely with the MR3. Only one unit was based in the north of the country, which was No. 206 Squadron that flew MR3s out of Kinloss.

Although the Avro Shackletons had given many years of good service they were coming to the end of their useful lives, but fortunately new equipment was on the horizon, the Hawker Siddeley Nimrod. The genesis of the HS801 Nimrod would begin in 1958 when an Air Staff Target was issued for a Shackleton replacement. While the Avro design had served the RAF its lack of modern features and expansion capabilities indicated replacement by a more modern design. Various civilian designs were put forward for a maritime aircraft based on the latest crop of civilian airliners, which included the de Havilland Trident, the Vickers VC 10 and the de Havilland Comet. After consideration of all the available designs Operational Requirement OR. 357 was issued, the contract going to Hawker Siddeley which had absorbed de Havilland in the meantime. The aircraft that emerged utilized a heavily modified Comet 4C airframe whose most visible alteration was the double bubble fuselage. The lower half contained the weapons bay and the radar scanner plus other systems while the upper deck housed the flight crew and the systems operators plus all the other facilities needed to carry out long endurance patrols. The wings were also heavily altered, especially the inner sections as the original Rolls-Royce Avons were replaced by the more powerful Rolls-Royce Spey engines. Not only did the Spey engines provide more power it was possible while on patrol to wind a pair down to minimum and use the other pair to carry out the patrol.

The Nimrod MR1 would replace the venerable Shackleton for maritime patrol duties and was based at Kinloss and St Mawgan. *(BBA Collection)*

The rear fuselage also underwent alteration as did the fin and rudder assembly. The former grew a MAD boom while the latter had a dorsal extension and an ESM pod mounted on the fin tip. As the overall weight of the aircraft had grown a much stronger undercarriage and support structure were needed.

The Ministry of Defence gave approval for the HS801 design in June 1966 for which purpose the last two unsold Comet 4C airframes were used for the development programme. The first prototype converted airframe, XV147, undertook its first flight from Chester on 23 May 1967 and would be used for performance and handling development while the second airframe, XV148, which first flew from Woodford on 26 June 1967, would be dedicated to systems development and testing. These two

No. 51 Squadron would operate the DH Comet R2 until it was replaced by the Nimrod R1 in 1971 by which time the squadron was at Wyton. *(BBA Collection)*

prototypes were followed by the first production Nimrod MR1, XV226, which undertook its maiden flight on 28 June 1968 from Woodford and quickly entered the flight and systems development programme. During the flight trials the aircraft was found to have a top speed of 575mph, a range of 1,200 miles, a loiter time of six hours and an endurance time of 12 hours. Take-off and landing was also excellent as the aircraft was capable of utilizing existing runways.

The first airframe of the forty-six ordered, XV230, was delivered to Strike Command in October 1969 entering service with No. 236 OCU at St Mawgan for crew training. The first unit to re-equip with the Nimrod was No. 201 Squadron at Kinloss who traded in its Shackletons from October 1970. No. 42 Squadron would equip with Nimrod MR1s during April 1971 at St Mawgan joining the OCU, also known as No. 38 Shadow Squadron. No. 206 Squadron, also based at Kinloss, would equip with the Nimrod MR1 in August 1970 being followed by No. 120 Squadron in October 1970. When the Strike Command units were fully formed they were allocated to No. 18 (Maritime) Group, which had replaced Coastal Command. So impressed with the Nimrod were Strike Command that the MoD would order a further eight airframes for delivery during 1975, although only five would enter service; the other three were placed in store at Kinloss in a basic equipment state.

During 1970–71 three further airframes, XW664 to 666, were built as Nimrod R1s for No. 51 Squadron at Wyton for use in the special electronics reconnaissance role, replacing the small fleet of elderly Comets. The first HS801R better known as the Nimrod R1 would undertake its maiden flight on 22 March 1971 with deliveries taking place during July. The new airframes operated alongside the venerable Comet C2Rs until these were retired in November 1974.

Like all platforms the Nimrod was under constant development, resulting in the MR2 model. Primary modifications included replacing the original ASV 21 radar with the EMI Searchwater system plus other upgrades. These other upgrades included AQS-901 acoustics package, the fitment of the FIN 1012 inertial navigation system, a Central Tactical System, and an Omega unit for long range navigation. Overall the modification programme took some ten years to complete. Eventually thirty-five of the original forty-six were converted to this new standard, the balance being allocated to another programme. The first aircraft to fly in its new configuration was XV147, which was quickly joined by three MR1s, all of which were converted to MR2 standard. Over the following two years over 1,000 hours were logged during the development and the data obtained were used to speed the conversion of the rest of the fleet. Those airframes chosen for conversion to MR2 standard were those with the lowest fatigue consumption; however the others were not scrapped as they would later be required for other purposes.

The first production MR2, XV236, undertook its maiden flight on 13 February 1979, being assigned to test flying with British Aerospace before joining No. 206 Squadron on 23 August. Unfortunately, the squadron would lose an MR2 on 17 November 1980 when XV256 suffered a multiple bird strike that wrecked three of the engines. The resultant crash would see the three flight crew killed, although the eighteen rear crew would escape with minor injuries. The pilot, Flt Lt Anthony, would be awarded the Air Force Cross while the co-pilot, Flt Lt Belcher, would be awarded the Queen's Commendation for Valuable Services in the Air. The final MR2 would be delivered to Kinloss on 19 December 1985 while the only brand-new aircraft, XV284, would also join the fleet. This airframe had been stored as an uncompleted MR1 and would replace XV256.

During its service the Nimrod would feature in the Fincastle Trophy that took place between crews drawn from the RAF, Australia, Canada and New Zealand. During the Nimrod years the competition took place at various venues around the world with the Nimrod winning twelve between 1971 and 2005.

As the MR2 was undertaking longer patrols it was decided by Strike Command engineering that a study of the fatigue life of the new model should be undertaken especially as the new equipment fitted to the MR2 had increased its basic weight. To that end XV227 was fitted out with a suite of monitoring systems known as the Nimrod Operational Flight Load Measurement Programme. The aircraft was modified at Kinloss and was ready for flight trials from 2 December 1981. Data gathered from these flights was collated by BAE Woodford, which helped with current and future modification programmes. Alongside the trials being undertaken by XV227 Nimrod XV241 was trialling another new system. In May 1978 the Nimrod was delivered to Woodford where the original ECM equipment mounted in the fin tip pod was replaced by the Loran Electronic Support Measures suite ESM.

In its new form XV241 undertook its maiden flight in September 1979 complete with ESM pods on the wing tips, although these were empty as they were undergoing aerodynamic trials. Once a bit of shape tweaking had been carried out to the shape of the pods the ESM suite would be fitted to both the MR2s and the R1s as the opportunity arose. XV241 would remain as a trials aircraft until returned to service in August 1986. Also involved in various trials was the Nimrod prototype XV148, which was moved from RAE Bedford to BAE Woodford where it had its nose and tail sections removed the remainder being used as a ground fatigue test specimen. Monitored by a sophisticated computer system this airframe was used to determine the fatigue consumption of the type and allowed any problems to be discovered quickly before they became widespread.

While the MR version of the Nimrod was an outstanding success the next model turned out to be an unmitigated disaster. Airborne Early Warning had become de rigueur for the majority of the world's air forces. From Britain's point of view, being an island, such a facility was a necessity. Originally such coverage had been provided on an ad hoc basis by the Fairey Gannet AEW3s of the Fleet Air Arm. The Fairey Gannet AEW3 was retired in 1978. With no AEW coverage available and an RAF replacement a long time in the future it was decided that another stand-in was needed. The solution to this problem was to fit the Gannet AN/APS.20 radar to a long-range land-based aircraft until a more modern system could be designed. The Nimrod MR1 was in squadron service, which allowed the recently retired Shackleton MR2 airframes to be fitted with the Gannet radar. When the type was cleared for operational service No. 8 Squadron was reformed at RAF Kinloss on 1 January 1972 and were equipped with the Shackleton AEW Mk 2. Royal Navy Gannets continued to operate from Lossiemouth, which was fifteen miles from Kinloss, supplying some coverage while the unit worked up to operational status. No. 8 Squadron joined them once the runways and taxiways at Lossiemouth had been strengthened.

The primary task of an AEW aircraft is to detect, direct and report thus Shackleton crew would detect and report the position of radar contacts by voice radio to ground radar sites and ships. This procedure was known as Voice Tell. Once a potential hostile aircraft was detected the Controller would direct friendly fighter aircraft onto the target. Fighter control was practised with F-4 Phantom and Lightning fighters over the North

Sea, operating in conjunction with the Sector Operations Centres at Buchan, Boulmer and Neatishead.

As well as having the ability to detect aircraft, the Shackleton radar could also detect ships. Therefore the crews had the ability to control attacking aircraft against potential enemy shipping. The Shackleton AEW2 also carried search and rescue equipment in its bomb bay and Lindholm dinghy drop procedures were regularly practised. This equipment allowed the aircraft to undertake its secondary task of air sea rescue that saved many a life.

For the majority of its operational life the Shackleton AEW operated as part of the UK Air Defence around Britain the zone extending north towards Iceland beyond the Faroe islands and towards Norway. Any Soviet aircraft entering this area had to be intercepted by UK fighters, and fighter squadrons took turns to hold Northern and Southern QRA. Tanker forces also held alert status to support the fighters and, if required, a Shackleton was also on call. The twelve crews of No. 8 Squadron maintained on two-hour alert, twenty-four hours a day, seven days a week. Once Soviet aircraft had been detected heading into the North Atlantic by Norwegian air defence sites, it was usual for the Duty Controller at RAF Strike Command to scramble the Shackleton to cover the Iceland-Faroe Gap. It could take up to three hours for a Shackleton to reach its barrier position and wait for the fighter scramble to take place. Often the intruders would turn back before reaching British airspace, although on occasion they would enter our airspace. The Shackleton operators would report the intruders via HF radio to one of the air defence stations – Saxa Vord, Polestar, on the Faroe Islands, Benbecula or Buchan. The controller would take control of the fighters and tanker and vector them towards the intruders. There was nothing more satisfying than to successfully prosecute a gaggle of Soviet Bear aircraft with a pair of Lightning fighters.

No. 8 Squadron would suffer a 50 per cent reduction in crews courtesy of the John Nott defence cuts of 1981, thus QRA became a Monday to Friday task with no replacement crew for the rest of the day once launch had taken place. QRA ceased at 17.00 hours on the Friday the result being that there was no AEW or rescue support cover until 07.00 hours on Monday morning. No. 8 Squadron would continue to operate the Shackleton AEW2 until June 1991 when the unit disbanded at Lossiemouth, although it would reform again the following month at Waddington as the operator of the Boeing AEW1 Sentry.

Prior to the decision to purchase the Boeing Sentry the British government decided to develop an in house aircraft. The chosen airframe would be the ten redundant Nimrods that had been excluded from the MR2 conversion process plus the singular stored airframe from Kinloss. Unlike the Boeing offering which utilized a rotodome mounted above the fuselage the modified Nimrods would have separate scanners housed behind enlarged radomes mounted at each end of the airframe. Hawker Siddeley Aviation would be given the Instruction to Proceed in April 1977 with Marconi- Elliott as the primary avionics contractor. To trial the aerodynamic shape for the nose radome and much of the avionics a Comet 4C, G-APDS, was purchased for use as a test bed. Registered as XW626 the Comet airframe was fitted with a Nimrod fin, rudder and ESM fin pod plus an enlarged radome to house the forward radar scanner. Prior to the fitment of this radome the shapes for both were extensively tested in a wind tunnel. The resultant shapes saw a pointed nose radome while that destined for the rear radome was of a more rounded shape, all of which helped smooth the airflow over the fuselage.

XW626 would make its maiden flight from Woodford on 26 June 1977. After initial flight trials from Woodford the aircraft was handed over to RAE Bedford for further trials work.

The configuration planned for the Nimrod AEW3 would see the redundant bomb bay being used for extra fuel tanks and cooling packages for the radar systems. The concept for the radar coverage was that the synchronized scanners would sweep 180 degrees in azimuth. Although the radar Marconi developed radar systems frequently worked well their speedy development meant that the systems were not as reliable as required. Of the eleven aircraft slated for conversion three were designated as development machines, these being XZ286, XZ287 and XZ281. XZ286 made its first flight on 16 July 1980 from BAE Woodford. British Aerospace had been the outcome of the merger between the British Aircraft Corporation and HSA in April 1977.

Initially the first conversion, designated DB1, was utilized for handling trials, although it was quickly joined by DB2 and DB3 both of which were handed over to Marconi- Elliot, later GEC Avionics, at Hatfield for the installation of the radar systems and other avionics. All three airframes would be heavily involved in the development programme, the intention being to return them to Woodford for upgrading to production standard. Even before the trials had been completed the other eight airframes were undergoing conversion. The trials of the radar systems did not proceed smoothly as the requirements originally specified by the RAF had changed significantly and the modifications could not be incorporated fast enough thus costs increased beyond the original estimates. Not helping the programme either was the industrial unrest at Woodford that also contributed to the delays. Other problems also began to rear their head; the planned cooling systems were not fully able to cope with the heat generated by all the electronics squeezed into the airframe while problems had been experienced with manoeuvring the aircraft on the ground when moving fully fuelled.

Even with all these problems, none insurmountable, the first production Nimrod AEW3, XZ285, undertook its maiden flight on 9 March 1982 from Woodford, although by this point the programme was two years behind schedule and vastly over budget. Delays were also experienced by equipment delivery problems, although these were cleared by the following years. By December 1984 the first Nimrod AEW3 was delivered to Waddington. This ex-V bomber base had been completely refurbished for the new type as flight simulators, technical support and other facilities had been provided. The new occupants, the Trials Evaluation Unit, would be the operator of the handful of aircraft delivered to Waddington. The three aircraft used by the TEU were flying with the 1983 avionics fit and computer software instead of the latest systems and upgrades that were becoming available. Eventually, only eight of the eleven Nimrod AEW3 airframes were completed to production standard, however the delays and mounting costs would see the entire programme cancelled in December 1986.

All of the converted airframes were then despatched to Abingdon for storage. Two airframes were removed; one was dismantled and transported to Finningly for use by the Air Engineers Training School while XZ282 was flown out to Kinloss on 14 September 1989. Although the remainder underwent some periodic servicing the decision was made to scrap the remainder, although this did not happen until all usable spares had been removed. Soon after the termination of the Nimrod AEW3 programme the RAF opted to buy the Boeing AEW3 Sentry, however GEC-Avionics would issue a statement to the effect that the Americans had leant upon the British government to scrap Nimrod and

The Westland Wessex HC1 replaced the Whirlwind HAR10 for air-sea rescue duties. XS675 was finished in the standard overall gloss yellow finish and wears the fin badge of No. 22 Squadron. *(BBA Collection)*

buy Boeing thus excluding British manufacturers from a lucrative world market. While Britain has lost its edge in designing and building aircraft and systems for its own use some of the technology and software has found use in other fields.

While the fixed wing side of Strike Command was experiencing some difficulties the upgrading of the rotary community was running quite smoothly. That old faithful of Air Support Command, the Westland Whirlwind, had left for another career in training and air-sea rescue. The replacement for the Whirlwind was the Westland Wessex HC2 that was more than capable of surviving the rough and tumble of combat operations. Within Air Support Command the Wessex helicopter unit was No. 72 Squadron based at Odiham, the first aircraft arriving in August 1964.

The upsurge of violence in Northern Ireland would find the Wessex heavily involved in supporting British forces especially in the inserting of troops into dangerous zones. This extension of the Wessex' duties plus the need for a replacement aircraft for SAR duties would see the Wessex fleet being stretched. The answer would be another helicopter and this would be another aircraft produced under an Anglo-French joint agreement. Initially the aircraft that would become known as the Westland Puma had been designed originally to cover French army requirements. The first of two Puma prototypes flew on 15 April 1965 being followed by six pre-production models, the last of which flew on 30 July 1968. The first production SA 330 Puma flew in September 1968 with deliveries to the RAF beginning in 1971. The first unit to form was No. 33 Squadron at Odiham under the command of Wing Commander FD Hoskins. The first of eleven aircraft arrived in June with the remainder having arrived in time for the official reformation on 29 September. A second unit would form at Odiham, No. 230 Squadron, which reformed in January 1972. This unit would remain as part of No. 38 Group until it was transferred to RAF Germany in October 1980.

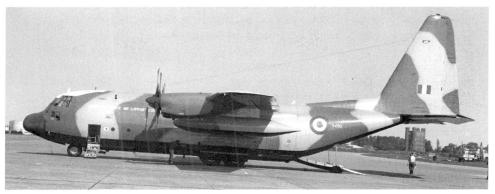

Photographed at Coningsby is Lockheed C-130 Hercules C1 XV190 of the Lyneham Transport Wing. The arrival of the Hercules into RAF service vastly improved its transport capabilities. *(BBA Collection)*

The Puma was intended to provide tactical support for the Army thus it could transport sixteen troops, an underslung load of 5,000lb, six stretchers and four medics or it could be used as a support gunship with a pair of 7.52mm general purpose machine guns mounted on one per side. As the Puma was designed to meet NATO specifications it could operate in the cold of Norway and the heat of the Mediterranean. As it was capable of being struck down for air transportation one could be carried by a C-130 Hercules while the Shorts Belfast could take three. The appearance of the Puma at Odiham would see the creation of No. 240 OCU to cover the conversion of both Puma and Wessex crews. The Puma was a different animal from the Wessex. While the latter could undertake a steep, tail down, hard landing, trying to do the same in a Puma would result in damage to the tail rotor. To cater for this eventuality the Puma was quickly fitted

Later in their career the Hercules fleet had its original desert type scheme replaced with a more temperate scheme as shown here on XV290. *(BBA Collection)*

The Westland Puma was introduced for the lighter tactical troop support role. Here an example from No. 33 Squadron based at Odiham scoots over the trees en route to its rendezvous. *(John Ryan Collection)*

with a tail bumper that would illuminate a light in the cockpit should it make contact with the ground first.

In service the Puma would soon be involved in numerous exercises that would see the type flying under similar conditions to the HSA Harrier thus the helicopter was designed to be easy to service under primitive conditions. To that end there was a minimum of lifed components, the systems contents gauges and refill points were at ground level while the engine access panels could be folded down for access to the powerplants and the gearboxes. Should an engine change be required a portable crane that was air transportable could be taken with the detachment. Extending the range of the Puma was a fairly simple operation as four 105-gallon tanks could be fitted in the cabin this providing another 800 miles of range.

The Puma would come into its own during the Rhodesian ceasefire after the protracted Lancaster House negotiations had finally reached fruition after fourteen years of hard bargaining. The basis of the ceasefire would see the guerrilla forces of ZANU and ZAPU congregate at specified locations to be disarmed and returned to civilian life. The biggest obstacle facing the establishment of these camps was supplying the occupants. As Britain was still nominally responsible for Rhodesia-Zimbabwe the government decided that the RAF would support the airlift of supplies to these camps. As this was purely an airlift operation the resources would come from No. 38 Group thus a detachment of Pumas was flown out to Salisbury while air freighting of personnel and supplies were despatched from both Brize Norton and Lyneham. Operation *Agila* would see the strategic airlift of supplies and materials being undertaken between 20 and

26 December 1979 with some extra help coming from the USAF who provided three Lockheed C-141 Starlifters and a C-5 Galaxy. During this short period over 860 tons of supplies and 1,398 personnel were moved during 63 missions. With all the equipment and personnel in place the deployment of the Commonwealth Monitoring Force plus the initial dispersion of supplies and materials to the camps was undertaken between 27 and 28 December with seven C-130s from the Lyneham Transport Wing undertaking twenty-six missions.

With the guerrilla camps fully established four of the seven LTW C-130s were returned to Lyneham. The three remaining aircraft all featured strengthened undercarriages while they were also given component life extensions of 150 flying hours so that no grounding for major servicing was required. All of these modifications enabled the C-130s to undertake arduous take-offs and landings from unprepared strips, although these rough surfaces did play havoc with the tyres their life being reduced by 70 per cent. While ground operations could be rough the crews also had to contend with hazards in the air; these including bird strikes and the occasional bullet fired by a freedom fighter who had not received the cease-fire message.

Of the 200 sorties planned from New Sarum before the C-130 Hercules detachment returned home on 1 February 1980 only one would be cancelled due to unserviceability, which was down to the hard-working dedication of the ground crew. The regular task for the C-130 detachment was to undertake ration delivery flights, known as the RATS Runs, to the various camps.

The six Pumas allocated to the task were drawn from Nos 33 and 230 Squadrons from Odiham. Their role was to provide light resupply coverage, Medevac and to transport troubleshooting teams whose role was to sort out little local difficulties such as interrupted water supplies and other problems that might have caused problems within the camps. As the Pumas were required to undertake much of their flying at low level it is surprising that only one aircraft was lost. The aircraft had hit some uncharted wires while on approach to Mtoko on 27 December with the loss of all three crew. The Pumas were dispersed between New Sarum and Thornhill, three helicopters being based at each airfield. Both detachments flew their Pumas to their limits with seven-hour sorties not being unusual. As with the Hercules the Puma sortie rate was high with few being lost to unserviceability. By 14 February 1980 the Puma flights had completed 600 hours of support flying having shifted over 143,000lb of freight, 1,600 passengers and 67 casevac cases. Once the elections had been held within Rhodesia-Zimbabwe, it was time for the RAF detachments to return to Britain. As before airlift was provided by Brize Norton and Lyneham with extra support coming from USAF as before. The Republic of Zimbabwe came into being on 18 April 1980 and has been sliding downhill ever since.

While the island of Cyprus is regarded as a holiday haven these days this has not always been the case. The majority of the population is mainly Greek with a strong Turkish enclave; this in conjunction with Greek-Cypriot desire for independence from Britain was always destined to be a hot bed of trouble. In January 1955 the National Organization of Cypriot Fighters, Ethniki Organosis Kyprion Agoniston (EOKA) was founded, their goal being to fight for independence from Britain. On 1 April 1955, EOKA began an armed campaign against British rule in a well co-ordinated series of attacks on police, military, and other government installations in Nicosia, Famagusta, Larnaca, and Limassol. This resulted in the deaths of over 100 British servicemen and personnel and some Greek Cypriots suspected of collaboration. These actions also greatly increased the tension between the Greek and Turkish Cypriot communities. By 1957 a Turkish resistance organization had been formed to protect the Turkish Cypriots from EOKA and began to take action in response to those of the Greeks.

By now the island was close to a full-scale civil war after several attempts to reach a compromise settlement had failed. In an effort to stop the war erupting representatives of Greece and Turkey met in December 1958 to open discussions on the Cyprus issue. The majority of these meetings were normally headed by the British and these finally yielded a compromise agreement that supported independence, laying the foundations for the Republic of Cyprus.

The location of the talks then moved to London, where the Greek and Turkish government representatives were joined by representatives of the Greek Cypriots and the Turkish Cypriots, Archbishop Makarios and Dr Fazil Kucuk and British officials. The outcome was the Zurich-London agreements that in turn became the basis for the Cyprus constitution of 1960 that was supplemented by three further treaties – the Treaty of Establishment, the Treaty of Guarantee, and the Treaty of Alliance. Under the Treaty of Establishment, Britain retained sovereignty over 256 square kilometres, which became the Dhekelia Sovereign Base Area, to the north-west of Larnaca, and the Akrotiri Sovereign Base Area to the south-west of Limassol. Cyprus achieved full independence on 16 August 1960.

While the foregoing seemed like a solution to the problems of Cyprus the low-level niggling and, in some cases warfare, continued between the Greek and Turkish Cypriot communities. This constant niggling would lead to the eventual breakdown of the basic functions of government. To get the basic functions up and running again a combined force of British, Greek and Turkish personnel were sent to the island to restore law and order. To further legitimize the peacekeeping force UN resolution 186 established a multinational force to keep the peace.

In November 1967, Cyprus witnessed its most severe bout of intercommunal fighting since 1964. In response to a major attack on Turkish Cypriot villages in the south of the island that left twenty-seven dead, Turkey bombed Greek Cypriot forces and appeared to be preparing itself for an intervention. Following international intervention, Greece agreed to recall General George Grivas, the Commander of the Greek Cypriot National Guard and former EOKA leader, and reduce its forces on the island. Capitalizing on the weakness of the Greek Cypriots the Turkish Cypriots proclaimed their own provisional administration on 28 December 1967. Head of state Archbishop Makarios immediately declared the new administration illegal, although the Archbishop began to accept that the Turkish Cypriots would have to have some degree of political autonomy.

In May 1968, intercommunal talks began between the two sides under the auspices of the UN Secretary-General, U Thant. Unusually, the talks were not held between President Makarios and Vice-President Kucuk. Instead, they were conducted by the presidents of the communal chambers, Glafcos Clerides and Rauf Denktas. During the first round of talks that lasted until August 1968, the Turkish Cypriots were prepared to make several concessions regarding constitutional matters, however Makarios refused to grant them autonomy in return. The second round of talks, which focused on local government, was equally unsuccessful. In December 1969 a third round of discussion started. This time they focused on constitutional issues. Yet again there was little progress and when they ended in September 1970 the Secretary-General blamed both sides for the lack of movement. A fourth and final round of intercommunal talks also focused on constitutional issues, but again failed to make much headway before they were forced to a halt in 1974.

It should be remembered that governments of both Greece and Turkey had great influence on events in Cyprus whatever the indigenous population may have felt. Turkey and its Prime Minister obviously felt that any further talks would not resolve the problems that beset Cyprus therefore a unilateral decision was made for Turkish forces to invade the island on 20 July 1974. Intense fighting between both sides would result in the Turkish forces holding 38 per cent of the island when the ceasefire was declared. Another result of this invasion was that Archbishop Makarios was deposed as head of state by Nikos Sampson, the Archbishop being forced to flee the island via the SBA at Akrotiri. Also departing the island during the fighting were the Avro Vulcans of NEAF. Comprising Nos 9 and 35 Squadrons the aircraft were flown to Waddington and Scampton respectively. Also leaving the island at the same time were the resident transports and the Nimrod detachment, although No. 56 Squadron and its Lightnings remained to ensure the safety of the Sovereign Base Areas (SBAs). To ensure that the Warsaw Pact could not make any gains from the Cypriot turmoil a Vulcan detachment was deployed to Luqa, Malta. No. 56 Squadron and its Lightnings returned to Wattisham in January 1975.

Eventually, the island would be divided along the Green Line with the Turks in the north while the Greeks occupied the remainder. While the division has reduced greatly any chance of racial integration, the southern part has successfully recovered from the fighting while the north still lingers in the past. From a British point of view both the SBAs remain under control although Akrotiri has assumed prominence as the airfield is used for Armament Practice Camps and a support base for operations throughout the Mediterranean and the Middle East.

Fortunately for those involved with the Cyprus crisis, whether evacuating civilians or service personnel and the families, the island of Malta GC was a very useful base for both these activities. Finally, on 21 September 1964, Malta obtained independence from Britain, although the incoming government signed a ten-year defence agreement with the UK that covered the use of Luqa plus other facilities on the island. However, after winning the 1971 elections the Labour government immediately requested the removal of all NATO and US forces from the island while the British government was asked to withdraw its forces by 1 January 1972. The deadline was later extended to 15 March and then 31 March of the same year. Although negotiations over the lease of Luqa were always under review, the Ministry of Defence would initiate Operation *Exit*, the removal of all service personnel out of Malta. No. 13 Squadron departed with its mix of Canberra PR7s and PR9s relocated to RAF Akrotiri while No. 203 Squadron, equipped with the Nimrod MR, moved to the US Navy base at NAS Sigonella in nearby Sicily. On 20 March a Nimrod from No. 203 Squadron made a low pass over Luqa as the RAF Ensign was lowered for what was then thought to be the last time.

During Operation *Exit* much of the equipment and facilities that could not be removed from the island in time were destroyed or rendered useless. However, a few days later a new agreement over the lease and its cost for the use of facilities in Malta was resolved. This new agreement, destined to expire on 31 March 1979, was formally signed. No. 203 returned to Luqa between 21 and 29 April supported by no fewer than twenty-five Hercules and nineteen Belfast sorties. These were bringing in new equipment to replace what was destroyed earlier. No. 13 Squadron returned later in October, although by this time their inventory was composed purely of Canberra PR7s.

With the return of the RAF to Luqa the usual round of Sunspots by bomber and fighter squadrons would resume and would continue until final withdrawal. Luqa was decommissioned as a RAF station on 29 September 1978 during which a special farewell programme was held. The RAF aerobatic team, the Red Arrows, together with a number of other RAF front-line aircraft such as the Harrier and Jaguar, gave a spectacular display in front of a very large crowd. Air Chief Marshal Sir David Evans KCB, CEB, RAF, was the reviewing officer. No. 13 Squadron would return to Wyton in October 1978, remaining as part of Strike Command until disbanding in January 1982. No. 203 Squadron on the other hand would be disbanded in December 1977, its aircraft being divided between St Mawgan and Kinloss. MR detachments would be provided by either base being deployed to either Cyprus or Malta as required.

When No. 13 Squadron returned to Britain to take up residence at Wyton it would join up with Nos 39 and 58 Squadrons. No. 39 Squadron had re-equipped with the Canberra PR9 in November 1962 while No. 58 Squadron had reverted to the PR7 retaining them until disbandment in September 1970. Possibly the most significant aircraft deployed at Wyton was the Shorts built Canberra PR9. Designed from the outset as a strategic reconnaissance asset the PR9 combined the equipment developed for the PR7 with a redesigned wing plus a redesigned front fuselage that bore a strong resemblance to the B(I)8 bomber model. The result was an aircraft that could cruise at a high altitude courtesy of its more powerful Rolls-Royce Avon engines. Unlike the bomber model the PR9 featured an ejection seat for the navigator housed in the nose, the front section of which swung open for access although any ejection took place through a frangible hatch above the occupant. In contrast to the bomber version access to the pilot's position was via an opening canopy instead of the original side-opening access hatch. The Avon engines being more powerful blessed the PR9 with a sprightly performance and these plus powered ailerons endowed the aircraft with fighter-like behaviour.

Altogether twenty-three Canberra PR9s were ordered of which twenty-one were delivered to the RAF; one had been lost before delivery while the other became the multi-pronged nose SC9 research aircraft. With the reshuffling of reconnaissance assets at Wyton the PR9s were eventually concentrated with No. 39 Squadron at Wyton while the remainder flew the far more numerous PR7. As they underwent further contractions the number of available PR9s was reduced to twelve and these were subject to various upgrade programmes between 1976 and 1980. One of the major upgrades would see the Decca Tactical Air Navigation System (TANS) installed, which was complemented by an improved Doppler radar unit and a Sperry Master Reference Gyro. The main visible change was courtesy of the ARI.18228/6 passive warning system whose receiver heads were mounted in a bullet on the front edge of the fin and a radome mounted on the extreme tip of the fuselage. As reconnaissance no longer required the hazardous dropping of flares to illuminate a target the redundant flare bay in the PR9 would become home for the ARI.5969/3. This was the designation for the Texas Instruments Infra Red Line Scan system that utilized the components removed from the reconnaissance pods originally built for the RAFG F-4 Phantoms. These modifications improved the aircraft's tactical low-level performance and capabilities. One further aircraft underwent the full modification process to replace two that were lost in 1977 and 1978.

While the PR9s undertook normal reconnaissance roles using conventional cameras the aircraft also undertook more secretive tasks using the System III equipment. Rumoured to be based around the American HR73 camera this was said to be capable of covering a large area and producing 3D images, all of which were exceptionally sharp. When the System III was installed in the PR9 it was housed in the flare bay this being covered by a bulged fairing. Within the British Isles the Canberra PR9 was utilized as part of Operation *Motorman,* which used the aircraft to undertake reconnaissance over the no-go areas of Belfast using infra-red film for the detection of hidden weapons. The PR9s also undertook a similar task over Sierra Leone as part of Operation *Silkman.*

As ever the spectre of defence cuts reared its head in 1981 when it was decided to reduce the number of reconnaissance Canberras long before their Tornado replacements were ready. In 1981 No. 13 Squadron would be completely disbanded while No. 39 Squadron would be reduced by half in January 1982 with full disbandment taking place in May. This was not the end for No. 39 Squadron as it would immediately reappear as No. 1 PRU, remaining as such until No. 39 Squadron was resurrected in July 1992, still based at Wyton. By November 1994 the unit had moved to Marham as Wyton was due for closure. As the final Canberra operator, No. 39 Squadron was responsible for its own conversion and continuation therefore it gained two Canberra T4s from the defunct No. 231 OCU and a pair of Canberra PR7s from No. 360 Squadron, which had also recently disbanded. With both these types in service the trainee pilots would use the T4 for basic conversion flying before moving onto the more powerful PR7; hopefully they were then capable of handling the PR9, a much more sprightly beast.

One of the most secretive units to operate the Canberra was No. 51 Squadron based at Wyton. Only four Canberra B6(RC)s were manufactured. These featured an extended nose that housed specialist electronic intelligence equipment. No. 51 Squadron's predecessor, No. 192 Squadron, received its first pair of Canberra B Mk 6s ,WJ775 and WT301, in December 1954, and then gained another, WT305, in May 1957. All three aircraft initially retained the same nose profile as the standard B Mk 6 bomber, although the original glazed nosecone was replaced by a dielectric radome of the same size and shape. The aircraft received a new, larger dielectric nose that was attached to frame 1. This first nose shape was followed by the T Mk 11 type needle nose. This had been chosen as it was flight cleared and offered sufficient space for a new steerable ELINT receiver.

Blue Shadow radar was also fitted to the aircraft on a temporary basis, before becoming a permanent fixture. Within the same time frame the aircraft gained a new fairing under the tail, behind the tail bumper, below and just behind the original Orange Putter tailcone. This housed the relocated Orange Putter active tail warning radar. The tailcone itself was replaced by a new, slab-sided, bluff ended tailcone with a sharp trailing edge, which accommodated a J/K/Ku-band passive tail warning system. In late 1965, the pointed T Mk 11 nose radome was replaced by a slightly shorter, round fronted radome that allowed better performance for the ELINT receiver in the nose. By 1966 the slab-sided tailcone had given way to one of a more conventional shape.

Systems carried by the four B Mk 6 (Mod) or (RC) included a Radio Research Laboratory AN/APR-4 superheterodyne radar intercept receiver with TN180 and TN181 tuning heads, an AN/ALR-8 comms band receiver, and a manually tuned R216 receiver plus twenty channels. The special operator's equipment rack formed the roof of a tunnel beside the pilot's seat, through which the systems operator and navigator had to squirm to reach their seats. These aircraft were retired on 1 July 1974 leaving No. 51 Squadron with a handful of Nimrod R1s on their inventory.

One aircraft, WT305, was returned to service in January 1976 for Project Zabra, with an American radiometer or infra-red radar unit mounted in a turret above the navigator's hatch. Un-named sources have suggested that the device was used to measure the IR signature of newly deployed Soviet fighters. Project Zabra ran from February until 14 October mainly flying from Laarbruch, after which the aircraft was retired from flying. Other Canberra operators during this period included No. 7 Squadron. Reformed at St Mawgan in May 1970 the unit flew the B2 version for conversion purposes plus the TT18 for the squadron's primary task, that of target towing. No. 7 Squadron would disband in January 1982 although the number plate would reappear soon afterwards as a Boeing Chinook operator.

When Strike Command formed No. 98 Squadron was part of Signals Command that later became No. 90 (Signals) Group with the aircraft then sporting this legend on their fuselages. As Watton was due for closure, No. 98 Squadron moved to Cottesmore in April 1969 from where it continued its duties. By August 1970 the squadron began to receive some long range Canberra E15s. The following year the unit retired its B2s remaining equipped purely with the E15. No. 98 Squadron continued flying its calibration duties until, following the reductions required by the 1975 Defence Review, it was finally disbanded at Cottesmore on 27 February 1976.

Having flown Victors up to September 1968 the No. 100 Squadron number plate was resuscitated in February 1972 at West Raynham with Canberra B2s and T19s. A move to Marham followed in January 1976 where the unit picked up some of the ex-98 Squadron B15s. A further move to Wyton followed in January 1982 where Canberra PR7s and TT18s were added to the inventory. Although much of its public tasking was concerned with target towing duties it did undertake some reconnaissance and calibration missions as well. By 1991 all of the Canberras had been retired to be replaced by the BAE Hawk T1.

While No. 51 Squadron was the secret face of ELINT a more public face was presented by No. 360 Squadron. Formed from a flight of No. 97 Squadron at Watton the unit was originally equipped with Canberra B2s, however these were soon replaced by the T17. This was a converted B2 whose bomb bay was stuffed with ECM equipment the jamming heads being mounted in a modified nose and a modified tail cone. Their primary role was to provide jamming capabilities for testing the British defence systems although in time of war such an asset could possibly used for jamming Soviet radar systems. No. 360 Squadron would move base to Cottesmore in April 1969 and remain there until April 1975 when Wyton became the unit's new home. Unusually for a unit with an RAF number plate the squadron was manned by both RAF and RN personnel with the commanding officer alternating between each service. The initial version of the T17 was later upgraded to T17A standard. This new version featured improved navigation aids, a spectrum analyser in place of the previously fitted AN/APR-20, and a powerful communications jammer. By 1991 the squadron had acquired some of the PR7s and TT18s from No. 100 Squadron, retaining these until the unit was disbanded in October 1994.

Another venerable aircraft was also giving good service to the RAF in the support role. Drawing on the American experience from Vietnam the RAF decided to form two units for weapons training purposes utilizing redundant Hawker Hunter FGA9s. Two units were formed for this purpose: the first was No. 45 Squadron, previously a Canberra operator. The squadron was reformed at RAF West Raynham on 1 August 1972 equipped with Hawker Hunters as a ground attack training unit. The squadron would disband in July 1976 after this role was taken over by the Tactical Weapons Unit. The second unit to form was No. 58 Squadron at Wittering from a nucleus of No. 45 Squadron in August 1973. No. 58 Squadron would also operate the Hawker Hunter FGA9, operating them until disbandment in July 1976 when the role was handed over to No. 1 TWU.

The Hunter would also see service with other second-line units, although these bore shadow squadron numbers. It would be No. 229 OCU that would be the primary second-line Hunter operator having three units under its wing these being Nos 63, 79 and 234 Squadrons. The role of the OCU was to prepare pilots for the ground attack role. Based at Chivenor the OCU was formed in June 1963 and would disband into the Tactical Weapons Unit when the OCU transferred to Brawdy in 1974. All three squadron number plates were retained after this move, the TWU remaining in operation until disbandment in August 1992.

The only veteran fighter still in service was the English Electric (BAC) Lightning of which the F3 and F6 fighters still remained in use while the T5 was the trainer version still in use. Only two units flew the Lightning, Nos 5 and 11 Squadrons, both utilizing all three available versions of the Lightning. As there was no operational conversion unit the Lightning Training Flight was formed using the F3s and T5s. All three units operated from Binbrook with the fighter squadrons operating in the air defence role. No. 5 Squadron would disband in December 1987, the LTF having gone in April. No. 11 Squadron would follow in April 1988 while Binbrook would be prepared for closure.

Having been founded during the Second World War to recover downed airmen of all nationalities the search and rescue organization of the RAF had evolved into a very workmanlike organization. Originally dependent on fixed wing aircraft that dropped dinghy packs to those in the water, for later retrieval by long range launches, the advent of the helicopter would alter the way rescues were performed. The first helicopter in

The Lightning was still in service during much of the 1980s. Based at Binbrook the type was flown by Nos 5 and 11 Squadrons. This is XR724 of No. 5 Squadron looking exceptionally clean after an overhaul. *(BBA Collection)*

The third unit to fly the Lightning at Binbrook was the Lightning Training Flight (LTF) and F3 XR713 'DD' was flown by that unit. *(BBA Collection)*

service with the then Coastal Command was the Westland (Bristol) Sycamore. This was followed by the widespread adoption of the Westland Whirlwind by both the Royal Navy and the RAF for deployment at bases near the coast. The two units involved were Nos 22 and 202 Squadrons, the former equipping with the Whirlwind HAR10 in August 1962 and being based at Thorney Island, Chivenor, Coltishall, Valley and Brawdy. In January 1976 the headquarters moved to Finningley, although the flights at Chivenor, Valley and Coltishall remained as part of No. 22 Squadron. No. 202 Squadron equipped with the Whirlwind HAR10 in 1964. Headquartered at Acklington the unit had flights at Boulmer, Leuchars, Coltishall and Lossiemouth. In September 1976 No. 202 Squadron joined No. 22 Squadron at Finningley to form a joint headquarters.

Resplendent in its coat of bright yellow Westland Wessex HC2 XR520 of No. 22 Squadron 'A' Flight Chivenor hovers off the Devon cliffs while undertaking a rescue. *(Bob Archer Collection)*

After the defence review of 1975 that saw cuts to British forces overseas there was a surplus of Westland Wessex helicopters available thus the opportunity was taken to re-equip the search and rescue units with a helicopter with an increased range and weight capability. In 1976 No. 22 Squadron was partly re-equipped with Wessex HC2s modified for the SAR role. C Flight 202 Squadron at Leuchars became B Flight 22 Squadron in April 1976 while D Flight of No. 72 Squadron at Manston became E Flight 22 Squadron in June 1976 while C Flight of No. 22 Squadron and its Whirlwind HAR10s were replaced by Wessex HC2s at Valley in June 1976. A and D Flights of No. 22 Squadron remained at Chivenor and Brawdy with their Whirlwind HAR 10s.

No. 202 Squadron remained an all Whirlwind unit with aircraft at A Flight Boulmer, B Flight Leconfield, C Flight Coltishall and D Flight Lossiemouth. In most respects the incoming Wessex was operated in a similar manner to the Standard Operating Procedures of the Whirlwind, although their crews exploited the Wessex's advantages to the full. The Wessex became a very capable and versatile search and rescue helicopter, although limited because it was still not normal to operate the aircraft over the sea at night. Initially the winch fitted to the Wessex had 100 feet of cable. Instead of a rope extension to the winch cable, previously used by the Whirlwind, a formal 120 feet tape was introduced to extend the effective length of the cable. The tape was used on both the Wessex and the Whirlwind. However, in 1977 a 300 feet cable was fitted to the Wessex negating the requirement for the tape. The Wessex remained in SAR service until its final replacement by the Sea King HAR3 at Valley in June 1997 plus the transfer of the Search and Rescue Training Unit at Valley from 18 Group to the Defence Helicopter Flying School, on 1 April 1997.

From October 1957 the Squadron Headquarters for 275, 228 and 202 (SAR) Squadrons had been at Leconfield, although from June 1956 until April 1974, No. 22

To supplement and later replace the Westland Wessex the RAF purchased the Westland Sea King HAR3. These were allocated to No. 202 Squadron headquartered at Finningly. This example is ZE368 seen at Fairford. *(BBA Collection)*

Squadron's Headquarters had originally been at St Mawgan, although a transfer was later made to Thorney Island. However, in January 1976 both Squadrons were brought together under the Search and Rescue Wing at Finningley while the No. 18 Group Standardization Unit (Helicopters), 18 GSU(H), also moved from Northwood. The Headquarters of the Search and Rescue Wing was located in prefabricated offices that housed the Officer Commanding, the Wing Adjutant and secretarial staff, the Officers Commanding 202 and 22 Squadrons with their training officers, pilots, navigators and winchmen, and the 18 GSU(H). The 2nd Line servicing for all the RAF SAR helicopters was carried out at the SAR Engineering Wing Headquarters. Thus the whole of the organization of the front-line RAF SAR Force had the advantage of being under one roof. The SAR Wing saw the introduction of the Wessex into SAR service in 1976 and the Sea King in 1978/9.

A dedicated search and rescue version of the Westland Sea King was developed for the RAF search and rescue squadrons as the HAR3. The Sea King entered service in 1978 replacing the Westland Whirlwind HAR10 with No. 202 Squadron at the same bases. Sixteenth aircraft was ordered soon afterwards. Following the Falklands War of 1982 three further aircraft were purchased to enable operation of a SAR flight in the Falkland Islands, initially operating from Navy Point on the north side of Stanley harbour and later from RAF Mount Pleasant. In 1992 another six aircraft were ordered to replace the last remaining Westland Wessex helicopters in the search and rescue role these entering service in 1996. The six Sea King HAR3As had updated systems, including a digital navigation system and more modern avionics. The Wessex remained in service with No. 22 Squadron until January 1997 while those operated by No. 202 Squadron used theirs between November 1982 to August 1983. The Sea Kings were deployed to St Mawgan, Chivenor, Leuchars, Wattisham, Valley and Coltishall with No. 22 Squadron while No. 202 Squadron deployed its aircraft to Finningley, Boulmer, Brawdy, Manston and Leconfield. The small group of aircraft dedicated to rescue duties in the Falkland Islands drew their crews from both squadrons, the unit initially being designated No. 1564 Flight, although this was later redesignated as No. 78

The arrival of the Boeing Chinook HC1 into RAF service would improve the heavy-lift capabilities of the tactical support force immensely. Pictured at Wyton is ZA714 'EX' of No. 7 Squadron based at Odiham. *(BBA Collection)*

Parked awaiting its crew is Vulcan B2 MRR, XH558, of No. 27 Squadron based at Scampton. This aircraft would eventually emerge as the only civilian-owned flying Vulcan. *(BBA Collection)*

Squadron in 1986 when No. 1310 Flight and its Chinooks at Mount Pleasant joined the Sea Kings.

The arrival of the Boeing Chinook into RAF service would enhance the service's lift capability in support of Army operations. The order for these machines was placed by the Ministry of Defence in February 1978. The original order covered thirty aircraft, although this was increased by a further three later. Strangely enough it had been planned for the service to acquire the type in March 1967, although this order was later cancelled due to defence cuts in August 1971. Two units would operate the Chinook, initially Nos 7 and 18 Squadrons. The latter would reform at Odiham in August 1981 while No. 7 Squadron would reform in September 1982 at the same base. No. 7 Squadron had replaced No. 18 Squadron as the unit had moved to Gütersloh as part of RAF Germany. The squadron would play an important part in the events of 1982.

As the decades swung over from the 1970s to the 1980s the strike/attack side of Strike Command was undergoing a massive change. The units involved were those flying the

Wrapped up well against the cold is Vulcan B2 XL426 complete with the leaping dingoes of No. 50 Squadron on the fin. The aircraft sports the new wraparound scheme first introduced in 1980. *(BBA Collection)*

Vulcan while the aircraft they were receiving was the Panavia Tornado. Scampton would be the first base to relinquish its famous deltas. It would be No. 617 Squadron that would say goodbye to its multi-seat bombers in December 1981 reforming with Panavia Tornado GR1s at Marham in January 1983. The second to go was No. 27 Squadron in March 1982, handing over its MRR role to the Nimrod fleet. The number would lie dormant until May 1983 when No. 27 Squadron reformed at Marham with the Tornado GR1. The last unit to disband and retire its Vulcans was No. 35 Squadron, which also disappeared in March 1982, although since that date its number plate has remained dormant. The four units at Waddington would have time to undertake participation in a Red Flag exercise before the disbandments began. The first unit to go was No. 9 'The Sleaford Road Detachment' Squadron, which disbanded in May 1982. Unlike the two Scampton squadrons No. 9 Squadron would reform as a Tornado unit in June 1982 at Honington before departing to Bruggen in 1986. This left Nos 44, 50 and 101 Squadrons still operational for much of 1982.

The aircraft that was destined to form the core of the RAF attack and defence squadrons two decades was the Panavia Tornado. Having proceeded through the AFVG, TSR2 and the F-111 BAC Warton was encouraged to continue its efforts to develop its swing wing designs for future RAF use. With help from Dr W Stewart at the Ministry of Technology BAC was by 1968 to confirm that the two main problems concerning swing wing technology had been solved. The primary was the swing wing pivot which after much development had been assembled about a Teflon bearing that demonstrated the required safe life for all kinds of flying plus an excellent fatigue life. Also developed was a full-scale wing box that was intended for a production model. The design engineers at BAC also cracked the other problem that faced swing wing operation, that of integrating the movements of the slats, flaps and spoilers with the wing and the aircraft's airspeed.

With these problems solved a team from BAC Warton had visited Munich, home of Messerschmitt-Bolkow-Blohm (MBB). This aviation combine had been formed to collaborate with Fairchild on the Advanced Vertical Strike aircraft. However, this project

One of the first units to receive the Panavia Tornado GR1 was the Tri-national Tornado Training Establishment based at Cottesmore. This aircraft is ZA375 B-05 of the British-commanded squadron. *(John Ryan Collection)*

was in deep financial, political and technical trouble and was on the verge of being cancelled. The AVS had been conceived when the NATO posture had been one of massive retaliation against any Soviet incursion; this had changed by 1967 to one of flexible response thus the AVS was not a viable proposition for this kind of task. After BAC's visit to Munich MBB was advised to look at non-vertical aircraft projects, and also asked to look at swing wing applications for a future combat aircraft.

The design projects of both Britain and Germany were now on a merging course thus meetings between government officials from Britain, Germany and Italy began in July 1967 concerning the design and production of an aircraft suitable for all three countries needs plus matching the needs of NATO. By May 1968 the three partners had been joined by the Netherlands, Belgium and Canada. The outcome of these discussions was that the Advanced Combat Aircraft was born based on the BAC studies for the UKVG. Helping to push forward the ACA/ MRA-75, Multi Role Aircraft, was the decision by Britain to withdraw from its commitments east of Suez. These changes resulted in an aircraft that was dedicated to operating within the confines of Europe although the fitment of a flight refuelling probe soon restored the aircraft's range flexibility.

By July 1968 the governments of all six interested nations had signed a Memorandum of Understanding (MoU) concerning the development of the MRA-75. Soon after the signing of the MoU three countries decided to withdraw; the Netherlands and Belgium were not overly concerned with the design and purchase of a new combat aircraft. In fact, after the initial enthusiasm both governments quickly cooled their ardour. Canada soon followed; although much of their aircraft industry was interested in the project, their armed forces were in the process of being rehashed into one service more dedicated to the peace-keeping role than that of national defence. Against this background the Canadians were unable to define the type of aircraft they might need in the future. By January 1969 the design work had started with the arrival of design teams from MBB, Fokker and Fiat at Warton to start the design work on the new aircraft. By this time the Rolls-Royce RB.199 had been chosen as the powerplant to power the new jet. Thus with all of these first steps having been completed without too much disagreement the formation of an overview organization was the next inevitable step. On 26 March 1969 Panavia GmbH was born with its registered offices in Munich. This would be the organization that would receive the production contracts for the aircraft that had by now become known as the Multi Role Combat Aircraft (MRCA).

The original MRCA was seen as two separate projects as the RAF and the *Marineflieger* wanted two-seat aircraft while the remainder were more interested in a single-seat version. Eventually the requirement for a single-seat version was dropped with the two-seater becoming the standard model. One feature of the MRCA that stood out was the extensive use of computing technology throughout the flight control and engine management systems. Hydraulics were also a major feature of the MRCA design, being used to drive the flight control system, differential tailerons, undercarriage, flight refuelling probe, brakes and canopy amongst others. It would be the CSAS, Command/ Stability Augmentation System that would be the greatest triumph for the MRCA. This was the first example of a triple redundancy fly-by-wire system installed in a European combat aircraft and this meant that should any of the fly-by-wire channels fail the other two would seamlessly pick up the load.

By July 1976 the three involved governments signed off on the MoU for series production to begin, the first contract covering forty aircraft. Prior to the production

The Lightning was due to be replaced by the Tornado Air Defence Variant. ZA254 would feature many of the production features of the production model, including the fuselage recesses for the Sky Flash missiles. *(John Ryan Collection)*

aircraft rolling off the line nine prototypes were constructed, followed by six pre-production aircraft. As the trials and development programme continued all fifteen airframes became heavily involved in testing various aspects of handling, avionics, engine management and weapons delivery. Production manufacturing was divided thus Britain received 385, Germany 324 and Italy 100, the ratios being Britain 48 per cent, Germany 40 per cent and Italy 12 per cent of the construction.

The first prototype would fly in August 1974 while the final pre-production machine would undertake its maiden flight in March 1979. Two months later the Tri-national Tornado Training Establishment (TTTE), to be based at Cottesmore, was authorized with the first aircraft, ZA320, which was delivered in July 1980. The TTTE began its first conversion course in January 1981. As the Tornado was a highly advanced aircraft it became obvious early in the programme that a dedicated weapons conversion unit was required. This came on line in June 1981 based at Honington with the reserve unit number of No. 45 Squadron being applied in 1984.

While the strike version of the Tornado was settled the RAF was on the hunt for a long-range interceptor to replace the remaining Lightnings and the Phantoms then in use. The answer was to develop the Tornado as the Air Defence Variant. The primary visible change was the extension of the forward fuselage to house extra fuel, while underneath troughs were created to house four Skyflash missiles. The extended radome was home to the Marconi/Ferranti AI.24 Foxhunter, although in the early days serious problems with this system meant that the initial aircraft were fitted with ballast weights

The first batch of Tornados were F2s, these being delivered to the OCU at Coningsby. Unfortunately, the radar system was causing problems therefore these aircraft flew with ballast in the nose better known as 'Blue Circle' radar. *(BBA Collection)*

known within the service as the Blue Circle radar unit. The two ADV prototypes both flew in 1980 and were used for initial development trials. Even as the RAF was re-equipping with its numerous new aircraft events would unfold in the South Atlantic that would stretch the service to its limits and accelerate the replacement of other types earlier than at first planned.

Chapter 6

The RAF at War in the South Atlantic

Many of this planet's conflicts seem to stem from the collision of minor actions and misunderstandings that need that one final spark to turn a niggle into all out warfare. This chapter is a tale of two governments both highly unpopular with their respective populaces. In Britain the Thatcher government had masterminded the greatest increase in unemployment and the largest financial crisis since the 1930s. Their answer had been to apply stringent cuts across the board; the net result was a mass outbreak of rioting across Britain that resulted in numerous arrests and extensive damage to property. The other antagonist in this scenario was Argentina. Throughout the period 1976 to 1983 Argentina had been under the control of a military dictatorship that had through ineptitude engineered a devastating economic crisis. The National Reorganization Process, as the Junta was known, had killed thousands of Argentine citizens for their political opposition to the government. This era becoming known as the Dirty War. Many of the victims simply 'disappeared', without any due legal process for opposing the corruption that had putrefied the upper echelon of the country.

The suppression of the Argentinian populace had continued under a succession of dictators following a coup that deposed President Perón with General Jorge Videla in power. Videla was followed by General Roberto Viola who was replaced by General Leopoldo Galtieri for a period. Before he started the Falklands War, Galtieri was subject to growing opposition from the populace, many of whom were openly protesting about the 'disappeared'. Galtieri retained power for eighteen months, although he had already been a key player in the slaughter and oppression of the Argentinians for many years. By 1981 inflation in Argentina had climbed to a record 600 per cent, while the GDP had fallen by 11.4 per cent, manufacturing output by 22.9 per cent and real wages by 19.2 per cent. The trades unions were gaining more support for a general strike every day and the popular opposition to the Junta was growing rapidly.

President Galtieri, as head of the military Junta, decided to counter public concern over economic and human rights issues by means of a speedy victory over the Falklands that would appeal to a popular nationalistic sentiment. Argentina began their campaign by exerting pressure on the United Nations dropping subtle hints of a possible invasion, however the British representatives either missed or ignored this potential threat in public and did not react. Mistakenly the Argentinians assumed that the British would not use force if the islands were invaded thus the Junta interpreted the failure of the British to react as a lack of interest in the Falklands due to the planned withdrawal of the Antarctic supply vessel, HMS *Endurance*, and by the British Nationality Act of 1981, that replaced the full British citizenship of Falkland Islanders with a more limited version.

In 1976 Operation *Sol Argentina* secretly landed a force of fifty military personnel, posing as scientists under the command of Captain Trombetta on the unoccupied island of Southern Thule. The Argentinean troops established the military outpost of Corbeta Uruguay on South Thule, part of the British South Sandwich Islands.. This led to a formal protest from the United Kingdom and an effort to resolve the issue through diplomatic rather than military means. This was followed by Operation *Journeyman*, the dispatching of a small military force to the South Atlantic in November 1977 by the Callaghan government that averted further action. Subsequent reports from the Joint Intelligence Committee (JIC) in 1977, 1979 and 1981 suggested that:

...as long as Argentina calculated that the British Government were prepared to negotiate seriously on sovereignty, it was unlikely to resort to force. However, if negotiations broke down, or if Argentina concluded from them that there was no prospect of real progress towards a negotiated transfer of sovereignty, there would be a high risk of its then resorting to more forceful measures, including direct military action.

While Argentina was uncertain over a possible reaction to such an invasion, events at home would appear to be forcing the Junta's hand. The Falkland Islands had been the subject of a sovereignty dispute since they were first settled in 1764, with Britain on one side, and successively France, Spain and Argentina on the other, although by 1833 the island was fully under British control. During a meeting between Admiral Anaya and General Galtieri on 9 December 1981, at Campo de Mayo barracks, the two discussed how and when to overthrow President Roberto Viola. Anaya offered the navy's support on the understanding that the navy would be allowed to occupy the Falkland Islands and South Georgia. They believed that the sight of the Argentine flag flying over Port Stanley on the 150th anniversary of Britain's 'illegal occupation of Las Malvinas' would lead to a renewed era of national pride and divert attention away from problems at home.

On 15 December Admiral Anaya flew from Buenos Aires to the main Argentine naval base at Puerto Belgrano to confirm Vice-Admiral Lombardo as the new Chief of Naval Operations. After the ceremony Anaya informed Lombardo to prepare a plan for the occupation of the Falkland Islands with Anaya stressing the need for absolute secrecy. The detailed planning for the invasion began in January 1982 under the command of Vice Admiral Lombardo, Commander-in-Chief Fleet, the participants including General Garcia, Commander Fifth Army Corps, and Brigadier Plessel, Air Force Staff. The operation would centre on an amphibious landing of 3,000 troops en masse to minimize bloodshed. The contingent of Royal Marines, British civil service officials and the more anti-Argentine among the Falklanders would be deported and the bulk of the invasion force would then return to their bases within forty-eight hours. A military governor and a gendarmerie of about 500 would be left to keep the remaining Falklanders in line. Also taken into consideration during the planning phase was the Argentine firm that had constructed a temporary runway near Stanley in advance of the building of a main runway at Stanley airport. The military Líneas Aéreas del Estado (LADE) airline was also flying regularly to the Falkland Islands. LADE was represented by Vice-Commodore Gilobert based in Port Stanley and he had been gathering intelligence for four years. The cargo ship ARA *Isla de los Estados* was on hire for commercial purposes by the island administration, and her captain, Capaglio, had detailed information on the Falkland coast, beaches and inner waters.

In January 1982 diplomatic talks over sovereignty of the islands finally ended without resolution. While the Falklands invasion had been in some respects a long-planned action, it became clear after the war that the subsequent defence of the islands had been largely improvised thus sea mines were not deployed at strategic landing locations, and a large part of the infantry forces sent to the Falklands consisted of conscripts, who had only begun their training at the beginning of that year. Confirmation that the decision to launch the invasion was a last-minute one is bolstered by the fact that the Argentine Navy were awaiting delivery of additional French Exocet airborne anti-ship missiles, Super Étendards and new ships being built in West Germany. Even the air force had been looking at new weapons, having sent a delegation to Britain to investigate the purchase of some retired Avro Vulcan B2 bombers plus a large spares package.

The Argentine Navy operated modern British built Type 42 air-defence destroyers of the type forming the bulk of the British Task Force's anti-aircraft defence. Training attacks on these revealed that over half of the Argentine aircraft might be lost in the process of destroying only a few British warships if they attacked at medium to high altitudes at which the Sea Dart missile was designed to engage thus the Argentine Air Force would employ low-level stand-off Exocet attacks when over blue water.

The Argentine Junta's original intention had been to mount a quick occupation, followed rapidly by a withdrawal, leaving only a small garrison to support the new military governor. This strategy was based on the assumption that the British would never respond with force. In fact, Argentine assault units were withdrawn to the mainland in the days following the invasion. However, strong popular support and the rapid British reaction forced the Junta to change their objectives and reinforce the islands. The Junta had badly misjudged the political climate in Britain, believing that democracies were weak, indecisive and averse to risk, and did not anticipate that the British would send their fleet halfway across the world to recover an overseas territory. They had also failed to understand that Premier Thatcher was in a similar predicament and that she saw an armed response as a way of boosting her popularity.

In 1980 Admiral Otero, once the notorious commander of the Navy Petty-Officers' School of Mechanics, where many of the 'disappeared' were tortured and executed, was the head of the Antarctic operations and sought to repeat Operation *Sol Argentina* in South Georgia by establishing a military base under the cover of Operation *Alpha*. Admiral Lombardo feared that Operation *Alpha* would jeopardize the secret preparations for the Falkland landings, however Admiral Otero had close links to Admiral Anaya who then approved Operation *Alpha* despite promising to Admiral Lombardo he would cancel the operation.

An Argentine entrepreneur, Constantino Davidoff, had gained a two-year contract regarding the removal of scrap at an old whaling station on South Georgia. In December 1981, he was transported by the icebreaker ARA *Almirante Irizar* to South Georgia for an initial survey. The party was landed without undertaking the courtesy visit to the British Antarctic Survey base at Grytviken, leading to formal diplomatic protests by the British Government. Davidoff later personally called the British Embassy in Buenos Aires to apologize, promising that his men would follow the correct protocols for landing in future. In return he received permission to continue with his venture, and on 11

March the naval transport ARA *Bahía Buen Suceso* departed carrying Davidoff's party of scrap workers. The group was, however, infiltrated by Argentine marines posing as civilian scientists. Operation *Alpha* had begun. Arriving on 19 March the party once again failed to follow the correct protocol, proceeding directly to Leith Harbour. The British Antarctic Survey (BAS) party sent to investigate this activity found that the Argentinian scrap metal workers had established a camp, defaced British signs, broken into the BAS hut and removed emergency rations, and had shot reindeer in contravention of local conservancy measures. The BAS party also reported a number of men in military uniform and that the Argentine flag had been raised.

A series of diplomatic exchanges then took place with the Falkland Island Governor and subsequently the Foreign Office passing a message to the BAS team to be forwarded to the captain of the ARA *Bahía Buen Suceso*. This was to the effect that the Argentine flag must be taken down and that they must report to the British administrator at Grytviken to have their passports stamped, although the party refused to do this as it would acknowledge British sovereignty over the islands. Eventually, the Argentine flag was lowered and the ARA *Bahía Buen Suceso* departed leaving a group of men behind. On 21 March HMS *Endurance* set sail with a party of twenty-two Royal Marines aboard to expel the men who remained at Leith, although to avoid further tensions the Foreign and Commonwealth Office ordered the *Endurance* to hold off. Taking advantage of the British pause, the Argentine Junta then ordered the ARA *Bahía Paraíso* to land a party of special forces led by Lieutenant Alfredo Astiz. Rather than force a confrontation the Royal Marines were ordered to set up an observation post to monitor the situation at Leith. The full party of Royal Marines was not landed until 31 March, by which time it became apparent that Argentine forces intended to seize the Falkland Islands. The Grytviken base was actually assaulted the day after the Falklands invasion as bad weather prevented an attack on the same day.

Falkland Islands Governor Sir Rex Hunt was informed by the British Government of a possible Argentine invasion on 1 April. At 3.30 p.m. that day he received a telegram from the Foreign and Commonwealth Office stating: 'We have apparently reliable evidence that an Argentine task force could be assembling off Stanley at dawn tomorrow. You will wish to make your dispositions accordingly.' On 2 April 1982, Argentine forces mounted amphibious landings of the Falkland Islands. The invasion involved landing Lieutenant-Commander Guillermo Sánchez-Sabarots' Amphibious Commandos Group at Mullet Creek, the attack on Moody Brook barracks and the battle and final surrender of Government House. It marked the beginning of the Falklands War.

The Governor summoned the two senior Royal Marines officers of Naval Party 8901 to Government House in Stanley to discuss the options for defending the Falklands. Major Norman, as the senior officer, was given overall command of the Marines, while Major Noott became the military advisor to Governor Hunt. The total military strength was sixty-eight Royal Marines and eleven naval personnel; this was greater than would normally have been available as the garrison was in the process of changing over. Both the replacements and the troops preparing to leave were on the Falklands at the time of the invasion. This initial strength was decreased to fifty-seven when twenty-two Royal Marines embarked aboard the Antarctic patrol ship HMS *Endurance* to observe Argentine soldiers based on South Georgia. The defensive numbers were reinforced by at least twenty-five Falkland Islands Defence Force (FIDF) members under the command of Major Summers. The FIDF was tasked with guarding key points such as the telephone exchange, the radio station and the power station. Skipper Jack Sollis, on-board the civilian coastal ship, operated his vessel as an improvised radar screen station off Stanley.

The Argentine amphibious operation began in the late evening of Thursday 1 April, when the destroyer ARA *Santísima Trinidad* disembarked special naval forces troops south of Stanley. The bulk of the Argentine forces would land some hours later from the amphibious warfare ship ARA *Cabo San Antonio* near the airport, on a beach previously marked by frogmen from the submarine ARA *Santa Fe*. The operation had originally been called *Azul, Blue*, during the planning stage although it was later renamed Operation *Rosario*. The very first action of Operation *Rosario* was the reconnaissance of Port William by the submarine ARA *Santa Fe* and the landing of fourteen tactical divers near Cape Pembroke, the reconnaissance mission began on 31 March.. The next day, the Argentinians became aware that the authorities in Stanley were aware of their intentions, so a change of plans was in order. Instead of landing right on Pembroke, the commandos would initially take a beach near Menguera Point, south of Kidney Island. After landing these forces planted navigation beacons for the main landing, then took over the airstrip and the lighthouse without resistance.

Over the night of 1–2 April, the destroyer ARA *Santísima Trinidad* anchored off Mullet Creek, lowering twenty-one Gemini assault craft into the water. These contained eighty-four special forces troops one of whose tasks was to capture Government House. The Argentine Rear Admiral Jorge Allara via a message radioed from *Santísima Trinidad* requested that Governor Rex Hunt negotiate a peaceful surrender, however the proposal was rejected. The Governor's residence had become the main concentration point for the Royal Marines and this would cause problems for the small force of Argentine troops sent to capture it. The first attack against this building started at 6.30 hours, barely an hour before the Yorke Bay amphibious landing, when one of platoons started to exchange fire with the British troops inside the house. In response and to stop casualties Hunt decided to enter talks with the Argentine commanders around 08.00 hours. The liaison for these negotiations was Vice-Commodore Hector Gilobert, the local commander of LADE, the Argentine government's airline company. Gilobert and a Governor's deputy went to the Argentine headquarters displaying a white flag. A ceasefire was put in place at that time, although this was occasionally breached by small arms fire.

Even though the Royal Marine troops had put up a strong resistance the Argentine Junta were still convinced that Britain would not respond. Obviously, the Argentine Embassy staff had failed to read the British press, the government was highly unpopular, plus the Defence White Paper for 1981–2 had proposed that much of the Royal Navy surface fleet be withdrawn. In light of this background Premier Thatcher would, with some help from the press, whip up some fervent patriotism even though many of the British populace thought initially that the Falklands were off the Orkneys!

Although the Royal Navy would bear the brunt of Operation *Corporate*, the recovery of the islands, the RAF and Strike Command would cover much of the long-range air operations plus any transport requirements. While events were unfolding 8,000 miles to the south the remaining Vulcan bomber squadrons were coming close to their disbandment dates that was scheduled to take place in June 1982. However, their disappearance would be delayed as the Vulcan was the only aircraft still in the active inventory capable of carrying a large quantity of bombs and other types of weapons over the distance to the Falklands. Even this had its drawbacks as the Vulcan would struggle

Famed for its role during the Black Buck missions to attack Argentine positions on the Falkland Island Vulcan B2 XM607 is seen here at the conclusion of Black Buck 1. The air conditioning hose is already in the cockpit as one of the ground crew hurries to collect the entrance door ladder. *(Mel James)*

to reach its target even with bomb bay fuel tanks installed and a light bomb load of 7,000lb, which was an inefficient use of such an asset. The answer was to reinstate the long dormant flight refuelling system that had fallen out of favour many years earlier due to leakage problems. Also lacking were the skills needed to undertake flight refuelling as the probe had few uses at that time being mainly used as a reference point for taxying and as an offset for the SFOM gunsight mounted in the co-pilot's position. Six aircraft were selected to have their flight refuelling systems reinstated by engineering personnel from Waddingtons Mechanical Engineering Aircraft Squadron (ME(A)S). These were XL391 and X597 (No. 101 Squadron), XM598 (No. 50 Squadron), XM607 and XM612 (No. 44 Squadron) and XM654 of No. 50 Squadron. All of these aircraft had other features in common; all had been built with the Skybolt missile pylon points as well as the ducting needed for the refrigeration system.

In preparation for Operation *Corporate* the Vulcans would undergo the work needed to make them suitable for their part in the retaking of the islands, although in the event XM654 would not take part in the raids being retained at Waddington for training purposes. To fly these bombers five crews were selected their qualification being that they had partaken in that year's Red Flag exercise held in February 1982. Two crews came from No. 50 Squadron while one crew each came from Nos 44 and 50 Squadrons and one from the recently disbanded No. 9 Squadron. Of the six chosen aircraft five were selected for the fitment of the Carousel Inertial Navigation System as installed in the British Airways Boeing 747 (XL391, XM597, XM598, XM607 and XM612), the intention being to improve the navigational accuracy over long distances. The first aircraft, XM597, was sent to Marham for conversion purposes as the Victor tankers were already fitted with this equipment. Marham also provided the necessary expertise for tanker training as none of the Vulcan crews were cleared for AAR (air to air). Intelligence gathering also revealed that the Argentine forces had put an effective air defence umbrella over the Falklands, which included control and detection radar, anti-aircraft guns and missiles. The radars, being of Western origin, could not be jammed by the ECM equipment carried by the bomber as it was geared towards the Soviet-based threat.

A close-up of the underwing pylon as fitted to the port side of the Vulcan, that on the starboard side was slightly deeper. *(Mel James)*

As the selected base for Vulcan operations would be Wideawake airfield on Ascension Island in the mid–Atlantic it was fairly obvious that any bombing mission could not be supported by any other aircraft type thus the Vulcan would have to provide its own suppression of enemy air defences (SEAD) capability. The answer would be to utilize the redundant Skybolt missile points already built into the aircraft wings, however none of the few pylons ever constructed for this programme still existed having been scrapped years earlier.

The solution would come from two Waddington engineering officers, Squadron Leaders Chris Pye and Mel James. Using a length of steel joist to which were added mounting shackles the first prototype pylon was built. Having successfully mated this latest addition to the Vulcan's capability in a trials machine the decision was made to construct a handful for at least three aircraft. These differed from the prototype in that they were built up to match the profile of the wing, had aerodynamic fairings fore and aft, and were fully equipped with the required electrical looms and weapons release shackles. The original weapon chosen to equip the Vulcan for the SEAD role was the Martel-guided missile, which was available in both television and radar guided form. The first aircraft fitted with a full set of pylons was XM597, which flew to the Aberporth ranges over 4–5 May 1982 for live firings of the radar-guided Martel. After four successful launches the Martel was reallocated to the Nimrod anti-submarine aircraft fleet as its versatility was seen as more useful to them. Searching for a replacement the MoD contacted their American counterparts who would offer the AGM-45 Shrike anti-radar missile. A few test firings later and the missile was cleared for operational service, a process that had only taken days instead of the usual weeks or months. The Vulcan fleet was also helping the remainder of the RAF in other ways as the flight refuelling probes were being removed from withdrawn aircraft for use by other types such as the Lockheed C-130 Hercules and the HS Nimrod. During these flights it was discovered that these pylons, in a similar manner to those for the earlier Skybolt, had no noticeable effect on the handling of the aircraft. Range extension was also investigated as in-flight refuelling plus the internal fuel load would give the bomber minimum time over target. To that end a design team from the RAF and British Aerospace arrived at St Athan. The aircraft chosen for the trials was XL389, currently standing in the scrapline, and the design team used a test pylon to check for clearances between the pylon and the main undercarriage doors and the intended fuel tank, which would be drawn from the remaining stocks of Hawker Hunter overload fuel tanks. Coupling up to the main aircraft system would have required extra pipework to be plumbed into the aircraft close to the number three tanks while extra electrical cabling and a pneumatic feed would also have been required. As well as improving the Vulcan's time over target time the installation of these tanks would also have reduced the number of Victor tankers needed to support each mission. Had such a system been adopted strikes against most of the Argentine mainland would also have been possible and it may have been as a result of forward planning against the possibility of the war requiring such attacks that these trials were undertaken. Once the RAF had been placed on full alert the decision was taken to stop the scrapping of the Vulcans. In the event the war ended quickly enough thus XL389 and the others on the scrapline met their ultimate fate.

While the various modification programmes were being undertaken the crews were using some of the other Vulcans at Waddington to practise live bombing and AAR, the latter taking place at Marham between 14 and 17 April. Two further modifications were undertaken to the chosen aircraft, one was the capability to carry the Westinghouse AN/ALQ-101 ECM jamming pod while the other was cosmetic as the squadron and Waddington badges were painted over while a coat of dark sea grey was applied to the underneath of each aircraft, contrasting somewhat with the shabby upper surface finish.

Modified, painted and trained the bombers and their crews prepared to depart from Waddington for the South Atlantic. On 29 April 1982 the first two Vulcans, XM598 and XM607, captained by Sqdn Ldr RJ Reeve and Flt Lt WFM Withers respectively lifted off from the tarmac and headed south. A third aircraft, XM597, also took off as an airborne spare, however it was not required and returned to base. After two Victor tanker refuels en route both aircraft landed safely later that day. After their arrival Sqdn Ldr AC Montgomery became the Vulcan bomber detachment commander. After the usual gamut of refuelling and maintenance both aircraft were prepared for a bombing raid against the Falkland Islands. During Black Buck 1 the first aircraft to depart was XM598 with Sqdn Ldr Reeve and crew aboard which departed Wideawake at around midnight local time,

Trundling towards the waiting crew chief is XM607 after its epic bombing mission down south. Of note is the ALQ-101 ECM pod under the starboard wing. Behind the Vulcan are a pair of Sea Harriers waiting for a lift south and a pair of Royal Navy Wessex vital for the movement of stores and equipment between ships before they too headed south. *(Mel James)*

With landing lamps fully down and the anti-collision lights flashing XM607 is being watched by the senior RAF commander on Ascension Group Captain Price. *(Mel James)*

followed by XM607 with Flt Lt Withers and crew aboard, which was intended to return once XM598 had successfully undertaken its first refuel. Supporting the mission were eleven Victor tankers that had taken off earlier and carried out a refuel relay to place a tanker at the final refuel point for the Vulcan. Once airborne XM598 began to experience pressurisation problems caused by a leak through the Captain's direct vision window, which had appeared to shut properly prior to take-off. As time was of the essence it was decided that XM598 should return to Wideawake while XM607 would undertake the mission. Aboard XM607 were the Withers crew plus Flt Lt RJ Russell, an AAR instructor seconded from Marham. A drop down to a lower level was undertaken some 300 miles short of the target, although a climb to 10,000 feet followed. While two miles from the target, Port Stanley airfield, the bomb doors were opened and the automatic bomb release system was activated. From the initial release point bomb after bomb departed the three carriers placing a diagonal slash of explosions across the airfield. Using this method ensured that at least one bomb would hit the runway while the others would cause collateral damage. It was also intended to show the Argentine occupiers that strikes against the islands long before the naval task force appeared were not only possible but would be prosecuted as often as needed. This attack also signalled that no more attempts at a diplomatic resolution were possible until Argentina withdrew. Over Stanley the Vulcan was 'painted' by one of the Argentine Sky Guard/ Fledermaus radar systems, however a quick burst from the ECM soon jammed it. Having released all twenty-one bombs successfully the code signal for success, 'Superfuse', was transmitted. Had things gone otherwise the codeword would have been 'Rhomboid'. Mission completed, the bomber turned north, completed a relay of refuels and landed at Wideawake complete with a surrounding stream of Victor tankers, the captain having been asked not to perform a victory roll. After taxying into the pan, followed by Victor XH672, which had stayed with the bomber for the greater majority of the mission, the Withers crew was greeted by a large welcoming party.

Preparation for Black Buck 2 would begin on Sunday 2 May when a full load of bombs was delivered by Hercules. The bombs were left to the front of the C-130 pan while their fuses were transported to the bomb dump, however this was a slow bumpy trip that lasted 1¾ hours. As the next raid was slated for the following day the decision was taken to arm the bombs close by the aircraft as a trip to the bomb dump and back would have delayed the mission significantly. Unfortunately, the fuzing data was not available and attempts to contact those in the know failed as much of the RAF had gone home for the weekend. Eventually, the signal specifying the fuzing details was eventually discovered and the arming of the bombs was started. Getting the bombs to the correct trolley ready for fitting to the carrier required the hiring of a crane owned by Pan Am. Eventually, just as dawn was breaking, the last bomb carrier was powered up onto its hangars just in time for a signal to arrive, which required that the whole lot be offloaded as the mission's fuzing details had been changed. Fortunately, a strong argument put forward by the engineering boss convinced the hierarchy that changing the fuses on the aircraft was possible as long as all relevant safety measures were covered. By midday on Monday 3 May both XM598 and XM607 were declared serviceable and would be moved to their combat ready positions at 22.40 hours local time. Engine start was fifty minutes later with both aircraft taxying out at quarter to midnight being allocated take-off slots three and five respectively. After take-off XM598 would follow XM607 up to the first airborne refuel point returning to Wideawake some 3½ hours later once XM607 had refuelled successfully. The crew aboard XM607 was the Reeve crew and Flt Lt PA Standing was the refuelling instructor. Black Buck 2 followed a similar pattern to that of the earlier sortie, although this time the bomb release height was 16,000 feet. Bomb release was undertaken on 4 May, although in this case the bombs completely missed the runway. Even so, the psychological effect was undeniable. Strike intelligence revealed that the bomb run along the runway had resulted in severe damage to the control tower and the adjacent hard standing while the petrol, oil and lubricants was destroyed. XM607 would return safely to Wideawake.

On 7 May both Vulcans were returned to Waddington for maintenance purposes. While in Britain XM597 and XM612 were fitted with Martel carriage points that allowed XM597 to undertake the further firing of a Martel missile over Cardigan Bay on 6 May. On 15 May XM607 was flown back to Wideawake to undergo preparation for Black Buck 3 joining XM612, which had flown in the previous day. This mission was later cancelled, by which time the port pylons had been removed as the crews had thought that this pylon was causing some increase in drag. XM607 returned to Waddington on 20 May with XM612 flying north three days later. While waiting for the next series of missions thoughts turned to the SEAD requirements as it was recognized that the Vulcans would not have an escort for missile and radar suppression. While the Martel system had been cleared for use on the Vulcan it was felt that this missile was far better employed on the Nimrod thus the offer of the AGM-45 Shrike was accepted. After flight trials with both two and four Shrikes the Vulcan was cleared for its operational use and some very hasty maintenance schedules were concocted before two bombers, XM598, the primary aircraft, and XM597, the secondary aircraft, departed from Waddington on 26 and 27 May respectively.

A hot mission debrief for Vulcan Captain Flt Lt Martin Withers by Group Captain Price, centre, and AVM Chesworth. After such a gruelling flight I bet the beer was most welcome! *(Mel James)*

Black Buck 4 was intended to be the first SEAD mission to depart from Ascension Island at midnight of 28 May. The chosen aircraft, XM597, was crewed by Sqdn Ldr CN McDougall and crew. After five hours airborne the bomber had to return to base as the centre Hose Drogue Unit on the lead Victor tanker had failed to operate correctly. The mission was rescheduled for 30 May with the same aircraft and crew allocated. The target was the Westinghouse AN/TPS-43F surveillance radar located at Port Stanley. This time round the refuels proceeded without incident, the Vulcan dropping down to 300 feet some 200 miles from the target, an altitude it remained at until it climbed up to 16,000 feet twenty miles from the target to start its run in. During the climb the Vulcan was painted by the target radar as the ARI 18228 indicated. It then appeared that the Argentine radar crew had switched the system off when, in fact, they had just reduced the output strength apparently in an attempt to draw the bomber towards the anti-aircraft guns defending the area. Orbiting slightly clear of the target the Vulcan remained in the vicinity of the target until it was switched on again at which point both missiles were launched; the first exploded close by the antenna causing some shrapnel damage while the second impacted quite a distance away. With the mission supposedly accomplished XM597 turned away and headed for home. Later it was learned that the radar was back on line twenty-four hours later while a sandbag revetment was constructed around the radar antenna. Black Buck 6 required the use of the same crew and aircraft and would begin on 2 June, only this time the bomber was carrying four Shrikes instead of the two carried on earlier missions. The target was the same as before

With the front bomb beam and its load of 1,000 bombs already loaded the 'plumbers' better known as armourers prepare to uplift the bomb beam with its load into the number two position. The beams were lifted using the hydraulic jacks inserted through the beam ends into the hangers. *(Mel James)*

and the Vulcan followed the same flight profile, undertaking its final run in during the early hours of 3 June.

As before the crew manning the AN/TPS-43F switched it off, and again the bomber crew orbited the target area before deciding that a dummy approach to Stanley airport might excite some interest. The run-in was effective as the bomber's Radar Warning Receiver (RWR) picked up the Stanley based Skyguard guidance radar, which was acting as the control unit for the anti-aircraft guns

A time honoured tradition even though the recipient will, hopefully, never read the messages. While there has been much debate concerning the effectiveness of the bombing missions it showed the Argentinians that Buenos Aires was well within range. *(Mel James)*

located around Port Stanley. Two Shrikes were launched at the radar and struck home successfully, after which the Vulcan stayed in the area in the hope of the primary target coming on line again. Eventually the aircraft's fuel state was reaching its safe minima thus the captain decided that a departure was required. En route north a Nimrod MR2 orbiting in the vicinity of the nearest tanker guided the Vulcan into its first refuelling nearly half way home to Wideawake.

Soon after making contact movement of the drogue snapped the tip of the bomber's refuelling probe. Fortunately, the non-return valves in the system ensured that no fuel flowed out of the ruptured pipeline. Even so the aircraft was obviously not going to reach Wideawake thus plans were made for a diversion airfield, Rio de Janeiro in Brazil. As the refuel had been undertaken at 20,000 feet the pilots calculated that staying at that altitude would consume so much fuel that the South American coast was out of range. The answer was to climb to 40,000 feet, which was the Vulcan's economical cruising altitude. Once sat at this height both Shrikes were fired as entering Brazilian airspace armed could cause a diplomatic incident. Just to compound the crew's misery only one missile fired correctly, the other remaining affixed to its mount. Slowing the aircraft down to entrance door opening speed the cabin was depressurized and the door was opened and a holdall containing the aircraft and crew's confidential documents was jettisoned. Having dumped the holdall problems were encountered in shutting the door, although after some attempts it finally closed and the cabin was repressurized.

Inbound into Brazilian airspace the crew contacted the Air Traffic Control centre at Rio de Janeiro requesting landing permission. As the purpose of the aircraft could not be revealed while diplomatic efforts to clear the aircraft were being made the crew were understandably evasive. In response the Brazilian Air Force launched a flight of Northrop F-5 Freedom Fighters to intercept the Vulcan and act as escort. After a small amount of the usual diplomatic wrangling permission was granted for the bomber to land at Galeao Airport near to Rio. Approaching the coast the aircraft descended to 20,000 feet as fuel margins were becoming tight and the captain made it clear that descending further before committing to a landing was not an option. Sighting the runway some six miles out a rapid spiralling text book descent was made with the airbrakes at high drag and the throttles returned to idle. At the one and a half miles out point the Vulcan was at an altitude of 800 feet but was travelling twice as fast as threshold speed. Raising the nose slowed the bomber down and it eventually lowered its undercarriage making a safe landing immediately afterwards. Taxying clear of the runway to a discreet parking place on the airfield the engines were shut down with no more than 2,000lb of usable fuel left in the tanks. Leaving the aircraft the crew made the Shrike missile safe before it was impounded along with the aircraft. Having gone through the official diplomatic motions the crew were treated well by their hosts who then offered them the chance to return home, however they declined, preferring to stay with their aircraft until it was released minus its missile on 10 June. On flying to Wideawake XM597 had its flight refuelling probe replaced before it returned home to Waddington on 13 June.

On 11 June 1982 XM607 departed Ascension Island to undertake Black Buck 7. This was a conventional bombing run manned by the Withers crew. The bombing run over the airfield was accomplished without incident, the aircraft returning to Wideawake safely. This would be the final mission for the Vulcan fleet as XM607 and XM598 returned to Waddington on 14 June. On that same date the Argentine forces occupying

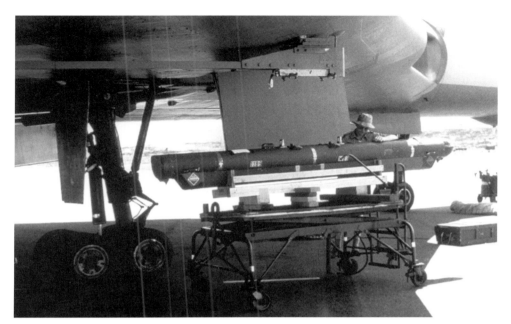

Can do – will do was the motto of the RAF at one time as exemplified by this locally made cradle for an ALQ-101 ECM pod being prepared for loading. *(Mel James)*

the Falklands surrendered having been outfought from the time the operations had begun.

With all the bombers returned to Waddington the continued rundown of the remaining Vulcan squadrons continued thus No. 101 Squadron disbanded on 4 August 1982 being followed by No. 44 Squadron on 21 December. The end for No. 50 Squadron was delayed as one glaring deficiency had become obvious during Operation *Corporate*: the RAF lacked enough tanking aircraft. During the Falklands bombing operations had required at least eleven Victors per sortie, however the Vulcan was not the only aircraft requiring their services as Nimrods and C–130 Hercules heading about their nefarious tasks also needed refuelling. All this extra work had put a great strain on the Victor fleet and consumed a lot of their remaining fatigue life. Steps had already been taken to augment the Victor fleet with the acquisition of the ex-British Airways Vickers VC 10 fleet for tanker conversion. All of this was in the future as the RAF cast about for a means of augmenting the existing tankers. Also driving this requirement was the fear that the fighting against Argentina might continue longer than it eventually did which in turn would put a greater strain on the Victors.

Yet again only one aircraft type was available and suitable for conversion – the Vulcan. Six aircraft were selected for conversion (XH558, XH560, XH561, XJ825, XL445 and XM571). The programme was known as Modification 2600 and required the reinstatement of the bomb bay centre position fuel tank connectors and the installation of six HDUs, hose drogue units, borrowed in the short term from the VC 10 conversion programme. The modification programme required that all of the ECM cans be removed as well as the VCCP pack and its exchange matrix cooler mounted on the

Without the Victor K2 tankers missions such as Black Buck could not have been launched. Much careful planning was undertaken to ensure that enough aircraft were available, not only to get the bomber to its target but to bring all the tankers home. *(BBA Collection)*

outside of the rear fuselage. The bomb bay fuel tanks chosen to fill the three positions were of the cylindrical type being drawn from the remaining stocks of 'A' and 'E' types. The modifications to the rear fuselage required that new mounting and structural support beams were fitted into the space once occupied by the ECM while the Flight Refuelling Mk 17 B HDU would be mounted onto this structure. Surrounding the section of HDU exposed to the airflow was a wooden fairing also known as the dog box. On the rear face of this assembly was the usual array of signalling and night illumination lights required for night-time refuelling. Forward of the HDU fairing was a new door that gave access to the fuel pipes and other parts of the system. Connecting the three bomb bay fuel tanks to the HDU was a completely new set of pipework that passed through the rear bulkhead using the cut-out once occupied by the Blue Steel missile. Mod 2600 required the Vulcan's fuel system to have extra pipe runs added. Not only were the bomb bay fuel tanks interconnected, but non-return valves were fitted into the bomb bay fuel galleries to ensure that fuel allocated for dispensing was not used by the tanker. As the bomb bay tanks contained 24,000lb of fuel that couldn't be burnt off in an emergency the decision was taken to install a fuel dump pipe that was powered by the tank pumps that could vent fuel at 360 gallons per minute. Control of the fuel tank pumps was through panel 5P, the retractable fuel control console, the switches covering each of the tanks separately while a further switch controlled the fuel jettison system. Also mounted in this panel were the magnetic doll's eye indicators that showed the status of the systems components. Changes were also undertaken to the nav plotter's panel to which a lighting control panel was added to the side of which was mounted an HDU monitoring panel. Unlike other tanker aircraft the Vulcan did not receive any form of camera equipment as the periscope at the AEO's position was deemed adequate enough to inspect the hose, drogue and keep an eye on any approaching aircraft. Completing the modification was an amendment to the undersurface paint scheme, which required that the centre section be painted white while dayglo striping outlined in black was applied to help guide the refuelling aircraft up to the drogue.

Everything is nice and quiet on Ascension as XM598 and XM607 bask in the sunshine. As the sun begins to fade the scene will resemble organized chaos as Victor tankers are prepared for their vital part in the Black Buck missions while around the Vulcans the pre-flights will be undertaken and the weapons loaded for that night's sorties. *(Mel James)*

Planning for Mod 2600 was first discussed at the British Aerospace Manchester Division offices on 30 April 1982 with the details being thrashed out and confirmed over the weekend of 1–2 May. The first aircraft slated for conversion, XH561, arrived at Woodford for conversion on 4 May being rolled out for its first flight on 18 June. After the usual selection of flight trials to confirm handling, centre of gravity and behaviour the Vulcan was cleared for service entry. Not all was straight forward as the HDU hose jammed in the out position, a not uncommon fault with this conversion. Even so, the redesignated Vulcan, now a K2, was released for operational service with No. 50 Squadron on 23 June. Such was the intensity of this programme that much of the data required to operate the Vulcan K2 was being completed as the aircraft arrived overhead Waddington.

The second conversion, XJ825, was flown into Woodford on 11 May undertaking its post conversion flight on 29 June and returning to Waddington on 1 July. The third conversion was XH560, which flew into Woodford on 15 June, undertaking its post conversion flight on 23 August. Five days later XH561 joined No. 50 Squadron. The fourth airframe, XM571, arrived at Woodford on 11 May for tanker conversion first flying as a K2 on 13 July. Instead of returning to Waddington the tanker was sent to Boscombe Down two days later to undertake clearance flying and the compilation of the modified pilots notes. XL445 underwent the conversion process from 25 May to 22 July, returning to Waddington that same day. The final airframe, XH558, landed at Woodford on 30 June being released for its first post-conversion flight on 3 September, although its delivery to Waddington was delayed until 12 October as it was retained for flight trials. Thirteen days later the aircraft was loaned to A&AEE at Boscombe Down for further flight trials before returning to No. 50 Squadron on 30 November.

Alongside the six tanker conversions No. 50 Squadron operated at least three standard Vulcan B2s, including XL426 for continuation training and other aircrew qualification tasks. During this final fling of the Vulcan the tankers were used purely in

Post *Corporate* the Vulcans were popular visitors at airshows in 1982. Here XM597 performs a flyby for the crowd. *(BBA Collection)*

the northern hemisphere in support of the UK Air Defence organization thus Phantoms were frequent customers as were Jaguars and Buccaneers, the latter involving a trail to Goose Bay in Canada. Tasking for the Vulcan tankers came from the Tanker Force Tasking Cell via the Tanker Force Cell housed in the Waddington Operations Centre. Handling of the tanker was very similar to that of the bomber, although the deepened rear fuselage meant that aerodynamic braking was no longer available to slow the aircraft down thus the pilots had to be very accurate in calculating the aircraft threshold speed, although should the touchdown speed have been slightly higher the tail braking chute was still available.

The use of the Vulcan as a tanker was always seen as a stopgap measure until the VC 10 conversions were made available thus when each of the Vickers machines was ready for its HDU a Vulcan tanker was withdrawn. The first to go was XJ825, which lost its

Back home at Waddington XM607 is towed out to the static line for an airshow. Of note are the mission markings on the nose. *(BBA Collection)*

HDU on 4 May 1983. Over the following eleven months the remainder of the aircraft would lose their HDUs, which would result in No. 50 Squadron being formally disbanded on 31 March 1984. The Vulcan tankers were formally handed over to the Waddington Station Flight who would retain the aircraft until they were disposed of. XH560 would eventually fly to Marham for spares recovery, XH561 departed to Catterick for use as a firemen's plaything, XJ825 remained at Waddington for battle damage repair training, and XL445 was flown to Lyneham for crash rescue training while XM571 flew out to Gibraltar for display and preservation.

This was not the end of the Vulcan flying in RAF colours and under RAF control as a further shorter chapter unfolded. While the Vulcan had officially finished with the RAF two aircraft were retained for flying preservation purposes, these being XH558 and XL426. The operator was the Vulcan Demonstration Team whose parent unit was No. 55 Squadron, a Victor tanker unit, at Marham. Unfortunately, XL426 was running out of hours the intention being to replace it with XH560, which was still extant. XH558 at Marham was undergoing spares recovery prior to disposal when close inspection of the aircraft's paperwork revealed that it had a reasonable amount of flying hours left before its next major servicing was due. As XH560 had only 160 hours left in comparison to the 600 hours available to XH558 it was decided to refit the latter to a basically safe state for flying. On 30 November 1984 XH558 was flown to Waddington to be converted to standard bomber configuration. As the aircraft still retained much of the structure associated with the tanker role a Service Embodied Modification had to be proposed to both Strike Command and British Aerospace at Woodford to convert it back to resemble a bomber. Once approved, XH558 would lose its HDU housing, the extra fuel system pipework and extra cable looms. In its place a set of ECM bay doors was fitted, however the whole of the rear fuselage was basically an empty shell as no ECM or Red Steer radar was fitted. This altered the aircraft's centre of gravity therefore to compensate a drum fuel tank containing 8,000lb of fuel was fitted in the rear position. The only way to differentiate between a 'proper' bomber and XH558 is by the lack of the VCCP cooling intake mounted on the rear fuselage. Two months and 1,200 hours later once the conversion work had been completed the aircraft underwent a minor servicing before being flown to Kinloss where much of the original paint work was sanded away after which a full coat of wraparound camouflage was applied. This differed from the norm in that it was high gloss to protect it from the worse of the British weather. In November 1985 returned to Waddington where it was placed in one of the hangars where it hibernated during the winter months. As for XL426, it was put up for sale being purchased by a preservation group based at Southend.

XH558 made its public debut in 1986 with Sqdn Ldr David Thomas and Flt Lt Paul Millikin as the two pilots. While thrilling the crowds at various airshows the MoD constantly reviewed the costs of running the aircraft as it was being paid for out of the No. 55 Squadron budget. The Vulcan Display Flight, as the organization was named, continued to show off the Vulcan. The final complete display season for XH558 would be 1992 as flying hours prior to its next major servicing were being consumed rapidly. After a flurry of speculation concerning a possible sale to a private organization the MoD announced in November 1992 that there were no plans at the time to sell XH558 and that the crew should remain current on the aircraft. However, this was a false hope as the MoD decided that retaining the Vulcan was not a viable proposition even though many concrete sponsorship proposals had been put forward to support the aircraft for further

Although the first VC 10 tanker conversion had flown during *Corporate*, delays with the programme resulted in six Vulcans being converted to K2 tankers. Although it still sports No. 101 Squadron markings the aircraft would be operated by No. 50 Squadron based at Waddington. *(NEAPG Collection)*

flying. Further to this the MoD announced that at the end of 1993 the remaining Victors would come to the end of their service and that the available experienced ground engineers would no longer be available to service the aircraft. The result was that in early 1993 the MoD announced that XH558 was again up for sale. At least the Ministry had the good grace to allow the aircrew to undertake continuation flying prior to the bomber being delivered to its new owners.

What it looks like heading towards a Vulcan tanker of No. 50 Squadron. Note the large areas of white under the Vulcan's wings and fuselage. *(NEAPG Collection)*

While the Vulcan would handle the long-range bombing role it would be the Sea Harrier that would cover the close air support task. It was obvious that the limited number of naval aircraft could do with reinforcements. To that end No. 1 (F) Squadron was warned to prepare for Operation *Corporate*. Their initial plan was to send the aircraft south aboard the *Atlantic Conveyer*, although this would be changed days later when it was decided to fly the aircraft south to Ascension Island instead using tanker support. The delay in departure allowed further training for the pilots while the ground crew prepared all the required spares and equipment for the deployment. Those Harriers selected for the trip south had their unit markings painted out while the aircraft codes were still carried in red. As it was intended that the Harriers would operate from HMS *Hermes* the aircraft were given training at Yeovilton on the ski jump between 14 and 23 April. Five aircraft were sent to Binbrook to undertake dissimilar air combat training with the Lightnings. A further detachment was sent to Metz to undertake further DACT against *Armée de l'Air* Mirages.

The ground engineers at Wittering were also doing their part modifying the Harriers for ship board life. Tie down rings were fitted to the outriggers while minor changes were made to the nozzle controls and steering nozzles. Extra drain holes were also drilled at the lowest points to enable any sea water to drain away. To enable the Harriers to operate safely within the fleet area the aircraft were fitted with I Band transponders mounted below the LRMTS fairing. Even the problem of setting up the INS was catered for as

As a precursor of things to come a Harrier GR3 prepares to touch down on HMS *Hermes* with its bombs still under the wings. *(BBA Collection)*

BAE and Ferranti developed the trolley-mounted Ferranti Inertial Rapid Alignment Equipment (FINRAE). This equipment could be plugged into the aircraft on start-up so that positional data could be fed directly into the INAS.

In order to improve the self defence capability of the Harrier it was decided to fit the aircraft with a modification kit that would allow the aircraft to carry an AIM-9G Sidewinder on the outer wing pylons as well as BL-775 Cluster Bombs, Pave Way laser-guided bombs, 1,000lb iron bombs or the Fleet Air Arm 2-inch rocket pods as the RAF SNEB pods were unsuited for shipboard use as they were not insulated from the potentially high electro-magnetic forces aboard ship. Fitting of the missile kit and its missiles would take two hours at most. The modification kit was cleared by the MoD on 22 April with the first fit taking place a few days later, the aircraft then departing to A&AEE Boscombe Down for a quick clearance programme. These were cleared quickly therefore five Harriers were despatched to Valley for live firing trials over Cardigan Bay at the beginning of May. BAE would eventually manufacture a total of eighteen missile modification kits for use in the South Atlantic.

Other defensive systems were developed and deployed for the Harrier GR3s before they deployed south. One of these systems was codenamed 'Blue Eric'; it was an ECM radar jammer that was mounted in the front of an Aden gun pod. It took no more than two weeks to complete these modifications the kits being ready by 21 May. Also fitted to the Harriers was the ALE-40 cartridge dispenser, which fired infra-red decoy flares when needed and was mounted aft of the airbrake on the fuselage. Unfortunately, this system had not been cleared in time to be fitted to the first half dozen aircraft before they deployed south. These aircraft had to make do with bundles of chaff mounted inside the airbrake and to the pylon bomb-release mechanisms.

The move south began on 1 May when a pair of C-130 Hercules from the Lyneham Transport Wing departed from Wittering with forty ground personnel aboard. Their route to Ascension Island was via Gibraltar and Dakar, the transports arriving in time for the detachment base to be set-up for receiving the inbound Harriers. Initially five Harriers were positioned at St Mawgan of which three would leave on 2 May with a Victor K2 for refuelling and to act as a mother hen for the 4,600 miles flight. Covering the entire flight was a Nimrod MR1 operating from Freetown, Sierra Leone, its task being to provide SAR cover. To increase the total fuel on each aircraft they were fitted with 330-gallon external tanks on the inboard pylons while the outboard pylons carried 100-gallon tanks, although these were empty as they were intended for use in combat. All three aircraft would make it to Ascension safely therefore the next two would depart from St Mawgan on early 3 May with a third following later that same day. Four more departed from St Mawgan the following day.

Of those aircraft that had reached Ascension Island six were flown onto the *Atlantic Conveyer* where they landed on a specially built pad before rolling into a space between two container walls. As the RAF Harriers were not designed for seaborne use further protective measures were required, a protective spray was applied to the entire airframe before each airframe was covered with plastic covers. The remaining three Harriers were assigned for air defence duties at Wideawake being armed with Sidewinders while the pilots were issued with night vision goggles to compensate for the lack of radar. This regime continued until 24 May when F-4 Phantoms from No. 29 Squadron arrived to take over the duty.

As the *Atlantic Conveyer* proceeded south four of the Harrier GR3s were flown off to join HMS *Hermes* while the final two staged through HMS *Invincible* for refuelling before proceeding to *Hermes*, all six being aboard by 20 May. Back at Wideawake the number of Harriers had increased to nine by 30 May, four of these aircraft using Victor tanker support would deploy to Hermes while four others were loaded aboard the *Contender Bezant* for onward transport. The final machine was returned to Britain as it was suffering from incurable fuel leaks.

First GR3 missions began from *Hermes* on 18 May with the first interception sorties being flown the following day the target being an Argentine Air Force Boeing 707. This would be the only air defence mission flown by the GR3s as the missiles and their rails were removed to be replaced with weapons carriers for ground attack duties. The air defence mission was handed over in total to the carrier's Sea Harriers. On 20 May the first ground attack mission was mounted against a fuel dump located at Fox Bay East on West Falkland using CBUs. Early the next day two aircraft attacked targets notified by the SAS to the north of Mount Kent. The targets were FAA helicopters. A Chinook was reported as destroyed, and a Puma badly damaged while a UH-1H Huey suffered minor damage. The afternoon mission was reduced to a single aircraft piloted by Flt Lt Glover whose aircraft was shot down over Port Howard on West Falkland after being hit by a Blowpipe Surface-to-Air Missile (SAM). Although the ejection seat was operated outside of its parameters the pilot survived, being picked up by some Argentine soldiers. Although injured Flt Lt Glover was well looked after and would later be despatched to Argentina before being released on 8 July.

On the late evening of 22 May four Harriers were launched from *Hermes* armed with CBUs, their intended targets being the POL dumps and Pucaras at Goose Green. The aircraft were subject to intensive anti-aircraft fire during this attack, although all escaped unscathed. The following days missions concentrated upon the various small airstrips dotted about the island the most important being on Pebble Island. Stanley Airport would be the focus of the attacks on 24 May; four Harrier GR3s were charged with destroying the runway and facilities while defence suppression was supplied by a pair of Sea Harriers. The airfield was the focus of attacks during the following day, although little success was reported. Unfortunately, 25 May was the day that the *Atlantic Conveyer* was sunk by an Exocet missile; the vessel was conveying bombs, spares plus much-needed Chinooks.

On 27 May seven Harriers were launched from *Hermes* in support of ground troops advancing on Goose Green and Stanley during which the Harrier piloted by Sqdn Leader Iveson was hit by anti-aircraft fire. The hit caused a systems fire also causing the controls to lock. Although the engine continued to run the pilot was forced to eject as the fire intensified. After successfully clearing his stricken aircraft Sqdn Ldr Iveson landed behind Argentine positions while the Harrier crashed in flames near Goose Green. After evading the occupying forces for three days Iveson was collected by a Royal Marines Gazelle helicopter and returned safely to HMS *Hermes*. The following day three of the Harriers were assigned to support British troops close by Goose Green as they were being delayed by an Argentine anti-aircraft gun that was being used effectively as an artillery piece. After an attack using CBUs and rockets the gun was destroyed thus clearing the way forward.

It would be Port Stanley that would bear the brunt of the attacks on 29 May. Although bad weather hampered most of the attacks a rocket attack was carried out against

Argentine positions near Mount Kent. The following day was a bad one for the *Hermes*-based Harriers. Four aircraft would depart the carrier in the early afternoon for further attacks against enemy positions in the Port Stanley area. During one of the attacks the aircraft piloted by Sqdn Ldr Pook was hit by small arms fire although at first there seemed to be no effect on the Harrier's performance. On the way back to *Hermes* Pook's wingman reported that his aircraft was losing fuel at an alarming rate. Trying desperately to return to the carrier Pook jettisoned all remaining weaponry and a climb to height was made. Even these measures failed to increase the range sufficiently thus Pook was left with no other option but to eject. His time in the water was short however as the pilots had called ahead for a rescue helicopter that lifted him out of the sea a few minutes later.

The last day of May would see the available Harrier force reduced to one as two of the available three aircraft had suffered battle damage during that day's activities. So that the single Harrier could still be used it was teamed up with Sea Harriers from No. 800 NAS to undertake attacks in the area around Mount Usborne. The first day of June would see the Harrier strength aboard *Hermes* increased by two as replacements were tanked to the ship by Victor tankers late aboard the carrier in the early evening. To increase the Harrier Force's capability a Forward Operating Base (FOB) was commissioned at Post San Carlos, although it was smaller than originally intended as much of the material had been lost aboard the *Atlantic Conveyer*. Even so an 850 feet runway was made available plus parking for four aircraft and a vertical take-off pad. Commissioned on 2 June the FOB had refuel facilities that were held in floating bags offshore, the fuel being pumped ashore as required. During the further prosecution of the war both the Harriers and Sea Harriers made use of the FOB, although they normally returned to *Hermes* every evening.

The FOB was put out of commission on 8 June when the Harrier piloted by Wing Cdr Squire suffered a partial engine failure. Attempting to land alongside the FOB strip the stricken Harrier slid across the runway closing the strip temporarily. The damaged Harrier, XZ989, was beyond local resources to repair thus it was used as a source of spares, eventually being scrapped upon return to Britain. To improve the strength of the Harrier force two more aircraft were tanked to *Hermes*, arriving on 8 June. The extras were much needed as one of the original aircraft was badly damaged by small arms fire leaving the pilot no option but to blow the undercarriage down on arrival at the carrier. Over the next couple of days the Harriers continued to support the forces advancing on Stanley, although some damage was caused by defending fire all of the aircraft returned to base safely. On 12 June attacks were carried out against Argentine positions on Sapper Hill, although one aircraft did return to *Hermes* with minor damage from enemy ground fire. While much of the Harrier force was engaged in attacking the remaining Argentine position one Harrier was undergoing modifications that would allow it to carry Shrike missiles, although the opportunity to exercise this option never arose.

It would be 13 June before a successful laser-guided bomb attack was carried out, the target being an enemy position on Tumbledown, while another was carried out at Moody Brook. Both attacks were successful. The final mission was launched from *Hermes* on 14 June. The target was Sapper Hill and the aircraft were carrying LGBs and rocket pods. When the Harriers arrived over the target the forward air controller told the aircraft to hold off as white flags had been seen flying over Port Stanley. After the surrender had been confirmed the aircraft returned to *Hermes* complete with weaponry. This concluded the part of No. 1 Squadron in Operation *Corporate* during which 150 sorties had been flown, either from the *Hermes* or *San Carlos* between 18 May and 14 June. At the conclusion of hostilities the aircraft were reconfigured for the air defence role being equipped with Sidewinder missiles instead of bombs. As for the pilots, they returned home to Britain for a well earned rest.

After hostilities the Harriers formed HarDet (Harrier Detachment) at RAF Stanley as the airport had been renamed, although the area had required much reworking to make it safe for operations. Not only were extra portable buildings built but the runway and a new apron were assembled using aluminium planking sections. HarDet would become No. 1453 Flight on 20 August 1983 utilizing crews drawn from all the operational squadrons and the OCU. The flight remained operational until replaced by a flight of F-4 Phantoms in May 1985 while the opening of basic facilities at Mount Pleasant improved the air bridge capabilities for those based on the islands.

Chapter 7

Operation *Corporate* – They Also Served

W hile the Harrier and the Vulcan were capturing the headlines for their ground attack prowess and the Black Buck raids respectively quite a few other types played a part in providing support to both types. Of these the most important were the Victor K2 tankers of Nos 55 and 57 Squadrons from Marham. Twenty-three of the original twenty-four aircraft were still available for use, which were the only strategic tankers available for front-line usage. Further tankers were undergoing conversion at the British Aerospace facility at Filton these being nine ex-British Airways VC 10s parked up at Abingdon. Although the inventory of Victors was shown as twenty-three it should be noted that two were undergoing major servicing at St Athan. These were finished as quickly as possible while the next two would go through using twenty-four-hour working to turn them out as early as possible. Strangely enough the first task for the Victors was not to be tanking, but Maritime Radar Reconnaissance. Training for this role plus low-level photo reconnaissance began soon after the invasion of the Falkland Islands. Three crews were involved utilizing XL192 as the initial aircraft, although XL163, XL164 and

When the VC 10 tankers finally became available they would make a few trips to the Falklands. Here ZA149 'H' of No. 101 Squadron taxies into Mount Pleasant in wintry conditions. Accompanied by three others the tankers were undertaking Operation *Lampuca*, the mass swap over of the F-4 Phantoms; the new birds had already arrived while those departing would leave the next day in very murky conditions. *(BBA Collection)*

XL189 were flown later. To fit the aircraft for their new role F95 cameras were installed in the nose bomb aimer's position many of which had been blanked off as no longer required. The Victors were also fitted initially with Carousel inertial navigation platforms for long-range navigation over water, although this was later replaced by an Omega system in some aircraft.

Prior to taking part in Operation *Corporate* the Victor fleet was utilized to tank eight Harrier GR3s across the Atlantic to take part in a Maple Flag exercise from the Canadian base at Cold Lake. Fortunately, all three Victors had returned to Marham on 15 April becoming available for *Corporate* duties. While the Victors were deployed to Ascension their duties were assumed by KC-135 tankers fitted with drogue adapters on the flying boom. By 18 April the first personnel had arrived at Wideawake to prepare for the arrival of the Victor detachment, the first five aircraft arriving later that day with four more arriving the following day. To ensure that enough fuel was available to reach Ascension or a diversion field each aircraft was refuelled by another Victor within British airspace. The Victors undertook their first missions the following day when XL192 plus four supporting tankers departed for a reconnaissance mission over South Georgia undertaking the radar reconnaissance at an altitude of 18,000 feet. Once XL192 was on its way home another four Victor tankers were sent to recover the aircraft, the Victor landing after covering more than 7,000 miles. Further reconnaissance missions were undertaken over 22–23 April using XL163 while XL189 undertook a similar mission during 24–25 April. These missions provided the small task force with the information required to retake South Georgia. Led by HMS *Antrim* Operation *Paraquat* was completed by 26 April.

The Victors at Marham were also fully occupied in supporting *Corporate*. Not only were they involved in training Vulcan crews in air-to-air techniques, a similar service was provided for the Sea Harriers and the first Nimrod fitted with an in-flight refuelling probe recovered from redundant Vulcans. Following on from the Nimrod the Victors were also employed in testing the newly probed Hercules C1P, both being cleared by early May. Even as these trials and support flight were being undertaken further tankers were being prepared for deployment to Ascension, which was undertaken between 23 April and 30 April. This brought the total strength of Victors at Wideawake to fourteen. This extra strength was brought into play when four aircraft were deployed to tank Vulcans XM598 and XM607 down to Ascension this being followed by a similar mission to refuel and escort six Sea Harriers of No. 809 NAS to Ascension.

The increased complement of tankers was vital to the first Black Buck mission that was undertaken from 30 April to 1 May. This required the use of fifteen aircraft and involved eighteen refuels. Both available Vulcans were prepared for the attack while eleven Victors were despatched to provide a refuel relay down to the Falkland Islands. Soon after take-off XM598 had to return to Ascension having developed a technical fault thus only XM607 and three Victors were to cover the final leg. The number of available Victors would drop to two when XL512 developed a fuel leak just after refuelling for the return journey. Fortunately, stand-by tankers had been prepared for just such an eventuality and XL512 was brought home safely. The two remaining aircraft, XH669 and XL189, continued south with XM607 with the latter refuelling the bomber, after which the tanker dispensed fuel to XH669. Unfortunately, the receiving Victor suffered a probe tip failure. As XL189 was intended to escort the Vulcan towards its target the damage to its probe meant that this was no longer possible, therefore all the fuel recently transferred was returned to XL189 while the other Victor headed back to Ascension. As the Vulcan could only use the centreline HDU a test prod was made to ensure that the probe tip from XH669 was not stuck in the drogue. Fortunately, the drogue was clear and the mission continued. The final Vulcan refuel was carried out some 3,000 miles from the Falklands after which the Victor began to trace its course for Ascension. Due to the re-ordering of the tankers XL189 was short of fuel and even with careful management it was estimated that there would be a shortfall of 400 miles.

Although a radio call to Ascension could have brought other Victors tankers to the rescue the aircraft's captain, Squadron Ldr Tuxford, decided to maintain radio silence until the callsign from XM607 signifying that the attack had been completed successfully. As soon as this had been transmitted the Victor transmitted its distress call resulting in Victors being despatched to deliver a much needed refuel. For his dedication to the task of getting XM607 to the Falklands Squadron Ldr Tuxford was awarded the Air Force Cross while the remainder of the crew all received the Queen's Commendation for Valuable Service in the Air.

A fast turn round for both the Victors and Vulcans followed so that Black Buck 2 could be mounted on 3 May. As before the entire complement of tankers were involved in either the outbound or return leg. Adding to the Victor fleet was XL160 that had arrived that same day being quickly turned round for that night's events. Once the mission was underway the two long-range tankers escorting the Vulcan were XL192 and XH669, the entire operation being undertaken without incident.

With extra reinforcements being moved south there was no respite for the Victors both at Marham and Ascension as nine Harrier GR3s of No. 1 Squadron required fuelling and escorting from Britain to Ascension. On 7 May the two Black Buck Vulcans returned to Waddington while two Victors returned to Marham. These returns were short-lived as the Vulcans would return later to resume further Black Buck missions against Argentine positions on the Falklands. The spare ramp space at Wideawake was quickly filled by Nimrod MR2P XV227, which arrived on 7 May. Two days later the Nimrod undertook its first long-range MRR mission prior to the start of Operation *Sutton*. Two other Nimrods arrived soon afterwards undertaking missions soon afterwards, although these were long-range missions one of which involved multiple refuels that required the entire Ascension-based Victor fleet. A further Nimrod mission was undertaken over 20–21 May that covered over 8,000 miles and required fourteen Victor sorties to be launched in support.

While the Nimrod missions were being undertaken the Victors were also engaged in providing support for the *Atlantic Conveyer*, which had departed Ascension on 7 May. Aboard the vessel was a mix of Harriers, Sea Harriers and helicopters with one of the Sea Harriers being maintained on a permanent QRA from the temporary pad fitted to the ship. Although the capabilities of the Victors were never needed missions were launched in support of the ship as it headed south, very much 'just in case'. The Vulcans also returned to Ascension, XM612 arriving on 13 May, while XM607 arrived the following day, both aircraft requiring Victor support. Both bombers had been deployed to undertake Black Buck 3, scheduled for 16 May, although this was later cancelled. Again the Victors were needed to support the Vulcans when they returned to Waddington on 20 and 23 May respectively. Adding to an already crammed flightline at Ascension was the arrival of the first probed C1P Hercules. The role for the Hercules initially was to undertake supply drops for ships operating within the Total Exclusion Zone. The first

The Nimrod MR2 undertook vital reconnaissance and anti-submarine missions during Operation *Corporate*. To that end an in-flight refuelling probe was fitted, although this required a ventral fin and finlets to be fitted to the aircraft to counter the effect of the probe. *(John Ryan Collection)*

supply drop mission was undertaken on 16 May, requiring three Victor tankers for both the outbound and return legs. This mission became a staple for the Victors not only during the conflict but for sometime afterwards.

Although the chances of the Argentine forces launching an air attack against Ascension were fairly slim it was felt that some form of air defence was needed especially as the Harriers initially previously employed had been deployed south with HMS *Hermes*. Their replacements were a trio of F-4 Phantoms from No. 29 Squadron normally based at Coningsby. As before, Victor tanker support was needed to get the fighters to the island. The first two arrived on 24 May with the third turning up on 26 May. No sooner had the Phantoms been settled in than the Victors were off, engaged in providing support for Vulcans XM597 and XM598, which arrived on 26–27 May. Two

Preparing to hook up are two Victor K2s. This tanking capability was essential in extending the range of the aircraft attacking Stanley airfield. *(John Ryan Collection)*

days later tanker support was needed for six Harriers of No. 1 Squadron that were deployed from the launch point at St Mawgan onwards to Ascension routeing via Dakar.

Another attempt was made on 28–29 May to undertake another anti-radar mission against positions around Stanley. Nominated Black Buck 4 the sortie had to be cancelled after the entire force had been airborne for several hours as the lead Victor had developed a fault with the centre-line HDU. Another Vulcan mission was launched on 30–31 May as Black Buck 5. This was more successful, requiring eighteen Victor sorties to be flown in support of the Vulcan with the longest taking over thirteen hours to complete.

The first day of June would see the Victors involved in providing support for a pair of Harriers bound for HMS *Hermes*, which required the use of eight Victors. A similar mission was undertaken six days later, the destination again being the Hermes. The next Black Buck mission, number 6, was undertaken by XM597 over 2–3 June, the target being various radar sites around Stanley using Shrike anti-radar missiles. Fourteen Victors were required to get the bomber to its target, although the return journey was not so easy as the tip of the Vulcan's probe broke off, requiring the bomber to make an emergency diversion to Rio de Janeiro. The final Vulcan mission, Black Buck 7, was undertaken by XM607 that had returned to the island on 10 June. The bomber and its supporting Victor cortege undertook the conventional bombing raid against Stanley Airport.

When the Argentine forces on the Falklands finally surrendered on 14 June there would be no slackening of the pace of Victor operations as both the Hercules and Nimrods still required support for their long-range operations, although this need dropped when the Nimrods departed on 18 August. This was followed by the opening of Stanley Airport as RAF Stanley, allowing much of the needed airpower to operate locally. The Hercules detachment still required tanker support as there was a constant airbridge running moving both personnel and stores to and from Ascension and the Falkland

The Nimrod was not the only type to remain at Ascension after hostilities ended. The Victor tankers still had a vital role to play in keeping the air bridge open. *(BBA Collection)*

The arrival of the Lockheed Tristar meant that trooping flights could be undertaken all the way to the Falklands with only a refuel stop at Ascension. Here C2 ZE704 sits outside the main hangar at Mount Pleasant. *(BBA Collection)*

Islands. Some of converted Hercules tankers helped to reduced the load on the Victor fleet, although Ascension would see a Victor detachment running until May 1985 when the runway and basic facilities became available at Mount Pleasant thus allowing the RAF Tristar fleet and the occasional British Airways 747 to operate down south without air refuelling.

Not long after the invasion No. 18 Maritime Group warned No. 42 Squadron at St Mawgan to prepare for deployment to Ascension. Initially two aircraft, three crews plus ground crew and spares were deployed on 5 April staging via Lajes and arriving at Ascension the following day. Strangely enough No. 42 Squadron was still operating the MR1 version while the Kinloss Wing had nearly completed re-equipping with the far more capable MR2. Operational flying began two days later, the mission covering surface reconnaissance and relaying orders to the Royal Nuclear submarines operating in front of the Operation *Corporate* fleet. Over the next few days both Nimrods undertook these missions, although by this time the need for a third crew had lessened thus its members were returned to St Mawgan. Both of the original Nimrods returned home after their last missions on 17 April being replaced by a pair of Nimrod MR2s from Kinloss. After returning to St Mawgan the aircraft of No. 42 Squadron had a further small part to play within Operation *Corporate* as they provided SAR cover for the Harriers en route to Ascension. To that end a detachment of aircraft were sent to Freetown in Sierra Leone to cover the southern part of the transit while St Mawgan were responsible for the northern section. This deployment lasted from 3 to 6 May. A further tranche of sorties were undertaken on 26, 29 and 30 May, although the southern operating base was Dakar in Senegal. As the Kinloss wing involvement increased No. 42 Squadron started to assume the normal duties including SAR, routine fishery patrols and the protection of the North Sea oil rigs as part of Operation *Tapestry*. No. 42 Squadron would make another deployment to Ascension Island after hostilities had ended; their role was to provide SAR cover for the Hercules aircraft operating the airbridge down to RAF Stanley.

The Kinloss Nimrod Wing consisted of three units, Nos 120, 201 and 206 Squadrons, who operated the aircraft on a pooled basis. The majority of machines at Kinloss were of the MR2 variant, although a handful of MR1s were still on strength awaiting their turn to enter the conversion line at Woodford. Fortunately, the MR2 avionics had been cleared for service use as intensive trials, including a maximum endurance sortie, had been completed in April 1982. By this time the Nimrods were returning to Kinloss in a new camouflage scheme of Hemp over light grey instead of the earlier finish of white over light grey. The first two Nimrod MR2s arrived at Wideawake on 13 and 17 April respectively. The first aircraft, XV230, undertook its first mission two days later being used to drop secret orders to HMS *Antrim* concerning Operation *Paraquat*, the retaking of South Georgia. Although the Nimrod detachment would become known for their extended long-range reconnaissance missions the aircraft also had another task that was just as important. As Ascension Island was the major staging post for Operation *Corporate* there was always a slim chance that Argentina might use some form of naval or special forces attack to cause disruption to operations from the island, although such actions would bring the wrath of the Americans upon their heads given the amount and type of equipment on the island. Therefore Nimrod patrols operated around the island in concert with a Royal Navy guard ship. Unfortunately, the radius of action for the Nimrod was 2,000 miles thus all the patrol efforts were concentrated in a southerly direction in support of the task force. Another task for the Nimrods was to act as a communications relay station between the Victor tankers supporting both the Harrier deployments and the Black Buck missions. Whilst engaged in this task the aircraft also covered the SAR role at the same time. This option was exercised fully from 30 April to 1 May during Black Buck 1 when a Nimrod MR2 was used to provide communications relay links between the Operation Centre on Ascension and the Vulcan and its supporting Victors.

The lack of range was affecting Nimrod operations thus investigations were carried out by British Aerospace at Woodford to see if such a fit was feasible. As in-flight refuelling was deemed possible BAE was given permission to commence a trial fit on 14 April using Nimrod MR2 XV229. To compensate for the installation of the refuel probe above the cockpit a ventral fin was fitted under the rear fuselage. The first flight of this aircraft as the aerodynamic model was undertaken on 27 April, although none of the pipework plus the associated valves were installed. The first aircraft to receive the full refuel fitment was XV238, which underwent trials with A&AEE at Boscombe Down. While the ventral fin compensated in part for the refuel probe it was found necessary to fit small fins above and below the tailplanes. In this new form the aircraft was designated the Nimrod MR2P. The first extended flight of XV238 took place on 6 May and involved a twenty-hour sortie.

The first Nimrod MR2P to deploy to Ascension was XV227, which departed from Kinloss on 7 May flying all the way without air-to-air refuelling. Within two days the aircraft undertook its first long-range mission, which took 12 hours 45 minutes to complete. On 12 May the next mission took over 14 hours to complete. By this time a second MR2 had arrived and this aircraft undertook some record breaking flight during this period. The first mission was launched on 15 May and took the Nimrod within 150 miles of Port Stanley for reconnaissance as satellite information was not available due to extensive cloud cover. After approaching the Falkland Islands the aircraft turned toward Argentina closing to within sixty miles of the coast. The run north up the coast allowed the Nimrod's Searchwater radar to confirm that all Argentine warships were still in port under the threat of sinking by Royal Navy submarines as part of the naval blockade. After a flight that had covered 8,300 miles and had required three tanker hook-ups the Nimrod landed safely at Wideawake.

Over the next few days the Nimrods undertook a continuous run of long-range reconnaissance missions, the longest of which was undertaken over 20–21 May. XV232 departed Ascension and headed south, stopping just short of the Falklands Islands before turning towards Argentina. Again the Nimrod ran up the coast checking again to confirm that the Argentine Navy was safely tucked up in port. At the conclusion of this sortie the Nimrod and its crew landed safely back at base having completed a flight that covered 8,453 miles with an airborne time of 18 hours 50 minutes, making this the longest combat mission of all time.

As the Nimrods and their crews were undertaking missions that were outside their normal training parameters steps were taken to train the crews in new tactics and weapons. It must have been some sight watching a Nimrod undertaking dissimilar air combat training, although it was a good idea as the Argentine air force was more than capable of getting airborne to intercept any nosey reconnaissance aircraft. The Nimrod had been designed from the outset to have underwing hard points mainly for the carriage of Martel missiles, although these had been earmarked for the Vulcans even though the AGM-45 Shrike was chosen instead. As they were an asset that was still available the design team at Woodford quickly designed a pylon adapter that could carry AIM-9 Sidewinders plus developed the required launch control and associated wiring looms. XV229 be employed on carriage and firing trials that began on 26 May, the entire programme being cleared for service use two days later. One of the Ascension Island deployed Nimrods, XV232, was returned to Woodford to have a Sidewinder kit fitted. This was completed by 31 May, the aircraft returning south on 5 June.

Besides the missile armament the Nimrod fleet was also cleared to carry a bomb load that included standard 1,000lb high-explosive bombs plus BL755 Cluster Bomb Units for which role a bomb sight was developed. Also cleared for Nimrod use was another

Although the Argentine surrender would mark the end of the violent part of Operation *Corporate* there were still patrols required over the ocean until the threat of any further reaction was deemed negligible. To that end Nimrods remained at Ascension for a short period after hostilities ended. *(BBA Collection)*

American weapon, the AGM–84A Harpoon, although this required some modifications to the bomb bay fitments. The first aircraft so modified was XV234, which undertook its post modification flight on 10 June with the missile being cleared for service use some two days later. The first Nimrod MR2P to be cleared for operations was XV237 on 19 June with deployment to Ascension taking place on 2 July. During the operational phase of Operation *Corporate* the anti-submarine Nimrods undertook 111 missions, although others were flown for a period after the Argentine surrender. The final Kinloss Nimrod sortie was undertaken on 17 August with the aircraft departing for Kinloss the following day. After routeing via Gibraltar the aircraft landed safely at Kinloss on 19 August.

Also deployed south for Operation *Corporate* was a single example of the Nimrod R1, although in line with the main Nimrod fleet it had an in-flight refuelling probe, ventral fin and tailplane finlets fitted. Very much a secretive unit and hence secretive aircraft the role of the Nimrod R1 and No. 51 Squadron are worth exploring.

In 1969 three Nimrods were ordered for use by No. 51 Squadron as Model HS 801Rs, although they were designated Nimrod R1s in service. The cost of developing the three specially configured aircraft plus systems was estimated at £2.38 million with airframe manufacture costing a further £11.34 million. Additional special equipment accounted for a further £1.25 million while additional COMINT equipment that included magnetic tape recorders, TR1986/1987 and R216 receiver replacements, an aerial distribution system and auto voice indicators added a further estimated £545,000.

Externally the airframe of the Nimrod R1 was the same as the Nimrod MR1/2 model minus the MAD boom, although internally the aircraft are completely different except for the flight deck. Due to the sensitivity of the equipment involved the aircraft were delivered as basic airframes to Wyton where they were fitted out with the requisite systems. The flight deck crew consisted of two pilots, two navigators and a flight engineer, however extra space is available for two supplementary crew to provide cover on long sorties. Given the nature of the Nimrod R1's task accurate navigation was essential thus the aircraft were fitted out with AD360 ADF, AD260 VOR/ILS, AN/ARN-172 TACAN, AN/ARA-50 UFH DF, LORAN, and a Kollsman periscope sextant. The ASV-21D radar from the MR1 variant was retained with a 32in diameter dish. Up to twenty-three, Signal Intelligence (SIGINT) specialists were accommodated at thirteen side-facing equipment consoles in the main fuselage; consoles 1 to 5 were located on the port side while consoles 6 to 13 were on the starboard side. Each console was designed to accommodate two 4 feet modules with provision for a single seat placed centrally, although these were able to slide on transverse rails. Consoles 1 to 4 plus 9 to 12 had provision for a pair of side-by-side seats. Three forward facing single-man consoles later augmented these double consoles.

The first Nimrod R1 airframe, XW664, was delivered to Wyton in July 1971 and required two years to fit out as any changes to the original layout for whatever reason required careful documentation. It should be noted that the electronics centre at Wyton was also required to fabricate all the internal fitment. Whilst many of the internal dimensions for the equipment racks had already been planned any alterations would also require notation thus increasing the into-service speed of the other two airframes The first training sortie was undertaken on 21 October 1973 with the first operational sortie being flown in May 1974. Two more Nimrod R1s entered service during late 1974, XW665 and XW666, this allowing the retirement of the remaining Comet R2s and Canberras. For flight crew training No. 51 Squadron also utilized a standard Nimrod

MR1, XZ283, that arrived during April 1976 and remained on strength until June 1978 after which it was returned to BAE for conversion to AEW3 standard.

During 1980 the aircraft underwent a modification programme that saw the ASV21 radar being replaced by an ECKO 290 weather radar that had displays on the flight deck. This allowed one of the radar navigator crew positions to be deleted. The workload of the remaining navigator was improved by removing one of the LORAN sets and replacing it with a Delco AN/ASN-119 Carousel IVA INS. As a result of this upgrade one of the LORAN external aerials was removed and a variety of other external antennas appeared, their purpose was believed to be that of direction finding. Wing tip pods, similar in appearance to the Yellow Gate Electronic Support Measures (ESM) fitted to the Nimrod MR2 were also fitted to XW664 and then later to the other two aircraft. The need for an in-flight refuelling capability became apparent as a result of Operation *Corporate*, the plan to recapture the Falkland Islands following the Argentine invasion in 1982, although only XW664 was reported with a probe. The remaining two aircraft probes were not fitted until *Corporate* had ended. Underwing pylons were also fitted to all three aircraft at the same time and these carried a modified BOZ pod that was believed to contain a towed radar decoys. It was rumoured that the aircraft were also fitted with a Marconi Master satellite communications system. The Nimrod R1 used during Operation *Corporate* was XW664, although where the aircraft operated from during the conflict is open to speculation, however some sources believe the aircraft operated from a base in Chile alongside a detachment of RAF Canberra PR9s from the recently disbanded No. 39 Squadron. In 1995 No. 51 Squadron would depart Wyton after thirty-two years of residency moving to Waddington from where it continues to operate.

Fortunately for the RAF the primary transport was the Lockheed C-130 Hercules, which was operated on a pooled basis by Nos 24, 30, 47 and 70 Squadrons plus No. 242 OCU, all known as the Lyneham Transport Wing. When Operation *Corporate* started some of the Hercules were undergoing a major conversion programme from the original short fuselage C1 to the longer C3. This programme had started in mid-1979 and

Initially the C-130 Hercules required that much of the internal cargo area was occupied by long-range fuel tanks in order to reach the Falklands. Eventually an in-flight refuelling probe was fitted that allowed the aircraft to conduct air bridge operations using Victor tankers. *(BBA Collection)*

required a plug to be inserted before and after the wing, which increased the length by 15 feet. The first conversion had been undertaken by Lockheed in the United States while the responsibility for the remainder was vested in Marshalls of Cambridge, the European Lockheed Agent. By March 1982 twelve of the conversions had been carried out while others would be fed into the programme on schedule even during *Corporate*.

While much of the bulky and heavy equipment and stores were moved to Ascension by ship the transfer of personnel and vital or smaller stores would be the responsibility of the Lyneham Transport Wing. The first four aircraft departed from Lyneham for Gibraltar on 2 April, this marking the start of an airbridge from Britain to Ascension that was operated on a daily basis. Routeings to the island were via Dakar, Banjul and Gibraltar and required a peak of sixteen Lyneham departures on 29 April requiring the use of all three staging posts.

Although the Hercules was the stalwart of the airbridge the aircraft was also employed in supporting the Task Force as the ships headed south. The first air drop was undertaken in late April using standard Hercules C1s. Initially the standard fuel contents were enough to get the aircraft to and from the ships. However, it was becoming obvious that as the ships headed further south they would go out of range of the transports. The answer was to dust off some old fuel tanks that had been built for the now retired Andover fleet. Lyneham Engineering Wing was charged with integrating two extra fuel tanks into the aircraft's fuel system, the tanks themselves being mounted in the forward fuselage. This initial installation extended the endurance of the Hercules by four hours while a similar four tank installation increased the range further, although the reduced payload available meant that these aircraft could only be used for high-value drops. In these configurations the aircraft were given a supplementary designation of L2R or L4R depending on the fit.

It would be Nos 47 and 70 Squadrons that would undertake the long-range support missions while the other two units concentrated on operating the vital airbridge to and from Ascension Island. The first extended-range Hercules would depart from Lyneham on 4 May proceeding directly to Wideawake with the first air drop mission being undertaken three days later. Unfortunately, the weather over the drop zone resulted in the drop being cancelled, although the entire mission lasted over eighteen hours. A further flight on 8 May lasted nearly as long and was successful all three drops being carried out. The final long-range drop mission was carried out on 24 May after which the aircraft returned to Lyneham.

Obviously the use of long-range fuel tanks, while acceptable in the short term, severely restricted the load-carrying capability of the Hercules. To that end Marshalls of Cambridge were charged with developing an in-flight refuelling probe installation for the C-130. Known as Modification 5308 the probe plus its installation pipework was first installed in XV200. The probe was mounted above the cockpit offset slightly to starboard while the required plumbing was mounted under a fairing that led from the probe to the starboard wing root. The conversion was carried out in ten days with XV200 making its first test flight on 28 April. This was successful and the aircraft was flown to A&AEE to undergo trials the following day. A Victor tanker was despatched by No. 57 Squadron to Boscombe Down for ground trials while the following day saw the first aerial link up between the C-130 and the Victor tanker. As there was a 20 knot discrepancy between the maximum speed of the Hercules and the Victor's minimum speed a unique method of refuelling was devised in which the entire refuel process was carried out during a gentle

Hercules C1(K) XV213 departs for another patrol mission around the Falkland Islands. This aircraft is complete with ESM underwing pods and flight refuelling equipment installed in the cargo area. *(BBA Collection)*

dive the rate of descent being fixed at 500 feet per minute, the whole process lasting approximately 15 minutes. After the successful completion of these trials XV200 was returned to Lyneham on 5 May for crew training before being deployed to Ascension on 14 May. A further five aircraft were fitted with refuelling probes before the conflict being redesignated as C1P afterwards. The first deployment was undertaken by a No. 47 Squadron crew on 16 May. Utilizing three Victor tankers , both outbound and inbound, the C-130 undertook a 6,300-mile round trip during which a large amount of stores and eight parachutists were dropped.

A second probed C-130, XV179, was flown from Lyneham to Ascension on 19 May undertaking its first mission two days later. Both aircraft were employed continuously on long-range drop missions, achieving a total of eight by 6 June. A third converted aircraft, XV196, was flown via Gibraltar to Ascension arriving on 5 June, its first mission being flown the next day. A fourth C1P, XV218, arrived at Ascension on 13 June departing the following day for a long-range air drop mission during which the surrender of the Argentine forces on the Falklands was broadcast. A further two conversions were completed by Marshalls just after the surrender. Both were deployed to Ascension and were used to undertake air drops to both the Falklands and shipping operating within the total exclusion zone. Fortunately once the runway at Stanley had been repaired the Hercules were able to land and deliver their stores, although a reversion to air drops was needed when the runway was closed for extension and strengthening from 14 August. During the two weeks that the runway was closed the Hercules operated an air snatch system that had been developed from an idea first used during the 1930s. Using a grapnel on the end of 150 feet of nylon rope the aircraft was required to run in at 50 feet, its aim being to grab a loop of nylon rope suspended 22 feet above ground on pylons placed some 50 feet apart. The concept was that the grapnel would engage with the loop and pull another cable with a mailbag attached that was pulled into the aircraft. The runway was reopened for business on 29 August, the first beneficiary being XV200.

Two further modifications were carried out by Marshalls, the first being the installation of an Omega navigation system under Mod.5309 while the second was more extensive. Mod.5310 was the installation of a Flight Refuelling Mk 17B hose drogue unit that was mounted on the ramp while a fairing for the drogue and refuel lights on the external surface of the door. During flight, with the drogue reeled in, the aircraft's fuselage remained pressurized although this changed when the drogue was deployed as developing a system that could retain fuselage pressurization would have taken longer to produce. Fuel for refuelling was drawn from the main fuel system instead of any tanks carried in the main cabin. These conversions were designated C1.K, the first being XV296. This aircraft undertook its first test flight on 8 June during which the drogue was successfully deployed. On 10 June the Hercules was delivered to A&AEE undertaking its first dry probe with an available Harrier. During this trial it was discovered that buffeting was being experienced by the receiver aircraft thus the C-130 was returned to Marshalls for modification. After observation of tufting stuck on the ramp area it was concluded that strakes fitted to the outer edges of the door would cure the buffeting problem. With these strakes fitted a further test flight was made during which a wet contact was made with a Buccaneer. Over the following week the aircraft was flown from Boscombe Down during which contacts were made with C-130s, Nimrods, Phantoms and Sea Harriers, all of which were concluded successfully. Eventually, a total of six Hercules were converted to tankers and were used almost exclusively on the air bridge from Ascension to the Falkland Islands. Eventually, a permanent detachment of Hercules was established at RAF Stanley – mix of tankers and probed aircraft. In August 1983 the C-130 detachment was designated as No. 1312 Flight. During Operation *Corporate* the Hercules undertook forty-four air drop missions that required more than 13,000 flying hours thus proving how successful the modified aircraft were.

While the Hercules was grabbing the long-range air drop missions the Vickers VC 10s of No. 10 Squadron based at Brize Norton were involved in *Corporate* missions almost from the beginning. The first mission was undertaken on 3 April when XV106 departed Brize Norton for Montevideo, the Uruguayan capital, routeing via Ascension to collect the Falkland Islands Govenor, Rex Hunt, and the Royal Marines that had been captured during the invasion of the islands. After collecting its passengers the VC 10 returned to Brize Norton on 5 April. Even as XV106 was returning XV109 was departing for Ascension carrying stores and personnel for the forthcoming deployment. Another run was undertaken to Montevideo on 18 April its purpose being to collect some of the Falkland Islanders that had been deported as possible trouble makers by the Argentine occupiers. Another repatriation flight was carried out a few days later to collect the remaining Marines from the Falklands plus those personnel captured when South Georgia was taken. After the recapture of South Georgia the captured Argentine personnel were transported by ship to Ascension. A suitably marked VC 10 from No. 10 Squadron complete with Red Cross insignia departed from Ascension taking its passengers to Montevideo to hand its occupants over to the Uruguay authorities for onward transfer to Argentina. The squadrons aircraft were also used to bring home the survivors from the sinking of HMS *Sheffield*.

The Boeing Chinook HC1 had only just entered service when the Falkland Islands were invaded. No. 18 Squadron had dispensed with its Wessex in December 1980 while based at Gütersloh. Training with the Chinook began in July 1981, the intention being that the unit would return to Germany in 1982. The need for a heavy lift helicopter for support duties during Operation *Corporate* would obviously delay this move, with transfer not taking place for nearly twelve months. When the squadron was declared operational it had thirteen helicopters on strength.

No.18 Squadron was warned for *Corporate* operations on 6 April, despatching three of its aircraft to Culdrose to provide heavy lift capability for the large amount of equipment, stores and personnel requiring movement onto the various vessels being prepared for the task force at Devonport. Five of the units aircraft were prepared at Odiham for despatch to the South Atlantic. These machines were Batch 2 aircraft that featured pressure refuelling systems and carbon fibre rotor blades. Modifications applied to these aircraft included Omega navigation systems and radar warning receivers. All five were ready for despatch on 23 April when they were flown to the RN base at Plymouth and were loaded onto the *Atlantic Conveyer* with some RN Wessex two days later. Accompanying the Chinooks was a small cadre of air and ground crew who were charged with caring for their charges. The greater majority of both air and ground crews were transported to Ascension by VC 10 from Brize Norton joining the Norland off the island on 7 May for transport down south. One of the Chinooks, ZA707, was offloaded from the *Atlantic Conveyer* to assist in the airlift of stores and equipment to the relevant ships in the task force flying over 100 hours with few technical defects. The remaining Chinooks departed for the TEZ having been joined aboard the *Atlantic Conveyer* by eight Sea Harriers and six Harriers GR3s. During the transit south the Harriers and Sea Harriers were flown off to the *Invincible* and *Hermes* when the ship reached the task force on 18 May. With the deck clearer the remaining Chinooks were prepared for disembarking. After a struggle to get the rotor blades fitted to ZA718 using a forklift truck the Chinook departed to undertake resupply flights to shipping in the area.

In the early evening of 25 May the *Atlantic Conveyer* was hit by an Exocet missile launched from an Argentine Navy Super Etendard. The missile struck close to the waterline on the port quarter causing an intense fire that saw the ship enveloped in dense black smoke. Although the damage control parties fought valiantly to control the resulting fires it became obvious that the vessel could not be saved and the order was given to abandon ship. Although most of those aboard managed to escape twelve of those aboard lost their lives, including the ship's master, Captain Ian North. All of the

The Boeing Chinook was an essential part of the British success in recapturing the Falklands even though only one machine arrived to provide support. Here HC1 ZA709 'A' is seen in calmer times operating from container city near Stanley. *(BBA Collection)*

helicopter personnel managed to escape unharmed, although on later inspection the three Chinooks had been destroyed alongside the Wessex and a single Lynx helicopter. Once the fires aboard the ship had finally died the ship was assessed as salvageable thus it was taken in tow by the tug *Irishman*, although the *Atlantic Conveyer* would break its back in heavy weather and sink on 28 May.

The surviving Chinook, ZA718, would find a new home aboard the *Hermes* from 26 May, although it would soon disembark to join the rest of No. 18 Squadron based at Landing Site Whale near Port San Carlos. The majority of the squadron's personnel had been landed that day from the assault ship HMS *Fearless*, having previously been aboard the *Norland* with No. 2 Para. Once the Army personnel had disembarked the squadron's personnel took over the air defence of the ship. Having moved to *Fearless* the squadron's personnel yet again undertook air defence duties and it's mooted that it was one of them that coined the phrase 'Bomb Alley' for the area around San Carlos Water that later appeared in official signals, task force messages and the popular press.

Once ashore the squadron's personnel were joined by the single Chinook, Bravo November, their task being to provide heavy lift to the Army as it proceeded towards Stanley. As there were far too many personnel to support one helicopter it was decided that two crews and seventeen ground crew would remain to support BN while the remainder would move out of theatre to await the arrival of the replacement helicopters already en route. As such the No. 18 Squadron was up against it, operating as they were with less than basic tools and equipment. However, as with all RAF ground crew the remaining engineers made do and mended as needed to keep the Chinook flying even though various entries in the F700 covered defective items such as windscreen wipers and minor cockpit instrumentation. While windscreen wipers would have been a nicety in the weather conditions the helicopters' main equipment kept functioning thus the ferrying of stores, ammunition, personnel and wounded was undertaken day after day until the end of the campaign.

As the British forces pushed forwards the SAS patrol operating in the area of Mount Kent discovered that the previous Argentine forces had withdrawn. As this was regarded as a strategic position the decision was taken to flying 85 troops from 42nd Commando plus three 105mm guns plus 22 tons of ammunition and supplies by helicopter. While the troops were flown in by Royal Navy Commando HC4s two of the guns were carried inside the Chinook while the third was taken as an underslung load. Upon arrival at Mount Kent the underslung gun was off loaded first while a low hover was needed to off load the other two guns plus personnel as the ground was too boggy to touch down fully. With the guns and personnel clear of the Chinook it began its high-speed low-level run back to the FOB near Port San Carlos settlement. In typical Falklands fashion the weather deteriorated into snow showers that reduced visibility to almost zero. Suffering slightly from disorientation the Chinook bounced off the water near Teal Inlet. Having scared the living daylights out of the crew the Chinook was flown back to base at a slightly higher altitude. Fortunately, the post-flight inspection revealed that little damage had been caused to the airframe.

On 2 June Major John Crossland of 2 Para used the local telephone network to contact Fitzroy settlement and discovered that the Argentine forces had abandoned the area. As the BN was the only available helicopter with enough room eighty-one fully armed troops were crammed into the cabin, far above Boeing's recommended loadings, and flown to Fitzroy in atrocious weather. After returning to San Carlos a further seventy-five troops were airlifted to the settlement again in deteriorating weather, both missions being without incident. The capture of Fitzroy would bring British forces within ten miles of Port Stanley.

Throughout the remainder of the campaign the solitary Chinook was worth its weight in gold as it continued to support the advance towards Stanley. In one direction supplies and ammunition were delivered to the front line while the reverse flight carried wounded and prisoners, the catter being flown out to the *Uganda* from San Carlos. This capability was tested to the limit after the attacks on the Landing Ships *Sir Galahad* and *Sir Tristram* on 8 June. During the period 27 May to 14 June this single Chinook had flown 109 flying hours during which over 550 tons of stores and ammunition plus 2,150 troops had been carried, the figure including casevacs and prisoners.

While Bravo November was undertaking its heroic efforts in the Falklands No. 18 Squadron was in the process of receiving some much needed replacement Chinooks. Three of the five new helicopters were prepared for despatch, arriving at HMS *Drake*, Plymouth, by 20 May when all three were loaded aboard the *Contender Bezant* for onwards transport to the South Atlantic. After a stopover at Ascension the ship entered the TEZ on 9 June. During the stopover Chinook ZA707 plus four Harrier GR3s were also collected plus a single Gazelle.

ZA705 was flown ashore via *Hermes* for a refuel stop and followed by ZA707, although this aircraft was forced to turn back as a spurious transmission warned of incoming enemy aircraft inbound towards the carrier. The Chinook finally departed for San Carlos on 16 June being followed by the final pair two days later. A further three Chinooks were prepared at Odiham for shipment down south flying to HMS *Drake* before embarking on the *Astronomer* on 7 June. This vessel had been converted as a temporary helicopter carrier to assist the Royal Navy carriers.

All three Chinooks plus five Wessex and some Army Westland Scouts were safely embarked on the ship departing in the early hours of 8 June. After a stopover at Ascension the *Astronomer* finally left for the Falklands on 18 June, although one of the Chinooks had been left behind to assist in loading other vessels destined for the Falklands. Both of the remaining aircraft were flown off on 27 and 29 June respectively. Although the Argentine forces had surrendered there was much work for them to do, not only clearing up the mess left behind after the conflict, but assisting in moving essential supplies around the islands. One of the primary stores that needed moving in quantity was aviation fuel required for the various Fleet Air Arm helicopters around the islands. On a normal day nearly 10,000 gallons were ferried each day, the fuel being carried in special bladder containers. A Sea King was capable of carrying one of the bladders while a Chinook was happy with four. After some 200,000 gallons had been moved in this manner the need dropped off as the refuelling facility became available at RAF Stanley. Following on from the fuel runs the Chinooks were used as flying cranes, mainly off loading containers from the stream of ships arriving in the harbour. Many of those containers are still located around Stanley, the airport and RAF Mount Pleasant to this day. Once the situation on the islands had become settled the original No. 18 Squadron helicopters were rotated back to Britain being replaced by others as they became available. Originally known as Chindet, the detachment set up a permanent home at Kelly's Garden near San Carlos where they remained until all of the flying units were centralized at Mount Pleasant in 1986. Before moving to Mount Pleasant Chindet had

While Bristow Helicopters provided much of the transport around the Falklands some RAF Sea Kings were sent south to provide SAR cover. *(BBA Collection)*

been renumbered as No. 1310 Flight, although upon arrival at Mount Pleasant the Chinooks and the Sea Kings were combined to form No. 78 Squadron.

Although no conventional fighters were deployed south to the Falklands during the conflict there was a requirement for air defence coverage over Ascension Island should, against all odds, the Argentine forces manage to mount an attack against the base. The unit chosen to provide this 'just in case' cover was No. 29 Squadron based at Coningsby. This unit had just returned from a Cyprus armament practice camp when they were warned to prepare for Operation *Corporate Duties*. Three aircraft were prepared for this deployment, losing their unit markings and fin code letters in the process. These three machines were flown from Coningsby to Wideawake using a relay of Victor tankers. The

RAF Stanley had various wrecks and relics around it such as this Macchi MB339. When the airfield was prepared for hand over to the civilian authorities all the detritus of war was removed. *(BBA Collection)*

first departure left on 24 May, the last aircraft landing at Ascension on 26 May. The early arrivals had taken over the air defence QRA on 25 May from the Harriers of No. 1 Squadron whose aircraft were needed for operations over the Falklands. The detachment maintained the QRA until 14 July when it ended, during this period the Phantoms were scrambled a handful of times to intercept unidentified aircraft heading towards Ascension. These were normally Soviet Air Force long-range reconnaissance aircraft keeping an eye on events in the South Atlantic. After the detachment was stood down the Phantoms were prepared for the return journey to Britain using the usual relay of Victor tankers. All three had landed at Coningsby by 20 July.

No .29 Squadron would finally reach the Falkland Islands in October as the runway had been extended and arrestor gear fitted to assist the Phantoms in stopping. Nine aircraft were selected for deployment to RAF Stanley these arriving during September. Once the required number of Victor tankers were available the transit south began with No. 29 Squadron taking over the air defence of the islands by 17 October 1982 under the command of Wing Commander ID Macfadyen. No. 29 Squadron completed its tour of duty at the end of 1983 handing over the duty to No. 23 Squadron. One consequence of using brake parachutes and the arrestor hook to stop the F-4s on landing was that the aircraft brakes took a long time to wear to their lower limits. The consequence was that to remove a seized-on brake unit required the undercarriage leg to be removed from the aircraft and transported to Component Repair Detachment (CompDet) where ministrations, sometimes violent, were needed to separate the assemblies.

No. 202 Squadron also played its part in Operation *Corporate*, initially providing a single Sea King HAR3 for search and rescue plus airlift duties. After preparation at Finningley XZ593 was flown down to Ascension aboard a Heavylift Belfast on 8 May. Operating alongside Chinook ZA707 and two Wessex HU5s this mix of helicopters allowed a particular aircraft to be assigned to specific tasks and ships. XZ593 ended its association with *Corporate* on 7 September when the helicopter landed aboard the carrier HMS *Invincible* for onward transit to Britain.

As the number of aircraft operating over and around the Falkland Islands increased it was decided that a SAR detachment would be required for coverage. Unlike those helicopters seen around the coast of Britain the three selected for deployment to the Falklands were given an overall coat of dark grey paint and low visibility markings. All three departed Finningley on 4 August leaving Britain on the *Contender Bezant* on 7 August. The ship arrived off Port William on 25 August, the helicopters flying off to their new base at Navy Point. Nearly a year after arrival the Sea King detachment was designated as No. 1564 Flight, a title it retained until 1986 when the Sea Kings were flown to Mount Pleasant where they joined the Chinooks to become part of No. 78 Squadron.

Much of the foregoing would indicate that the airfield on Ascension Island was a fully up to speed facility that could cope with numbers of aircraft and personnel that arrived in support of Operation *Corporate*. Nothing could be further from the truth as the island was home to a NASA, and other agencies, satellite tracking station and the BBC relay station. This meant that the number of visiting aircraft was few and far between, consisting mainly of USAF and USMC transports, while the population consisted of those charged with looking after the equipment, a few small settlements, some goats and a large quantity of small black crabs that spent much of their lives jumping great distances sideways!

The number of personnel that could be accommodated was basically limited by the water supply available this in turn being governed by the capacity of the two water plants to deliver as the island has negligible rainfall. The original capacity was limited to approximately 2,800 extra persons for no more than two weeks. Even with careful management some water conservation was required, which remained the norm until two reverse osmosis plants were flown in and brought on line. Even with these available there was little water to waste especially when the military population had reached over 1,500. Actual accommodation for the number of personnel based on the island and those in transit was also under pressure. Most of the accommodation was of very poor standard. Even after renovation and the addition of tented accommodation the number of personnel living in below standard accommodation could have resulted in serious health and safety implications had not comprehensive briefing been given to those arriving on the island.

Given the length of many of the sorties being flown by the various aircrews they obviously could not share the normal accommodation and they were subject to the hurly burly of everyday service life. Originally the crews were accommodated in the USAF accommodation, however these arrangements were at best temporary and any American requirement took priority. A partial cure was affected by the arrival of USAF supplied accommodation modules known to many as 'Concertina City'. Even this solution had its problems as the power supply generators made their usual penetrating noise that disturbed rest. Extending the power cables and creating earth noise dams helped to dampen the effects, although the noise was still loud enough to penetrate sleep. Eventually the use of temazepam was authorized, allowing desperately tired crews to sleep.

Catering was also a problem as can be imagined with a large and fluid population. Meals were originally prepared in the USAF Mess Hall plus three field catering kitchens located near the camps at English Bay, Two Boats and at the Airhead. Further facilities were courtesy of the USAF Commissary who provided a regular supply of meals, some of which were ad hoc.

The actual flight operating conditions were at best minimal even though Wideawake boasted a 10,000 feet runway and a large apron capable of handling twenty-four large aircraft. The main problem facing the planners was that the only easy access was to Runway 14, this being the only direct access, while Runway 32 required any aircraft to taxi down the runway and turn round to face back up the way it had come. This meant that should it reverse direction, which it does occasionally, then it would have been impossible to launch multi-aircraft formations such as those required for the Black Buck mission and the Nimrod long-range reconnaissance flights. As Ascension is basically an extinct volcano risen above the sea the main problem facing the aircraft operators was the volcanic dust that constantly blows across the islands, which is harmful to both engines and airframes. Runway sweepers were quickly flown in to help keep the dust under control, but even so the compressor blades on many of the aircraft were showing signs of polishing by the end of the conflict.

Aircraft parking was also a problem as part of the available area was tarmac and given the heat and the fact it was not stressed for heavily loaded aircraft to sit on for long periods of time, the inevitable happened: the aircraft began to sink. To counter this any aircraft scheduled to depart from the tarmac area was tugged forward a few feet prior to engine start. Fuel availability was also a problem at the start of operations as Ascension only boasted a single bulk fuel installation (BFI), more than enough to cope with the normal air traffic arriving at the island. Given the scale of intended operations it was obvious that more capacity would be needed and quickly. The island's BFI was located at Georgetown some five miles from the airfield. This caused time delays in getting enough fuel down to the flightlines as only a single bowser could be bulked at a time. Also militating against a speedy transit between the BFI and the airfield was the abrasive nature of the road, which wore its way through tyres quickly. To improve fuel availability a pipeline was installed from the BFI to the airfield by the Royal Engineers during the end of April and the beginning of May these feeding into a fuel farm that eventually had a maximum capacity of a million gallons of AVTUR.

Airfield buildings are few and far between at Wideawake, these being dedicated to Pan Am use, thus tented accommodation was erected for basic operational usage while inflatable rubber hangars, better known as rubs, were erected for the servicing of components that needed a cleaner atmosphere for delicate work. Even these facilities were unable to cope with the volcanic dust that penetrated everywhere while the ultra-violet light from the strong sunlight also caused problems. The civilian operator Pan Am managed to provide extensive help to the military as they attempted to turn a quiet airfield into a front-line combat base. Kudos should go to the two air traffic controllers who managed much of the airfield's movements throughout April until RAF air traffic control personnel could be drafted in.

Overall, all of the personnel involved in setting up Ascension Island as a combat base undertook their task with great alacrity and strangely enough there was not a single Health and Safety muppet in sight!

Chapter 8

Farewell to the Old – Hello to the New

After its success during Operation *Corporate* that delayed its withdrawal it was time for the Vulcan to retire. The three remaining units were still based at Waddington and the first to disband would be No. 101 Squadron, which would disband in August 1992. No. 44 Squadron would hang on for a while longer until December of that year. It would be No. 50 Squadron that would gain a reprieve, although they would change their role from that of bomber to aerial refuelling tanker. The need for extra tankers had become obvious during Operation *Corporate* plus the length and number of missions flown had eaten deep into the remaining lives of the Victor tanker fleet. Even as Operation *Corporate* was progressing some of the retired British Airways VC 10 fleet were undergoing conversion to tanker status. Unfortunately, this programme had encountered a few teething problems thus a short-term solution was required.

The original request to pursue a possible conversion of some of the remaining Vulcan B2s into tankers had first been mooted at the end of April 1982 after a request from the RAF. A meeting between representatives of the RAF and British Aerospace Woodford

Abingdon was the home for those Super VC 10 airframes scheduled for conversion to K4 standard. Although looking pretty grotty the effect was courtesy of the anti-corrosion compound applied to the airframe. Eventually four engines would be installed, checks carried out to ensure that the flying controls functioned correctly and an airframe flown very carefully to Filton for conversion. *(BBA Collection)*

No. 50 Squadron would be the last operator of the Vulcan in both B2 and K2 forms, although it would cease flying in March 1984 by which time the last HDU had been removed for installation in the emergent VC 10K fleet.*(BBA Collection)*

soon thrashed out a development plan and how it would be executed. The layout for the K2 would be very simple and would result in the creation of a single point tanker. The bomb bay would be home to three 8,000lb fuel tanks plumbed into the bomb bay fuel galleries, although these were isolated from the main system instead of retaining the previous connection to the aircraft fuel system. The selected drogue package was the Flight Refuelling FR17B, which were diverted from the VC 10 tanker programme until those airframes were ready to accept them. The hose drum unit (HDU) would be mounted in the space previously mounted occupied by ECM cans and the Vapour Cycle Cooling Pack (VCCP), while the connection hose passed through the space previously occupied by the X–Band equipment if fitted. Much of the HDU was housed in a wood and aluminium construction under the ECM bay being known as the dog box. The coloured refuel lights were on the rear face of the assemblage.

The aircraft chosen for conversion were all Olympus 200 engines airframes and those selected also had a reasonable Fatigue Index available. Waddington and No. 50 Squadron were already gearing up for the arrival of the tanker conversion utilizing a small number of bombers to maintain crew currency. Each Vulcan was flown to Waddington by an RAF crew entering the conversion hangar after defuelling with a maximum of three in there at any one time. The first conversion, XH561, still wearing its No. 101 Squadron fin badges, undertook its maiden flight in K2 form on 18 June, however the HDU hose would jam on both the first two deployments. Eventually, it would operate correctly on the third flight. It would be the AEO who would control much of the refuelling process as his position was the only one equipped with a periscope. XH561 would finally be delivered to Waddington on 23 June being quickly followed by XJ825 while XH560 was delivered to A&AEE at Boscombe Down for trials and service clearance. The final three

This is a close-up of the Vulcan HDU 'dog box' manufactured from a mix of hardwood and aluminium as part of mod 2600. In common with all tanker aircraft it has a set of controlling traffic lights mounted in fairings each side of the box. *(Mel James)*

aircraft, XM571, XL445 and XH558, went through the conversion process on schedule, the last being delivered to Waddington during October 1982.

Not only did the aircrew have to learn new operating techniques, the ground crew also had much to learn. They were not helped by the nomadic existence of No. 50 Squadron as Waddington was undergoing a great upheaval and much rebuilding as it had been designated as the new base for the AEW Nimrod. Scampton would be their new home in March 1983, shades of 1973 when Waddington was shut for refurbishing, while a relocation to Coningsby was undertaken a few weeks later. The squadron returned to Scampton again where they remained until a return to Waddington was made later in the year. From an operator's point of view the Vulcan tanker was a success even though it was only a single point tanker. The airframe proved a very stable platform and most of the time the HDU worked correctly, although on one occasion the hose cutter was employed at least once when the hose failed to retract and had to be cut just over the boundary of Waddington airfield.

As the VC 10 conversions were being declared ready for service use so the Vulcan K2s were being grounded so that the HDUs could be installed in the VC 10s as they became ready for use. Eventually, No. 50 Squadron was disbanded on 31 March 1984 having flown over 3,000 hours in the tanker role.

Another aircraft type that was undergoing a reduction was the Blackburn Buccaneer, although this had been forced upon the RAF after the fatal crash involving XV345 in February 1980 whilst flying a low-level Red Flag mission. The cause of the accident was later determined to be failure of the inner wing spar ring. This saw the entire Buccaneer fleet grounded for inspection of the inner wing spar rings. Those found to be fully serviceable were placed back on alert duties in RAF Germany while the remainder would be assessed and a decision made concerning their fate. Extensive NDT on the affected area of each would reveal which of those could be quickly recovered while others could be brought back to life with an inner wing spar change. Those that could be recovered quickly would have access holes drilled close to the affected areas then each crack would be blended out carefully using a variety of rotary tools and pastes until each crack was confirmed as removed by NDT checking. The inner wing change programme required an extensive rebuild of the chosen aircraft and required two teams; one would remove the damaged spar section from the selected aircraft while another would undertake the removal of the same ring from the donor aircraft. Eventually, after an almost complete rebuild, the Buccaneer could be returned to service. Those aircraft that had acted as donors would be held in another hangar and slowly stripped for spares before being dragged over to Pickerston for final destruction.

During 1978 the RAF issued a requirement for nine dedicated tanker aircraft that were sorely needed to support the forthcoming Panavia Tornado F3 fleet in its air defence role. After a successful feasibility study it was decided that converting ex-civil VC 10s that were becoming available was a viable option. At the time BAE had several VC 10s available as it had recently repossessed the four remaining East African Airways Super VC 10s after the bankruptcy of the airline while Gulf Air had also terminated its VC 10 operations. Successful negotiations saw these nine aircraft sold to the RAF, and a contract was awarded to British Aerospace Filton to convert the airframes. The RAF specification was extensive calling for three refuelling points, extra fuselage fuel tanks, commonality with the existing C Mk 1 fleet, self-supporting capabilities plus a small passenger capability for the transportation of support personnel. Two types of VC 10 were involved in the programme, which were ex-BOAC/Gulf Air Type 1101s, designated K2 after conversion, and EAA Type 1154s, designated K3s after conversion. The modification programme was carried out in the Brabazon hangar at Filton. Prior to entering the programme the airframes were completely stripped of all paint so that a full inspection of the airframe structure could be carried out. Aircraft awaiting conversion were protected by 'Driclad' bags with internal dehumidification that still allowed for the movement of the aircraft if needed. Up to six airframes would be inside the hangar at any one time for the modification programme.

The resultant aircraft had five cylindrical fuel tanks mounted inside the fuselage holding 3,500 UK gallons. The K3 still retained its cargo door that was used to manoeuvre the fuel cells into the fuselage after which it was sealed. However, for the K2 a section of the top fuselage skin and supporting structure was removed to get the cells inside. As this was a tricky operation each airframe had to be carefully jacked and trestled until the installation was complete. The rear cargo bay area was modified to mount the fuselage HDU, although the area had to be strengthened while new pressure bulkheads were mounted fore and aft of the HDU with a pressure floor above. To carry the wing-mounted refuel pods new structural frames were mounted between the front and rear spar in the outer wing section to support the fixed pylons that were to carry the underwing refuelling pods.

To bring the K2 into line with the remainder of the fleet they were fitted with Rolls-Royce Conway Mk 550 engines while thrust reversers were fitted to the outboard engines only. The rear end of the fuselage of both tanker versions was modified to house a Turbomeca Artouste APU that would provide electrical power and bleed air for engine starting. This gave the tankers a certain measure of independence from ground equipment when operating away from base. At the other end of the fuselage a flight refuelling probe was installed on the nose to enable the tanker aircraft itself to be refuelled. Management of flight refuelling operations required a CCTV camera to be installed in an under- fuselage dome, which covered both the centreline HDU and the underwing pods. Further visual control was provided by traffic lights and spotlights that illuminated the refuelling points fitted to the fuselage and wing trailing edge. Initially the port front entrance door was converted to enable crew members to exit the aircraft by parachute in case of emergency. This meant that the right front service door would be the main entrance door.

The first K2 conversion, ZA141, undertook its first flight on 22 June 1982 and flew most of the trials flights for the new tankers. This was the only one finished in a grey and green camouflage scheme, although this was not adopted for the VC 10 tanker fleet, the remaining aircraft being finished in an all over hemp colour. ZA141 entered service as the only camouflaged VC 10 tanker, although it was later repainted to match the other VC 10 tankers. Due to the time needed to undertake each conversion it took several years for all the aircraft to slowly advance through the process, however in May 1987 the last K3 was delivered to No. 101 Squadron. The BOAC/Gulf Air airframes were the oldest VC 10s still flying thus they were also the first to be withdrawn. First withdrawals of the K2s began with ZA141, which was withdrawn in 1999 to St Athan and finally scrapped in 2002. In March 2001 ZA142 made the last flight of an operational K2 and was later flown to St Athan for scrapping after spares recovery.

By early 1981 the last of the British Airways VC 10s had been retired with fourteen being purchased by the RAF, along with a supply of parts and engines all for possible conversion to tankers. As the Victor K2 fleet was nearing the end of its fatigue life, the RAF would again be facing a shortage of tankers. As the K2 and K3 conversions were still being undertaken, there were no slots available to convert these aircraft, thus they were stored at RAF Abingdon and Brize Norton. The airframes were wrapped in 'Driclad' bags, although when they had been torn to shreds by the prevailing winds they were later covered in a PX -based sealant preservative that resulted in layers of grime covering the external surfaces.

In 1989 the MoD invited tenders for the conversion of five of the Super VC 10s to K4 standard plus the upgrading of the No. 10 Squadron VC 10 C Mk 1s to C Mk 1 Ks. After much negotiation BAe was awarded the primary contract in early 1990 while FR Aviation at Hurn would act as a subcontractor for the C Mk 1 conversions. Prior to departing Abingdon the airframes were inspected by the BAe Woodford division who discovered that the long years in storage had caused severe corrosion problems and the MoD were soon made aware that major structural work was needed. The major corrosion problem was centred upon the wing torque box that required rectification prior to the ferry flight to Filton. After a trial repair using VC 10 G-ARVJ, which was lying on the RAF Brize Norton scrap dump minus its wings, the conclusion was reached that through careful stress jacking of the fuselage the repair to the centre-section torque box was feasible and could be done economically. Readying the airframes for the ferry to Filton meant that lots of spares started arriving at RAF Abingdon to prepare the first aircraft, ZD242, for its first flight in years. The ferry flight took place on 27 July 1990 the aircraft flying with the undercarriage locked down. The slats and flaps were hand wound out and locked

After their sterling effort during Operation *Corporate* some of the Victor airframes were running close to their maximum fatigue lives. To compensate the remaining VC 10 airframes of No. 10 Squadron were fitted with flight refuelling underwing pods as shown on XR103, by now designated as a C(K)1. *(BBA Collection)*

while the tailplane was set to a fixed setting for 210 knots at 6,000 feet. Against the doubts of many naysayers this VC 10 made a safe landing at Filton. Soon after arrival the engines plus many other components were removed and sent back to Abingdon for use in the next airframe scheduled for flying out.

Within several weeks, the five aircraft selected for conversion had been flown to Filton being given a thorough structural inspection prior to entering the conversion programme. This would follow a similar process to that of the previous K2/K3 conversions; however there were large differences between the programs. The K2s and K3s had been airworthy aircraft. However the K4s had stood idle for years therefore many modifications that had been incorporated in the other VC 10s in RAF service would have to be incorporated in the conversion programme to bring the airframes up to the same standard. This required each airframe to be completely stripped down to bare metal and completely rebuilt again. When the first airframe emerged from the hangar in its new colours the RAF took delivery of a completely re-lifed aircraft.

There were some changes compared with the earlier conversions though the most obvious was the decision not to incorporate the extra fuselage tanks. To install these a section of the upper fuselage would need removing in a similar manner to the K2 conversion. Given the high hours on these airframes the RAF did not want to possibly weaken the primary structure of the airframe. The K4 did, however, retain the fin fuel tank that holds 1,750 gallons, even so the K4 is a very capable refuelling platform. When the aircraft were delivered to No. 101 Squadron they were fitted with the latest equipment on the flight deck, including extra radios that were installed in the K4s. These were much appreciated during a busy sortie.

When the C1 modification programme was initiated the aircraft were actively flying with No. 10 Squadron therefore all the airframes had already been modified up to the latest standard, thus the major changes needed to fit the two underwing refuelling pods and their pylons were restricted to the outer wing sections. These were strengthened to accept the weight of the underwing pods and extra fuel lines were installed to connect these to the refuel/defuel gallery. Four new pumps were added to the main tanks to feed the fuel to the refuelling pods. Monitoring the refuelling operation is the task of the flight engineer and his cockpit station has been modified for this purpose. The first conversion, XV101, flew in June 1992 while the last, XR808, was delivered in October 1996. The aircraft have retained their full transport capabilities, and the new refuelling capabilities will only be used when other assets are unavailable.

In December 1982 further tanker purchases were announced as part of the £1,000 million post Falklands War re-equipment expansion. Included within this package was the purchase of six ex-British Airways L1011 Tristar 500 series airframes to which was added a further three airframes purchased from Pan Am. As the Lockheed Service Agent for the rest of the world Marshalls of Cambridge were appointed to convert the six ex-BA aircraft into tankers. Four of the airframes were designated as KC1s while the remainder emerged as K1s. The KC1 model featured the twin HDU system mounted in the rear cargo compartment while the forward cargo compartment was occupied by fuel tankage. The upper passenger deck was capable of being used for passengers and their luggage or for moving freight all the while being capable of refuelling other aircraft en route. Unlike normal airline Tristars the need to carry freight on the upper deck required a wide cargo door to be cut into the port side of the fuselage. This was a very delicate operation that required the airframe to be carefully jacked and trestled. As some of the structural strength of the fuselage had been removed by cutting a large hole in the side, a large external strengthening frame was riveted around the opening while the door itself was also built as a structural member. The installation of this door allowed the KC1s to be role changed as needed as just inside the door was a roller deck leading off from which were mounting rails for pallet panels. Seating, galleys or flat floor panels could be loaded in a variety of mixes as needed. Forward of the roller deck was seating for the support ground crew normally carried down route. The only internal fitments to escape change were the rear bank of toilets and the crew toilet just aft of the flight deck.

The two K1s underwent a similar conversion, although the upper deck retained much of its seating aft of the centre doors while the forward seating section was used to carry the passenger baggage, which was loaded into lockable bins that were in turn locked into their mounting rails. Again, seating for travelling ground crew is placed forward of this section. Initially Marshalls undertook a feasibility study concerning the possibility of fitting underwing refuelling pods. Unfortunately, after consulting with Lockheed Burbank the idea was dropped as the manufacturer stated that it could no longer guarantee the behaviour of the wing and its flight control software should the wings be modified. As an aside Lockheed guaranteed the airframe against structural failure overall for life, a proud boast. The three Dash 500s purchased from Pan Am were destined from the outset to be utilized in the passenger role as they lacked a second cargo access door in the rear fuselage. Given this state of affairs it would be British Airways who would mentor both the aircraft and those chosen to maintain them. Until BA finished their contract with the RAF all of those who worked on the C2s, as this version became, had to be registered on the BA Maintenance system as engineers and required training in the use of civilian engineering paperwork. Only two of these aircraft, ZE704 and ZE705, were placed in service while the third, ZE706, was flown to Marshalls for external storage where it was known locally as the 'corrosion control specimen'. Initially, these aircraft sported a basic Pan Am finish from which the logos had been removed; these were replaced by RAF roundels and fin flashes with the serials on the rear upper fuselage.

It would be No. 216 Squadron that was chosen to operate the Tristar fleet having disbanded in 1980 after a short time as a Buccaneer operator. The Tristar C2s were the first to enter service in March 1985 being employed from the outset in the twice weekly runs to the Falkland Islands, alternating when needed with British Airways Boeing 747s. The run south would begin at Brize Norton stopping at Ascension to take on fuel and other sundries before departing to the Falkland Islands. Each crew and its supporting engineers were normally deployed on this duty for an average of ten days after which the aircraft and crew would return to base. The tanker versions would enter service from 1986 when the Tristar K1s joined the squadron with the fully convertible versions, the KC1s, entering service in 1989. Such was the capability of this model that they soon became known as 'sheds'.

The Tristars would soon be used for long-range tanking flights for the aircraft that had become the primary fighter and attack type during the 1980, the Panavia Tornado. The Tornado ADV had its origins in Air Staff Requirement 395 that called for a long-range interceptor to replace the Lightning F6 and Phantom FGR2. Although initially it was suggested, the attack variant of the Tornado was not suited to the specialized interception role as its radar and engines were more suited for the low-level attack role. As there were no other takers for the ADV model the MoD decided to proceed with the ADV's development, which was approved on 4 March 1976, with British Aerospace providing three prototypes. The first prototype was rolled out at Warton on 9 August 1979, making its maiden flight on 27 October 1979. The second and third development aircraft made their first flights on 18 July and 18 November 1980 respectively.

The difference between the ADV and the IDS included a greater sweep angle on the inboard fixed wing sections, deletion of the Krueger flaps, a longer radome for the Marconi/Ferranti AI.24 Foxhunter airborne interception radar, and a fuselage stretch of over four feet to allow for the carriage of four Sky Flash semi-active radar-homing missiles. The port cannon from the attack variant was also deleted. Also improved was the software suite that managed the aircraft's systems. The extended Tornado front fuselage was constructed in Britain, which helped to reduce drag plus created space for

When the Phantom finally finished its work it too would be replaced by the Tornado F3 in the Falklands as seen here as ZG799 'D' formates with the tanker aircraft. *(Bob Archer Collection)*

an additional fuel tank, Tank '0', carrying 200 Imperial gallons of fuel. The definitive Tornado F3 undertook its maiden flight on 20 November 1985 powered by Rolls-Royce RB.199 Mk 104 engines, which were optimized for high-altitude use with longer afterburner nozzles, the capacity to carry four underwing Sidewinder missiles rather than two, and automatic wing sweep control. The F3's primary weapons when it entered service were the short-range Sidewinder and medium-range Sky Flash, a British-built missile based on the American AIM-7 Sparrow.

Realizing that in its current form the F3 would not continue as an effective air defence platform up to its planned out of service date of 2010, the MoD began the Capability Sustainment Programme (CSP). This programme, announced in March 1996, covered many aspects, including the integration of ASRAAM and AMRAAM air-to-air missiles and radar upgrades to improve multi-target engagement. Additionally, pilot and navigator displays would be improved, along with the introduction of new processor and weapon management computers. The CSP would see the removal of many of the anomalies within the Tornado F3 fleet especially that concerning the Foxhunter radar, all of which required upgrading to the final Z standard.

In what was criticized as a short-sighted move at the time, the F3 could not exploit the full capabilities of either the AMRAAM or ASRAAM missiles. AMRAAM required two mid-course updates after launch to refresh target information prior to its own seeker taking over. The CSP, as announced, did not include the data link to provide this capability, it being subject to budget cuts. In addition, the ASRAAM was not fully integrated, which prevented the full off-boresight capability of the missile being exploited. Despite becoming operational before 2002 the F3 force deployed on combat operations with the Sky Flash, not AMRAAM, leading to the supposition that the decision not to fully integrate the missile made it no more effective than the original missile. On 8 June 2001, the MoD signed a contract for a further upgrade to the F3 force to allow these midcourse updates. The upgrade to give full AMRAAM capability, together with an updated IFF, known as the AMRAAM Optimisation Programme was incorporated in the remaining Tornado F3 fleet between December 2003 and September 2006. A further upgrade, not revealed until early 2003, was the integration of the ALARM anti-radiation missile to allow suppression of enemy air defence missions (SEAD). The F3's existing radar warning receivers formed the basis of an extremely effective Emitter Location System, that is used to locate radar antennas. The modified aircraft were then given the new designation Tornado EF3, being operated by RAF No. 11 Squadron RAF.

The Tornado F3 was operated at three separate airfields, north of the border in RAF Scotland, Leuchars and Nos. 43 and 111 Squadrons would trade in their F-4 Phantoms in September 1989 and June 1990. Further south at Leeming, for many years home to Jet Provosts, Nos 11, 23 and 25 Squadrons would set up home at a revamped airfield. No. 11 Squadron had finally said goodbye to its Lightnings in April 1988 while No. 23 Squadron had returned on paper from Mount Pleasant in the Falklands in October 1988 the Phantoms down south being renumbered as No. 1453 Flight. In contrast No. 25 Squadron had not operated aircraft since the Javelins had been withdrawn in 1962 this being followed by a period as a Bloodhound missile operator between 1973 and October 1989. The final base to receive the Tornado F3 was Coningsby, once home to the mighty Phantom. Two units would be based there with the F3, Nos 5 and 29 Squadrons, the former being a Lighting operator until December 1987 while the latter flew the F-4 until April 1987.

Seen departing from Honington is this Tornado GR1 of the Tornado Weapons Conversion Unit sporting the markings of No. 45 Squadron on the nose. *(BBA Collection)*

The Tornado F3 and Tristar fleet would be given a thorough workout during Exercise Golden Eagle 1988 that involved four F3s from No. 29 Squadron plus tanker support from No. 216 Squadron while the Lyneham Transport Wing provided a C-130 to carry the majority of large spares plus attendant ground equipment. The four F3s departed Coningsby on 21 August 1988 landing at Seeb in Oman some 9½ hours later. The four fighters plus tanker and spares support departed Seeb and headed towards the Australian base at Butterworth in Malaysia. After arrival the detachment undertook various air combat exercises against Singapore Air Force Northrop F5 Freedom Fighters and F-18 Hornets of the Australian Air Force. While the RAF was showing off its new aircraft officials from the defence sales organizations were undertaking negotiations with the various local governments in the region some of which would later result in contracts being issued for various weapons systems. After Butterworth, the detachment moved to Korat Air Base in Thailand where the RTAF indulged in various air combat exercise against their Thai hosts. A move to Singapore followed where various presentations concerning the Tornado were made to local officials. There would be a changeover of personnel on 5 October when a No. 216 Squadron Tristar landed at Kuala Lumpur. From Singapore the detachment decamped to the wilderness that is RAAF Darwin for a night stop. After Darwin the aircraft flew further south to Williamstown where the F3s would take part in the Australian Bicentennial Air Show centred around RAAF Richmond. Departing Australia the detachment headed for Pago Pago in Western Samoa. After a night stop the aircraft headed for Hickam AFB on Hawaii, yet another night stop. A further leg took the detachment to Travis AFB then onto Goose Bay. The final leg was across the Atlantic and back to Coningsby, Brize Norton and Lyneham after eleven weeks away and 26,000 miles of travel.

The attack equivalent of the F3 was the Tornado GR1, based at Honington and Marham. Marham was the home of Nos 27 and 617 Squadrons, both being ex-Vulcan squadrons. No. 27 Squadron had disbanded in March 1982, reforming in May 1983 to operate the GR1. No. 617 Squadron had disbanded in December 1981, the number plate remaining dormant until it reformed in January 1983. At Honington No. 9 Squadron, another ex-Vulcan operator, would re-equip with the Tornado GR1 in June 1982 having relinquished its Vulcans in May 1982 at Waddington. The squadron would depart

Preparing to depart Fairford are two Tornado GR4s of No. 617 Squadron based at Lossiemouth; of note are the fin codes that celebrate the exploits of the original 'Dambusters'. *(Bob Archer Collection)*

Honington in October 1986, moving to Bruggen as part of RAFG. The final unit to form in Britain was No. 13 Squadron at Marham, although it was a late starter not reforming until January 1982. Given its previous history as a reconnaissance unit its aircraft were Tornado GR1As. These differed from the basic attack model in that their primary role was reconnaissance although full attack capability was retained. Instead of the usual fuselage-mounted cannon the space was dedicated to housing three Vinten infra-red Linescan sensors.

Although the Harrier GR3 had given good service during Operation *Corporate* its load carrying limitations had become noticeable. The answer to this problem had already begun in August 1969 when Hawker Siddeley formalized a partnership with McDonnell Douglas to build the Harrier GR1 as the AV-8A. By 1973 both companies were studying an expanded version of the Harrier for use by the RAF and the United States Marine

No. 1 Squadron based at Wittering would be operating the Harrier GR7 by 1992 when this example, ZD470 '60', was photographed. Eventually, a good majority of the airframes would be converted to GR9 standard. *(BBA Collection)*

Corps. The result was a more complicated version of the Harrier that was eventually cancelled as no taxpayers' funds were forthcoming. McDonnell Douglas, MDD, would eventually take the lead in the design and development of the Harrier II. The start line was the premise that a lighter airframe would be capable of carrying a greater weapons and fuel load; this coupled to a larger area wing looked like a possible winner. Flying of what would become the AV-8B began in 1979 these aircraft featuring improved intakes and new types of flaps called positive circulation flaps. Coupled to these improvements were a new nozzle gearbox and improved forward nozzle that were more effective. Much of the fuselage and the wing were made from carbon composites this reducing the aircraft's basic weight by at least 480lb.

By this time British Aerospace, having absorbed Hawker Siddeley, had been involved in developing their own large wing for the Harrier featuring Leading Edge Root Extensions. As both Britain and the United States were looking for a replacement for their earlier Harriers the combination of both the MDD and the British Aerospace designs meant that both governments would be satisfied as the overall costs for each would be lower.

There were significant changes between the RAF and USMC versions the GR5 being fitted with twin new design 25mm Aden revolver cannon, each with a rate of fire of up to 1,850 rounds per minute and a muzzle velocity of over 1,000 metres per second. The RAF also required a Sidewinder launch rail under the landing-gear outriggers and the British aircraft incorporated additional protection against bird strikes to support low-level operations.

The GR5 had also a different avionics fit, the ARBS from the AV-8B this incorporating a Ferranti moving-map display, British radio equipment and IFF system plus different countermeasures. The countermeasures system included a Marconi Zeus ECM system, a Plessey Missile Approach Warning (MAW) system plus Swedish Bofors BOL chaff dispensers. The Zeus included an RWR that could identify 1,000 different types of emitters and activate its self-defence jammer automatically to meet a specific threat. The MAW can automatically dispense chaff when a missile attack is detected.

When the BAES Harrier GR5 was delivered to Strike Command it was finished in this attractive two-tone green scheme as carried by ZD404 '07' of No. 1 Squadron at Wittering. *(John Ryan Collection)*

The GR5 was fitted with an infra-red camera for all-weather reconnaissance in addition to the Forward Looking Infra Red, housed in a chin fairing, although this was later cancelled and the chin housing remained unfilled.

The first GR5 flew from Dunsfold on 30 April 1985 with service acceptance taking place in 1989, replacing the earlier GR3. Forty-one GR5s were built followed by a further batch of twenty-one GR5As that were similar to the GR5, although they had minor modifications that made them easier to convert to the next planned version, the GR7. The GR7 was the RAF equivalent of the Night Attack Harrier II, although as before it used British specified avionics, including a GEC-Marconi 1010 FLIR in a small fairing on top of the nose; a Smiths Industries wide-angle HUD; a GEC-Marconi colour map display, updated mission software; and an Night Vision Goggle compatible cockpit. When the GR7 entered service the Martin-Baker Mark 12 ejection seat was updated to a Type 12 Mark 2 ejection seat that had a connection to the pilot's helmet to blow off his NVGs with a compressed air charge before ejection. The initial GR7 prototype flew on 20 November 1989 with deliveries to operational squadrons beginning in late 1990. Thirty-four new-build GR7s were manufactured while fifty-eight GR5s and GR5As were upgraded to GR7 specification. Although all GR5 and early GR7 production featured the 70 per cent LERX, the seventeenth new-build GR7 was fitted with the 100 per cent LERX with earlier production aircraft being refitted with them as they became available. Only one unit within Strike Command would be equipped with the BAE Harrier GR5, No. 1 Squadron at Wittering, the new model arriving in 1988. They remained in service until 1992 when they were replaced by the GR7. Alongside the single-seat Harriers the RAF also received thirteen two-seat Harrier T10s, not only for squadron use, but for training usage by No. 233 OCU.

Also subject to modifications during this period was the Sepecat Jaguar fleet regarded by some senior RAF officers as an aircraft without a mission to perform; as events would prove, they were completely wrong. Having entered service in the mid-1970s it was becoming obvious that the Jaguar's capability was no longer comparable to its contemporaries. Therefore in 1983 an avionics upgrade programme was started that

During any conflict the Harriers of No. 1 Squadron were charged with supporting British forces deployed to Norway. To that end their aircraft were painted with this disruptive scheme of white over the basic two-tone grey finish that replaced the earlier two-tone green. *(John Ryan Collection)*

would encompass all of the surviving Jaguar GR1s. The modifications would see the original Elliott MCS 920M computer replaced by the Ferranti FIN 1064 Inertial Navigation and Attack System (INAS), NAVWASS II, which was smaller and lighter than the previous unit. Flight trials began in July 1981 with deliveries beginning to No. 54 Squadron in 1983 with the Jaguar GR1A. All of the conversions were carried out at the Jaguar Maintenance Unit at Abingdon where they entered for either a major or minor servicing. Overall, eighty-nine aircraft were upgraded to this standard.

Another new system fitted to the GR1A was the Ferranti Total Avionics Briefing System (TABS), which allowed the pilot to plot his course and way points plus other information before take-off. A hard copy was then printed off for the pilot for reference while the electronic version was down loaded into the Ferranti Portable Data Store (PODS), which was similar in concept to the modern thumb drive. This could be inserted into an interface that allowed the stored data to be downloaded onto the aircraft's computer. Protection capability was also improved by the fitment of a Westinghouse ALQ-101 jamming pod on the port outer pylon while the starboard was wired for the Phimat chaff dispenser and Tracor flare dispensers were mounted on the engine doors. An AIM-9 Sidewinder missile capability was added at the same time. The original Adour Mk 102 engines were replaced with the uprated Mk 104 version. Also subject to the same upgrade programme were the two-seat Jaguar T2s, although this was mainly confined to the engines and the NAVWASS II.

While the attack side of Strike Command was being upgraded some of the more venerable aircraft were slowly heading to retirement. One of these was the F-4J(UK), fifteen of which had been purchased from surplus US Navy stocks to replace those aircraft despatched to the South Atlantic. Prior to delivery to Britain the aircraft were overhauled and modified at NAS North Island, California, before delivery to the RAF. The F-4J(UK) aircraft retained their original J79 engines and most of their American avionics. However, a number of US Navy systems, such as the AN/ASN-54 Approach Power Compensator System, the AN/ASW-25 data link system, and the AN/ALQ-126 countermeasures set, were removed and replaced by their British equivalents. The

The Sepecat Jaguar was a slowly shrinking community, even so enough remained available to maintain three squadrons and an OCU. Sporting the markings of No. 16 Squadron is 'A' of the OCU. *(BBA Collection)*

Due to the need to deploy a Phantom-based unit to the Falkland Islands further aircraft were required to fill the gap in Britain's air defence. Fifteen low-time US Navy F-4Js were supplied from US stocks in 1984. Operated by No. 74 Squadron they remained in use until 1991. *(BBA Collection)*

prominent electronic countermeasures antenna fairings on the upper sides of the air intakes remained on the aircraft, although no equipment was installed.

The first three F-4J(UK) aircraft were delivered to Britain in August 1984. They equipped the newly reformed No. 74 Squadron based at RAF Wattisham. These aircraft were intended to serve in the air defence role pending the introduction of the Tornado F Mk 3. In later years, the aircraft were made compatible with the BAe Sky Flash air-to-air missile. The F-4J(UK) Phantoms were eventually retired in early 1991 when some low-time Phantom FGR Mk 2 fighters became available to re-equip No. 74 Squadron. As the original British Phantoms were being replaced by the Panavia Tornado F3s, the first unit to lose its F-4s was No. 29 Squadron being followed by Nos 23 and 43 Squadrons. By 1990 No. 111 Squadron also at Leuchars had traded in its Phantoms for the Tornado F3. This left only Nos 56 and 74 Squadrons at Wattisham equipped with the F-4, although both units would be gone by late 1992.

Another old favourite would also disappear from British skies, the BAC, English Electric Lightning F3, T5 and F6. The first Binbrook-based unit to disband was the Lightning Training Flight, which was running its last course at the start of 1987 after which the LTF began retiring some of its last remaining airframes, with several F3s being dispatched to Leuchars and Wattisham respectively for battle damage repair training in early March. The LTF flew its final sortie on 16 April, when it performed an eight aircraft flypast with two F3s, the unit's single F6 and five T5s. After this event the remaining T5 airframes were split between both Nos 5 and 11 Squadrons and the Aircraft Servicing Flight for short-term storage.

Almost all the remaining F3s were retired and gradually underwent spares recovery, with the exception of two airframes, these last two airworthy F3s being passed on to No. 5 Squadron for air display duties throughout the year. Meanwhile, the two remaining Squadrons were kept busy with operational flying and training commitments, both units taking part in regular air defence exercises. No. 5 Squadron undertook a one-way squadron exchange with the General Dynamics F-16s of 350 Squadron from the Belgian Air Force, based at Beauvechain, in May while both units also undertook the last ever

The Lightning F6s based at Binbrook were still undertaking their fair share of air defence duties although their end was drawing near. Here XR763 'AP' of No. 5 Squadron awaits its next pilot on the squadron flight line. *(BBA Collection)*

Armament Practice Camp deployments by Lightnings to RAF Akrotiri, where they undertook aerial gunnery practice firing at the banners towed behind Canberras from 100 Squadron. As No. 5 Squadron was due to disband first the unit managed to squeeze two trips to the sunnier climate of Cyprus, the first deployment took place during February, while No. 11 Squadron followed, deploying for a whole month during mid May, followed again by No. 5 Squadron which deployed again towards the end of June. Unfortunately, during its last detachment the unit lost one of its F6s when it suffered an engine failure and crashed on final approach to Akrotiri, the pilot thankfully ejecting safely.

One of the most welcome announcements of 1988 was the news that Binbrook would host one last open day to mark the retirement of the Lightning towards the end of August. Binbrook had already emerged intact from plans to turn it into a prison several years before. However, the MoD had announced that the airfield would close after the end of Lightning operations and that it would become a Relief Landing Ground (RLG) for the Central Flying School, based at RAF Scampton. On Saturday 22 August the hoped for sunny day was cancelled and replaced by torrential rain, although it did ease off later. Even so, with the skies still leaking the aircrew headed to their aircraft amongst whom was the last Station Commander of RAF Binbrook, Group Captain John Spencer, who flew his personalized Lightning F6 'JS'. Other Lightnings included the now well known red and black finned squadron commanders' aircraft of Nos 5 and 11 Squadrons. Altogether, eleven aircraft taxied down to the end of runway 21 before making a thunderous take-off. The Lightnings then departed in the direction of Mablethorpe to form into the nine-ship formation, before heading north towards Immingham, finally turning inbound for Binbrook. With a slight improvement in visibility the formation flew across the airfield with moisture streaming from the wing tips as they went. And then a surprise came in the form of the two airspares, who flew across the field at high speed creating a truly memorable image of a pair of Lightnings almost shrouded in moisture. After that the formation did the traditional run and break before landing.

In August 1987 Binbrook would announce the 'Last Last Lightning Show'. Unfortunately, it rained heavily that day but even so the locals managed to undertake some flying. XR763 'E' of No. 11 Squadron is seen in sunnier times trundling down the Binbrook taxiway. *(BBA Collection)*

After the Last Last Lightning Show the retirement of the fleet now got underway, with the scrapping of the airfield decoys taking place at the end of September. These were quickly replaced by more retired airframes that had been stripped of any usable spares. No. 5 Squadron held a families' day and aircrew reunion at the beginning of November before finally disbanding and converting to the Tornado F3 at Coningsby in December. No. 11 Squadron was disbanded at the end of April 1988, performing a final nine-aircraft formation over Binbrook and Coningsby. The remaining aircrew undertook the task of delivering the last few airworthy airframes to museums and various RAF bases for battle damage training or display. And thus the Lightning had gone.

The 1980s were very much a period of austerity again and as before the Armed Forces bore much of the pain. Such circumstances give rise to ingenuity thus the RAF cast around for a way of improving its fighter defences. The answer was to improve the capability of the BAE Hawk T1s assigned to the Tactical Weapons Unit at Brawdy. Beginning in 1983, eighty-eight aircraft were put through a modification programme that added missile pylons to the inner wing pylons that could carry a single AIM-9 Sidewinder missile while a gun pod was developed for the centreline position under the fuselage. The final aircraft was completed in 1986 the plan being to create a mixed fighter force that would see either a Phantom or Tornado F3 acting as the lead aircraft using its radar to point its smaller brethren towards any incoming enemy aircraft. When the Cold War ended the need for these aircraft ended although they acquired another role: that of aggressors in air to air combat exercises.

While the fighter and tanker communities had been undergoing a revamp other aircraft within the Strike Command community had found themselves in more perilous circumstances. In September 1983 the BRITFORLEB troops arrived in Lebanon as part of a United Nations peacekeeping force. The Lebanon was still being torn apart by

Parked up at Lyneham is Hercules C3 XV222 that had originally been delivered as a short-bodied C1. Conversion work to create this new model was carried out at Marshalls of Cambridge. *(Bob Archer Collection)*

both religious and political differences that had wracked the country for many decades. Support for the ground forces was centred upon Akrotiri, Cyprus, as Beirut airport was again out of action as the runway had been damaged by shelling. This left the RAF with only one option: to fly the loads in by C-130 Hercules from Lyneham where they would be broken down into smaller loads for onwards shipment by Chinook. Three of these heavy lift helicopters were deployed to Cyprus: two had been supplied by No. 7 Squadron while the third had come from No. 18 Squadron. To reduce the possibility of being hit by random gunfire all three soon sported large Union flags on the rear rotor pylon. Unlike previous occasions when the Chinooks were deployed those assigned to the detachment were flown to Cyprus stopping at Brindisi, Italy, en route.

To improve the Chinooks chances while flying around Beirut each aircraft had been fitted with chaff and flare dispensers for self defence while the useful Nightsun searchlight had been mounted under the nose. Later in the detachment an infra-red landing light was installed in each airframe this allowing for night operations. As the Chinook was also required to undertake other tasks while in theatre one was fitted with an external hoist that could be used for air sea rescue duties. All three aircraft had been upgraded to the latest modification standard, which included pressure refuelling and composite rotor blades.

When the Chinooks undertook flights into Beirut they would stop en route to refuel aboard the RFA Reliant as the facilities available at the airport were considered dangerous to use and the purity of the fuel itself was suspect. Having departed the ship the inbound helicopter was required to ask for diplomatic clearance during which updates concerning the areas of fighting were supplied. With this information available the Chinook crew contacted the Forward Air Controller on top of the British HQ, after which a high-speed low-level transit was made to the designated landing pad. Once on the ground the aircraft is cleared and reloaded as fast as possible: throughout the aircraft's rotors are kept turning. Once reloaded the helicopter would depart the area as fast as possible, reversing its course as it headed back to Akrotiri.

To provide British forces on the ground with support a detachment of Buccaneers was also deployed to Cyprus, the aircraft being drawn from Nos 12 and 208 Squadrons. Soon after their arrival the Buccaneers undertook three flights over Beirut city just to let the local forces know that the ground troops had air support available if needed. Six aircraft were deployed to Cyprus with one being kept fully fuelled and armed on QRA. Held in reserve the five remaining aircraft undertook numerous training exercises over the sea as well utilizing the local bombing ranges for practice attacks. They also indulged in some air combat flying against squadrons on deployment for armament practice camps as well as utilizing the Victor tankers on detachments for refuelling practise. The BRITFORLEB force was withdrawn in 1984.

This would also be the period when security and NATO were toned down, the former was more orientated towards the activities of various Irish terrorist groups while the latter was a much needed reaction to the increase in Soviet air attack capability. RAF Germany would, for obvious reasons, undergo this process first with hardened aircraft shelters (HAS) springing up all over each airfield while green paint became the colour of the day for virtually everything. In Britain the Strike Command airfields also began to see the same changes although the larger aircraft were still left outside on dispersals instead of being placed under cover. Even so, the brightness of the concrete had a substance applied to reduce its glare. Some of the items painted green utilized an infra-red component, however due to funding shortages the modified vehicle lights and goggles were never supplied. Airfield security in general was also beefed up; on most bases the perimeter was fairly open. This state of affairs soon changed when some were given perimeter fencing all round. Much of this not only had an outer overhang, but also had an inner overhang. When asked by a member of the ground crew why this should be the security officer replied that 'it was to keep you buggers in when your aircraft have departed towards Russia'.

Training exercises also took on a more realistic tone, not only was the annual TACEVAL beefed up but smaller local exercises increased in reality as all ranks

Presaging events to come Victor K2 XH672 is chased by a pair of Buccaneer S2s from No. 208 Squadron and a Tornado GR1 from No. 12 Squadron. *(John Ryan Collection)*

The Canberra PR9 would continue to provide the British Armed Forces with much needed real time reconnaissance albeit their numbers were dwindling. PR9 XH135 lifts off from Wyton at the start of another mission. *(Bob Archer Collection)*

struggled to get to grips with the consequences of decisions and orders as they passed through the chain of command. Even the threat and reality of extreme bad weather was not allowed to curtail these operations while aircraft required for alert duties were still kept on line.

Representative of the exercises was Elder Forest 90, which was held between 23 and 27 April 1990. This was an air defence exercise therefore the attacking force, Orange Force, consisted of Tornado GR1s, Canberras, Buccaneers and Hawks while some NATO forces also featured, these including *Luftwaffe* Phantoms and Alpha Jets, French Jaguars and Mirages, F-16s from various European air forces plus USAF F-111s and B-52s. To simulate the electronic support available to any incoming enemy air attack the USAF provided EF-111s and EC-130H Hercules while Norway and Italy provided further aircraft.

Opposing the Orange Forces was Blue Force, comprising the Tornado F3s flying from Coningsby, Leeming, Leuchars and Stornoway. Also taking part were the Phantoms from Leuchars and Wattisham while Hawk T1As operated from Scampton and Wattisham. One of the exercises objectives was to fully test Britain's air defences, which included mixed fighter force tactics, Rapier missile point defence and the Bloodhound area defence surface to air missiles. Airborne early warning was also given a thorough workout, which included the Avro Shackleton AEW2 from No. 8 Squadron, while the Boeing E-3A Sentries from NATO were also involved. Tanker support was provided by the Victor K2s from Marham plus the Vickers VC 10 tankers from Brize Norton operated by No. 101 Squadron. USAF KC-135 tankers were also involved.

The Royal Navy involvement was limited to the Type 42 destroyers HMS *Glasgow* and HMS *Nottingham* whose task was to provide extended radar coverage across the North Sea and warn of incoming enemy forces. Unlike a genuine war the incoming raiders were allowed to continue their attacks once they had been confirmed as intercepted. This gave their targets a hard time as raid after raid hit the target airfields before peeling off to undertake a simulated nuclear attack over the various weapons ranges before returning to their home bases. Each air raid brought with it different scenarios, including the usual nuclear, biological and chemical attacks plus the usual plethora of unexploded bombs scattered around the airfield. Although most of these raids took place in daylight some were carried out at night and for some strange reason they always took place at meal times or shift changeovers. While in a real war most of the flying criteria would be quietly shelved, as this was a training exercise the usual minima of 250 feet and a maximum speed of 450 knots was rigidly observed. While on a personnel basis there may have been some competition between the opposing sides the purpose of the exercise was to test the capability of Britain's air defences after which the various groups would undertake an extensive debriefing in order to iron out any problems encountered during this period.

One of the aircraft involved in Elder Forest would be the venerable English Electric Canberra. Three units still operated the Canberra, the type having entered service in the 1950s. Their tasks were varied and included reconnaissance, target facilities and ECM training. The reconnaissance role was undertaken by No. 39 Squadron based at Wyton. Having disbanded under mysterious circumstances during Operation *Corporate* the unit would reappear as No. 1 Photographic Reconnaissance Unit (PRU), commemorating the first such unit formed at Benson during the Second World War. The unit's number plate would finally be resurrected as No. 39 (1 PRU) Squadron in 1992. All through this period the unit had remained the only strategic reconnaissance platform available to Strike Command.

No. 100 Squadron had originally been a Victor bomber unit before disbanding in 1968. The number plate remained dormant until 1972 when the unit was reformed at West Raynham as a Canberra operator. Its role was to provide a variety of target facilities for aircraft undertaking armament practice camps in Cyprus and to act as intruders and decoys in exercises. In the target towing role the Canberras flew with a target banner attached to a hook on the rear fuselage for the training fighter pilots to shoot at, the Canberra crew always hoping that none would hit them. Fortunately few such occurrences took place and thus the attacking pilots were able to fly alongside the banner to check their scores, after which the aircraft would drop its banner on the airfield approaches before landing. During its existence as a Canberra operator No. 100 Squadron would fly the B2, T19, E15, PR7 and TT18 models before trading its mixture in for the BAE Hawk in late 1991 at Wyton. During its time with its mixed Canberra fleet the squadron had moved to Marham in 1976 and thence to Wyton six years later. Eventually, the unit would pitch up at its current base of Leeming in 1995.

When the Canberra was required for a new role that was outside the basic specification of the airframe the answer was to graft on a new nose to contain the new equipment. Mostly these would see the aircraft growing a pointy nose, however in the case of the T17 the new proboscis was more bulbous with added blisters to house the aerials. The sole operator of the Canberra T17 and its upgraded sibling the T17A was No. 360 Squadron based at Wyton. The unit, manned by both RAF and Royal Naval personnel, was to provide ECM training during air defence exercises and for the Royal Navy and its surface vessels. While it was mainly equipped with the T17 the squadron also operated some other versions, including Canberra PR7s and E15s that were inherited from No. 100 Squadron. Even such a useful airframe as the Canberra T17/ T17A would have a finite life therefore the decision was taken to disband the unit in October 1994. After disbandment the ECM spoofing role was handed over to a civilian contractor.

Although the HSA Andover C1 had been a victim of the defence cuts in the 1970s when the only British-based unit, No. 46 Squadron, had been disbanded some of the stored Andovers would have a second life. This would be with No. 115 Squadron whose Argosy E1s were due for replacement. To replace these elderly transports Andover C1s were converted to E3 standard after removal from No. 5 MU at Kemble and delivered to No. 115 Squadron based at Brize Norton. The squadron would utilize their new mounts in the airfield calibration role, as had been the case with the Argosies. This would not only involve the aircraft undertaking controlled approaches towards the runway aids undergoing checking before breaking off to overshoot at a predetermined point. Sometimes a member of the crew would be dropped off complete with a theodolite, which was used to check the angle of descent of the Andover. Like many aircraft the Andovers of No. 115 Squadron were utilized to fly spares and personnel around Britain during Operation *Corporate*. In January 1984 No. 115 Squadron would leave Brize Norton for Benson as pressure on space at the former was increasing with the arrival of the Tristar and VC 10 tanker fleets. The squadron remained operational at Benson until it was disbanded in October 1993.

The Andover was also still in service with the Queen's Flight that had previously been the Northolt Communications Squadron based at Northolt. When renamed the Queen's Flight the unit moved to Benson where it occupied a secured compound to protect the aircraft and personnel from attack. During its existence the unit flew the Andover CC2, Whirlwind HCC12 Wessex HCC4 and the BAE 146 CC2. In April 1995 the Queen's Flight became part of No. 32 Squadron this adding various marques of HS125 to the operating fleet. Throughout its existence the unit has been used to fly members of the Royal Family, senior politicians and senior military officers throughout Britain and across to Europe as needed. One other unit would fly the Andover C1, the Open Skies unit. The unit operates converted Andover C1(PR) XS596. This is the British-designated aircraft under the Treaty on Open Skies and is based at Boscombe Down. This aircraft has been fitted with cameras and video recording equipment for recording purposes. This was an east-west understanding brought into force after the numerous disarmament treaties and negotiations finally resulted in both sides involved in the cold war reducing both their conventional and nuclear weaponry. Although some of this could

Having dispensed with its Lightnings No. 5 Squadron would re-equip with the Tornado F3 in January 1988 at Coningsby. In this splendid portrait ZE295 'CC' looks good against the clouds. *(Bob Archer Collection)*

Before it was reborn as a Tornado operator No. 12 Squadron would be one of the last Buccaneer users. Resplendent in its new tactical grey finish is XW543. *(Robbie Shaw Collection)*

be checked using satellites some confirmations of destruction needed a closer look thus both sides designated a small fleet of aircraft for Open Skies flying. These aircraft were allowed access to all areas of the old enemy's territory to confirm the destruction of military material.

By 1990 Strike Command was in pretty good shape, although there had been some rationalization due to defence cuts overall capability had been improved by the introduction of new aircraft. Air defence was the responsibility of the F-4 Phantom and the Tornado F3. The former was still in service with Nos 56 and 74 Squadrons, the latter flying the F-4J plus the Phantom Training Flight, all being based at Wattisham. Only one other unit would operate the type, No. 1435 Flight based at Mount Pleasant in the Falklands. The Tornado F3 was operated by Nos 5 and 29 Squadrons as well as No. 229 OCU, all being based at Coningsby, while Nos 11, 23 and 25 Squadrons were based at Leeming with Leuchars housing Nos 43 and 111 Squadrons. Except for Nos 5 and 11 Squadrons, which previously operated Lightnings, the remainder had flown the Phantom.

Strike and attack was the province of the Buccaneer, Harrier, Jaguar and Tornado GR1. Although it was coming to the end of its operational life the Blackburn Buccaneer still had an important role to play within Strike Command. Only two operational units were flying the type in 1990, Nos 12 and 208 Squadrons, plus No. 237 OCU and all were based at Lossiemouth. All three units also operated the Hunter T7 in the conversion role. The primary task for both squadrons was that of maritime strike and reconnaissance for which task the Sea Eagle missile had been developed. The Harrier was operated by one unit within Strike Command, No. 1 Squadron, based at Wittering where it flew alongside No. 233 OCU. Having flown the original model of Harrier the GR5 had been received in 1988. Outside of Britain the original Harriers were still operated by No. 1417 Flight based at Belize before disbanding in July 1993. Coltishall would be the main base for the Sepecat Jaguar that still equipped Nos 6, 41 and 54 Squadrons in 1990 while the training unit was No. 226 OCU, although this was based at Lossiemouth.

The type with the greatest number in service was the Panavia Tornado, although the majority were operated by squadrons based in RAF Germany. Those allocated to Strike Command included Nos 27 and 617 Squadrons based at Marham while Honington was

Creating the inevitable cloud of smoke on touchdown is Tristar KC1 ZD952 of No. 216 Squadron based at Brize Norton. Kissing the tarmac it isn't. *(BBA Collection)*

home to No. 13 Squadron, which flew the reconnaissance version, the GR1A. The GR1 was also flown by the Tri-national Tornado Training Establishment at Cottesmore plus the Tornado Weapons Conversion Unit that had the shadow designation of No. 45 Squadron.

Supporting all of these units plus any other aircraft with a refuelling probe were the Tristar, VC 10 and Victor tankers. Both the Tristar and VC 10 tankers were based at Brize Norton while the Victors were based at Marham. Also based at Brize Norton were the VC 10 C1s of No. 10 Squadron, the strategic transport unit. At Lyneham the ubiquitous C-130 Hercules ruled the skies. Operated by Nos 24, 30, 47 and 70 Squadrons and No. 242 OCU, the type was used extensively to support both RAF and Army operations, the latter being the province of No. 47 Squadron whose primary duty was special operations. Only one other unit would fly the Hercules, No. 1312 Flight based at Mount Pleasant. At this location the Hercules undertook a multiplicity of roles, including refuelling the defending fighters, maritime patrols and freight hauling when needed.

Around the British Isles and out over the Atlantic the primary maritime patrol aircraft was the Nimrod MR2. The greater number were located at Kinloss, the home of Nos 120, 201 and 206 Squadrons, while St Mawgan was home to No. 42 Squadron and No. 236 OCU, also known as No. 38 (Shadow) Squadron. The only other Nimrod operator was No. 51 Squadron based at Wyton where it was co-located alongside the Electronic Warfare Avionics Unit. The squadron undertook the operational intelligence flying while the EWAU designed, developed and installed the equipment for the aircraft.

Strike Command also had a wide range of helicopters at its disposal in 1990, including the Chinook, Puma, Sea King and the Wessex. The Boeing Chinook HC1 was operated in Britain by No. 7 Squadron at Odiham, which also housing No. 240 OCU that operated a mix of Chinooks and Pumas for conversion purposes. The type was also operated by No. 78 Squadron at Mount Pleasant, the other flight comprising Westland Sea Kings. The Westland Puma was also based at Odiham where it equipped No. 33 Squadron, although the unit also provided crews and aircraft for No. 1563 Flight in Belize. Unlike the Royal Navy the RAF purchased the Sea King HAR3 for air-sea rescue duties with No. 202 Squadron where it replaced the Westland Wessex. The British-based Sea Kings were based at Boulmer, Brawdy, Manston and Lossiemouth while other

Also scheduled to disappear post *Corporate* was the venerable Avro Shackleton AEW2 of No. 8 Squadron based at Lossiemouth. WL756 is seen here undertaking a high power flyby. You can just imagine those Griffons roaring! *(BBA Collection)*

aircraft were based at Mount Pleasant. The Westland Wessex, while becoming long in the tooth, was still providing good service to the RAF. Air-sea rescue was the primary role of No. 22 Squadron whose bright yellow aircraft were based at Chivenor, Leuchars, Valley and Coltishall while No. 72 Squadron based at Aldergrove used its aircraft to transport troops and supplies around Northern Ireland.

In 1990 the AEW fleet consisted of the five remaining Avro Shackleton AEW2s based at Lossiemouth with No. 8 Squadron, although these were slated for retirement in mid-1991. Their replacement was the Boeing Sentry AEW1 that would be based at Waddington, the No. 8 Squadron number plate transferring from that date.

On 9 November 1989 the Berlin Wall came down. The leaders of the West decided that there would be a peace dividend and a great reduction in the arms held by the West. How wrong their projections were as the remaining years of Strike Command would prove.

Chapter 9

War in the Desert – Operation *Granby/Desert Storm*

At the beginning of August 1990 the forces of Iraq under the command of Saddam Hussein began their invasion of the small neighbouring oil-rich country of Kuwait. At that time the author was on the flight deck of Tristar ZE705 listening to the news while in transit between Ascension and Mount Pleasant. This series of transport flights ended a few days later with the Tristar and its crew returning home to Brize Norton. The reason for the invasion given by the Iraqi regime was that Kuwait had been stealing oil from an oil field that both countries shared. The countries around Iraq, especially Saudi Arabia, were worried that they would be next on the list; the West too was also seriously concerned as much of their oil needs were supplied by Kuwait and Saudi Arabia. The latter would request help to defend their borders from the Western powers and their neighbours while the invasion of Kuwait would be referred to the United Nations Security Council who would pass Resolution 660 that demanded that Iraq remove its forces from Kuwait immediately. The war to relieve Kuwait of its invaders would also be the most filmed in the history of warfare giving those back home a view of the work that their armed forces carry out on their behalf.

With the UN Resolution in place the Allied Coalition would form in order to drive the invaders out of Kuwait and to render the Iraqi forces harmless. Britain's involvement in *Desert Shield*, the build-up and the protection of Saudi Arabia, would begin on 9 August when the Defence Secretary, Tom King, confirmed that the British forces would participate. Historically Britain has always had strong links with the area: in 1962 Iraq moved forces to the Kuwait border to which Britain responded by sending an aircraft carrier plus other forces to the Gulf. Fortunately, the regime in Iraq saw sense and withdrew its forces back to barracks.

The air component would initially see the transport element heavily involved with Brize Norton and Lyneham heavily involved. From Brize Norton the VC 10s of No. 10 Squadron would be heavily involved in moving personnel into theatre their task being to prepare the various bases assigned to the fighter and attack forces. No. 216 Squadron and its Tristars would be involved in moving stores and equipment into Riyadh: the KC1s being the most versatile would move these items while the two C2s would transport personnel and their kit into theatre. As both the Tristar C2s were involved in these operations the twice weekly run to the Falkland Islands was taken over by civilian airlines, this remaining the case until well after hostilities ended. The Lyneham

Pictured at Coltishall just after returning home is Jaguar GR3A XZ356 *Mary Rose* of No. 41 Squadron. As an aircraft assigned for reconnaissance duties as well as normal attack missions the aircraft sports a mix of symbols signifying both types of missions as well as a reconnaissance pod under the fuselage. *(Bob Archer Collection)*

Transport Wing would despatch aircraft from Nos 24, 30 and 70 Squadrons for use in theatre for the more conventional transport flights while No. 47 Squadron would concentrate upon the special operations work. The overall commander of British Forces Arabian Peninsula was Air Vice Marshal Wilson while the commander of British Forces Air at Riyadh was Group Captain Peacock-Edwards.

On 11 August 1990 the fighter and attack aircraft began to arrive in theatre. The fighter element was designated as No. 5 (Composite) Squadron and would be based at Dhahran in Saudi Arabia. Commanded by Wing Commander Black the Tornado F3s plus air and ground crews were drawn from Nos 5 and 29 Squadrons while a further ten aircraft were held at the Akrotiri post, an APC detachment. Thumrait in Oman would be the home during Operation *Granby* for the Sepecat Jaguars drawn from the wing at Coltishall. Known as No. 6 (Composite) Squadron the unit was commanded by Wing Commander Connolly and consisted of twelve aircraft that included four from No. 41 Squadron fitted out with reconnaissance equipment. Prior to deploying all of the Jaguars were given an overall coating of Pink Panther desert camouflage. The following day Oman would receive further visitors when Nimrod MR2s from Kinloss were deployed to Seeb. Commanded by Wing Commander Neil, their purpose was to enforce the maritime blockade in the Gulf. Fortunately, the Nimrod crews drew on Exercise Magic Roundabout, these being the regular deployments to the region in support of the Armilla Patrol. Whilst in theatre the Nimrods also received some upgrades and modifications that made their task easier, including: self defence systems, a turret-mounted infra-red system for night operations and the installation of a partial Link 11 system that allowed the aircraft to contact and receive data from US Navy vessels operating in the area. Other upgrades included software changes to the radar systems and the electronic support measures. Seeb would see further arrivals on 12 August when No. 101 Squadron would use the base as its headquarters during the conflict although some of their aircraft would be detached to Riyadh and Bahrain. By 17 August six Phantoms from the Wildenrath fighter wing would arrive at Akrotiri to undertake the air defence of the island should it be needed. Their arrival allowed the ten Tornado F3s that had been held

Air Defence assets deployed to the Gulf included Tornado F3s from the Leeming Fighter Wing. This aircraft is ZE764 'DH' and during peacetime was the mount of the Officer Commanding No. 111 Squadron. *(BBA Collection)*

there after completing their APC to return to Britain. Also arriving at Akrotiri during this period were a pair of Nimrod R1s from No. 51 Squadron based at Wyton; their purpose was to undertake intelligence gathering in the Gulf area. From 10 September the Nimrods began patrols that concentrated on the north-west corner of the Persian Gulf, which allowed the aircraft to radar map the Kuwaiti coast and check on the Iraqi assets known to be there. By this time the Nimrods in common with the remainder of the British aircraft deployed to the Gulf had been fitted with the Mk 12 IFF with Mode 4 security, which stopped the American forces from continuously challenging the aircraft.

By October the Nimrods had the SAR component added to their patrol duties, although they were fully versed in oversea search and rescue: to this was added combat

The Nimrod R1s of No. 51 Squadron provided ELINT services during Operation *Desert Shield/Storm*. The nearest of the pair seen is XW665, both being photographed at Akrotiri. *(BBA Collection)*

SAR overland in the event of an allied aircraft crashing in the desert. While the SAR mission was important, that of monitoring the Gulf was still the primary task, although this would drop off by November 1990 as at last the Iraqi realized that it would be impossible to run a ship through the gauntlet of allied ships and aircraft. In order not to waste such a valuable asset as the Nimrod it was decided to employ them as part of the aerial screen that protected the US Navy carrier battle groups in conjunction with the US Navy P-3s already on station. During *Desert Storm* the Nimrods detachment flew 86 sorties that consumed 616 flying hours. At the conclusion of hostilities the Nimrods continued to undertake patrols over the Gulf before the last returned home to Kinloss on 17 April.

On 23 August the MoD announced that a dozen Tornado GR1s would be sent to Muharraq where they arrived four days later already bedecked in a coat of desert pink. Routeing was via Akrotiri where the Tornados night stopped before proceeding onwards the next day. Designated as No. 14 (Composite) Squadron the commander was Wing Commander Morris while the Air Commander at Muharraq was Group Captain Goodall.

It was also a time of changeover for the Tornado F3 fighters as a replacement force of updated aircraft were ordered to the Gulf as No. 11 (Composite) Squadron commanded by Wing Commander Hamilton. The fighters would depart Leeming on 29 August for Akrotiri using Victor tankers for support. The onward journey would be supported by a tanker of No. 216 Squadron, the fighters splitting off inside the borders of Saudi Arabia for Dhahran while the Tristar landed at Riyadh. Not only was Riyadh operating as a civilian airport, it was also the major military transport gateway for the allied forces. Throughout the conflict the threat of enhanced SCUD missiles fired by the Iraqis was always a threat and numerous air raid warnings would be experienced. Trying to change into an NBC suit, gasmask and tin helmet in the boiling hot hydraulic bay of a Tristar is not recommended! Having brought the first six Tornado F3s into theatre the supporting tanker would return to base to collect a further six at a later date.

Complete with a full complement of bombs, pods, missiles and fuel tanks Panavia Tornado GR1 ZA471 'E' Emma/Snoopy Airways taxies out at Muharraq on its way to attack another target in Iraq. The aircraft eventually returned home adorned with thirty-two mission marks. (*Bob Archer Collection*)

On 14 September a further six Tornado F3s were ordered for deployment to Dhahran while five days later an initial batch of six Tornado GR1s were despatched to Bahrain as part of No. 671 (Composite) Squadron under the command of Wing Commander Iveson. After a night stop at Akrotiri the Tornados departed from their new base the next day. These initial six were followed by a similar number on 26 September. Further changeovers for the Tornado F3 force took place on 22 September when a further six aircraft were deployed to Dhahran, which allowed the last few initially deployed aircraft to return to Britain. As the build-up in the Gulf states continued a senior commander was appointed this being Lt General Sir Peter de la Billière who was appointed as Commander British Forces Middle East on 1 October with Air Vice Marshal Wilson as the deputy commander.

With the number of Tornado GR1s building up at Bahrain it was decided to transfer the aircraft of No. 617 (Composite) Squadron to Tabuk in western Saudi Arabia. Other transfers were also taking place involving the transfer of No. 7 Brigade from Germany to Saudi Arabia, the advance party arriving on 11 October. This heralded the start of the main airlift on 16 October that involved Tristars, VC 10s and Boeing 747 airliners from British Airways. Other flights operating out of Gütersloh included a No. 216 Squadron Tristar KC1 departing Germany with a full load of fuel plus an upper deck full of JSP 233 bomblet dispensers needed for the Tornado GR1s. The total all-up weight of the Tristar on take-off was just short of one million kilograms, and we needed every ounce of power and every inch of runway to get airborne. Even before the full military build-up began a Hercules detachment was in place by 30 October 1990. Designated as the RAF Air Transport Detachment this unit was based at King Khaled international Airport at Riyadh. Originally using three C-130 Hercules the whole premise was to use the airport as a hub with all the other transports feeding their freight and personnel in for redistribution. The Hercules would act as the spokes transporting everything and everyone to their final destinations.

A further deployment of Jaguars would depart from Coltishall on 23 October, the first seven departing on that date being followed by a further five on 2 November. A further singleton aircraft was tanked to Akrotiri by a Tristar KC1 en route with passengers to Akrotiri during this period. During the build-up and the following air war the RAF tanker aircraft played a vital part in getting aircraft into theatre and subsequently on towards their targets. The key role of air-to-air refuelling came to the fore during Operation *Corporate*; without the Victor fleet the Black Buck and long-range Nimrod patrols could not be carried out. Fortunately, the RAF had a good spread of tankers that included Handley Page Victors, getting a bit long in the tooth but still capable, Lockheed Tristars and VC 10Ks tankers, the latter two not joining the inventory until after *Corporate*. No. 101 Squadron would detach two of its VC 10s to the Jaguar base at Thumrait to provide direct support for the aircraft based there. From a VC 10 operator's point of view Thumrait was not an ideal operating base thus on 29 August the two aircraft relocated to Seeb. A further two VC 10s were sent to Muharraq on 27 August their purpose being to provide training and support for the Tornado F3s and GR1/1As deployed to the region. Eventually, seven of the nine VC 10Ks were deployed overseas, the K2s were based at Muharraq while the K3s operated out of Seeb. The remaining two aircraft remained at Brize Norton to complete some crew training, although they would soon be deployed to the Middle East.

During Operation *Desert Shield* the Jaguars from No. 41 Squadron were flown without overwing missile pylons, although XZ355 of No. 41 Squadron does carry an ECM pod under the port wing. *(USAF)*

As the various air assets built up in theatre the VC 10s began to settle into a tasking pattern from October. Fortunately, many of the squadrons' crews were familiar with the American system of Air Tasking Orders that was adopted throughout the theatre. The build-up of air assets also raised another problem, that of getting the tankers to rendezvous with the attack aircraft en route to their targets. This would be especially difficult at night therefore much time and effort was spent in training so that tankers and bombers would be in the right bit of sky at the right time at night. All of this had to be conducted under radio silence; the Tornados meeting up with the tankers and following them to the cast off point having refuelled just prior to that. After reaching their target the tankers would then meet up with the returning Tornados at a predesignated point for a post attack refuel before the attackers departed for home. Having undertaken these training missions both the VC 10 and Tornado crews would utilize this mission profile during the actual air war. Even an aircraft failure would not delay a mission; during a full

Captured above the mountainous area of Saudi Arabia this Tornado F3 has just refuelled from its tanker in this case Tristar K1 ZD951 *Perky*. *(BBA Collection)*

weight take-off from Muharraq a VC 10 suffered an engine failure. The crew would send a revised rendezvous time to Tabuk so that the Tornado crews could rebrief for the changed time. The VC 10 would successfully make a three-engined landing back at base, the crew quickly swapping to the standby aircraft. Their transit time was spent filling in the paperwork for the engine failure on the previous aircraft.

Few modifications were carried out to the tankers at the beginning of the deployment. Have Quick radio systems were fitted plus secure Mode 4 IFF while minor modifications internally catered for the crew should they need to fly wearing NBS equipment. Later in the conflict a Marconi Sky Guardian radar warning receiver was fitted as was a second TACAN unit that incorporated an airborne beacon facility and the Autocat automatic radio relay equipment.

No.101 Squadron would vacate Muharraq on 17 December to make way for the Victor tankers, the VC 10s moving to the international airport at Riyadh. Here they shared a partly built terminal building with the air transport detachment, other air organizations, a large field hospital and the incoming SCUD attacks of which there were many indicated by the air raid sirens. As soon as the squadron was settled it promptly resumed its various refuelling roles while planning for the forthcoming air war. When the first air strikes were launched the tankers found themselves airborne supplying fuel to the JP 233 armed Tornados heading into Iraq. Once the low-level JP 233 attacks had been cancelled the VC 10s would then support the Buccaneer Tornado strike groups undertaking laser-guided bomb attacks. During the air war all of the RAF tankers were also cleared to refuel aircraft from other air forces; in fact the list basically covered anything with a probe. After the intensive flying carried out during the air war, the Iraqi surrender after the short sharp ground war would see No. 101 Squadron hit a short lull. This was short-lived as refuelling tracks were quickly set-up to get the Jaguars and Tornados home to their bases. Soon it would be the turn of No. 101 Squadron to return home to Brize Norton. After a night stop at Palermo Airport, Sicily, the first four aircraft, complete with their BP – The Empire Strikes Back badges – overflew Brize Norton in formation before landing and taxying up to the terminal to be greeted by the waiting families and the media. The remaining tankers would return the following day to a similar sort of welcome.

When Operation *Granby* began five of the eight Tristars of No. 216 Squadron were immediately available; one was at Marshalls of Cambridge undergoing maintenance, while another was deployed on a Medman (Medicine Man in Canada) flight while the last was undertaking the Mount Pleasant to Ascension back and forth runs. As quickly as possible each aircraft was integrated into *Granby* operations, the two C2s starting the move of personnel to their Middle East bases. A similar role was assigned to the two K1s, although they were also refuelling inbound aircraft either to Akrotiri or onto the Middle East. The four KC1s, being more flexible, would find themselves moving personnel, freight, and weapons whilst also refuelling aircraft en route. Such was the workload that at one point five of the squadrons aircraft were on the ground at Akrotiri, four were heading east while the fifth was en route to Brize Norton. All five had disappeared by midnight local time leaving the pan quiet and empty. A detachment would later be sent to Gütersloh in December 1990 to collect weapons for the Tornado force many being JP233 dispensers. During the build-up and the air war there was only one day when all eight Tristars were back at base. This was Christmas Day and the last Tristar passing through picked up the Gütersloh troops; to say the aircraft was packed to the rafters was an understatement.

On Boxing Day the Tristars would resume their tasks of moving men, materials and aircraft into theatre. In mid-January the two K1s were sent to Marshalls of Cambridge for a coat of desert pink to be applied. After returning to Brize Norton they were immediately christened the 'Pink Pigs' with ZD949 becoming 'Pinky' while ZD951 became 'Perky'. Both resumed their transport tasks alongside the remainder of the fleet. By this time all the Tristars were not only carrying warlike materials, they were also carrying mail and any newspapers that could be scrounged up. On the reverse flights letters, 'blueys' were moved back to Brize Norton for onward distribution to their families. Prior to the air war starting it was decided to deploy the K1s overseas, ZD949 would be permanently detached to Riyadh for fighter refuelling duties while ZD951 would undertake the transit trails between Palermo, Sicily, and the Middle East. The inbound bombers and fighters would leave the tanker over the Nile while the Tristar would head into Riyadh. Unless there was an outbound trail the next day there was every chance that ZD951 would be used to undertake a night refuel for the permanent CAP. On one inbound trail ZD951 was escorted for a short while by an RSAF F-5F fighter glorious in gloss black. Once the air war started the two K1s continued their refuel duties while the remainder of the fleet continued to move men and materials into and out of the theatre of operations.

At the conclusion of hostilities the Tristar fleet was heavily involved in returning everything and everyone home as soon as possible. This required each aircraft to land at Brize Norton or Gütersloh, for Germany based personnel, then to undertake a quick turnaround before returning for more people to bring home. One of the largest outbounds from Brize Norton was undertaken on 15 March 1991, Red Nose Day, with three of the Tristars managing to leave before the powers that be insisted that they be removed from the final two aircraft. One of the returning aircraft would come back in freight configuration complete with a pair of Arab Stallions, these being a gift from the King of Saudi Arabia to the Queen. However, this raised quite a few questions about animal welfare, antiseptic cleaning of the freight deck and how to get rid of some half dozen aircraft drip trays with a rather toxic horsey load without contaminating the

A moment of quiet at Brize Norton as ZD951 and ZD949 wait for their deployment to Saudi Arabia. During all phases of Operation *Granby* most of the unit's aircraft were down route somewhere moving personnel or stores into theatre. *(BBA Collection)*

Pictured at Palermo, Sicily, is Tristar K1 ZD951 *Perky* of No. 216 Squadron. The tanker was tasked to collect inbound aircraft from the escorting Victor K2 and take them onto their destinations. *(BBA Collection)*

aircraft. Eventually the veterinary service did their work and the Tristar was cleaned and returned to service.

For the Victor tanker fleet Operation *Granby* would be a last hurrah before retirement after many years of invaluable service. Only No. 55 Squadron was still operating the type as No. 57 Squadron had disbanded in June 1986. When *Granby* began many of No. 55 Squadron's tankers were supporting a Jaguar deployment to Bergstrom AFB Texas, USA, at the Reconnaissance Air Meet. Within twenty-four hours of the invasion of Kuwait the Victors were recalled back to Marham beginning tanking tasking forty-eight hours later. Having completed the required tanker trails of Tornados and Jaguars in concert with Tristars and VC 10Ks No. 55 Squadron were finally deployed to Muharraq on 14 December 1990 to take over the slot previously occupied by No. 101 Squadron. Within two days four Victors were at Muharraq plus six crews. Once they were settled

As well as being a major international airport Riyadh was also home, on a temporary basis, to many allied aircraft. In this view four VC 10K tankers can be seen, including ZA147 'F', ZA148 'G', ZA148 'J' and ZA149 'H'. *(BBA Collection)*

in the Victors began refuelling RAF aircraft undergoing training over the desert. As the number of aircraft in theatre from all nations began to build up it became obvious that keeping each country's tankers just for their own use was seriously impractical. The answer was to clear all probed aircraft to use any available tanker asset. This in turn would see the Victors undertaking trails all over Saudi Arabia refuelling anything that came along.

Further Victors would arrive at Muharraq on 16 January 1991 this bringing the force up to six aircraft and eight crews plus a full supporting cast of ground crew. Over the next four days the Victors undertook further training sorties until 16 January when two aircraft were launched to support a force of Tornados heading towards Iraq. The tankers would fly the Olive Low Trail south of the Iraqi border, although the tankers would cast off the Tornados as they headed north on the racetrack. This location would be the main area of operations for the Victors throughout the entire air war; not only did they refuel target bound aircraft the tankers would also be in place to collect the returnees and refuel them for their final journey back to base. Initially on these sorties the Victors would be fully fuelled for take-off, although this would increase the fatigue life consumption threefold. As experience was gained the fuel load was adjusted downwards this in turn reducing the fatigue life consumption. Three days after the start of the air war another Victor was deployed to Muharraq in order to spread the workload as a minimum of fourteen sorties were being flown every day. During the air war the Victors flew nearly 300 sorties with each crew flying at least thirty-three missions each.

The next deployment would be announced by the MoD on 24 October and would involve Westland Puma helicopters. Three pink Pumas were collected by a USAF Lockheed C-5 Galaxy from Brize Norton on 1 November being followed by a further eight the following day, while another four would follow on 3 November. All were destined for No. 230 (Composite) Squadron based at Ras Al Ghar, the base commander being Group Captain Hunt. The Pumas had been fitted with infra-red jamming equipment, chaff and flare dispensers plus enhanced navigation equipment. From this date the Hercules force based at Riyadh began flying to all the bases within theatre

Seen on the ground at Muharraq is Victor K2 XH672 *Maid Marion*. This war was also the swansong for the type as the Victor would leave service soon afterwards. Fortunately this aircraft is preserved at Cosford. *(Bob Archer Collection)*

moving personnel and supplies to wherever they were required. It would be the turn of the Chinooks to follow next on 24 November, these too requiring airlifting into theatre by C-5 Galaxy. As with other aircraft in theatre these helicopters were painted desert pink and had similar updates fitted to those installed on the Pumas. Some of the Chinooks were also fitted with night vision goggles for special operations usage. While the first handful of Chinooks were delivered to No. 7 (Composite) Squadron at Ras Al Ghar the remainder were sent by sea, departing from Southampton on 23 December.

During the end of November and the beginning of December the various RAF commanders in the Gulf were rotated home thus the Dhahran Tornado F3 force would become No. 43 (Composite) Squadron under the command of Wing Commander Moir while the Jaguars at Murharraq would change from No. 6 (Composite) Squadron to No. 41 (Composite) Squadron under the command of Wing Commander Pixton. Also at Murharraq the Tornado GR1s were renumbered from No. 14 (Composite) Squadron to No. XV (Composite) Squadron commanded by Wing Commander Broadbent. The Tornado force at Tabuk was also renumbered with No. 617 (Composite) Squadron becoming No. 20 (Composite) Squadron commanded by Wing Commander Heath while the station commander at Muharraq became Group Captain Henderson and Group Captain Hedges took over at Tabuk.

Muharraq was becoming a very busy place and adding to the number of aircraft there was the arrival of the first Victor K2 from No. 55 Squadron based at Marham. The first would arrive on 14 December while a further three arrived the following day, the whole being commanded by Wing Commander Williams. Further reinforcements were despatched by sea on 23 December. The vessel was the new *Atlantic Conveyer* and its load included four Pumas, eight Chinooks and twelve Royal Navy Sea Kings. *Atlantic Conveyer* arrived at Al Jubayl in Saudi Arabia on 8 January.

On 30 December the MoD would announce that a third squadron's worth of Tornado GR1s would be despatched to Saudi Arabia. By 2 January 1991 six Tornado GR1s would depart from Bruggen for Dhahran where they would form the core of No. 31 (Composite) Squadron under the command of Wing Commander Witts. Further aircraft

Complete with desert filters for the engines, chaff and flare dispensers, infra-red decoy equipment, a machine gun in the forward door position and a paint scheme sufficient to give you nightmares is Chinook HC1 ZA720 fully configured for special operations duties. *(Bob Archer Collection)*

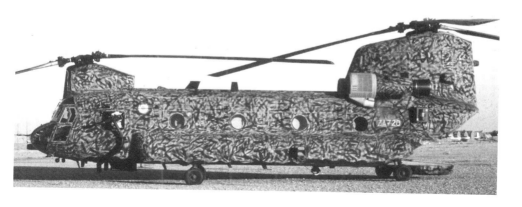

A less gaudy machine is Chinook HC1 ZD982 'I' seen at Riyadh complete with sand filters for the engines. The inverted V signifies an allied aircraft. *(Bob Archer Collection)*

would be tanked into the region over the following two days. Unlike the earlier deployed aircraft these featured uprated engines, a new IFF, provision for 495-gallon underwing tanks plus GPS navigation equipment. A further tranche of Tornados would follow on 14 January, although these were the GR1A reconnaissance arriving at Dhahran the following day to form No. 2 (Composite) Squadron commanded by Wing Commander Threadgould. The first three aircraft deployed were ZA371, ZA372 and ZA373, which made the flight nonstop courtesy of a Tristar tanker from No. 216 Squadron. Soon after arrival the Tornados undertook a series of test flights from Dhahran to trial the upgraded equipment, fortunately the imagery produced was acceptable. On 15 January another GR1A, ZA370, arrived at Dhahran, followed the next day by ZA397 and ZA400. Throughout the greater part of the conflict the reconnaissance Tornados undertook the majority of their missions at night even when their bomber counterparts had switched to daylight operations. By this time there were forty-two Tornado GR1s/GR1As deployed in theatre. On 16 January 1991 Tristar K1 ZD941 would be flown to Marshalls

This gaggle of Tornado GR1As includes ZD719 'AD' *Check Six*, ZA374 'CN' *Miss Behavin* and ZA457 'CE' *Bob*, all operating out of Dhahran, Saudi Arabia. *(Bob Archer Collection)*

Captured inbound is Victor K2 XL164 *Saucy Sal* of No. 57 Squadron based at Marham. Fortunately, the nose of this aircraft has been preserved. *(BBA Collection)*

of Cambridge to have a coat of desert pink applied to the fuselage and fin, although the blue cheat line would remain. It was quickly followed by the other K1, ZD951, both becoming known as the Pink Pigs and individually named as *Pinky* and *Perky* respectively.

The aircraft deployed to the Gulf underwent further modifications to fit them better for combat thus the Tornado F3s were late-build aircraft fitted with the latest AI.24 Foxhunter radar absorbing materials on the leading edges. In addition, Tracor AN/ALE-40(V) flare dispensers were mounted on the rear lower fuselage. During their transit flight the aircraft used their normal underwing fuel tanks, although these were replaced by the larger type used by the GR1 version in order to improve loiter time. Further modifications were applied to the air conditioning system to enhance its capability in the desert while short-range combat capability was improved by the purchase of Raytheon AIM-9M Sidewinder missiles instead of the normal AIM-9Ls

Awaiting its next task is Puma XW220 'H'. During *Desert Storm* the Pumas were used to move troops forward to the battle area. Note the white stripes edged in black on the tail boom. *(Bob Archer Collection)*

Lacking any sort of allied identity markings is Puma HC1 ZA937 'O' complete with a full suite of self defence equipment. *(Bob Archer Collection)*

normally used. During the conflict Dhahran would maintain a continuous twenty-four-hour Combat Air Patrol (CAP), the task being divided between the RAF, USAF and the Royal Saudi Air Force. Tanker support for the fighters flying the patrol racetrack was normally provided by the VC 10 tankers of No. 101 Squadron, although the Tristar tankers of No. 216 Squadron were utilized if needed. Although the airborne CAP could become boring after a while to stop this happening some of the F3s were fitted with smaller fuel tanks borrowed from the GR1 force. Although these were limited to subsonic speeds they did have a higher 'g' rating. With these fitted the F3s were able to carry out simulated interceptions of attack aircraft training for missions over Iraq.

When the Jaguar force was initially deployed to the Gulf a few enhancements were added that included a revised mounting tray to accept the fitment of the Mk 12 IFF (Identification Friend or Foe), changes to the ALE-40 flare/chaff system, removal of some nonessential instruments to improve forward visibility plus a series of changes to aid cooling of both equipment and pilot. Subsequently this initial work became known as Stage 1. The Stage 2 programme started at the beginning of September 1990 and comprised two dedicated tracks working a two-shift system varying between eight and twelve hours each as circumstances dictated. As the aircraft came off the modifications line they were fed into the training programme to give the aircrew experience of the new equipment and to shake down the modifications. All twelve Stage 2 aircraft were completed by the end of October with the deployment taking place at the end of that month and early November. The programme incorporated all the Stage 1 enhancements and, in addition, a new radar warning receiver (RWR), together with an improved cockpit display, limited night vision capability, a video camera fitted to the Head-Up Display for rapid post attack and training sortie analysis, and an ability to dispense flares from the ALE-40 in a manner that better matched the threat from heat-seeking missiles. There were also engine performance modifications to recover some of the thrust lost because of the high ambient temperatures in the Gulf. Stage 2 also saw the introduction of overwing pylons for the AIM-9 Sidewinder missiles. The design and manufacture of these pylons, machined by British Aerospace from solid billets of metal within two weeks of the order being given, was a major achievement.

Initial approval for the Jaguar enhancements covered a total of twenty-eight aircraft and thus the Stage 3 programme covered the update of sixteen more aircraft, eight of these having just returned from the Gulf. Also at this time one of the most successful weapons to be used by the Jaguar became available, the high-velocity Canadian Rocket Vehicle (CRV-7), and arrangements were made to clear it for use on the inboard pylons so that training with it could begin in the Gulf. Another modification was GEC-Ferranti's upgrade to the weapon aiming computer software to cater for the ballistics of the US CBU-87 cluster bomb, which was quickly cleared for use with the Jaguar. This weapon was capable of being dropped from medium level thus endowing the Jaguar crews with a new operational option; one that they subsequently used extensively. Whilst work continued on the aircraft at home, further enhancements capable of installation in-theatre were developed and modification kits were sent to the Gulf. Principal amongst these was a second VHF/UHF radio to improve communications with AWACS, and the ability to fire the CRV-7 from both inboard and outboard pylons, separately or together. Work on the Stage 3 programme was finally completed on 14 February.

When the aircraft deployments were first mooted there was no intention for the Buccaneer to become involved. However, it was quickly realized by Strike Command that the aircraft was the only one in the inventory that could use the AN/AVQ 23E 'Pave Spike' pod, for use with laser-guided bombs, in the case of the Buccaneer this was the CPU-123/B Paveway 2. Modifications for Gulf deployment included the fitment of extended wing tips to improve hot and high performance plus an Mk XII Mode 4 IFF, Have Quick II secure radios, AN/ALE-40 chaff/flare dispensers plus a complete re-spray in Desert Pink.

The air war, codenamed *Desert Storm*, would begin in the early hours of 17 January with the despatch from Muharraq of the Tornado GR1s based there. Fitted with Hunting JP233 bomblet dispensers their task was to use this weapon to crater the infrastructure of the Iraqi airfields. Known as the L2 Mk 1, each pod contained 30 SG357 runway cratering bomblets plus 216 HB876 area denial munitions, resulting in an overall weight of 5,158lb. During these attacks Tornado ZD971/BG was shot down by a Roland surface-to-air missile, the crew ejecting safely although they would become prisoners of war. This was also the debut of the BAE ALARM anti-radar missile whose service pre-release trials would be cut short for use during the air war. I had possibly the best trials situation for any new weapon as it was carried into battle by No. IX Squadron aircraft, ZB810/AA, this being the first of fifty-two Suppression of Enemy Air Defences (SEAD) missions flown that night. The ALARM missile is designed to home in on the signal generated by a ground radar installation. Should the emitter switch off after launch the missile will climb to height and remain airborne courtesy of a parachute. Once the emitter restarts the parachute is ejected, and the secondary motor starts driving the missile onto its target.

Chasing SCUDs kept the GR1As occupied over the night of 17–18 January with ZA400 and ZA371 successfully tracking down a missile launcher while flying at low level. Unfortunately, no allied aircraft were available to attack this choice target and all the reconnaissance aircraft got for their troubles was a bullet through one of their fins. Unlike the other Tornados involved in attack missions those involved in reconnaissance were sometimes called upon at short notice to undertake a mission. The aircraft sometimes had to launch with four fuel tanks aboard due to the lack of tanker availability, however under more normal circumstances only the underwing tanks were carried while

Muharraq was a very busy place during Operation *Desert Shield*, while XZ396 awaits its next pilot an F-15E Eagle from Seymour-Johnson AFB taxies behind. *(USAF)*

the other pylons were occupied with a Sky Shadow ECM pod and a BOZ-107 chaff and flare dispenser.

The Jaguar would be engaged in *Desert Storm* operations from Day 1, its targets being Iraqi installations inside Kuwait. As the Jaguars were based in Bahrain in-flight refuelling was a necessity thus Victors or VC 10 tankers were always on hand to provide fuel when needed. The first Jaguar mission was launched from Muharraq using four aircraft. Their intended target was an Iraqi Army barracks in Kuwait, the bomb load comprising two 1,000lb bombs on the centreline pylon. This layout only lasted a few days, however, as a load of two bombs was considered too light to be of effective use thus the centreline became home to a fuel tank while the inner wing pylons were fitted with bomb beams thus doubling the bomb load at a stroke. On 18 January, the second day of the air war, the Jaguars concentrated on targets within the south-east corner of Iraq their primary targets being the mobile SCUD launchers plus any anti-aircraft positions that they came across while the following day would see them hitting SAM missile launchers.

Protection for the allied air strikes was provided by the Tornado F3s supplied by No. 43 (Composite) Squadron from Dhahran, although no Iraqi resistance was encountered. During the first daylight raids it would be the turn of the Muharraq-based Jaguars to undertake their first attacks using the newly deployed CRV-7 rocket pods. However, these were not fully effective initially until Ferranti worked round the clock to integrate the weapon into the computer weapon-aiming system. This was completed within two weeks and turned the rocket into a devastating weapon that could be fired singly or by rippling. The effectiveness of this weapon has more to do with its speed of entry, Mach 4, than its warhead, which is quite light.

The air movements side of *Desert Storm* was also fully occupied from the start moving army personnel to their designated start positions. Due to the lack of proper airfields the C-130s were required to use rough strips in the desert to deliver their loads. In order that quick role turnarounds could be carried out the aircraft were configured for combat loading with the inside of the fuselage gutted of seats and other equipment. In the case of personnel movements this required the troops to sit on the floor and to hang on to whatever was available – mainly each other!

Preparing to depart from Brize Norton en route to the Gulf is Hercules C1P XV306 *The Baron* complete with Snoopy artwork. *(BBA Collection)*

During *Desert Shield* and the subsequent *Desert Storm* the C-130 fleet flew 7,400 sorties that used nearly 3,000 flying hours. The number of passengers flown reached nearly 23,000 while freight tonnage reached nearly 20 million tons. After the ceasefire the air transport detachment began to fly into Kuwait International Airport, the first aircraft touching down on 28 February 1991. Some of these were incredibly dicey as visibility was obscured by oily black smoke that was emanating from burning oil wells. Once the situation had settled the Hercules began to run as a mini airline transporting personnel, equipment and freight to Al Jubayl, Tabuk, Muharraq, Dubai and Kuwait City, all flights starting from Riyadh.

Day 2 of the air war would see a second Tornado, ZA392/EK, shot down during an airfield attack, although in this case the crew were posted as missing. This was also the day when Iraq launched its first SCUD attack against Saudi Arabia, the target being Dhahran. During a raid by Tornados on another airfield an Iraqi Mirage F1EQ was destroyed while taxiing out to take off. Again the Tornado F3s were airborne providing air cover; a pair were called away by an orbiting USAF Boeing E-3 AWACS to protect a flight of Fairchild A-10 Thunderbolts from a detected incoming air attack. As the Tornados approached at high speed the incoming Iraqi aircraft turned away and fled back to their base.

Over the night of 18–19 January Tornado GR1As undertook a reconnaissance over Iraq that revealed a mobile SCUD launcher whose missile was pointed towards Israel. While the SCUD missiles were militarily insignificant their political clout was massive. Given the concern raised prior to *Desert Storm* about a possible response by Israel if the country was attacked every effort was made to destroy these launchers and their support vehicles. Prior to their deployment the six aircraft chosen from No. 2 Squadron for deployment were subject to modification by Computing Devices Co. in an effort to improve the imagery captured by the GR1A's systems. Known as Granby 2 some improvement in image quality was revealed but even so it required the skills of good interpreters of the Reconnaissance Intelligence Centre to get the best from each image.

On Day 3 the weather had improved as previous operations had been hampered by rainfall. This clearance allowed the Jaguars to undertake a full range of attacks against Iraqi positions near the Kuwait border. The Jaguar pilots also showed a great degree of cunning. Determined to hit a missile launcher before it packed up and disappeared into the desert again the Jaguars lurked in the cloud cover before reaching time on target after which they dropped rapidly through the cloud and destroyed the target, not bad for an aircraft with no radar fitted. From the outset the Jaguars flew with a pair of AIM-9 Sidewinders on overwing pylons, an ALQ-101 ECM pod on the port outer underwing pylon, a Phimat pod carried on the starboard underwing pylon, and a fuel tank on the fuselage centreline pylon while both inner pylons carried 1,000lb bombs or other weapons of choice. Unfortunately, the day was marred by the loss of another Tornado GR1; the pilot was reported as missing while the navigator became a POW.

By Day 4 the RAF had flown 300 missions against targets in western and southern Iraq, the majority of which were airfields, and other targets in south-east Iraq and Kuwait. During that day's raids Tornado GR1, ZD893/AG, suffered a control restriction on take-off; the crew successfully jettisoned weapons in the hope of bringing the aircraft back to base. Unfortunately, this was not possible and the crew ejected safely. The following day it was confirmed that the Tornado fleet would undertake its attack missions from a greater altitude in order to reduce losses. The MoD also announced that four more Tornado GR1s would be flown to join those already in theatre.

On 22 January the RAF would suffer another Tornado loss when ZA467/FF was shot down over Iraq, with the crew being reported as lost. It was from Day 7 that the Tornado force had begun to use laser-guided bombs and it was also revealed that all three tankers types had completed 700 sorties with 100 per cent reliability. This would also be the day that another Tornado, ZA403/CO, was lost while carrying a full load of 1,000lb bombs. The following day the RAF nearly lost another Tornado when a SAM exploded near the aircraft flipping it over. Fortunately the crew regained control of ZD843/DH and after dumping its remaining stores limped back to Dhahran badly damaged. The GR1A 'Scudbusters' were still chasing the SCUD launchers, their missions taking them down to 200 feet at a speed of nearly 580 knots. Normal sortie lengths were between two and three and a half hours, although on 24 January the sortie time for ZA371 was nearly four and a half hours. The MoD would announce that a half squadron of Buccaneers from Lossiemouth would be sent to operate in the target marking role for the Tornado fleet. Two would be prepared at Abingdon while the remainder would come from Lossiemouth.

On Day 10, 26 January, the allied air forces began to concentrate on Iraqi troop concentrations in order to destroy their structure and morale. The RAF Tornados began to concentrate on the elite Republican Guards located near the Iraq-Kuwait border. From this date the media began to show swathes of Iraqi troops, mainly conscripts, throwing away their weapons and surrendering to any kind of vehicle, including helicopters. The Jaguar force were concentrating on destroying various anti-aircraft and anti-ship missile positions, and on this day a Silkworm battery was destroyed on the Kuwait coast. Further reinforcements would also enter theatre these being the first two Buccaneers to Muharraq with Wing Commander Cope in command. The following day would see another pair arrive while the final pair landed on 28 January. The six Buccaneers were XX899, XX892, XW547, XW533, XX889 and XW530, their fin codes spelling PIRATE.

Over 26/27 January sixteen Tornado GR1s undertook overnight attacks against radar site, command and control facilities and ammunition storage dumps with great success. The GR1As were not idle either as a sortie was launched at the USAF's behest to assess the damage to bridges as cloud cover was hiding them from satellite reconnaissance. As before the tanker fleet was undertaking support missions not only in support of RAF

Muharraq was a busy place during the Gulf War as the author can testify. Aircraft of all types and all nations were to be seen as were the various airlines to whom the airfield was better known at Bahrain International. Tucked away in a corner is Buccaneer XW533 'A' awaiting preparation for its next mission. *(Bob Archer Collection)*

aircraft, but virtually anything with a refuelling probe. Also using this facility on a more consistent basis were the Tornado F3s as these were undertaking CAPs over Iraqi airspace. This was also the day that much of the Iraqi Air Force flew en masse to safety in Iran. The original total was given as thirty-nine, although this was later updated to sixty-nine. The fleeing of the aircraft would guarantee that allied air supremacy was almost complete.

Over the following night the Tornado GR1s were back in action again, although on this occasion they were toting ALARM missiles as they were providing support to RSAF Tornados engaged in bombing raids against targets in Iraq. During Day 12 it was announced that the oil refineries were now regarded as strategic targets and thus open to bombing, although Saddam Hussein would beat them to it on many occasions.

It would be the Jaguar fleet that would take centre stage as they continued their attacks on Silkworm missile sites, the attacks being carried out in conjunction with other aircraft attacking vessels of the Iraqi Navy. It was during these attacks that American supplied CBU-87 cluster bombs due to a shortage of Hunting-manufactured BL755 weapons. The overnight raids by the Tornados struck at the air bases at Al Taqaddum and Ubay bin al Jarh plus the fuel storage dump at Ad Diwaniyah.

The closing days of January would see the Jaguars in action again when a pair of Jaguars were directed towards some naval targets by a circling AWACS. The vessels were some Iraqi Polnocny C- Class landing craft, which were sunk with CRV-7 rockets and cannon fire. Others attacked an artillery position north of Kuwait while to the south a command bunker was also destroyed. Most of these rocket attacks were undertaken from a range of 1,000 metres, although as a high velocity weapon the rockets had a range of 6,000 metres. Further attacks against artillery positions were undertaken by Jaguars in southern Kuwait with some success. Raids over the next two nights would be the preserve again of the Tornados whose targets included fuel and the remaining oil refineries causing massive explosions while others struck at the airfields at Al Taqaddum and Habbinyah to the west of Baghdad.

Surrounded by ground equipment and with ground crew in attendance Buccaneer XX889 'T' sports a pirate flag on the nose plus a Pave Spike pod under the wing. Eventually named Longmorn and sporting fourteen mission marks this aircraft is currently with the Jet Age Museum. *(Bob Archer Collection)*

Day 16, 1 February, would see the combat debut of the Buccaneers carrying the Westinghouse AN/AVQ- 23E Pave Spike laser designator whose first use was against a bridge over the River Euphrates, which was bombed by two Tornados that loosed six Pave Way bombs against the target. Jaguars would also be in action this day attacking a ZSU-23/4 anti-aircraft vehicle and destroying it with cluster bombs, although only two were carried per aircraft. While these weapons were effective against all soft targets their effects were, to say the least, devastating. Eventually, international pressure would see the global banning of these weapons.

On 2 February the Buccaneers, rejoicing in the self-given name of Sky Pirates, undertook their first mission, which was the target marking of the As Samawah bridge. The aircraft flying the mission were XX899 and XW530. This was also the biggest day for the RAF operations in the Gulf, involving Buccaneers, Jaguars and Tornados whose targets were airfields, fuel dumps, weapons dumps and Silkworm missile sites.

The Tornado force were again in action over the night of 2/3 February when they attacked a crude oil pumping plant in western Iraq while others bombed three petro-chemical plants with great success and others bombed an Iraqi air base. The following day Jaguars were in action again striking against ammunition dumps south of Kuwait City with spectacular results while others dropped 1,000lb air burst bombs on artillery positions on the island of Faylakah, clearing the way for its recapture by Allied forces.

From Day 18 the Tornado force began undertaking its bombing raids during the day with Iraqi barracks in Kuwait being the target. This was followed by an attack on a bridge across the Euphrates, each end being target marked by supporting Buccaneers. Belatedly on Day 21, 6 February, an RAF spokesman confirmed the destruction of four bridges and a SCUD launcher. This was also the day when the GEC-Ferranti TIALD, (Thermal Imager And Laser Designation) pod was first deployed to the Gulf theatre. Had Operation *Granby* not arrived the service trials would have taken longer, however it was reasoned that the Gulf air war was as good a place as any to trial the new equipment and to sort out any faults. Getting the pods ready for deployment was not without tribulations. The trials pod had been undergoing flight trials under the wing of a trials

Buccaneer. This was quickly removed and despatched to Ferranti in Edinburgh for refurbishment while a second unit was assembled from spares. Manufacture of a third pod was begun, although it was not ready for use before hostilities ended. While the pods were being brought up to speed Honington was modifying five Tornados to use the TIALD. Most of the modifications were centred upon the port under fuselage pylon, which required extra wiring for control purposes plus another for power supply purposes. Five modified Tornados, ZA393, ZA406, ZD739, ZD844 and ZD848, flew direct from Honington to Tabuk using in-flight refuelling support. With the arrival of TIALD, five Tornados from No. IX Squadron, including ZD739/AC *Armoured Charmer*, formed a TIALD flight. Altogether, thirty-six designaed missions were flown by this small unit out of the total of designated sorties overall. The following days' operations were highlighted courtesy of a Nimrod MR2 that had detected an Iraqi ship close to the estuary of the Shatt al Arab. Originally, a Royal Navy Lynx was called into attack, however the helicopter was beaten to it by Grumman A-6 Intruders of the US Navy that sank the vessel.

The Sky Pirates were in action again this time the target being the Muftul Wadam railway bridge in concert with eight Tornados, some of which also attacked Tall Al Lahm ammunition dump. The Buccaneers were XW547 and XW530. Further reinforcements were announced for Gulf deployment these being another six Buccaneers from Lossiemouth. The aircraft departed on 9 February and were escorted by a Victor tanker. The Victor handed over its flight of three chicks over to a Tristar Pink Pig not far from Palermo. The Tristar escorted the Buccaneers, XV863, XX885 and XX894, towards Oman before turning away to land at Riyadh in Saudi Arabia.

On Day 19, 4 February, the target was Al Madinah bridge, the target markers being XX899 and XX889, although this was aborted due to the failure of one of the Pave Spike pods. The second mission flown that day was aimed at An Nasiriyah railway bridge plus the Nasiriyah power station, the spikers being XW547 and XW530 while four Tornados were the bomb carriers. Further attacks were carried out the following day against strategic infrastructure targets. The first was the As Samawah road and rail bridge using

Scrapped in 1992 Buccaneer XW533 'A' rolls out to start another mission. After a few weeks in theatre the special finish has become tatty and stained. On the port side of the nose the Buccaneer sports the pirate flag while the starboard wore eleven bomb symbols while the names *Miss Jolly Roger*, *Fiona* and *Glenfarcas* were also applied. *(Bob Archer Collection)*

After hostilities had ceased No. 216 Squadron was tasked to send five aircraft to Riyadh to bring military personnel back to Britain. As it was Red Nose day we managed to get three away before the powers that be issued a cease and desist order reference dayglo cut outs on the nose radome. One that escaped was the ZD 951, pictured here. *(BBA Collection)*

XW533 and XX899 as the spikers, followed by XW547 and XX899 operating against the Al Kut bridge and dam. The final mission of the day was against As Samawah road bridge, the markers being XX892 and XW530, although the mission was aborted due to the failure of the Pave Spike pod on the latter aircraft. The An Nasiriyah bridge was the target for XX899 and XW530 on 6 February while the second raid of the day was against Albu Salih bridge using XW547 and XX899 marking for six Tornados.

Bridges were the target again on 7 February, the first to receive attention being the Ar Ramadi bridge that was attacked by XW547 and XW530, followed by the Al Fallujah bridge being attacked by XX899 and XW533 while XW530 and XX889 attacked the Al Khidr bridge.

While the extra Buccaneers were in transit the Tornados would concentrate mainly on troop concentrations on 8 February, the Republican Guard plus tanks and artillery being the primary targets. In contrast the Buccaneers continued their campaign against bridges with those at Ar Ramadi, As Samawah, Al Rumaylah and Al Busalih receiving the attentions of XW547, XX892, XX895, XX899, XX889, XW547, XV863 and XX885. The following day, Day 24, would see the Tornados concentrating on fuel storage dumps while it was the turn of the Jaguars to attack the Republican Guards for which they used air burst bombs. For the Buccaneers it was a mix of targets on Day 24 of the campaign. Two aircraft, XX892 and XW530, attacked the As Samawah rail bridge and the Ad Dawaniyah POL dump, although this was aborted due to bad weather. Following on from these attacks XX899 and XW533 launched an attack against the An Nasiriyah pontoon bridge that had replaced the previous structure and the As Samawah POL dump, both of which were also aborted due to the weather. The Bayji production facility attack was more successful using XX895 and XW547 while XW530 and XW547 were successful against the An Nasiriyah bridge. It was also announced that the RAF had flown 2,900 missions by this date. Having made a good service debut with the Buccaneers the TIALD pod would make its debut with the Tornado force on 10 February. Using this equipment four bridges were successfully destroyed using LGBs while a direct hit was made on a HAS that was wrecked as was the aircraft lurking within its environs.

Tango and Echo, XX889 and XW530, respectively streak across the desert on a training mission as the underwing tanks reveal, although both are sporting ECM pods on the starboard pylons. (*Bob Archer Collection*)

The TIALD-equipped Tornados were launched in earnest against the large H3 south-west airfield in Iraq on 10 February using a marker aircraft plus four bombers carrying CPU-123B Paveway 1,000lb bombs, although only three of these weapons could be carried by each bomber due to the increased size of the bomb courtesy of the fin and tail additions. As experience increased it was soon discovered that two such bombs were enough for a HAS while three were needed for a bridge or similar structure. Two days later an attack was mounted against Ruwayshid airfield, however one of the marker aircraft TIALD pods suffered from nodding dog syndrome that saw the seeker head oscillating wildly caused by a glitch in the software.

Buccaneer operations were initially hampered by bad weather on 10 February with missions against the Ar Ramadi and Al Fallujah bridges being cancelled. The next two slated for that day were more successful as four aircraft would attack the east and west bridges at As Samawah – XX899, XX895, XX889 and XW547. Bridges were again the briefed targets for 11 February with Al Amarah bridge and Qal'at Salih pontoon being bombed by XW547 and XW530 while the bridge at Ataq was struck by XV352 and XX901, although the second bomb dropped missed even though they went round again. Two attempts were made against the Al Amarah bridge, although the first was cancelled due to aircraft unserviceability while that carried out by XX892 and XW533 was more successful. On 13 February the Desert Cats were in action again when five Astros multiple rocket launchers were destroyed while further attacks the next day saw further artillery weapons destroyed by the Jaguars. On 11 February the Jaguar detachment also began to run a pair of aircraft configured purely for the reconnaissance role; much of this was intended for the Jaguar attack aircraft although some were carried out on behalf of other agencies. Normally these Jaguars operated as a pair; one was fitted with a Vinten LOROP (long range oblique photography) pod while the other sported the standard BAE pod with an F126 survey camera fitted. While the LOROP revealed great imagery its narrow field of view meant that it was difficult to determine the exact location of the image hence the need for another system to assist the RIC personnel with their task of interpreting the images provided. The Jaguar Detachment would start to head for home on 13 March to Coltishall where they received an emotional welcome having flown over 600 missions that consumed over 921 flying hours.

By now the air war was entering its final phase thus the Tornados switched their attention to HASs on the various Iraqi airfields on Day 27 while the following day would see them destroying a SCUD rocket fuel plant. The Buccaneers would also be scheduled to attack HASs at Wadi Al Khirr and Al Asad, the former receiving the attentions of XV352 and XX901 while the latter was attacked by XX899, XX892, XX889 and XW547. The following day was similar as the airfields at Al Taqaddumand Al Asad were raided by XV352, XX901, XX892 and XW530 while XW547 and XX899 bombed Al Fallujah railway bridge. Having had a clear period free from losses the Tornado force would lose another aircraft on 14 February. Further airfield attacks were mounted by the Buccaneers on 14 February when Al Taqaddum and Ubaydah Bin Al Jarrah airfields were raided by XX889, XX895, XV863, XV901, XW530 and XV352 while XX899 and XW533 took care of the latter. The Muharraq Tornados would undertake their 1,000th sortie involving TIALD, not only overnight but into the following day. Their targets were the airfields and their hardened aircraft shelters.

A further assault on Iraqi airfields took place the following day when Kut Al Hayy East, Tallil, As Salman and Jalibah South East airfields were bombed by XW530, XX892, XX899, XW547, XX895, XX894, XV863, XX901, XV352 and XX895. Of the five missions planned for 16 February three were not completed due to technical failures, however the airfields at Qal'at Salih, Al Amara New Airfield were bombed by XW547, XV352, XX889,XX895, XV863 and XW530. A quieter day was experienced by the Sky Pirates on 17 February when the only mission flows was against Kut Al Hayy East airfield by XV863 and XX895 where the runway was the focus. Further missions were mounted against the airfields at Jalibah South East and Tallil using XX895, XW533, XX899,XX885, XX892 and XW530. Unfortunately, the weather cancelled the remainder of that day's sorties. Alongside the Buccaneers the Tornados would join in the bridge strike missions, although they would switch targets back to airfields between 20 and 23 February. The TIALD Tornados undertook their final missions against Al Asad and Habbaniyah airfields with ZD739 acting as the guidance aircraft. Altogether eleven aircraft departed on the raids both of which were successful; at the latter base helicopters were destroyed in a hangar. Overall, seventy-two TIALD missions were launched before the war ended and the aircraft returned home to Honington.

The weather would also play a part in the sorties planned for 19 February when two missions were cancelled, although the airfields at Shaibah and Ubaydah Bin Al Jarrah were bombed by XV352, XW530, XX885, XW533, XW547, XX889, XX895 and XW530. Continued bad weather would lead to the cancellation of all the sorties planned for 20 February while a similar situation saw many of those planned for the following day cancelled. Those that did go ahead included strikes against Kut Al Hayy East and Qal'at Salih airfields using XW547, XW530, XV863, XX885 and XX895. The following six days saw further attacks on the Iraqi airfields,including Ar Rumaylah South West, Kut Al Hayy East, Qalat Sikar, Al Amara, Al Taqaddum Jalibah South East and Qal'at Salih; this involved the majority of the Buccaneer fleet. Unfortunately, some missions were cancelled because of drifting smoke from burning oil wells and bad weather. The Buccaneers flew their final missions on 27 February with airfields again being the targets. Those struck included Al Taqaddum, Shayka Mazhar and Habbaniyah airfield with the aircraft involved including XX895, XX885, XX899,XV863, XX894, XW533 and

XW530. Two of the Buccaneers, XX901 and XX894, managed to claim two aircraft destroyed on the ground at Shayka Mazhar, one being a captured Kuwait Air Force C-130 and an Iraqi Air Force Antonov AN-12 Cub. On 17 March the Sky Pirates would depart from Muharraq in three waves of four en route for Lossiemouth.

The Tabuk-based Tornados would have greater luck than their Buccaneer counterparts on 19 February. The target was Al Jarrah airfield and ZD844 would hit the bull's eye when its laser-guided bombs hit an ammunition dump that disappeared in one great tumultuous explosion

Possibly the largest and shortest land assault would begin on 24 February when Operation *Sword* was launched. This involved all the available allied forces. Prior to the launch of the ground war the GR1As concentrated their efforts on those sites located near the Syrian and Jordanian borders thus clearing the way for the ground forces. Also covered by the GR1As were the Republican Guard positions in the same area plus the bridges over the Euphrates were checked for the damage caused by laser-guided bombs. On Day 42, 26 February, the Iraqi forces left in great haste from Kuwait City and headed for Basra. Unfortunately, the American command decided that a statement needed to be made therefore A-10 Thunderbolts would destroy the top and tail of the ten-mile column, after which all available attack aircraft in the area proceeded to destroy the entire convoy, even those that attempted to flee across the desert. The final missions flown by the GR1A detachment took place over the night of 25/26 February, the final aircraft (ZA397) landing just as day was breaking. During their deployment the Tornado GR1A detachment had completed 128 missions while notching up 300 flying hours. With an assault that was rolling up the Iraqi forces from both the north and south and the entire military structure of the country in total disarray the Iraqi High Command sued for a ceasefire on Day 43 (28 February). By 3 March, Day 46, the Iraqi government agreed in full to the Allied ceasefire terms after it had been pointed out that the entire military machine was still in place and that it would take less than twenty-four hours to complete a full occupation of Iraq.

About to get an emotional welcome from the waiting families VC 10K2 ZA144 'E' of No. 101 Squadron taxies towards the terminal at Brize Norton. The tanker still sports its BP badge and 'The Empire Strikes Back' inscription on the nose. *(BBA Collection)*

Chapter 10

Onward to the Future and the End

At the conclusion of Operations *Granby* and *Desert Storm* the defence programme put forward in 1990 as Options for Change would proceed as planned. From Strike Command's point of view this would see the number of bases in Germany reduced to two while the McDonnell Douglas F-4 Phantoms would finally be retired. The reduction in RAFG and the return of its assets to Britain would see the command becoming part of No. 2 Group. The disappearance of the two F-4 Squadrons would leave only two units flying the type, both based at Wattisham. No. 56 Squadron would finally disband in July 1992 while the other unit, No. 74 Squadron, would disband in January 1993. This was not the end of Britain's air defence as a new shape was on the horizon.

First revealed as the European Fighter Aircraft (EFA), the aircraft's genesis began in 1971 when an investigation regarding a new multi-role fighter began. The first glimmer of interest was sparked by the issue of Specification AST 403, which was issued by the Air Staff in 1972. Running alongside the British search for a new fighter was the West German requirement that eventually led to the development of the TKF-90 concept. This featured a cranked delta wing design with forward canard controls and computer control artificial stability. As both nations required a similar type of aircraft discussions were held between British Aerospace (BAe) and Messerschmitt-Bölkow-Blohm (MBB) to thrash out a joint design, although the BAE designers rejected some of its advanced features such as vectoring engine nozzles and vented trailing edge controls. By 1979, MBB and BAe presented a formal proposal to their respective governments for the ECF, the European Collaborative Fighter also known as the European Combat Fighter. In October 1979 Dassault joined the ECF team for a tri-national study, resulting in the project becoming known as the European Combat Aircraft. It was at this stage of development that the Eurofighter name was first attached to the aircraft. While the respective governments tried to foster co-operation the development of different national prototypes continued. France produced the ACX while Britain produced two designs; the P106 was a single-engined lightweight fighter, while the P110 was a twin-engined fighter. The P106 concept was rejected by the RAF, on the grounds that it had half the effectiveness of the twin-engined aircraft at two-thirds of the cost. West Germany continued to refine the TFK-90 concept. The ECA project finally collapsed in 1981 for various reasons that included differing requirements, Dassault's insistence on the project design leadership and the British preference for a new version of the RB199 to power the aircraft versus the French preference for the new Snecma M88.

The future is the Eurofighter Typhoon. Here T1 ZJ800 'AC' sporting the marks of No. 17 Squadron trundles down the taxi way at Coningsby. *(BBA Collection)*

With the dissolution of the original design partnership the Panavia partners, MBB, BAe and Aeritalia, launched the Agile Combat Aircraft (ACA) programme in April 1982. The ACA was very similar to the BAe P110, having a cranked delta wing, canards and a twin tail, although one major external difference was the replacement of the side-mounted engine intakes with a chin intake. The ACA would be powered by a modified version of the RB199. The German and Italian governments would later withdraw funding while the Ministry of Defence agreed to fund 50 per cent of the cost with the remaining 50 per cent to be provided by industry. MBB and Aeritalia signed up with the aim of producing two aircraft, one at Warton and one by MBB. In May 1983 BAe announced a contract with the MoD for the development and production of an ACA demonstrator, the Experimental Aircraft Programme. In 1983 Germany, France, UK, Italy and Spain launched the Future European Fighter Aircraft (FEFA) programme. This aircraft was to have short take-off and landing (STOL) and beyond visual range (BVR) weapons capabilities. During 1984 France reiterated its requirement for a carrier capable version of the design and demanded a leading role in the programme. As a result of the French demands Britain, West Germany and Italy opted out and established a new EFA programme. In Turin on 2 August 1985, Britain, West Germany and Italy agreed to go ahead with the Eurofighter; and confirmed that France, along with Spain, had chosen not to proceed as member of the projects. Despite political pressure from France, Spain rejoined the Eurofighter project in early September 1985 while France officially withdrew from the project to pursue its own ACX project that later became the Dassault Rafale.

By 1986 the cost of the programme had reached £180 million. When the EAP programme had started the cost was supposed to be equally shared by both government and industry in each country, however the West German and Italian governments wavered on the agreement and the three main industrial partners had to provide £100 million to stop the programme from ending. In April 1986 the BAe EAP was rolled out at BAe Warton; by this time it had received partial funding from MBB, BAe and Aeritalia. The EAP demonstrator first flew on 6 August 1986. Design work continued over the next five years using data from the EAP flight test programme. Initial production requirements for each nation were, Britain: 250 aircraft, Germany: 250, Italy:

165 and Spain: 100. The share of the production work was divided among the countries in proportion to their projected procurement thus DASA received 33 per cent, British Aerospace 33 per cent, Aeritalia 21 per cent, and Construcciones Aeronáuticas SA (CASA) 13 per cent. In a similar manner to the Tornado programme it was decided to establish an organization to manage the new aircraft. This would be Eurofighter Jagdflugzeug GmbH based in Munich, which was established in 1986 to manage development of the project while EuroJet Turbo GmbH, the alliance of Rolls-Royce, MTU Aero Engines, FiatAvio and ITP, was established to development the EJ200 powerplant. The aircraft was originally known as the Eurofighter EFA from the late 1980s before it was renamed the EF 2000 in 1992.

By 1990 the selection of the aircraft's radar had become a major problem as Britain, Italy and Spain favoured the Ferranti Defence Systems' ECR-90 while Germany preferred the MSD2000 based on the APG-65, which was a collaboration between Hughes, AEG and GEC-Marconi. An agreement was reached after UK Defence Secretary Tom King assured his West German counterpart Gerhard Stoltenberg that the British government would approve the project and allow GEC to acquire Ferranti Defence Systems from its troubled parent. The maiden flight of the Eurofighter prototype took place in Bavaria on 27 March 1994, flown by DASA Chief Test Pilot Peter Weger. On 9 December 2004, Eurofighter Typhoon IPA4 began three months of Cold Environmental Trials at the Vidsel Air Base in Sweden, to verify the operational behaviour of the aircraft and its systems in temperatures between –25 and 31°C. The maiden flight of Instrumented Production Aircraft 7 (IPA7), the first fully equipped

Complete with 1,000lb bombs on the centreline, chaff dispensers on the engine doors, overwing AIM-9 Sidewinders, PHIMAT flare pod and ECM pod is Jaguar GR1A XZ357 'EK' of No. 41 Squadron patrolling over Iraq. *(Bob Archer Collection)*

Tranche 2 aircraft, took place from EADS Manching airfield on 16 January 2008. In May 2007 EDA 5 made the first flight with the CAESAR demonstrator system, a development of the Euroradar CAPTOR that incorporated Active Electronically Scanned Array (AESA) technology. The production version of the CAPTOR-E radar was being proposed as part of the Tranche 3 build of the Typhoon from 2012 as the Tranche 2 aircraft use the non–AESA, mechanically scanned Captor-M that incorporates weight and space provisions for possible upgrade to CAESAR, AESA, standard in the future.

The first production contract was signed on 30 January 1998 between Eurofighter GmbH, Eurojet and NETMA. The agreed procurement totals were as follows: Britain 232, Germany 180, Italy 121, and Spain 87. Production was again allotted according to procurement: British Aerospace 37.42 per cent, DASA 29.03 per cent, Aeritalia 19.52 per cent, and CASA 14.03 per cent. On 2 September 1998 a naming ceremony was held at Farnborough that saw the Typhoon name formally adopted. In September 1998 contracts were signed for production of 148 Tranche 1 aircraft and procurement of long lead time items for the Tranche 2 aircraft. In March 2008 the final aircraft out of Tranche 1 was delivered to the German *Luftwaffe*, with all successive deliveries being to the Tranche 2 standard. On 21 October 2008, the first two of ninety-one Tranche 2 aircraft, ordered four years earlier, were delivered to RAF Coningsby.

With a new fighter on the horizon the MoD was also on the lookout for an airborne early warning aircraft to provide control. After the fiasco of the Nimrod AEW2 programme the venerable Avro Shackleton AEW2 and its equally venerable APS-20 radar were in dire need of replacement. Without spending most of the nation's gross national product the only viable option was the Boeing E-3 Sentry already in service with the USAF and more crucially with NATO. The RAF model would enter service with No. 8 Squadron at Waddington in July 1991. The contrast in technologies is almost impossible as the RAF had missed out completely in an entire generation of AEW systems. The Sentry AEW1 has a far more capable radar system that can orbit quite happily at 30,000 feet. Like the Shackleton the Sentry has an unrefuelled endurance of

Sepecat Jaguar GR3A XX974 'GH' is pictured on patrol as part of Operation *Warden*. The aircraft carries live AIM-9 Sidewinders on the overwing rails plus a live bomb on the underfuselage pylon. *(Bob Archer Collection)*

twelve hours, crucially however, the newer aircraft comes complete with a refuelling probe plus the equipment for boom refuelling. Although the squadron formed properly in July the first operational sortie was undertaken in May, lasting for nearly nine hours.

During the recent Gulf War the RAF Tornados gained extensive experience with the USAF E-3s that would stand them in good stead when the Sentry AEW1s finally took over control of the defence of British airspace. The crews of No. 8 Squadron had a lot to live up to as their American counterparts virtually ran the war in the air as they guided attacking forces into Iraq, helped manage the tanker tracks and guided aircraft back to their bases if needed. The first post reformation sortie took place on 4 July 1991 and involved the control of Jaguars, Harriers and Tornados acting as the attackers plus the control of the defending Hawks and Tornado F3s. While the aircraft of No. 8 Squadron would be primarily confined to the detection of incoming aircraft there was still a NATO commitment that required aircraft to undertake tasks assigned to it by the NATO-AEW Force headquartered at SHAPE.

Although *Desert Storm* had drawn much of Saddam Hussein's military teeth his regime still retained enough hardware to cause grief to those around him. Two of his favourite targets were the Marsh Arabs in the south and the Kurds in the north. With the weakening of Iraqi control there was an uprising in northern Iraq in 1991 that resulted in an Iraqi military response towards the rebels in both northern and southern Iraq. Fearing a massacre similar to that of the 1988 Anfal campaign, millions of Kurds fled towards the Turkish border. In response, on 3 March General Norman Schwarzkopf warned the Iraqis that Coalition aircraft would shoot down Iraqi military aircraft flying over the country. This was verified on 20 March when an American F-15C Eagle fighter shot down an Iraqi Air Force Su-22 Fitter fighter-bomber over northern Iraq. On 22 March, another F-15 destroyed a second Su-22 and the pilot of an Iraqi PC-9 trainer baled out after being approached by American fighters.

On 5 April the United Nations passed Resolution 688, calling on Iraq to end repression of its population, followed on 6 April by the start of Operation *Provide Comfort* that began to bring humanitarian relief to the Kurds. A no-fly zone was established by the US, the UK and France north of the 36th parallel. This was enforced by American, British and French aircraft. Included in this effort was the delivery of humanitarian relief and military protection of the Kurds by a small Allied ground force based in Turkey.

To ensure that Iraq complied with the UN resolutions a Coalition Task Force patrolled the area. This was encouraged by the Turkish government who joined the coalition of Britain, France and the USA. Based at Incirlik AB, in southern Turkey, many of the patrolling aircraft were provided by USAF with Britain and France providing the reconnaissance assets. This disparate collection of aircraft was managed by a Combined Forces Air Component HQ. The French aircraft were Mirage F1CRs while the RAF despatched eight Jaguar GR1s as their part of the force. The RAF part of this operation began in August 1991, codenamed Operation *Warden* and under the command of Group Captain Morley. The eight selected aircraft were drawn from all three Coltishall squadrons all of which were painted in the familiar Desert Pink finish. The first four aircraft departed Coltishall on 4 September with the remainder following five days later. Tanker support for the deployment was provided by a pair of VC 10K tankers from No. 101 Squadron while all of the support personnel, spares plus the Reconnaissance Interpretation Centre were moved over twelve Hercules transport flights. Pilots from

This excellent portrait is of VC 10K2 ZA143 'D' of No. 101 Squadron. All of the K2s have since been retired. *(BBA Collection)*

Nos 6 and 54 Squadrons were trained in the use of the reconnaissance equipment, which allowed all three squadrons to cover the task. The Jaguar deployment ended in February 1993, the task being assumed by Harrier GR7s from RAFG. In 1997 Operation *Warden* would become part of Operation *Northern Watch* and would see Tornado GR1s deployed to the region. The entire operation would be wound down in May 2003.

The Marsh Arabs in the south of Iraq were not so lucky; their uprising was based on the thought that the coalition forces would provide them with support. Unfortunately, this was not forthcoming therefore the Iraqi forces repressed the rebellion ruthlessly using gas against the Arabs. This lack of support would colour the indigenous population's attitude against the coalition once Operation *Telic* was launched in 2003. During the Iraqi repression thousands of Marsh Arabs fled from the attacks therefore in August 1992 the United Nations imposed a no-fly zone over southern Iraq below the 33rd parallel. The operation to protected the Arabs was named *Southern Watch* and this

A pair of Tornado GR4s of No. 12 Squadron depart from Lossiemouth to undertake another training sortie. The nearest aircraft sports a TIALD pod on the underfuselage pylon while its companion carries 28lb smoke and flash bombs in light store carriers. *(USAF via DR Jenkins)*

would last until February 2003. The RAF contribution to this operation was six Tornado GR1s at Al Kharj in Saudi Arabia with a further twelve based at Ali Al Salem, although this level was not sustainable as the Tornado fleet was undergoing a mid-life update. This would see the GR1s replaced by the Tornado F3 at Al Kharj in February 1999.

During December 1998 Operation *Desert Fox* was launched in response to increased incursions by the Iraqi forces. The air strikes would last from 16 to 19 December and would concentrate on targets around Baghdad plus Tikrit in the North and Basra in the south. The Tornado GR1s were supplied by No. 12 Squadron who flew 250 missions, mainly dropping laser-guided bombs. Other aircraft deployed for the operation were VC 10Ks from No. 101 Squadron while a single Nimrod was supplied by the Kinloss Wing for patrol and support duties. The RAF would undertake a further adventure over Iraq in 2003. Codenamed Operation *Telic* this assault upon Iraq and its final defeat has been surrounded by political controversy. The background was the fear that both Britain and the United States had of the spread of the media-named 'weapons of mass destruction'. Also, Saddam Hussein and the Iraqi regime had consistently obstructed and hampered the United Nations Weapons Inspectorate in its attempts to find evidence of such weapons. Annoyed by the Iraqi response to its effort the United Nations passed Resolution 1441 that called for the regime to co-operate or face the consequences.

Britain's part in the final assault on Iraq began on 20 March 2003 by which time Nos 9 and 31 Squadrons from Marham with Tornado GR4s flew to Ali Al Salem Air Base, Kuwait, reinforcing those forces already building up there as Operation *Resonate South*. A few days later a further batch of Tornado GR4s drawn from Nos 12, 14 and 617 Squadrons would be deployed to Al Udeid Air Base, Qatar, while a deployment of Harrier GR7s from Nos 1, 3 and 4 Squadrons based at Cottesmore would be deployed to Al Jaber Air Base, Kuwait. Air defence assets were provided by Leuchars who despatched Tornado F3s drawn from Nos 43 and 111 Squadrons that were deployed to Prince Sultan Air Base in Saudi Arabia. Further air assets were also deployed to the area these comprising of six Nimrod MR2s, four Tristar tankers, VC 10K tankers based in Saudi Arabia, four Sentry AEW1s plus VC 10 transports held at Akrotiri for the

Vital to both Britain's air defence and any overseas adventures is the E-3 Sentry AEW1. This aircraft is flown by No. 8 Squadron, normally based at Waddington, although here the aircraft is operating in Saudi Arabia. *(USAF)*

aeromedical role. The support helicopter role was covered by Chinooks and Pumas drawn from the units at Odiham.

The air war began in the mid-afternoon of 19 March 2003 when allied aircraft including RAF Tornados undertook raids on Iraqi artillery batteries near the border to clear the way for allied ground forces. The following day would see the expiration of President Bush's ultimatum to the regime to comply with the UN resolution. As the regime decided to ignore this ultimatum the United States launched what it claimed to be a 'shock and awe' attack on targets within Iraq. With the initial assault over RAF Tornados were again in action while Harriers were tasked to hunt down SCUD missile launchers that had fired missiles at the allied troop concentrations in Iraq. That same day the Turkish government approved the use of their airspace so that attacks could be launched from the north. The following day, 21 March, would see an increase in the assaults upon Iraqi facilities and troops with the presidential palaces being attacked as well as communications and control centres. Both the Tornados and the Harriers were involved in these attacks, their task being to provide support for the ground forces. As a result of the operations to this date the commander of the 51st Division based near Basra decided to surrender the whole of his unit following suit. The level of explosive violence would increase markedly when Boeing B-52 Stratofortress bombers attacked Baghdad while other aircraft and guided missiles were launched towards Kirkuk, Mosel and Tikrit. The Tornados of No. IX Squadron had a vital part to play in this assault using their Air Launched Anti-Radiation Missile (ALARM) missiles against Iraqi radar.

Tornado GR4A ZA553 'DI' of No. 31 Squadron based at RAF Marham. Not only is the aircraft carrying a TIALD pod the other pylon is home to a Paveway bomb. (USAF)

On 22 March air operations were also flown during the day as well as at night. The following day the RAF suffered its first combat loss when a Tornado was shot down by an American Patriot missile. Further air operations would continue over the next few days with Baghdad being surrounded by allied forces on 6 April. Entry into the capital city would follow in the next three days with the local population showing their support for the military action by destroying statues of Saddam Hussein. Operations also continued against Tikrit, Saddam Hussein's hometown, as well as consolidating the capture of Baghdad. With the collapse of the defence of Baghdad and the virtual destruction of the Republican Guard units it was the turn of the regular Iraqi Army units to see sense and surrender. While much of Iraq had surrendered there were still pockets of resistance and these were attacked by air using Storm Shadow missiles. The Storm Shadow long-range air-launched and conventionally armed missile equips the Tornado GR4 squadrons and made its operational debut with No. 617 Squadron in 2003 during combat in Iraq, prior to entering full service in 2004. Post Telic deployment analysis demonstrated the missile's exceptional accuracy, and the effect on targets was described as devastating.

Feasibility studies on a possible UK requirement for a Long Range Stand-Off Missile started in 1982, although the development work was eventually subsumed in 1986 into the NATO seven-nation Modular Stand-Off Weapon programme. This project was, however, aborted, and the UK subsequently withdrew. With the end of the Cold War the UK's continued need for a stand-off requirement was reviewed and endorsed as part of the 'Options for Change' exercise. An international competition was launched in 1994 to meet the UK's Conventionally Armed Stand Off Missile (CASOM) requirement, and seven companies responded.

The MBDA (UK) Storm Shadow missile was selected with a development and production contract being awarded in 1997. Storm Shadow is equipped with a powerful UK-developed warhead and is designed to attack important hardened targets and infrastructure, such as buried and protected command centres. Mission data, including target details, is loaded into the weapon's main computer before the aircraft leaves on its mission. After release, the wings deploy and the weapon navigates its way to the target at low level using terrain profile matching and an integrated Global Positioning System. On final approach to the target the missile climbs, discards its nose cone and uses an advanced infra-red seeker to match the target area with stored imagery. This process is repeated as the missile dives onto the target, using higher resolution imagery, to ensure the maximum accuracy.

On 1 May 2003 President Bush declared that the major combat operations in Iraq were complete. For the RAF this meant that many of the units involved in the fighting would be returned to their home bases, although replacements were supplied to maintain an air support capability should it be required.

The wind down of RAF Germany began in 1992 when Wildenrath closed with both of the F-4 Phantom units, Nos 19 and 92 Squadrons, disbanding at the same time, although both number plates would be resurrected as part of Support Command. Also departing Wildenrath was No. 60 Squadron, the RAFG communications unit. Transferred to Benson the squadron was reformed as a Westland Wessex operator, although this resurrection was short-lived as the unit disbanded in March 1997. The Harrier base at Gütersloh would be the next base to close, although it would be transferred to the Army. The based units, Nos 3 and 4 Squadrons flying Harrier GR7s, would transfer to Laarbruch in 1992 as did No. 18 Squadron with its mix of Chinooks and Puma HC1s. It would be the turn of Laarbruch to wind down in 1999, although this base was home to numerous units. The Tornado units at the base had been drastically reduced after Operation *Granby* with No. XV Squadron disbanding in December 1991, although the number plate would be applied to the TWCU, which had previously been No. 45 (Shadow) Squadron. The squadron then transferred to RAF Lossiemouth where it was declared to SACLANT in the maritime strike role. The other nuclear strike unit at Laarbruch, No. 16 Squadron, would disband in September 1991, although it would quickly reappear as a reserve unit operating Sepecat Jaguars, this being No. 226 OCU renumbered. Having initially flown its new mounts at Lossiemouth the unit moved to Coltishall in 2000, although it would disband in 2005 as the retirement of the Jaguar approached. The number plate was finally applied to a unit flying Grob Tutors, a great contrast to the heavy metal of a few years previously. The third Tornado unit was No. 20 Squadron that had reformed in 1984 being assigned to SACEUR as a nuclear strike unit. The squadron would disband in September 1992, although its number plate would be applied to the Harrier OCU. The Harrier GR7 units, Nos 3 and 4 Squadrons, would move to Cottesmore in mid–1999 where they were soon joined by No. 1 Squadron and the OCU. The final unit was No. 18 Squadron that would relocate to Odiham in August 1997 and is currently operational.

Bruggen would be the last station to close in 2001 and was home to three Tornado units. All four would return to Britain, including No. IX Squadron, which began its transfer from Bruggen in July 2001 and completed its move to Marham in September. No. 14 Squadron had already departed Bruggen for its new base at Lossiemouth in January where it remained active specializing in the use of the TIALD bombing pod. No. 17 Squadron would not return to Britain for further service with the Tornado being disbanded instead, although it would be resurrected in 2002 at BAE Warton for formation as the first Eurofighter Typhoon unit.

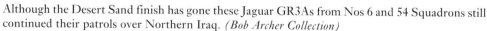

Although the Desert Sand finish has gone these Jaguar GR3As from Nos 6 and 54 Squadrons still continued their patrols over Northern Iraq. *(Bob Archer Collection)*

On 4 May 1980 Marshal Josef Tito, the leader of a united Yugoslavia, would die in Belgrade. While Yugoslavia remained together initially, the more dominant Serb population took exception to the other nationalities trying to break away and form independent states. This would result in 1989 in the breakdown of the talks between Serbia, Croatia and Slovenia. The latter two states would declare independence and the ten-day war broke out in 1991 with Slovenia in which the Slovenes were victorious. Further warfare between the Serbs and the other two states would begin in earnest and would lead to some of the greatest atrocities committed against humanity since the days of the Third Reich, even though the media would dumb it down by calling it ethnic cleansing.

Eventually, the United Nations would decide to intervene and issued a series of resolutions calling on all parties to cease and desist their fighting. In the end there was no other option but to send in armed forces to separate each of the warring parties. Participation by the RAF and Strike Command would include Operations *Agricola*, part of *Joint Guard*, *Allied Force*, *Cheshire*, *Deliberate Force*, *Deliberate Forge*, *Deliberate Guard*, *Deny Flight*, *Engadine*, *Grapple*, *Hampden*, *Lodestar*, *Palatine*, *Radome*, *Resolute* and *Sharp Guard*.

In October 1992, at the beginning of the Bosnian War, the UN Security Council passed Resolution 781 prohibiting unauthorized military flights in Bosnian airspace. Following the resolution NATO began Operation *Sky Monitor* during which NATO forces monitored violations of the no–fly zone, without taking any military action against the violators. By April 1993 NATO forces had documented more than 500 violations of the no–fly zone. In response to these violations of Bosnian airspace the UN Security Council issued Resolution 816.

Resolution 781 prohibited only military flights while Resolution 816 prohibited all flights in Bosnian airspace, except for those expressly authorized by the UN Flight

Still lacking unit markings is Panavia Tornado GR4 ZD714 AJ-W *Johnny Walker* of No. 617 Squadron undertaking training for Operation *Telic*. *(Bob Archer Collection)*

Co-ordination Centre in Zagreb. The resolution also authorized UN member states to take all necessary measures to ensure compliance with the no–fly zone restrictions. Therefore in response to this resolution, NATO commenced Operation *Deny Flight* on 12 April 1993. Initially *Deny Flight* was intended only to enforce the no–fly zone, however several NATO members, including the USA, were eager to find ways to end the war and improve the situation of the civilian population and hoped that military action could do so.

The Strike Command commitment included fighters, attack and tanker aircraft. The fighters would begin their deployment in 1993, the chosen aircraft being the Tornado F3 while the crews were drawn from Nos 43 and 111 Squadrons. The strike attack role was covered initially by the Coltishall Jaguar Wing with the pilots coming from Nos 6, 41 and 54 Squadrons. All of the deployed airpower was based at the Italian air base at Gioia Del Colle as this was the nearest air base to the Balkans. Given the distance to the theatre of operations No. 101 Squadron would deploy VC 10K tankers to Italy while transportation was provided by the Lyneham Transport Wing and the Tristars of No. 216 Squadron who also supplied tanker capability when needed. During 1995 Nos 5 and 29 Squadrons replaced the aircraft from Leuchars while the Jaguars were replaced by Harriers and crews provided by Nos 1 and 4 Squadrons.

The situation in Bosnia deteriorated further when Bosnian Serbs captured 370 UN peacekeepers that were then used illegally as human shields around sensitive targets. In July 1995 a brutal assault on Srebrenica would finally push the entire international community to finally decide that enough was enough. Fortunately, AFSOUTH, part of NATO, had already identified many targets within the Bosnian Serb enclave and thus planning for air strikes could proceed quickly. Possibly advancing the decision to attack the Serbs was the explosion of a mortar bomb in a Sarajevo market place on 28 August 1995 resulting in the deaths of sixty-eight civilians. As was the norm for this entire unhappy episode the Serb government blamed the Muslims for the attack as a means of hastening NATO action.

After many years stored at Marshalls the RAF finally received Tristar C2A ZE706 for operational use with No. 216 Squadron. Unlike the other C2s this aircraft has analogue avionics fitted in common with the other ex-British Airways aircraft. *(BBA Collection)*

Assigned to No. 6 Squadron is Jaguar GR3A XX737 'EE', which has just dropped clear of the tanker. *(Bob Archer Collection)*

In the early hours of 30 August an aerial force of 220 aircraft and 70 support aircraft launched an attack on Bosnian Serbs positions and facilities as Operation *Deliberate Force*. Drawn from NATO members forces the attacks were launched in packages, four or five packages each day when the weather allowed. Not only were Serbian positions in Bosnia attacked, so were those opposite Croatia where the Serbs were preparing to launch an armoured attack. RAF support during this operation included nine Jaguars to Italy while the Harrier GR7s already deployed in theatre were made available for air operations. The former were carrying TIALD pods and used them to guide the LGB bombs carried by the Harriers. During the period 30 August to 14 September the Harrier GR7s undertook 144 missions during which 48 LGBs and 32 × 1,000lb bombs were dropped. Tasks covered included air interception, close air support and tactical reconnaissance. Fighter top cover was provided by Tornado F3s while aerial refuelling was courtesy of No. 216 Squadron and its Tristar tankers while Sentry AEW1s worked in concert with the E-3s of NATO and USAF. During *Deliberate Force* the RAF flew 326 sorties that covered 9.3 per cent of the overall sortie rate.

The missions flown during *Deliberate Force* would finally force the Bosnian Serbs to the negotiating table thus a ceasefire was announced in October 1995. America would sponsor the following peace talks that occupied much of November and December that would finally lead to the Dayton Peace Accords. This document agreed the partition of Bosnia- Herzegovina between the Bosnian Serbs and the Croatian Muslims. To ensure this was complied with a NATO Implementation Force (IFOR) was put in place, the Strike Command contribution being six Harrier GR7s based in Italy. In December 1996 IFOR would be renamed the Stabilization Force (SFOR), while Operation *Decisive Edge* running in concert with IFOR, was replaced by Operation *Deliberate Guard*. In February 1997 the Harriers were replaced by Coltishall Wing Jaguars. By April 1998 the situation in the region had stabilized enough to allow for the withdrawal of the Jaguar and Tristar assets although a Sentry AEW1 aircraft remained on station until 2000.

Although the situation in Bosnia-Herzegovina had stabilized that in Kosovo was still in full flux especially as the ethnic Albanians formed the greater part of the population. President Milosevic of Serbia would inflame the situation by encouraging Serbians to move to Kosovo and ease the local Albanian population out by any means of persuasion

Photographed during Operation *Telic* is Harrier GR9 ZG505 '76' complete with mission marks on the nose. (Bob Archer Collection)

possible. To counter the Serbian incursions the Albanians formed the Kosovo Liberation Army (KLA) to counter the efforts of the Serbs. By the summer of 1998 the KLA was having great success with their countermeasures thus the Serbian president ordered troops and police units into the area to brutally repress the Albanians. Having already failed to get involved to stop the Bosnian genocide NATO was determined to become involved as soon as possible. Initially diplomatic efforts were to the fore, however, as ever, dealing with the Serbs these were doomed to failure. In order to reinforce the talks NATO undertook Exercise Determined Falcon in June 1998 during which eighty-five fighters, attack and support aircraft overflew Albania and Macedonia to show the Serbs that there was enough airpower in the region already to undertake aerial attacks if needed. During this over flight four Jaguars were involved.

Operation *Allied Force* would begin on 24 May 1999, which was a joint NATO operation; the RAF involvement included No. 1 Squadron operating 16 Harrier GR7's,

Waddington is also home to No. 51 Squadron and its intelligence-gathering aircraft, one of whose Nimrod R1s, XW665, is preparing to depart for another mission. *(BBA Collection)*

No. 8 Squadron flying Sentry AEW1s, No. 14 Squadron with Tornados, Nos 27 and 33 Squadrons flying Chinooks and Pumas, No. 101 Squadron with five VC 10 tankers and No. 216 Squadron deploying four Tristars. Reconnaissance assets were supplied by No. 51 Squadron who deployed a single Nimrod R1 while No. 39 Squadron supplied a pair of Canberra PR9s.

Aerial attacks on Serbian positions would take place between 24 to 26 May, although those scheduled for the Saturday were hampered by bad weather thus the allied forces resorted to guided missile attacks. Further attacks took place over the ensuing week with RAF Tornados becoming involved on Sunday 4/5 May while the Harriers made their combat debut on 5 May. The result of these attacks and their intensity would see the Yugoslav government asking for a ceasefire; however NATO rejected their offer saying that the Yugoslav plan did not meet their requirements concerning a complete withdrawal from Kosovo. With this rejection NATO resumed its air strikes against Serbian troops operational within Kosovo.

Over 6/7 April there were reports that a great number of Kosovo Albanians had vanished from the border with NATO being concerned about their fate. Air strikes continued against Yugoslav targets, especially troop formations operational in Kosovo. Adding fuel to the flames a statement by the speaker of the Russian parliament on 9 April revealed the fact that Russia had targeted its missiles on NATO countries, although this was quickly denied by the Russian military. Russia continued to oppose the air strikes and warned the NATO allies not to send in ground troops or it might force Russia to get involved militarily. The Russian President, Boris Yeltsin, warned of another European, possibly world war. The following day the Chinese also added their voice to the argument surrounding the air strikes. The UK announced that the aircraft carrier HMS *Invincible* would be sent to the region while the USA announced another eighty-two aircraft were being sent to the region. On Sunday 11 April Albania ceded its ports, airspace and military installations to NATO control. After this announcement Serbian artillery fired across the Albanian border killing two civilians and wounding several more.

Aerial attacks were mounted against the headquarters of the Serbian police while the following night the Serbian TV station in Belgrade was bombed. The Serbian

This Harrier GR9 is certainly armed for business complete with gun pods, and Sidewinder missiles. The aircraft is ZG479 '69' and sports a shark's mouth on the nose. *(Bob Archer Collection)*

government then put forward a peace proposal that involved unarmed UN peace keepers entering the region, although this was rejected by NATO as insufficient. At the fiftieth anniversary summit of NATO, an oil embargo was announced against Yugoslavia while NATO announced it was seeking a UN resolution calling for Serbian troops to withdraw from Kosovo and an autonomous government be set up for the province.

On 3 May the Harrier force was in action against Serbian military and police units in Kosovo, the aircraft flying seventeen missions. The following day the Harriers flew another eight sorties and by 6 May it was reported that RAF aircraft had flown 800 plus sorties for NATO. On 7 May the Harriers attacked Sjenica airfield with 1,000lb bombs although adverse weather conditions continued to disrupt other combat missions. RAF Harriers flew sixteen sorties the following day during which they destroyed a radio relay site outside Pristina. With an improvement in the weather on 10 May Harriers and Tornados undertook further attacks against Serbian targets, followed by another twenty missions being flown by Harriers followed by a similar number on the 12 May. On 4 June the Serbian parliament accepted a G8 peace agreement therefore talks between Serbian and NATO generals covering the Serbian withdrawal from Kosovo began on 5 June at an Albanian border town, and the Serbian evacuation of Kosovo was to be completed within seven days. NATO bombing against Serbian troops and installations continued until evidence of Serbian withdrawal was confirmed. Serbia finally signed the G8 Peace Plan on Thursday 10 June therefore NATO air strikes were suspended on Friday. During Operation *Allied Force* it was reported that NATO had mounted 38,004 air strikes in 10,484 sorties, the British having contributed 1,618 strikes in 1,008 sorties during which 23,614 air munitions were dropped

On 9 September 2001 terrorists later identified as belonging to al-Qaeda flew airliners into the twin towers of the World Trade Center in New York destroying them utterly. While the more radical fundamentalists in the Muslim world rejoiced to see America humbled they were unaware of the retaliation that would be unleashed. In concert with the Joint Chiefs of Staff President Bush identified those countries that were responsible for sponsoring terrorism; also identified as the leader of al-Qaeda and the man responsible for 9/11 was Osama bin Laden, a Saudi Arabian national.

After the Soviet withdrawal from Afghanistan the Taliban seized upon the resulting power vacuum to form an Islamic government from 1996 to 2001. Their extreme interpretation of Islamic law prompted them to ban music, television, sports, and dancing, and enforce harsh judicial penalties with amputation an accepted form of punishment for stealing while public executions could often be seen at the Kabul football stadium. They drew further criticism around the world when they destroyed the Buddhas of Bamyan, historical statues nearly 1,500 years old, because they were considered idols.

In 1996 Osama bin Laden had moved to Afghanistan upon the invitation of the Northern Alliance leader Abdur Rabb ur Rasool Sayyaf. When the Taliban came to power, bin Laden was able to forge an alliance between the Taliban and al-Qaeda. It is understood that al-Qaeda-trained fighters known as the 055 Brigade were integrated with the Taliban army between 1997 and 2001. On 20 September 2001 the US government stated that Osama bin Laden was behind the 11 September attacks in 2001 therefore they delivered a five-point ultimatum to the Taliban. These demands included the delivery of the leaders of al-Qaeda, the release of all imprisoned foreign nationals, the closure of every terrorist training camp, the handing over of every terrorist to appropriate authorities plus giving the United States full access to terrorist training camps for inspection.

The following day the Taliban completely rejected this ultimatum, stating there was no evidence in their possession linking bin Laden to the 11 September attacks. This stance would result in the United Arab Emirates and later Saudi Arabia withdrawing their recognition, on 22 September 2001, of the Taliban as the legal government of Afghanistan, leaving neighbouring Pakistan as the only remaining country with diplomatic ties. In an effort to stave off the attacks that were obviously forthcoming it is believed that the Taliban covertly offered to turn bin Laden over to Pakistan for trial in an international tribunal that operated according to Islamic shar'ia law. This was followed, on 7 October 2001, by a Taliban offer to try bin Laden in Afghanistan in an Islamic court. This proposition was immediately rejected by the US government.

Operation *Enduring Freedom* would begin on 7 October 2001 against identified al-Qaeda training camps and assets within Afghanistan; not only were the resident terrorists targeted, the Taliban were also deemed as legitimate targets. As with the previous operations the first attacks were aerial. There was no real need to establish air superiority, however air attacks were preferred as it was hoped that this would reduce casualties. While much of the bombing was carried out by the USAF the RAF would deploy aircraft in the support role under the title of Operations *Fingal* and *Veritas*. Air assets deployed by Britain included No. 39 Squadron whose Canberra PR9s were used for reconnaissance missions while Kinloss Wing Nimrod MR2s provided patrolled over the sea in order to protect naval vessels engaged on operations. No. 8 Squadron also despatched Sentry AEW1s to assist in the command and communications roles.

Air transport and tanking assets deployed at this time included the Tristars of No. 216 Squadron, the VC 10s of both Nos 10 and 101 Squadrons plus the newly delivered Boeing Globemasters recently delivered to the No. 99 Squadron based at Brize Norton. Also operating in theatre were those airlift stalwarts, the C-130 Hercules of the Lyneham Transport Wing. The initial operation was adjudged a success as the northern part of the country was cleared quite quickly and Kabul, the Afghan capital, fell to the allies on 14

Playing to the crowd is VC 10 C(K)1 XV101 of No. 10 Squadron. As this, the original fleet, was run down these aircraft were transferred to No. 101 Squadron and No. 10 Squadron was disbanded. *(Robbie Shaw Collection)*

The Tristar KC1 is the most versatile of all the three variants as its role change internal fit can be adapted for any task while the aircraft can still operate in the tanker role. *(Robbie Shaw Collection)*

November 2001 as Taliban forces, heavily battered by aerial attack, retreated south to Kandahar province.

While the initial victories against the Taliban and al-Qaeda were achieved quickly there were still elements of both in the south of the country. Throughout the following years the aircraft of RAF Strike Command would play a significant part in quelling the insurgents, although not without loss of life. The British operation in Kandahar province was designated *Herrick* and would commence in October 2002 at the conclusion of Operation *Fingal*.

The RAF deployment to Afghanistan is based at Kandahar airport and the managing organization is designated No. 904 Expeditionary Wing. The first offensive aircraft deployed to Afghanistan were six Harrier GR7s from No. 3 Squadron that arrived in August 2004. When British troops arrived in theatre in 2006 and took the war to the Taliban the Harriers stopped acting as a show of force aircraft and conducted the war for real. During the period May to October 2006 the Harriers dropped over 500 dumb bombs on various targets while using their cannons to provide suppressing fire. The role of the aircraft in theatre included close air support plus tactical reconnaissance and they frequently operated in attack packages that frequently included Fairchild A-10s and Boeing B-52s of USAF. Initially combat flying was carried out during daylight hours, although as the fighting intensified the Harriers began undertaking night operations as well. To cope with this extra load the number of Harriers was increased to seven while flying hours also increased to some 480 per month. The detachment would eventually consist of 16 pilots and 125 engineering staff who normally worked 12-hour shifts. The task was later handed over to No. 800 NAS who continued to operate the Harrier GR7s, the government having short-sightedly decided to retire the Sea Harrier F/A2s of the Fleet Air Arm.

When first deployed the Harrier Force used the TIALD pod to mark targets but as they were frequently employed on strikes against targets within suburban areas this pod was found wanting. To counter this an Urgent Operational Requirement was issued in late 2006 requesting a new targeting pod with better definition capabilities. The result was the Lockheed Martin AN/AAQ-33 Sniper Advanced Targeting Pod that was first test flown on a Harrier GR9 in December 2006.

Tornado GR4s would also operate over Afghanistan as needed although they were initially based out of theatre as the runway at Kandahar was in no fit state to operate this type of aircraft. In theatre air transport support was provided by the four squadrons of the Lyneham Transport Wing while helicopter support was courtesy of No. 1310 Flight whose eight Chinook HC2s and crews were drawn from Nos 7, 18 and 27 Squadrons while the five Westland Merlin HC3s were managed by No. 1419 Flight whose aircraft and crews were drawn from Nos 28 and 78 Squadrons. At various times the Tristars of No. 216 Squadron have been involved in the movement of personnel and aircraft into theatre. During operations over Afghanistan the RAF inevitably suffered some aircraft losses. The first would occur in June 2005 when a special forces C-130 with the new British Ambassador aboard caught fire after landing at Lashkar Gah, although no casualties were reported. Kandahar would be the next locale when a Harrier GR7 was destroyed and another damaged during a Taliban rocket attack in October.

In May 2006 another LTW Hercules would crash while landing at a dirt landing strip outside the town of Lashkar Gar. All nine crew and twenty-six passengers aboard were safely evacuated, although the aircraft was burned out. The most serious loss took place 2 September when a Nimrod MR2 caught fire and crashed after an in-flight refuelling. The subsequent inquiry would eventually lead to the premature retirement of the Nimrod fleet. Only one aircraft was lost in 2007, another special forces aircraft of No. 47 Squadron that was badly damaged on landing at a rough strip in Afghanistan, although no casualties were reported. Such was the extent of the damage that all usable and sensitive equipment was removed before the airframe was blown up.

Throughout this final period of Strike Command's existence many of the aircraft in service underwent upgrades to fit them for new tasks. Possibly one of the most developed aircraft was the big wing Harrier. The first of these was the GR5 that made its maiden flight on 30 April 1985, entering service with No. 233 OCU in July 1987. Altogether forty-one of this model were built before production switched to the GR5A model. This version consisted of nineteen aircraft with a further three converted from GR5s. Changes were minor, the primary one being the provision of Forward Looking Infra Red (FLIR) mountings. These aircraft never entered service, being converted to the later and more capable GR7. These aircraft featured a GEC-Marconi 1010 FLIR sensor housed in a small fairing above the nose. Other avionics changes included a Smiths Industries wide angle Head Up Display (HUD) plus a GEC-Marconi colour map display, all fitted in a Night Vision Goggles, (NVG) compatible cockpit. The GR7 undertook its maiden flight on 20 November 1989. Production of new-build aircraft reached thirty-four while a further fifty-three were reworked from Harrier GR5 and GR5A airframes. As production of the new aircraft was being undertaken the Leading Edge Extensions (LERX) were increased in area from 70 per cent to 100 per cent, the whole fleet eventually receiving this modification. While the NVGs improved the aircraft's capability they did pose some safety problems for the pilot in the event of ejection. Due to the weight of the goggles their retention by the pilot during the ejection would cause either death or serious injury due to the forces exerted. To remedy this the Martin-Baker MB 12 Type 2 seat was fitted with a compressed gas source that would blow the goggles clear of the pilot prior to ejection.

The GR7 entered service with No. 4 Squadron RAFG in September 1990 having moved straight across from the earlier Harrier GR3. The only Strike Command unit to receive the type was No. 1 Squadron at Wittering, which received its first aircraft in June

Converting pilots to the new versions of the Harrier required the services of a dedicated trainer hence the arrival of the T10. This is ZH664 in the original green finish wearing the marks of No. 4 Squadron that would soon be borne by the OCU aircraft. *(BBA Collection)*

1992, finally relinquishing the GR5s in November 1992. During 1992 the GR7s made their combat debut over northern Iraq during Operation *Warden*, which was followed by operations over the former Yugoslavia. Further modifications would be applied to the fleet in the light of these combat operations thus the centreline pylon was fitted for the carriage of a Vinten reconnaissance pod or a TIALD pod as required. The GR7 was also cleared to fire the AGM-65G2 Maverick air-to-ground missile. This gave the Harrier a much-needed standoff capability, a need that was recognized after operations over Kosovo.

In 2000 the Joint Harrier Force was formed, bringing both the RAF and RN Harrier fleets together under a single command. This unit was added to the Joint Rapid Deployment Force. By 2003 the Harrier Force was again embroiled in hostilities, this time over Iraq as part of Operation *Telic*. This would be followed in 2004 by Operation *Herrick* with the GR7s giving sterling service in the war against the Taliban and the insurgents. The Harriers would be replaced in 2010 by Tornado GR4s.

Having undertaken both combat operations and shipboard deployments it had become obvious that the Harrier really needed a more powerful engine. Rolls-Royce would oblige with the Pegasus 11-61 Mk107 powerplant rated at 23,800lb. This engine was ordered in 1999 and the initial batch was fitted to twenty GR7s making them GR7As. This was seen as an interim update while the GR9 details were confirmed. Known as JUMP (Joint Update and Maintenance Programme), this £500 million project would start in mid-2006 when the first aircraft passed through a normal maintenance period during which software upgrades were applied to the communications systems, the ground proximity warning system and the navigation systems while AGM-65 Maverick was also integrated. Other new systems fitted included the Rangeless Airborne Instrumentation Debriefing System (RAIDS), the Raytheon Successor IFF (SIFF), the Digital Joint Reconnaissance Pod (DJRP), plus the capability to carry and drop Paveway IV guided weapons was also integrated. This upgrade programme was intended to keep the Harrier at the cutting edge of technology until the much-vaunted F-35 Lightning II entered service.

The first GR9 entered service in September 2006, and eventually forty GR7s were upgraded to GR9 standard with the first operational deployment taking place in January 2007 as part of the NATO International Security Assistance Force (ISAF). Later that year an £84 million contract was awarded to BAE Systems for the installation of the Tactical Information Exchange System (TIES), the first GR9 so fitted undertaking its maiden flight on 29 June 2010 from Warton. Using this equipment the Harrier pilot was able to establish communications links between a ground station and an orbiting AWACS aircraft. One final upgrade and maintenance programme was awarded the BAES in April 2009 that covered any needed upgrades and repairs that would see the aircraft fit for service until 2018. By March 2010 the final Harrier GR7 was retired from service leaving the GR9 as the only operational combat version. Although slightly outside of the scope of this work it should be mentioned that one of the first actions of the incoming Conservative government would be to retire one of the most capable aircraft in the RAF inventory, possibly one of the stupidest things ever done by a political party. The given reason was that the Harrier GR9 lacked any form of gun armament, which had been removed in yet another politically inspired move.

In 1984 the UK Ministry of Defence began studies of a Mid-Life Update (MLU) of the Tornado to rectify the shortcomings of the GR1. This update, to Tornado GR4 standard, would improve capability in the medium-level role while maintaining the Tornado's exceptional low-level penetration capability. The GR4 upgrade was approved in 1994 after it had been revised to include lessons learned from the GR1's performance during the 1991 Gulf War. The contracts were signed with British Aerospace (later BAE Systems) in 1994 for the upgrade of 142 GR1s to GR4 standard; work began in 1996 and was finished in 2003.

These modifications enabled the GR4 to fly automatically at low level using Terrain Following Radar (TFR) when poor weather prevents visual flight. The aircraft is also equipped with FLIR and is NVG compatible. This gives it a unique all-weather night capability, as well as making it an impressive platform for mounting passive night electro-optical operations. For navigation purposes, the Tornado is equipped with an integrated Global Positioning Inertial Navigation System (GPINS). The GR4 also has a Ground Mapping Radar (GMR) to identify fixed way points and the update navigation systems as well as providing an air-to-air search facility. The GR4 is also equipped with a Laser Ranger and Marked Target Seeker (LRMTS) that can be used to locate targets designated on the ground or can provide accurate range information to ground targets. The GR4 normally carries a maximum of five Paveway IV smart weapons or two Stormshadow cruise missiles, but can be configured with various weapons, targeting pods and reconnaissance pods simultaneously, including the Dual Mode Seeker Brimstone, ALARM Mk 2 missile, Litening III targeting pod and the Reconnaissance Airborne Pod TORnado (RAPTOR).

The RAPTOR pod is one of the most advanced reconnaissance sensors in the world and greatly increases the effectiveness of the aircraft in the reconnaissance role. Its introduction into service gave the GR4 the ability to transmit real-time, LOng Range Oblique Photography (LOROP) to commanders or to view this in cockpit during a mission. The standoff range of the sensors also allows the aircraft to remain outside heavily defended areas, thus minimizing the aircraft's exposure to enemy air-defence systems. Additional capability in the Non-Traditional Intelligence Surveillance and Reconnaissance (NTISR) role is provided by the Litening III RD and the use of the ROVER data link for providing tactical operators with real time Full Motion Video (FMV).

All GR4 aircraft are capable of carrying the ALARM missile, which homes on to the emitted radiation of enemy radar systems and can be used in the Suppression of Enemy Air Defences (SEAD) role. The GR4 is capable of carrying up to nine ALARMs or a mixed configuration of ALARMs and bombs. The self protection capability of the GR4 has recently been upgraded by the integration of the ASRAAM short range air-to-air missile. Infra-Red and Radio Frequency countermeasures are provided by a BOZ-107 pod on the right wing to dispense chaff and flares and a Sky Shadow-2 electronic countermeasures pod on the left wing. The aircraft is also equipped with an integral 27mm Mauser cannon capable of firing 1,700 rounds per minute. In addition the Tornado GR4 Force trains and maintains a capability with legacy weapons such as 1000lb class dumb weapons, legacy Paveway II and III as well as enhanced variants and the AIM-9L Sidewinder. The Tornado GR4 is currently operated from two bases at Lossiemouth, in Scotland, which houses No. 15 (Reserve) Squadron that acts as the OCU, No. 12 (Bomber) Squadron and No. 617 Squadron, while Marham is the home of the GR4s of No. II (Army Cooperation) Squadron, No. IX (Bomber) Squadron and No. 31 Squadron. The Tornado GR4 has been successfully deployed since 1990, seeing service over Iraq, Kosovo and Afghanistan.

The Sentinel R1 is a modified Bombardier Global Express powered by two Rolls-Royce Deutschland BR710 turbofan engines. The first flight of the modified prototype took place in August 2001 confirming that the aerodynamic changes for housing the radar were viable. The first production Sentinel R1 undertook its hour-long maiden flight on 26 May 2004 with the aircraft entering operational service with No. 5 Squadron based at Waddington.

The aerial platform involved five aircraft that were matched to eight mobile ground stations, six of which are wheeled all terrain vehicles while the other two in air transportable containers. Supporting the active squadron is a synthetic training facility at Waddington. The Sentinel cockpit has a centrally mounted pull-down screen capable of displaying a moving map, Link 16 data link information and defensive aids subsystem (DASS) data. The DASS comprises a towed radar decoy, missile approach warning system and chaff and flare dispensers and can be operated in automatic, semi-automatic or manual mode. The main radar is a Raytheon Systems dual-mode Synthetic Aperture/Moving Target Indication (SAR/MTI) radar. Strangely enough while the programme suffered from delays it is one of few procurement projects to be delivered below cost estimates.

The aircraft normally operates at an altitude of 15,000m (40,000ft) ensuring a high-resolution view of a large battlefield area. It is crewed by a pilot, co-pilot, an Airborne Mission Commander (AMC) and two image analysts. Mission endurance is approximately nine hours. While the image analysts can analyse the images presented to them on-board it is expected that, unlike the USAF JSTARS, the actual battle management will take place on the ground. The British government's Strategic Defence and Security Review announced its intention to withdraw the Sentinel airborne ground surveillance aircraft once it is no longer required to support operations in Afghanistan, although it is proposed to find a larger aerial platform to transfer the equipment to.

Having been impressed with the Boeing Chinook the MoD would investigate the next-generation Chinook, the CH-47D, that entered service in 1982. Improvements from the earlier model included uprated engines, composite rotor blades, a redesigned cockpit to reduce pilot workload, redundant and improved electrical systems, an advanced flight control system (FCS) and improved avionics. The RAF returned their original HC1s to Boeing for upgrading to CH-47D standard, the first of which returned to Britain in 1993. Three additional HC2 Chinooks were ordered with delivery beginning in 1995, while another six were ordered in 1995 under the Chinook HC2A designation; these differed from the standard HC2 by having the front fuselage strengthened to allow an aerial refuelling probe to be fitted in future.

In order to strengthen the fleet eight Chinook HC3s were ordered in 1995 as dedicated special forces helicopters. The HC3s include improved range, night vision sensors and navigation capability. The eight aircraft were to cost £259 million and the forecast in-service date was November 1998. Although delivered in 2001 the HC3 did not receive airworthiness certification as it was not possible to certify the avionics software. The avionics were unsuitable due to poor risk analysis and the necessary requirements omitted from the procurement contract. Without the certification, the helicopters were only permitted to fly in visual meteorological conditions and subsequently were stored in climate-controlled hangars while a decision regarding their fate was made.

Originally it was proposed that the Defence Aviation Repair Agency would install the Thales TopDeck avionics system. However, the MoD announced in March 2007 that this programme would be cancelled, and instead it would refit the helicopters' avionics to the Chinook HC2/2A specification. This programme was estimated to cost £50–60 million, however in June 2008, the National Audit Office issued a scathing attack on the MoD's handling of the affair, stating that the whole programme was likely to cost £500 million by the time the helicopters entered service.

One of the results of the 1998 Strategic Defence Review wash the identification of a requirement for a strategic airlifter. The Short-Term Strategic Airlift (STSA) competition commenced in September of that year, however tendering was cancelled in August 1999 as some bids were identified by the MoD as too expensive, including the

Rotating from Mildenhall is Boeing C-17 Globemaster III, one of the most versatile airlifters available today. This example, ZZ172, belongs to No. 99 Squadron, based at Brize Norton. *(USAF)*

Boeing/BAe C-17 bid. Even so the project continued, with the C-17 seen as the favourite, therefore in the light of continuing delays to the Airbus A400M program, the Defence Secretary, Geoff Hoon, announced in May 2000 that the RAF would lease four C-17s at an annual cost of £100 million from Boeing for an initial seven years with an optional two-year extension. At this point the RAF would have the option to buy the aircraft or return them to Boeing. The UK committed to upgrading the C-17s in line with the USAF so that in the event of their being returned to Boeing the USAF could absorb them without modification costs.

The first C-17 was delivered to the RAF at Boeing's Long Beach facility on 17 May 2001 later being flown to Brize Norton by a crew from the newly reformed No. 99 Squadron that had previously trained with USAF crews to gain experience on the type. The fourth C-17 was delivered to the RAF in August 2001. The RAF aircraft were some of the first to take advantage of the new centre wing fuel tank fitted to Block 13 aircraft. In service the RAF declared itself delighted with the C-17. Although the Globemaster fleet was intended to be a fallback for the A400M, the MoD announced in July 2004 that they had elected to buy their four C-17s at the end of the lease, even though the A400M appeared to be moving closer to production. They also announced there would be a follow-on order for one C-17, with possible additional purchases later.

In August 2006 the MoD announced that they had ordered an additional C-17 and that the four aircraft on lease would be purchased at the end of the current contract in 2008. The fifth aircraft was delivered in February 2008 while the MoD announced later in 2006 that it planned to acquire three more C-17s, bringing the total to eight, with delivery intended for 2009–2010. In addition, in July 2007 the MoD announced that it intended to order a sixth C-17 to cover operations in Iraq and Afghanistan. Given the work load of the fleet in service it came as no surprise that the MoD announced a further contract, in December 2007, for a sixth C-17 that was delivered in June 2008.

While the early-build C-130 Hercules had served the RAF faithfully many of the airframes were coming to the end of their useful lives. And it appeared that the only replacement for Hercules was a newer Hercules. The C-130J is the newest version of the Hercules and the only model still in production. Externally similar to the classic

The only replacement for the Hercules is another Hercules. Here C4 ZH879 departs en route to its home base at Lyneham. (BBA Collection)

Hercules, the J-model features considerably updated technology. These differences include new Rolls-Royce AE 2100 D3 turboprops with Dowty R391 composite scimitar propellers, and digital avionics that include HUDs for each pilot, thus reducing crew requirements. The J-model is available in a standard-length or stretched -30 variant. Lockheed Martin received the launch order for the J-model from the RAF, who ordered twenty-five aircraft, with first deliveries beginning in 1999 as Hercules C4 ,C-130J-30, and Hercules C5 ,C-130J. The first was delivered to Lyneham in November 1999 while the last was delivered in June 2001. The RAF trains its C-130J crews in a purpose-built simulator system, also being supplied by Lockheed Martin. Since entering service the C-130Js has been used in a variety of operational missions, including action in the former Yugoslavia, Afghanistan and Iraq.

As part of Delivering Security in a Changing World, the UK's vision for the future of the armed forces, on 21 July 2004, Defence Secretary Geoff Hoon detailed plans to reduce the number of Tornado F3 squadrons by one to three squadrons. This was the first stage in the transition to the F3's replacement, the Eurofighter Typhoon, which entered operational service with the RAF in 2005. The first unit to disband would be No. 23 Squadron at Leeming, although this would be resurrected at Waddington as a Sentry AEW1 operator. No. 23 Squadron at Coningsby would follow in 1998 later reappearing in 2003 as a Typhoon F2 squadron. Coningsby would also say farewell to No. 5 Squadron in 2003, although re-equipment with the Bombardier Sentinel followed in 2008.

It would be the turn of Leeming next to lose a Tornado unit when No. 11 Squadron was disbanded in 2005, later receiving the Typhoon fighter at Coningsby in March 2007. Two other units would disband during this period, the first being No. 39 Squadron, which finally said farewell to its last three Canberra PR9s in July 2001, although the unit has since become a reconnaissance drone operator. The age of the RAF VC 10 fleet would also see reductions in the available aircraft as the transport versions began to be withdrawn in 2000. Given the reduction in the overall fleet it was decided that No. 10 Squadron should disband this taking place in October 2005.

On 1 April 2007 RAF Strike Command ceased to exist when it was merged with Personnel and Training Command to form the rather anonymous Air Command.

Appendix I

Comparative Strengths

Strike Command strength 1968

No. 1 Squadron
West Raynham
Hawker Hunter FGA9

No. 5 Squadron
Binbrook
English Electric Lightning F6

No. 9 Squadron
Coningsby
Avro Vulcan B2

No. 10 Squadron
Fairford
Vickers VC 10 C1

No. 11 Squadron
Leuchars
English Electric Lightning F6

No. 22 Squadron
St Mawgan
Westland Whirlwind HAR10

No. 23 Squadron
Leuchars
English Electric Lightning F3

No. 24 Squadron
Lyneham
Lockheed Hercules C1

No. 27 Squadron
Scampton
Avro Vulcan B2

Strike Command strength 2007

No. 1 Squadron
Cottesmore
BAES Harrier GR7/7A, GR9/9A, T10

No. 2 Squadron
Marham
Panavia Tornado GR4/4A

No. 3 Squadron
Coningsby
Eurofighter Typhoon F2/T1A

No. 4 Squadron
Cottesmore
BAES Harrier GR7/7A, GR9/9A, T10

No. 5 Squadron
Waddington
Bombardier Sentinel R1

No. 6 Squadron
Coningsby
Sepecat Jaguar GR3A/T4

No. 7 Squadron
Odiham
Boeing Chinook HC2

No. 8 Squadron
Waddington
Boeing E-3D Sentry AEW1

No. 9 Squadron
Marham
Panavia Tornado GR4

Strike Command strength 1968

No. 29 Squadron
Wattisham
English Electric Lightning F3

No. 30 Squadron
Fairford
Lockheed Hercules C1

No. 35 Squadron
Coningsby
Avro Vulcan B2

No. 36 Squadron
Lyneham
Lockheed Hercules C1

No. 41 Squadron
West Raynham
Bristol Bloodhound II

No. 42 Squadron
St Mawgan
Avro Shackleton MR3

No. 44 Squadron
Waddington
Avro Vulcan B2

No. 46 Squadron
Abingdon
HSA Andover C1

No. 47 Squadron
Fairford
Lockheed Hercules C1

No. 50 Squadron
Waddington
Avro Vulcan B2

No. 51 Squadron
Wyton
DH Comet R1

No. 53 Squadron
Fairford
Shorts Belfast C1

Strike Command strength 2007

No. 11 Squadron
Coningsby
Eurofighter Typhoon F2/T1A

No. 12 Squadron
Lossiemouth
Panavia Tornado GR4

No. 13 Squadron
Marham
Panavia Tornado GR4/4A

No. 14 Squadron
Lossiemouth
Panavia Tornado GR4

No. 18 Squadron
Odiham
Boeing Chinook HC2

No. 22 Squadron
Chivenor and detached flights
Westland Seaking HAR3/3A

No. 23 Squadron
Waddington
Boeing E-3D Sentry AEW1

No. 24 Squadron
Lyneham
Lockheed Hercules C1/C3/C4/C5

No. 25 Squadron
Leeming
Panavia Tornado F3

No. 27 Squadron
Odiham
Boeing Chinook HC2

No. 28 Squadron
Benson
Augusta/Westland Merlin HC3/3A

No. 30 Squadron
Lyneham
Lockheed Hercules C1/C3/C4/C5

Strike Command strength 1968

No. 54 Squadron
West Raynham
Hawker Hunter FGA9

No. 55 Squadron
Marham
Handley Page Victor K1A

No. 57 Squadron
Marham
Handley Page Victor K1A

No. 58 Squadron
Wyton
English Electric Canberra PR7/PR9

No. 72 Squadron
Odiham
Westland Wessex HC2

No. 83 Squadron
Scampton
Avro Vulcan B2

No. 98 Squadron
Watton
English Electric Canberra B2/E15

No. 99 Squadron
Lyneham
Bristol Britannia C1/C2

No. 100 Squadron
Wittering
Handley Page Victor B2

No. 101 Squadron
Waddington
Avro Vulcan B2

No. 111 Squadron
Wattisham
English Electric Lightning F3/F6

No. 115 Squadron
Watton
Armstrong Whitworth Argosy E1

Strike Command strength 2007

No. 31 Squadron
Marham
Panavia Tornado GR4

No. 33 Squadron
Benson
Westland Puma HC1

No. 43 Squadron
Leuchars
Panavia Tornado F3

No. 47 Squadron
Lyneham
Lockheed Hercules C1/C3/C4/C5

No. 51 Squadron
Waddington
BAES (HSA) Nimrod R1

No. 70 Squadron
Lyneham
Lockheed Hercules C1/C3/C4/C5

No. 78 Squadron
Mount Pleasant
Westland Sea King HAR3/Boeing Chinook HC2

No. 99 Squadron
Brize Norton
Boeing C-17 Globemaster III

No. 101 Squadron
Brize Norton
BAC VC 10 C1K/K3/K4

No. 111 Squadron
Leuchars
Panavia Tornado F3

No. 120 Squadron
Kinloss
BAES(HSA) Nimrod MR2

No. 201 Squadron
Kinloss
BAES(HSA) Nimrod MR2

Strike Command strength 1968

No. 120 Squadron
Kinloss
Avro Shackleton MR3

No. 139 Squadron
Wittering
Handley Page Victor B2

No. 201 Squadron
Kinloss
Avro Shackleton MR3

No. 202 Squadron
Leconfield and detached flights
Westland Whirlwind HAR10

No. 206 Squadron
Kinloss
Avro Shackleton MR3

No. 210 Squadron
Ballykelly
Avro Shackleton MR2

No. 214 Squadron
Marham
Handley Page K1A

No. 216 Squadron
Lyneham
DH Comet C4

No. 267 Squadron
Benson
Armstrong Whitworth Argosy C1

No. 511 Squadron
Lyneham
Bristol Britannia C1/C2

No. 617 Squadron
Scampton
Avro Vulcan B2

Total: 44 operational squadrons

Strike Command strength 2007

No. 202 Squadron
Boulmer and detached flights
Westland Seaking HAR3

No. 216 Squadron
Brize Norton
Lockheed Tristar K1/KC1/C2/C2A

No. 230 Squadron
Aldergrove
Westland Puma HC1

No. 617 Squadron
Lossiemouth
Panavia Tornado F3

Total: 37 operational squadrons

Aircraft and Operating Squadrons

Armstrong Whitworth Argosy C1

General characteristics
Crew: Four – pilot, co-pilot, navigator, air engineer
Capacity: Up to 69 troops, 54 paratroops, 48 stretcher cases or 29,000lb (13,154kg) of cargo
Length: 86ft 9in (26.44m)
Wingspan: 115ft 0in (35.05m)
Height: 29ft 3in (8.92m)
Wing area: 1,458ft² (135.5m²)
Empty weight: 56,000lb (25,401kg)
Loaded weight: 97,000lb (43,999kg)
Useful load: 29,000lb (13,150kg)
Maximum take-off weight: 105,000lb (47,627kg)
Powerplant: 4 × Rolls-Royce Dart RDa.8 Mk 101 turboprops, 2,470ehp (1,843kW) each

On approach to land at Benson is AWA Argosy C1 XP443 of No. 269 Squadron, part of RAF Transport Command. When the Argosy fleet wound down XP443 was withdrawn in October 1971 and later scrapped. *(John Ryan Collection)*

Performance
Cruise speed: 253mph (220 knots, 407km/h)
Range: 3,450 miles (3,000 nmi, 5,552km)
Service ceiling: 23,000ft (7,010m)

Avro Shackleton MR3

General characteristics
Crew: Ten
Length: 87ft 4in (26.61m)
Wingspan: 120ft (36.58m)
Height: 17ft 6in (5.33m)
Wing area: 1,421ft^2 (132m^2)
Empty weight: 51,400lb (23,300kg)
Maximum take-off weight: 86,000lb (39,000kg)
Fuel capacity: 4,258 imperial gallons (19,360 litres)
Powerplant: 4 × Rolls-Royce Griffon 57A liquid-cooled V12 engine, 1,960hp (1,460kW) each

Performance
Maximum speed: 260kn (300mph, 480km/h)
Range: 1,950nmi (2,250 miles, 3,620km)
Endurance: 14.6 hours
Service ceiling: 20,200ft (6,200m)

Avro Shackleton MR3 WR971 'E' was assigned to No. 120 Squadron based at Kinloss when photographed. *(John Ryan Collection)*

Avro Vulcan B2

General characteristics
Crew: Five – pilot, co-pilot, AEO, navigator radar, navigator plotter
Wingspan: 111ft 0in
Length: 99ft 11in
Height: 27ft 1in
Wing area: 3,964 ft^2
Maximum take-off weight: 204,000lb

Wearing the gloss anti-flash finish complete with matching markings is Vulcan B2 XL360 of No. 617 Squadron, pictured at Scampton. *(Martyn Chorlton)*

Performance
Cruising speed: Mach 0.86 (610mph)
Maximum speed: Mach 0.92 (625mph)
Range: 4,000nmi
Service ceiling: 60,000ft
Engines: 4 x Bristol Siddeley Olympus 201 or 301
Fuel capacity: 9,250 imp gallons

Armament
1 × Blue Steel missile or
2 × WE.177 free-fall nuclear bomb or
21 × 1,000lb (450kg) conventional bombs

BAe Harrier GR7

General characteristics
Crew: One
Length: 46ft 4in (14.12m)
Wingspan: 30ft 4in (9.25m)

Pictured just prior to engine shut down is BAE Harrier GR7 ZD438 '50' assigned to No. 1 Squadron at Wittering and later Cottesmore. *(BBA Collection)*

Height: 11ft 8in (3.56m)
Wing area: 343ft² (22.6m²)
Empty weight: 12,500lb (5,700kg)
Loaded weight: 15,703lb (7,123kg)
Maximum take-off weight: 18,950lb VTO, 31,000lb STO (8,595kg VTO, 14,061kg STO)
Powerplant: 1 × Rolls-Royce Pegasus Mk 105 vectored thrust turbofan, 21,750lb (96.7kN)

Performance
Maximum speed: 662mph (1,065km/h)
Combat radius: 300nmi (556km)
Ferry range: 2,015 miles
Service ceiling: 50,000ft (15,000m)
Rate of climb: 14,715ft/min (74.8m/s)

Armament
Guns: 2 × 30mm ADEN cannon pods under the fuselage
Hardpoints: Eight with a capacity of 8,000lb (3,650kg) of payload and provisions to carry combinations of:
    Rockets: 4 × LAU-5003 rocket pods (19 × CRV7 70mm rockets each) or 4 × Matra rocket pods (18 × SNEB 68mm rockets each)
    Missiles: 6 × AIM-9 Sidewinders or 4× AGM-65maverick
    Bombs: ordnance such as Paveway series of laser-guided bombs, unguided iron bombs

BAe Nimrod MR2

General characteristics
Crew: Twelve
Length: 38.65m (126ft 9in)
Wingspan: 35.00m (114ft 10in)
Height: 9.14m (31ft)
Wing area: 197.05m² (2,121 sqft)
Empty weight: 39,009kg (86,000lb)

HSA Nimrod MR2 XV260 '60' was assigned to the Kinloss Wing. Normally squadron markings are not carried, however the aircraft here is wearing celebratory markings on the fin for No. 120 Squadron. *(Martyn Chorlton)*

Maximum take-off weight: 87,090kg (192,000lb)
Powerplant: 4 × Rolls-Royce Spey turbofans, 54.09 kN (12,160lbf) each

Performance
Maximum speed: 923km/h (575mph)
Cruise speed: 787km/h (490mph)
Range: 8,340–9,265km (5,180–5,755 miles)
Service ceiling: 13,411m (44,000ft)

Armament
Hardpoints: 2 × underwing pylon stations and an internal bomb bay with a capacity of 20,000lb (9,100kg) and provisions to carry combinations of:
   Missiles:
      Air-to-air missile: 2 × AIM-9 Sidewinder
      Air-to-surface missile: Nord AS.12, Martel missile, AGM-65 Maverick, AGM-84 Harpoon
   Bombs: Depth charges, US-owned B57 nuclear depth bombs
   Other:
      Air-dropped Mk 46 torpedoes, Sting Ray torpedoes
      Naval mines
      Sonobuoys

Blackburn Buccaneer S2

General characteristics
Crew: Two – pilot and observer
Length: 63ft 5in (19.33m)
Wingspan: 44ft (13.41m)
Height: 16ft 3in (4.97m)
Wing area: 514.7ft² (47.82m²)
Empty weight: 30,000lb (14,000kg)
Loaded weight: 62,000lb (28,000kg)
Powerplant: 2 × Rolls-Royce Spey Mk 101 turbofans, 11,100lbf (49kN) each

HSA (Blackburn) Buccaneer S2 XV349 sports the original finish the type was delivered in. Here it sports the markings of No. 12 Squadron, underwing fuel tanks and practice bomb carriers on the outboard pylons. *(BBA Collection)*

Performance
Maximum speed: 667mph (580 knots, 1,074km/h) at 200ft (60m)
Range: 2,300 miles (2,000nmi, 3,700km)
Service ceiling: 40,000ft (12,200m)

Armament
Hardpoints: 4 × under-wing pylon stations & 1 × internal rotating bomb bay with a capacity of 12,000lb (5,400kg) and provisions to carry combinations of:
  Rockets: 4 × Matra rocket pods with 18 × SNEB 68mm rockets each
  Missiles: 2 × AIM-9 Sidewinders for self-defence, 2 × AS-30Ls or 2 × AS-37 Martel missiles or 4 × Sea Eagle missile
  Bombs: Various unguided bombs, laser-guided bombs, as well as the Red Beard or WE.177 tactical nuclear bombs
  Other: AN/ALQ-101 ECM protection pod, AN/AVQ-23 Pave Spike Laser designator pod, buddy refuelling pack or drop tanks for extended range/loitering time

Boeing C-17 Globemaster III

General characteristics
Crew: Three – 2 pilots, 1 loadmaster
Capacity: 134 troops with palletized seats or
  102 troops with standard centreline seats or
  36 litter and 54 ambulatory patients or
Payload: 170,900lb (77,519kg) of cargo or a mix of palletized cargo and vehicles
Length: 174ft (53m)
Wingspan: 169.8ft (51.75m)
Height: 55.1ft (16.8m)
Wing area: 3,800ft² (353m²)
Empty weight: 282,500lb (128,100kg)
Maximum take-off weight: 585,000lb (265,350kg)
Powerplant: 4 × Pratt & Whitney F117-PW-100 turbofans, 40,440lbf (180 kN) each
Fuel capacity: 35,546 US gal (134,556 L)

When the Shorts Belfast was withdrawn due to defence cuts the RAF was left without a heavy lifter. This was finally rectified when the Boeing C-17 Globemaster III was delivered to No. 99 Squadron at Brize Norton. *(BBA Collection)*

Performance
Cruise speed: Mach 0.76 (450 knots, 515mph, 830km/h)
Range: 2,420nmi (2,785 miles, 4,482km)
Service ceiling: 45,000ft (13,716m)
Take-off distance at MTOW: 7,600ft (2,316m)
Landing distance: 3,500ft (1,060m)

Boeing E-3 Sentry AEW1

General characteristics
Crew: Four
Mission crew: 13–19
Length: 152ft 11in (46.61m)
Wingspan: 145ft 9in (44.42m)
Height: 41ft 4in (12.6m)
Wing area: 3,050ft² (283.4m²)
Empty weight: 185,000lb (73,480kg)
Loaded weight: 344,000lb (with aerial refuelling) (156,400kg)
Maximum take-off weight: 347,000lb (156,150kg)
Powerplant: 4 ×: Four CFM 56 2A-3 turbofans, 24,000lb each

Performance
Maximum speed: 530mph (855km/h, 461 knots)
Range: 4,000nmi (7,400km) (8hr)
Service ceiling: 41,000ft (12,500m)

The faithful Avro Shackleton AEW2 was eventually replaced by the Boeing Sentry AEW1, which was a quantum leap in technology. Captured taking off from Waddington is ZH103 of No. 8 Squadron. *(Bob Archer Collection)*

Boeing Chinook HC1

General characteristics
Crew: Four – pilot, co-pilot, one or two air loadmasters depending on role
Length: 30.1m (98ft 9in)
Rotor diameter: 18.3m (60ft 0in)

Prior to the application of inverted V allied identifying markings the Boeing Chinook HC1 detachment was fairly anonymous. When the *Desert Storm* air war began ZD982 'I' would be so marked. Later converted to HC2 standard, the aircraft is operated by No. 18 Squadron at Odiham. *(Bob Archer Collection)*

Height: 5.7m (18ft 8in)
Empty weight: 10,185kg (22,450lb)
Loaded weight: 12,100kg (26,680lb)
Maximum take-off weight: 22,680kg (50,000lb)
Powerplant: 2 × Honeywell T55-GA-712 turboshaft, 2,800kW (3,750 hp) each

Performance
Maximum speed: 295km/h (183mph)
Service ceiling: 2,590m (18,500ft)
Rate of climb: 10.1m/s (1,980ft/min)

Bristol Britannia

General characteristics
Crew: Four
Capacity: 113 passengers plus 53 stretcher cases and six medical attendants
Length: 124ft 3in (37.88m)
Wingspan: 142ft 3in (43.36m)
Height: 37ft 6in (11.43m)
Wing area: 2,075ft² (192.8m²)
Empty weight: 86,400lb (38,500kg)
Maximum take-off weight: 185,000lb (84,000kg)
Powerplant: 4 × Bristol Proteus 255 turboprops, 4,450 ehp (3,320kW) each

Performance
Maximum speed: 397mph (345 knots, 639km/h)
Cruise speed: 357mph (310 knots, 575km/h) at 22,000ft (6,700m)
Range: 4,430 miles (3,852nmi, 7,129km)
Service ceiling: 24,000ft (7,300m)

The Comet C2s purchased for RAF Transport Command usage were assigned to No. 216 Squadron at Lyneham. Like the other Comet C2s XK669 'Taurus' would be replaced by the Comet C4s being scrapped at Brize Norton in 1967. *(John Ryan Collection)*

DH Comet C4

General characteristics
Crew: Four – two pilots, flight engineer and radio operator/navigator
Capacity: 56–81 passengers
Length: 111ft 6in (33.99m)
Wingspan: 114ft 10in (35.00m)
Height: 29ft 6in (8.99m)
Wing area: 2,121ft² (197m²)
Empty weight: 75,400lb (34,200kg)
Maximum take-off weight: 162,000lb (73,500kg)
Powerplant: 4 × Rolls-Royce Avon Mk 524 turbojets, 10,500lbf (46.8 kN) each

Performance
Maximum speed: 526mph (457 knots, 846km/h)
Range: 3,225 miles (2,800nmi, 5,190km) (with 16,800lb (7,620kg) payload)
Service ceiling: 42,000ft (12,800m)

English Electric Canberra B2

General characteristics
Crew: Three – pilot, 2 navigators
Length: 65ft 6in (19.96m)
Wingspan: 64ft 0in (19.51m)
Height: 15ft 8in (4.77m)
Wing area: 960ft² (89.19m²)
Empty weight: 21,650lb (9,820kg)
Loaded weight: 46,000lb (20,865kg)
Maximum take-off weight: 55,000lb (24,948kg)
Powerplant: 2 × Rolls-Royce Avon R.A.7 Mk.109 turbojets, 7,400lbf (36 kN) each

Having served with Nos 18, 61 and 50 Squadrons respectively, Canberra B2 WJ728 would spend time with No. 231 OCU at Bassingbourn as shown here complete with dayglo striping over basic light grey. *(BBA Collection)*

Performance
Maximum speed: Mach 0.88 (580mph, 933km/h) at 40,000ft (12,192m)
Combat radius: 810 miles (700nmi, 1,300km)
Ferry range: 3,380 miles (2,940nmi, 5,440km)
Service ceiling: 48,000ft (15,000m)

English Electric Lightning F6

General characteristics
Crew: One
Length: 55ft 3in (16.8m)
Wingspan: 34ft 10in (10.6m)
Height: 19ft 7in (5.97m)

Although the Lightning F6 was the primary fighter for the Binbrook squadrons some F3s were retained for training purposes. Here F3 XP741 'AR' sports the markings of No. 5 Squadron based at Binbrook. *(BBA Collection)*

Wing area: 474.5ft² (44.08m²)
Empty weight: 31,068lb (14,092kg)
Maximum take-off weight: 45,750lb (20,752kg)
Powerplant: 2 × Rolls-Royce Avon 301R afterburning turbojets
   Dry thrust: 12,530lbf (55.74 kN) each
   Thrust with afterburner: 16,000lbf (71.17 kN) each

Performance
Maximum speed: Mach 2.0 (1,300mph, 2,100km/h) at 36,000ft. 700 KIAS at lower altitude
Range: 850 miles (1,370km) supersonic intercept radius: 155 miles (250km)
Ferry range: 920 miles (800nmi, 1,660km), 1,270 miles (1,100nmi, 2,040km) with ferry tanks
Service ceiling: 54,000ft (16,000m)

Armament
Guns: 2 × 30mm ADEN cannons
Hardpoints: 2 × under-fuselage for mounting air-to-air missiles, 2 × overwing pylon stations for
   260 gal ferry tanks and provisions to carry combinations of:
   Missiles: 2 × de Havilland Firestreak or 2 × Hawker Siddeley Red Top

Eurofighter Typhoon F2

General characteristics
Crew: One
Length: 15.96m (52.4ft)
Wingspan: 10.95m (35.9ft)
Height: 5.28m (17.3ft)
Wing area: 51.2m² (551 sqft)
Empty weight: 11,150kg (24,600lb)

Eurofighter Typhoon T1 ZJ699 has spent much of its time as a development aircraft with BAES at Warton, although squadron service may follow at a later date. *(Bob Archer Collection)*

Loaded weight: 16,000kg (35,000lb)
Maximum take-off weight: 23,500kg (52,000lb)
Powerplant: 2 × Eurojet EJ200 afterburning turbofan
Dry thrust: 60kN (13,000lbf) each
Thrust with afterburner: 89kN (20,000lbf) each
Fuel capacity: 4,500kg (9,900lb) internal

Performance
Maximum speed:
  At altitude: Mach 2 (2,495km/h, 1,550mph)
  At sea level: Mach 1.2 (1,470km/h, 910mph)
  Supercruise: Mach 1.1–1.5
Range: 2,900km (1,800 miles)
Combat radius:
  Ground attack, lo-lo-lo: 601km (325nmi)
  Ground attack, hi-lo-hi: 1,389km (750nmi)
  Air defence with 3-hr combat air patrol: 185km (100nmi)
  Air defence with 10-min. loiter: 1,389km (750nmi)
Ferry range: 3,790km (2,350 miles)
Service ceiling: 19,810m (64,990ft)
Rate of climb: >315m/s (62,000ft/min)
Wing loading: 312kg/m^2 (64.0lb/ft^2)

Armament
Guns: 1 × 27mm Mauser BK-27 cannon with 150 rounds
Hardpoints: Total of 13: 8 × under-wing; and 5 × under-fuselage pylon stations; holding up to
  7,500kg (16,500lb)
Missiles:
  Air-to-air missiles:
    AIM-9 Sidewinder
    AIM-132 ASRAAM
    AIM-120 AMRAAM
    IRIS-T
  Air-to-surface missiles:
    Storm Shadow
    Brimstone
  Bombs:
    6 × 500lb Paveway IV
    Paveway II/III/Enhanced Paveway series of laser-guided bombs
  Others:
    LITENING III laser targeting pod
    Up to 3 drop tanks for ferry flight or extended range/loitering time

Eurohelicopters (Augusta-Westland) Merlin HC1

General characteristics
Crew: Four
Capacity:
  24 seated troops or
  45 standing troops or
  16 stretchers with medics

Length: 22.81m (74ft 10in)
Rotor diameter: 18.60m (61ft 0in)
Height: 6.65m (21ft 10in)
Empty weight: 10,500kg (23,150lb)
Useful load: 5,443kg (12,000lb)
Maximum take-off weight: 15,600kg (32,188lb)
Powerplant: 3 × Rolls-Royce Turbomeca RTM322-01 turboshafts, 1,725kW (2,312shp) each

Performance
Never exceed speed: 309km/h (167 knots, 192mph)
Range: 1,389km (750 nmi, 863 miles)
Service ceiling: 4,575m (15,000ft)

Handley Page Hastings C1

General characteristics
Crew: Five
Length: 82ft 8in (25.20m)
Wingspan: 113ft 2in (34.4m)
Height: 22ft 6in (6.85m)
Wing area: 1,408ft² (130.8m²)
Empty weight: 48,427lb (21,966kg)
Loaded weight: 80,000lb (36,287kg)
Powerplant: 4 × Bristol Hercules XVI radial engine, 1,615hp (1,205kW) each

Performance
Maximum speed: 282mph (454km/h) at 13,500ft (4,115m)
Range: 1,860 miles (3,000km) combat
Service ceiling: 24,000ft (7,315m)

Handley Page Victor K2

General characteristics
Crew: Five – pilot, co-pilot, navigator radar, navigator plotter, AEO
Length: 114ft 11in (35.05m)
Wingspan: 117ft 0in (35.66m)
Height: 28ft 1½in (8.57m)
Wing area: 2,580ft² (223.5m²)
Empty weight: 114,050lb
Maximum take-off weight: 238,000lb (107,957kg)
Powerplant: 4 ×19,750lb Rolls-Royce Conway 2010 each

Performance
Maximum speed: 627mph (545 knots, 1,009km/h) at 36,000ft (11,000m)
Range: 6,000 miles (5,217nmi, 9,660km)
Service ceiling: 56,000ft (17,000m)

While the Victor tanker fleet was in service, its primary home base was Marham. Handley Page Victor K1A XA932 was assigned to No. 214 Squadron when photographed. *(BBA Collection)*

Hawker Hunter F6

General characteristics
Crew: One
Length: 45ft 11in (14.00m)
Wingspan: 33ft 8in (10.26m)
Height: 13ft 2in (4.01m)
Wing area: 349ft² (32.42m²)
Empty weight: 14,122lb (6,405kg)
Loaded weight: 17,750lb (8,050kg)
Maximum take-off weight: 24,600lb (11,158kg)
Powerplant: 1 × Rolls-Royce Avon 207 turbojet, 10,145lbf (45.13kN)

Performance
Maximum speed: Mach 0.94, 620 knots (715mph, 1,150km/h) at sea level
Combat range: 385nmi (445mi, 715km)
Ferry range: 1,650nmi (1,900mi, 3,060km) with external fuel
Service ceiling: 50,000ft (15,240m)

Armament
Guns: 4 × 30mm (1.18in) ADEN cannons in a removable gun pack with 150rpg
Hardpoints: 4 underwing with a capacity of 7,400lb (3,400kg) and provisions to carry combinations of:
 Rockets: 4 × matra rocket pods (each with 18 × SNEB 68mm (2.68in) rockets)
 Bombs: a variety of unguided iron bombs
 Other: 2 × 230 Gallon drop tanks for extended range

Hawker Siddeley Andover C1

General characteristics
Crew: Four – pilot, co-pilot, navigator, loadmaster
Capacity: 44 troops or 14,000lb (6,350kg) of cargo
Length: 78ft (23.77m)

Sporting the fin markings of No. 46 Squadron is HSA Andover C1 XS605 based at Thorney Island. Once the unit shut down XS605 had a second career with No. 115 Squadron as an E3 employed in the airfield calibration role. *(John Ryan Collection)*

Wingspan: 98ft 6in (30.02m)
Height: 30ft 1in (9.15m)
Wing area: 811ft² (75.4m²)
Empty weight: 25,524lb (11,577kg)
Loaded weight: 40,000lb (18,000kg)
Maximum take-off weight: 51,000lb (23,100kg)
Powerplant: 2 × Rolls-Royce Dart 12 Mk 201 turboprop, 3,245shp (2,420kW) each

Performance
Maximum speed: 320mph (512km/h)
Range: 1,624 miles (2,613km)
Service ceiling: 25,000ft (7,600m)

Hawker Siddeley Harrier GR3

General characteristics
Crew: One
Length: 46ft 10in (14.27m)
Wingspan: 25ft 3in (7.70m)
Height: 11ft 11in (3.63m)
Wing area: 201.1ft² (18.68m²)
Empty weight: 13,535lb (6,140kg)
Maximum take-off weight: 25,200lb (11,430kg)
Powerplant: 1 × Rolls-Royce Pegasus 103 turbofan with four swivelling nozzles, 21,500lbf (95.6kN). Four vertical flight puffer jets use engine bleed air, mounted in the nose, wing tips, and tail.

HSA Harrier GR3 XV758 '34' had been delivered to the RAF as a GR1 before conversion. During its service career the aircraft served with the RAFG squadrons as well as No. 1 Squadron before joining No. 233 OCU whose markings it wears. *(BBA Collection)*

Performance
Maximum speed: 730mph (635 knots, 1,176km/h) at sea level
Combat radius: 230mi (200nmi, 370km) lo-lo-lo with 4,400lb (2,000kg) payload
Ferry range: 2,129 miles (1,850nmi, 3,425km)
Endurance: 1hr 30 min (combat air patrol – 115 miles (185km) from base)
Service ceiling: 51,200ft (15,600m)

Armament
Guns: 2 × 30mm (1.18in) ADEN cannon pods under the fuselage
Hardpoints: 4 × under-wing & 1 × under-fuselage pylon stations with a capacity of 5,000lb (2,268kg) and provisions to carry combinations of:
  Rockets: 4 × Matra rocket pods with 18 × SNEB 68mm rockets each
  Missiles: 2 × AIM-9 Sidewinder air-to-air missiles
  Bombs: A variety of unguided iron bombs, BL755 cluster bombs or laser-guided bombs
  Others: 1 × reconnaissance pod, 2 × drop tanks for extended range/loitering time

Lockheed Hercules C1

General characteristics
Crew: Five – two pilots, navigator, flight engineer and AIR loadmaster
Capacity:
  92 passengers or
  64 airborne troops or
  74 litter patients with 2 medical personnel
Payload: 45,000lb (20,000kg)
Length: 97ft 9in (29.8m)
Wingspan: 132ft 7in (40.4m)
Height: 38ft 3in (11.6m)
Wing area: 1,745ft^2 (162.1m^2)
Empty weight: 75,800lb (34,400kg)
Maximum take-off weight: 155,000lb (70,300kg)
Powerplant: 4 × Allison T56-A-15 turboprops, 4,590shp (3,430kW) each

Sporting the first camouflage scheme applied to the Hercules C.1s soon after delivery is XV212. The aircraft was eventually converted to C.3 standard serving with the LTW. *(John Ryan Collection)*

Performance
Maximum speed: 320 knots (366mph, 592km/h) at 20,000ft (6,060m)
Cruise speed: 292 knots (336mph, 540km/h)
Range: 2,050nmi (2,360 miles, 3,800km)
Service ceiling: 33,000ft (10,060m) empty; 23,000ft (7,077m) with 42,000 pounds (19,090kg) payload
Rate of climb: 1,830ft/min (9.3m/s)
Take-off distance: 3,586ft (1,093m) at 155,000lb (70,300kg) max gross weight; 1,400ft (427m) at 80,000lb (36,300kg) gross weight

Lockheed Hercules C4/C5

General characteristics
Crew: Three – two pilots, and AIR loadmaster
Capacity:
    92 passengers (128 for C-130J-30) or
    64 airborne troops (92 for C-130J-30) or
    6 pallets (8 pallets for C-130J-30) or
    74 litter patients with 2 medical personnel (97 litters for C-130J-30)
Payload: 42,000lb (19,090kg) ; for C-130J-30: 44,000lb/ 19,900kg
Length: 97ft 9in, 29.79m (for C-130J-30: 112ft, 9in, 34.36m)
Wingspan: 132ft 7in (40.41m)
Height: 38ft 10in (11.84m)
Wing area: 1,745ft^2 (162.1m^2)
Empty weight: 75,562lb (34,274kg)
Maximum take-off weight: Up to 175,000lb (79,378kg); normal 155,000lb (70,305kg)
Powerplant: 4 × Rolls-Royce AE 2100D3 turboprop, 4,637shp (3,458kW) each

Performance
Maximum speed: 362 knots (417mph, 671km/h)
Cruise speed: 348 knots (400mph, 643km/h)
Range: 2,835nmi (3,262 miles, 5,250km)

Captured departing Kandahar is Lockheed Hercules C5 ZH880, originally based at Lyneham.
(Bob Archer Collection)

Service ceiling: 28,000ft (8,615m) with 42,000 pounds (19,090 kilograms) payload
Take-off distance: 3,127ft (953m) at 155,000lb (70,300kg) gross weight

Lockheed Tristar K1

General characteristics
Crew: Four – captain, co-pilot, air engineer, air loadmaster
Capacity: 187 passengers
Length: 50.05m (164ft 3in)
Wingspan: 50.09m (164ft 4in)
Height: 16.87m (55ft 4in)
Wing area: 329.0m² (3540ft²)
Empty weight: 105,165kg (242,684lb)
Maximum take-off weight: 245,000kg (540,000lb)
Powerplant: 3 × Rolls-Royce RB.211-524B turbofans, 50,000lbf (222.4 kN) each
Maximum fuel load: 136,080kg (300,000lb)

Performance
Maximum speed: Mach 0.90
Cruise speed: Mach 0.83 (483 knots, 894km/h)
Range: 4,200nmi (7,785km) with maximum passenger payload
Service ceiling: 43,000ft (13,000m)

McDonnell Douglas Phantom FGR2

General characteristics
Crew: Two – pilot, navigator
Wingspan: 38ft 4.5in (11.71m)
Length: 57ft 11in (19.00m)
Height: 16ft 6in (5.02m)
Wing area: 530ft² (49.2m²)
Empty weight: 30,328lb (13,757kg)
Loaded weight: 41,500lb (18,825kg)
Maximum take-off weight: 61,795lb (28,030kg)
Powerplant: 2 × Rolls-Royce Spey, 17,845lbf (79.4kN) each

Seen on the pan at Brize Norton is Lockheed Tristar KC1 ZD950 of No. 216 Squadron. When originally delivered the aircraft was minus a refuelling probe, although this was quickly added during the build-up period for *Desert Storm*. *(BBA Collection)*

Performance
Maximum speed: Mach 2.23 (1,472mph, 2,370km/h) at 40,000ft (12,190m)
Cruise speed: 506 knots (585mph, 940km/h)
Combat radius: 367nmi (422 miles, 680km)
Ferry range: 1,403nmi (1,615 miles, 2,600km) with 3 external fuel tanks
Service ceiling: 60,000ft (18,300m)

Armament
4 × AIM-7 Sparrow/Skyflash in fuselage recesses
4 × AIM-9 Sidewinders on wing pylons;

Panavia Tornado GR4

General characteristics
Crew: Two – pilot,navigator
Length: 16.72m (54ft 10in)
Wingspan: 13.91m at 25° wing sweep, 8.60m at 67° wing sweep (45.6ft / 28.2ft)
Height: 5.95m (19.5ft)
Wing area: 26.6m² (286ft²)
Empty weight: 13,890kg (31,620lb)
Maximum take-off weight: 28,000kg (61,700lb)
Powerplant: 2 × Turbo-Union RB199-34R Mk 103 afterburning turbofans
   Dry thrust: 43.8kN (9,850lbf) each
   Thrust with afterburner: 76.8kN (17,270lbf) each

Performance
Maximum speed: Mach 2.2 (2,400km/h, 1,490mph) at 9,000m / 30,000ft altitude; 800 knots, 1,482km/h, 921mph indicated airspeed near sea level
Range: 1,390km (870 miles) typical combat
Ferry range: 3,890km (2,417 miles) with four external drop tanks
Service ceiling: 15,240m (50,000ft)
Rate of climb: 76.7m/s (15,100ft/min)

Complete with Paveway bombs on the underfuselage pylons Panavia Tornado GR4A ZA405 'Y' of No. 2 Squadron rolls down to the perimeter track towards its parking spot. *(Bob Archer Collection)*

Armament
Guns: 2 × 27mm (1.063in) Mauser BK-27 revolver cannon internally mounted under both sides of fuselage, each with 180 rounds (Panavia Tornado ADV has 1 × BK-27)
Hardpoints: 4 × light duty + 3 × heavy duty under-fuselage and 4 × swivelling under-wing pylon
stations holding up to 9,000kg (19,800lb) of payload, the two inner wing pylons have shoulder launch rails for 2 × short-range AAM (SRAAM) each
Missiles:
    Air-to-air missiles:
        AIM-9 Sidewinder or IRIS-T or AIM-132 ASRAAM for self-defence
    Air-to-surface missiles:
        12 × Brimstone missiles
        2 × Storm Shadow
    Anti-ship missiles:
        2 × BAe Sea Eagle
    Anti-radiation missiles:
        9 × ALARM missile
    Bombs:
        5 × 500lb Paveway IV
        3 × 1,000lb (UK Mk20) Paveway II/Enhanced Paveway II
        2 × 2,000lb Paveway III (GBU-24)/Enhanced Paveway III (EGBU-24)
        Hunting Engineering BL755 cluster bombs
        Up to 2 × JP233 or MW-1 munitions dispensers (for runway cratering operations)
        Up to 4 × B61 or WE.177 tactical nuclear weapons
    Others:
        Up to 4× drop tanks for ferry flight/extended range/loitering time

Raytheon Sentinel R1

General characteristics
Crew: Five
Length: 30.3m (99ft 5in)
Wingspan: 28.5m (93ft 6in)

Height: 8.2m (27ft 0in)
Wing area: 94.9m² (1022ft²)
Empty weight: 24,000kg (54000lb)
Gross weight: 42,400kg (93500lb)
Powerplant: 2 × Rolls-Royce BR710, 65.6kN (14,750lbf) thrust each

Performance
Maximum speed: Mach 0.75
Range: 9250km (5800 miles)
Endurance: 9 hours
Service ceiling: 12,200m (40,000ft)

Sepecat Jaguar GR1A

General characteristics
Crew: One
Wingspan: 28ft 6in (8,69m)
Length: 50ft 11in (15,52m)
Wing area: 258ft² (24,0m²)
Height: 16ft (4,89m)
Empty weight: 7,000kg (15,432lb)
Loaded weight: 10,954kg (24,149lb)
Maximum take-off weight: 15,700kg (34,612lb)
Powerplant: 2 × Rolls-Royce/Turbomeca Adour Mk 102 turbofans
  Dry thrust: 22.75kN (5,115lbf) each
  Thrust with afterburner: 32.5 kN (7,305lbf) each

Performance
Maximum speed: Mach 1.6 (1,699km/h, 917 knots, 1,056mph) at 11,000m (36,000ft)
Combat radius: 908km (490nmi, 564 miles)
Ferry range: 3,524km (1,902nmi, 2,190 miles)
Service ceiling: 14,000m (45,900ft)

Parked outside its HAS at Coltishall is Sepecat Jaguar GR1A 'H' of No. 41 Squadron complete with a reconnaissance pod under the fuselage. *(BBA Collection)*

Armament
Two internal 30mm Aden Mk 4 cannons with 150 rounds per gun
4763kg (10,500lb) of disposable stores, including AIM-9 Sidewinders, air-to-surface missiles, anti-radar missiles, free-fall or guided bombs, cluster bombs, dispenser weapons, rocket launchers, ECM pods, drop tanks and TIALD or recce pod, carried on five or seven external hardpoints.

Shorts (English Electric) Canberra PR9

General characteristics
Crew: Two – pilot, navigator
Length: 67ft 10in (19.96m)
Wingspan: 67ft 10in (20.06m)
Height: 15ft 8in (4.77m)
Wing area: 960ft^2 (89.19m^2)
Empty weight: 21,650lb (9,820kg)
Loaded weight: 46,000lb (20,865kg)
Maximum take-off weight: 55,000lb (24,948kg)
Powerplant: 2 × Rolls-Royce Avon Mk 206, 11,250lbf (42kN) each

Performance
Maximum speed: Mach 0.88 (580mph, 933km/h) at 40,000ft (12,192m)
Combat radius: 810 miles (700nmi, 1,300km)
Ferry range: 3,380 miles (2,940nmi, 5,440km)
Service ceiling: 48,000ft (15,000m)

Finished in the final hemp and light grey scheme is Canberra PR9 XH168 'AD' of No. 39 Squadron whose winged bomb badge is on the fin. No. 39 Squadron would disband in July 2006 leaving the RAF without a manned strategic reconnaissance aircraft. *(BBA Collection)*

Shorts Belfast XR362 *Samson*, operated by No. 53 Squadron, performs a flyby. Although initially plagued by problems the aircraft eventually proved to be a useful heavy lifter. *(John Ryan Collection)*

Shorts Belfast C1

General characteristics
Crew: Five – pilot, co-pilot, air engineer, navigator and air loadmaster
Capacity: 11,750cu.ft
Payload: 80,000lb (36,288kg)
Length: 136ft 5in (41.70m)
Wingspan: 158ft 10in (48.1m)
Height: 47ft (14.33m)
Wing area: 2,466ft² (229.1m²)
Empty weight: 130,000lb (59,020kg)
Maximum take-off weight: 230,000lb (104,300kg)
Powerplant: 4 × Rolls-Royce Tyne R.Ty.12, Mk 101 turboprops, 11.250ehp (4,270kW) each

Performance
Cruise speed: 358mph (576km/h)
Range: 5,200 miles (8,368km) with capacity fuel load of 80,720lb
Service ceiling: 30,000ft (9,100m)
Range with maximum payload: 970 miles (1,560km)

Vickers VC 10

General characteristics
Crew: Four
Capacity: 150 passengers plus 76 stretcher cases and 6 medical attendants
Length: 133ft 8in (48.36m)
Wingspan: 146ft 2in (44.55m)
Height: 39ft 6in (12.04m)
Wing area: 2,851ft² (264.9m²)
Empty weight: 146,000lb (63,278kg)
Loaded weight: 323,000lb
Powerplant: 4 × Rolls-Royce Conway Mk 301 Turbofan, 22,500lbf (100.1kN) each

Parked outside the main hangar at Mount Pleasant, Falkland Islands, is VC 10 ZA142 'C' of No. 101 Squadron based at Brize Norton. *(BBA Collection)*

Performance
Maximum speed: 580mph (933km/h)
Range: 5,850 miles (9,412km)
Service ceiling: 43,000ft (13,105m)

Westland Belvedere HC1

General characteristics
Crew: Three
Capacity:
   19 fully equipped troops or
   12 stretchers with two seated wounded and a medical attendant
Payload: 6,000lb (2,700kg)
Length: 54ft 4in (16.56m)

Although not the safest of helicopters the Westland (Bristol) Belvedere HC1 would finally be bullied into behaving itself. This aircraft is XG459 of No. 72 Squadron at Upavon prior to the application of camouflage. *(John Ryan Collection)*

Rotor diameter: 48ft 11in (14.9m)
Height: 17ft 0in (5.18m)
Empty weight: 11,350lb (5,159kg)
Maximum take-off weight: 19,000lb (8,600kg)
Powerplant: 2 × Napier Gazelle turboshaft, 1,465hp (1,092kW) each

Performance
Cruise speed: 138mph (120 knots, 222km/h)
Range: 460 miles (400nmi, 720km)
Service ceiling: 12,000ft (3,660m)

Westland Puma HC1

General characteristics
Crew: Three
Capacity: 16
Length: 18.15m (59ft 6½in)
Rotor diameter: 15.00m (49ft 2½in)
Height: 5.14m (16ft 10½in)
Empty weight: 3,536kg (7,795lb)
Maximum take-off weight: 7,000kg (15,430lb)
Powerplant: 2 × Turboméca Turmo IVC turboshafts, 1,175kW (1,575hp) each

Banking sharply away from the camera is Westland Puma ZA940 'CY' of No. 230 Squadron based at Aldergrove, Northern Ireland, although a move to Benson took place in November 2009. *(John Ryan Collection)*

Performance
Never exceed speed: 273km/h (147 knots, 169mph)
Maximum speed: 257km/h (138 knots, 159mph)
Cruise speed: 248km/h (134 knots, 154mph)
Range: 580km (313nmi, 360 miles)
Service ceiling: 4,800m (15,750ft)
Rate of climb: 7.1m/s (1,400ft/min)

Westland Wessex HC2

General characteristics
Crew: Two pilots and air loadmaster
Capacity: 16 troops or 8 stretchers
Length: 65ft 10in (20.07m)
Rotor diameter: 56ft 0in (17.07m)
Height: 15ft 10in (4.83m)
Empty weight: 8,340lb (3,767kg)
Loaded weight: 13,500lb (6,136kg)
Powerplant: 2 × Rolls-Royce Gnome H.1200 Mk110/111 turboshaft, 1,350shp (1,007kW) each

Performance
Maximum speed: 132mph (115 knots, 213km/h)
Cruise speed: 122mph (106 knots, 196km/h)
Range: 310 miles (270nmi, 499km)
Service ceiling: 12,000ft (3,660m)
Rate of climb: 1,650ft/min (8.4m/s)

Even the dismal weather cannot damp the bright colours of Westland Wessex HCC.4 XV732 assigned to the Queen's Flight, Benson. After retirement the aircraft was preserved in the RAF Museum, Hendon. *(John Ryan Collection)*

The Westland Sea King HAR3 is a vital part of the air–sea rescue organization around the British coast. Aircraft XZ594 was assigned to No. 202 Squadron at the time. *(BBA Collection)*

Westland Sea King HAR3

General characteristics
Crew: Two to four, depending on the mission
Length: 55ft 10in (17.02m)
Rotor diameter: 62ft 0in (18.90m)
Height: 16ft 10in (5.13m)
Empty weight: 14,051lb (6,387kg)
Loaded weight: 21,000lb (9,525kg)
Maximum take-off weight: 21,400lb (9,707kg) (overload weight)
Powerplant: 2 × Rolls-Royce Gnome H1400-2 turboshafts, 1,660shp (1,238kW) each
Five bladed rotor

Performance
Maximum speed: 129mph (112 knots, 208km/h)
Range: 764 miles (664nmi, 1,230km)
Service ceiling: 10,000ft (3,050m)
Rate of climb: 2,020ft/min (10.3m/s)

Westland Whirlwind HAR10

General characteristics
Crew: Two pilots and air loadmaster
Length: 64ft 4in
Rotor diameter: 53ft 0in (19.25kg)
Height: 15ft 7½in (4.27kg)

Empty weight: 5,993lb (2,724kg)
Maximum take-off weight: 7,800lb (3,538kg)
Powerplant: 1 × Bristol Siddeley Gnome, 1,050shp

Performance
Maximum speed: 109mph (95 knots, 175km/h)
Range: 334 miles (290nmi, 534km)
Service ceiling: 13,000ft (3,960m)

Bibliography

Butler, Phil & Buttler, Tony (2009) *Aerofax: Handley-Page Victor*, Midland Publishing, ISBN-13: 978-1857803112.

Clemons, John (1993) *English Electric Canberra*, Midland Publishing, ISBN-13: 978-0904597738.

Chartres, John (1985) *Postwar Military Aircraft: Avro Shackleton*, Ian Allan Publishing, ISBN-13: 978-0711015135.

Darling, Kev (2008) *English Electric/BAC Lightning Mks 1–6*, Lulu.com, ISBN-13: 978-1435715561.

Jefford, C.G. (1988) *RAF Squadrons: A Comprehensive Record of the Movement and Equipment of All RAF Squadrons and Their Antecedents Since 1912*, Airlife Publishing Ltd, ISBN-13: 978-1840371413.

Thetford, Owen (1988) *Aircraft of the Royal Air Force Since 1918*, Putnam Aeronautical Books, ISBN-13: 978-0851778655.

Index